REACHING BEYOND:
*Chapters in the History
of Perfectionism*

REACHING BEYOND: CHAPTERS IN THE HISTORY OF PERFECTIONISM

Stanley M. Burgess, Editor

HENDRICKSON
PUBLISHERS
PEABODY, MASSACHUSETTS 01961-3473

CONTENTS

Preface

SINCE THE BEGINNING of recorded history, indeed even in that
long and shadowy past before men began to tell their story,
certain individuals have chosen to reach beyond their fellows in
the hope of achieving a state of perfection as they have defined
it. This volume presents glimpses into both the prehistory and
the history of this perfectionist impulse, for the purpose of providing a better understanding of the nature of, and motivations
for, such attempts in the history of Christianity.[1]

The first problem faced by scholars working in the history of
perfectionism is the extreme difficulty of defining the terms
"perfection" and "perfectionism." Perfection is viewed by
some as the possibility or actuality of freedom from sin and of
the attainment of moral likeness to God in this life. Others insist that, because of natural and inevitable human
limitations—especially the infirmity of human knowledge—it is
more realistic to strive after a religious rather than an ethical
perfection. To these (who might better be called "perfection
aspirants" than perfectionists), perfection is an ideal to be
sought, but never a reality to be achieved completely in this
life. It is not uncommon for perfectionists to argue that the
ideal state is not realizable so long as man is entrapped in
human flesh. Their problem is to elevate themselves above
matter in order to emulate their god-model. They tend to be
mystical, seeking escape from the temporal-material world and
striving for eventual union with God—a realization of the ideal
harmony of the phenomenon with its ideal expression. Given
these preconceptions, perfection usually is conceived of as a
journey or a way, the attainment of an end or something pursued through to the end.

Despite these definitional differences, nearly all perfectionists find common ground in arguing that perfection is a higher level of completeness. This definition, therefore, will serve for our purposes. "Perfectionism" as used in this volume is the disposition to regard anything other than the perfect state as unacceptable and the resultant drive to reach beyond to complete actualization.

The perfectionists' motives are equally varied as are their definitions of perfection. Often their impulse derives from a reaction against comfortable, popular religion. Whether or not this perfectionist drive is a conscious expression of unacknowledged opposites such as despair and social marginality, as Francis H. Touchet has suggested,[2] there is no denying that a high percentage of those who reach beyond also disdain the world around them. They then tend to follow two very different courses. One is the active role which seeks to impact the world while living therein, and which also may include a vow of poverty. The prime example is Francis of Assisi who attempted to achieve Gospel perfection by imitating Christ. The second is the path of full asceticism, in which there is a voluntary separation from the world's pollution and an assumption of a life of self-denial—an attempt to put off the temporal and material while striving to be united with God who is both eternal and transcendent. Such an individual was Symeon the New Theologian.

Perfectionists often are motivated by primitivist urges and desire to return to primordial origins which they consider ideal. In certain cases this involves an effort to return to Garden of Eden pristine purity and goodness, for others the setting of greatest appeal is the first century A.D., when the Church was dynamic and was assumed to be unspoiled and still actualizing Christ's injunctions to Gospel perfection.

The perfectionist's drive also can spring from an overwhelming desire for greater knowledge of God and of self. Thomas Aquinas viewed man's capacity to think about things divine as the highest level of human activity. He reasoned that human reason, when so directed and when coupled with love, allows one to attain the highest perfection attainable in the mortal state. But for the mystics such a knowledge of God is impossible. Their search for perfection centers on the potential for union with a transcendent deity who is to be encountered, not through human reason, but in a cloud of unknowing.

Apocalypticism also has motivated the perfectionist's impulse, although its expression has varied widely. For example, the Montanists pursued a life of holiness as defined by their prophets in anticipation of the parousia. Joachim of Fiore predicted the coming of a final age of the Holy Spirit which would usher in a worldwide paradise of perfection. Modern Pentecostals combine a striving for holiness, which is a reaction against the worldliness of contemporary society, with a strong emphasis on preparation for the second coming of Christ.

Those who strive after perfection share several common denominators. The first is a tendency, which would seem inseparable from their effort, to rank spirituality in a hierarchic fashion, with those who are said to have attained perfection placed at the top. The second is the belief that the effort to attain perfection will result in greater completeness or wholeness—a new level of fulfillment and maturity. This implies conversely a reaction against limitation, inadequacy, incompleteness or evil. The third common denominator is the tendency to cling to a method for obtaining the perfect life, often to such an extent that the method itself becomes a type of perfection. While the drive for perfection can provide that prime energy that leads to a higher synthesis of forces, when perfectionism becomes ossified into a mere method or code it can impale adherents on its sharp demanding thrusts.

Clearly, the drive for perfection is an enduring feature in the history of religion, including that of Christianity, which must be reckoned with. *Reaching Beyond: Chapters in the History of Perfectionism* highlights the concept of perfection in primitive man, in both Old and New Testaments, and in a variety of perfectionist individuals and movements throughout Christian history, including the Montanists; three of the early church fathers—Clement of Alexandria, Origen, and Gregory of Nyssa; the Eastern medieval mystic, Symeon the New Theologian; the medieval apocalyptist, Joachim of Fiore; the rationalist, Thomas Aquinas; the Western medieval mystic, Bonaventure; John Calvin and his followers; early modern Anabaptists, Puritans and later primitivists; and the modern holiness-Pentecostal tradition. While this study by no means is exhaustive, it will provide the reader with representative examples of those throughout Christian history who have attempted to "reach beyond."

Stanley M. Burgess

NOTES

1. Two of the more important earlier studies in the history of Christian perfectionism are R. Newton Flew, *The Idea of Perfection in Christian Theology* (New York: Humanities Press, 1968), and H. K. LaRondelle, *Perfection and Perfectionism* (Berrien Springs, MI: Andrews University Press, 1971).

2. Francis H. Touchet, "Perfectionism in Religion and Psychotherapy: Discerning the Spirits," *Journal of Psychology and Theology* 4, no. 1 (Winter 1976): 25–26.

Karl W. Luckert

Karl W. Luckert is a Professor of the History of Religions at Southwest Missouri State University. A native of Germany, he studied philosophy at the University of Kansas and the history of religions at the University of Chicago where he earned his M.A. and Ph.D. degrees. As a student of Mircea Eliade he became interested in primitive and prehistoric religions and wrote a dissertation on the "Mythical Geographies of the Dead in Melanesia." He lived ten years in Arizona where he taught at Northern Arizona University and did field research in American Indian religions, especially among the Navajo Indians. His work was supported, in part, by the National Endowment for the Humanities, the Rockefeller Foundation, Wenner-Gren Foundation, Rockefeller Brothers Fund, Northern Arizona University, and the Smithsonian Institution. He has recently been invited by Aarhus University, Denmark, to a Fulbright lectureship in the field of American Indian religions.

Luckert's field work in Stone Age hunter traditions and in the religions of primal domesticators, and his inquiry into "grand domesticator" or civilizational religions, have enabled him to revise his perspective on the broader subject of religious evolution. The present essay on "Perfectionism in Human Evolution" is a preliminary step toward publishing his general synthesis of "Religion in Evolution," a larger study which he expects to finish soon. What is offered here is a preview of the author's larger perspective which he acquired during extensive investigations in the field. Even though this essay is written for general readers in the Religious Studies field, thus without footnotes and technical documentation, the student who wishes to engage in more serious inquiry is not without recourse. He may find ethnographic support for most of the writer's points—for his broad evolutionary sequence as well as for his theories on primal guilt and divine justification—in the writer's published works: *The Navajo Hunter Tradition* (1975), *Olmec Religion—a Key to Middle America and Beyond* (1976), *Navajo Mountain and Rainbow Bridge Religion* (1977), *A Navajo Bringing-Home Ceremony* (1978), and *Coyoteway—a Navajo Holyway Healing Ceremonial* (1979). In addition, a number of innovative suggestions and interpretations can be found in editor's notes, introductions, postscripts and footnotes in monographs in the "American Tribal Religions" series— published by the University of Nebraska Press—of which Luckert is founder and editor. His recent introductory essay, "Coyote in Navajo and Hopi Tales," in Volume Nine (1984) of that series, is especially helpful for understanding the writer's present direction in history of religions hermeneutics.

1

PERFECTIONISM IN HUMAN EVOLUTION

Karl W. Luckert

ORIGINAL SIN BETWEEN HEROISM AND MYSTIC SURRENDER

> But the serpent said to the woman,
> "You will not die.
> For God knows that when you eat of it
> your eyes will be opened,
> and you will be like God,
> knowing good and evil."
>
> Genesis 3:4-5

THIS CHAPTER does not engage in a creationist/evolutionist controversy. The origin story from which our introductory quotation has been chosen affirms who created the world and who therefore owns it. In comparison, the concept of human evolution implies neither the presence nor the absence of a personal creative power; it implies only an elongated perspective on human time and on processes of change. The time span of human evolution contains our portion of known history as well as our prehistory, as it increasingly comes into focus with the help of archaeological data. While this essayist is ordinarily in the habit of postulating for his perspective a probable human chronology of roughly three million years, the actual length of his evolutionary epochs are unimportant for the task at hand. This delineation of "perfectionism" in evolution requires only the assumption of relative sequences. Stone Age hunters preceded domesticators, and the domestication of plants and animals preceded the formation of cities, empires, and so-called civilizations.

Our introductory quotation and the origin narrative in Genesis reflect a significant moment in the history of religions in the Near East. They refer to a historical context and to a time when human beings had already changed from a hunter-gatherer to a domesticator economy. People in that time and at that place told their story about the origin of the world from the perspective of human keepers of animals and cultivators of plants. They knew about gardens with fruit trees, about the watering of plants, and about the necessity of weeding thistles and thorns. They were also familiar with the possibility that gardens might be surrounded with insurmountable walls and that armed guards could be stationed at their gates. As planters of gardens and as keepers of sheep they offered firstfruits and firstborn animals in payment to the Creator-god who, as a fellow "maker," had blessed them and had given them title to the property which they tended. At the same time their God, as this story presents him, showed a preference for the diet and lifestyle of herders. While he rejected the vegetable produce of Cain the farmer, he accepted Abel's offering of meat. When in due time the first farmer killed the first herder, this origin story refers to a time in Near Eastern history when obviously the preferred people of the narrator were good herders. These herders were somewhat envious of the farmers' standard of living and were, apparently in return, regarded contemptuously by the more civilized citizens of settled communities, by craftsmen and tillers of the soil.

While our Genesis passage is thus assignable in a sequence of linear time, while it can be traced with reasonable accuracy to an economy of advanced domesticators and possibly to scribes employed at temples and at royal courts, it nevertheless carries a timeless human theme. In all periods of human evolution the norm, the challenge as well as the temptation of perfection could be summed up in those same words: "You will be like God, knowing. . . ."

Knowledge is that specific human attribute which, since ancient times, has been used in some manner to explain humankind. Modern "souls" have defined themselves even more precisely than the ancients as *Homo sapiens*, Man-who-thinks. Similarly in the Genesis narrative, human intelligence is associated with the beginnings of human time, that is, with a fruit that in the beginning had been plucked from a forbidden tree. Whether or not in that tradition the fruit(s) of knowledge and life grew on two separate trees becomes a mute question in light of the fact that in every *Homo sapiens* culture the tree of knowledge poses as a tree of life. "Learn and live better" our educators are saying. But in the end both knowledge and life are lost on account of the human appetite for more knowledge and more life—on account of craving for perfection. Predator knowledge invariably leads to death, it implies a world in which death is possible; and knowledge which in the end defeats itself may not be as worthwhile as all along it seems. The Genesis story, a narrative with masterful strokes of irony, rises to the height of a profound paradox. Inasmuch as the paradisiac tree of life and knowledge has been rediscovered by "perfected" and godlike men, it offers them only the fruit of death. This is, indeed, a curious happenstance for enlightened mortals to smile and to tell each other about.

The notion of perfection, at any point in human evolution, has quite likely always dawned first in relation to peak experiences in the climactic-heroic quest for food, for survival, and for power. Second, this heroic quest was subsequently modified and sublimated into a sportive perfection of skills and into the steady improvement of technological means. Third, when they were freed of the advantages of technology and economics, those sportive and inventive skills could be further refined toward the perfection of artistic talent. Finally, freed of all ambitions and pride, the ideal of human perfection was rediscovered, with added humility, as something contained only in the character of a divinity. In this final setting the human aspiration to religious perfection always necessitates the death of ego, namely, a mystic blending of human individuality with some greater-than-human and more perfect dimension of reality. To the extent that an individual ego nevertheless insists on surviving as a self-conscious entity, it must do so by presenting itself a little wiser, a little greater, and a little better than it has been up to the points of its habitual or natural surrenderings. In order to survive, a conscious ego must strive to be at least as knowledgeable as the God who threatens to control and to absorb its individuality.

In order to facilitate this discussion in a worldwide evolutionary context, religion will be defined here as the response of humankind to so-conceived greater-than-human configurations of reality. Since living organisms' *experiences* immediately turn into *responses*, the same terminology can be used to delineate both. Thus, religious experiences of, and responses to, so-conceived greater-than-human realities range in degree from mild fascination to awe, to trembling, fear and trance, and with further increase in intensity to total tranquility and surrender.

In a religious context, perfectionism not only means that a human ego surpasses its previous levels of performance, but it also implies aspirations to what hitherto seemed greater-than-human status—aspirations to divine power and knowledge. The resulting psychological dilemma is obvious. No sooner than a *Homo sapiens* is convinced that he has obtained greater-than-human rank, and as soon as he has surveyed his newly reached

biblical

plateau of godlike perfection, he faces an abyss. He discovers a void exactly at the point where his own ego has displaced the divine model which, in his quest for perfection up to that moment, he strove to imitate. Unbeknown to the thus "perfected" imitator, the divine model whose superior rank he has assimilated has at the same time disappeared as "model," has been usurped by, and has been absorbed into his own personhood. As a perfected and now greater-than-ordinary human being, the former imitator stands frightfully alone. Where formerly his divinely sanctioned efforts at devout imitation, i.e. his anticipational identification with the deity, have inflated his imitator ego, there is now nothing left. In this sense, ego-centeredness becomes the foil of mysticism—as in every mystic's life "union with the One" gets interrupted by ego-induced "visions of the abyss."

Faced with this emptiness of "fulfilled" selfhood and having exhausted goals of ambitions, the usurper of divine roles has become ripe and vulnerable to encounter, to recognize, and to accept new and greater divine realities. These greater revelations will in due time help him put again his own fascinations, his feelings of awe, his fears and surrenders into perspective. As a primate who can do nothing better than imitate, and as one who by virtue of his appetite is doomed to eat and to think, man has no alternative but to adjust his methods and to sharpen his responses to ever new and greater realities. He must learn to respond to them as to his gods, with imitational humility, with competitive similarity, and with realistically accepted surrender. As a *Homo sapiens* he naturally expects to come up with a meaningful explanation for the entire scale of his experiences and responses.

Homines sapientes are "mosting" creatures, thoroughly possessed by the necessity of wanting to surpass themselves together with all else. The *Book of World Records* attests to the fact that in our time no imaginable activity is immune to the human habit of wanting to discover norms of perfection above those which are already thinkable. In their drive to surpass themselves, and in their greedy pursuit of continuous ego-addition, they not only change themselves but also the world around them. Nevertheless, in order to keep the scope of this essay sufficiently narrow and manageable, only the four general types of perfectable human activities introduced earlier will be discussed here: conquest, sports, arts, and extreme religion.

These four categories correspond to four personality types whose ambitions and perfectability can be analyzed along a graduated scale accomodating both the dimensions of ego-assertion and retreat. This simplified typology is used to present in an evolutionary sequence at least that many types of perfection. *Heroes* fight and conquer for the sake of existential advantages and for human survival; *athletes* play to win and to display respectable specialized physical skills; *artists* develop sensitivities and skills in a more individualistic manner for their personal satisfaction, for the expression and the communication of inspirational beauty; and *mystic saints* surrender the aspirations of their human egos, they abandon them for states of perfect happiness which lie beyond the reach of ordinary sensual enjoyment or rewards.

A hero operates at one end of the spectrum extending between the point of conquest and the point of total surrender. He establishes himself as a successful conqueror while, at the other end of the spectrum, the mystic saint surrenders all. The hero assumes the perfectability of his individual self, while, by contrast, the mystic saint dissolves into a greater reality, which, by faith, he has accepted as being more perfect than he himself had been all along. Whereas in the performance of his feats the hero uses all available means, the mystic saint renounces not only the hero's means but he also rejects all his goals. Along that same scale—a graduated scale of aggression and retreat—but moving toward the middle from heroes and mystics, operate athletes and artists. Athletes register approximately halfway from the middle of the scale toward the heroic extreme, while many inspired artists function halfway between the scale's middle and the point of mystic surrender.

Athletes submit selectively to certain rules of sportsmanship. Certain technological and scientific advantages are purposely excluded from sports contests. The athlete's goal is to demonstrate his superiority in specialized skills. Apart from providing entertainment and establishing norms (i.e. records) for his own specialized skills, the athlete provides no tangible benefits for his fans. While his ego is nourished by, and often dependent on, applause from fans, and although it is sustained by his achievement of applauded victories, he rises only to the height of a greater-than-ordinary non-utilitarian model. As long as his athletic records are being broken, and as long as he submits to societal rules of sportsmanship, an athlete will rise to hero or god status only for children who blend his image with that of a great parent.

Athletic performances, in accordance with societal rules of sportsmanship, nevertheless become important symbols of *limited* human retreat. The voluntary forfeiture of technological advantages, the glorification of non-utilitarian skills, together with the egalitarian exchange of handshakes before and after contests, remove the athlete and such fans as cheer him from the red-in-tooth-and-claw world of heroics. Inasmuch as specialized athletes actually practice "sportsmanship," they help sublimate humanity's raw struggle for survival. Admired by groups of fans they climb specialized peaks of perfection. With many fighters and many winners thus given a chance to win and to reach their peaks, cheered on and imitated partways by many audiences, the chances for having massive battle scenes in the valleys beneath those peaks are significantly reduced. Of course, as one observes the frequency with which grandiose civilized sports events erupt into bloody brawls, one can easily see that athletic perfection still lingers far too dangerously close to the gore of raw heroism. Sportsmanship is far too selfish and aggressive an activity for it to function as a sufficient check and balance that would assure a decent human survival. More severe types of retreat from heroic perfection, to milder types of perfection, are therefore necessary.

Though still far from the goal of mystics, an artist's retreat from heroic aggressiveness is more thoroughgoing than the retreat of athletes. Like athletes, artists develop skills of performance and perception. Furthermore, most artists profess that their motives are purer than are those of sportsmen—that their ambitions transcend the athletes' hunger for public vainglory. This motivation, of course, varies from artists to artisans and from craftsmen to actors in commercialized showbusiness. We are introducing here general types, not the entire gamut of human possibilities. And still, the presence of popular "stars" who posit public norms of perfection, short of sportsmen's legitimized level of violence, represents, suggests, and teaches an additional step toward religious retreat. It certainly was not without good reason when during the 1960s certain "hippie" groups espoused artistic ideals to symbolize their level of personal retreat from industrial and commercialized modernity and aggression.

During early phases of religious evolution, as one might conclude on hand of ethnological and archaeological reconstructions, human conquests, sports, arts, and religions were still very much of one piece. Running after his next meal, the primitive hunter did not have the luxury of choosing whether or not to become a perfect conqueror, athlete, artist, or mystic. Surely, he had to compromise regularly among many types of conflicting norms of perfection. Usually the humanoid hunter, to the extent that he had become aware of his mortality, could only come as close to a type of perfection as his greater-than-human tutelary had chosen to sponsor his attempts. And to the extent that the latter sponsored him, it was he who determined and defined the type or norm of such perfection.

The godlike honors and monetary rewards which modern cultures bestow on select athletes and artists demonstrate our perpetual human need to concretize our adored and imitable norms of perfection. Athletic peak performances in specialized skills, the perfect ease with which our star actors manage to escape present limitations by becoming someone else, together with extravagant remuneration, move far beyond the mere establishment of artistic retreat stages. These renunciant but disciplined winners in sports and in the arts succeed in spite of, and because of, the retreat posture to which they have restricted themselves. They spite the rewards of full-scale aggression and are therefore rewarded by the people who instinctively know that they themselves would not survive in a world of full-blown heroes without rules. Certain successful leaders of populous religious movements demonstrate the same societal dynamic; they ride popular tides of promised comfort, security, and simple universalistic game rules. Athletic, artistic, and religious retreats become in varying degrees the mothers of hope which, fertilized by human and greater-than-human egotism, eventually give birth to new rounds of aggressiveness. All those people who are caught at mediocre levels of human existence see their athletes or artists as reasonably imitable models. People who have been kicked below the level of mediocre survival, who can not afford participation in sports and arts events, will have to begin their recoveries at more extreme positions of religious retreat. For their rationally intelligent religious perspectives, on paths suited for retreat as well as for reemergence, the world's oppressed have always depended on saints who, accustomed to mystic surrender and poverty, nevertheless radiate happiness and hope. When flesh-and-blood heroes are discovered by humankind as being threatening tyrants, then specialized achievers and athletes replace them in business, sports, and in the cult. When specialized athletic achievers are disclosed as being still too egotistic or irrelevant, then less selfish artistic beautifiers contribute new style, rhythm, form, color, and glitter. When the rhythms of music only deafen the ear or fail to inspire direction and orderly movement, and when forms, words, and colors only add bewilderment to the patterns of sustainable comfort and excitement, then mystic surrender to some greater-than-human dimension remains the last reasonable alternative.

Of course, heroic conquerors, athletes, artists, and mystic saints are in this essay mentioned only to represent ideal benchmarks for discussion. They are not the only personality types on earth who aspire to perfection. The fact that one can ponder all four types together, can research and write about them, suggests the possibility that the writer has all along been leading up to another norm of perfection. But then, here in a scholarly essay on perfectionism, the introduction of the notion of the perfection of scholarship would seem self-serving at best. It would certainly confuse the scholar's medium of exposition with his subject matter. Moreover, "perfect" scholars or writers deserve to be abandoned at least as regularly as any one of the four perfectable personality types introduced above. Human balance and survival must be worked for continually along the entire scale of human experiences and responses— from control, experimentation, hypothetical rearrangement, analysis, familiarity, fascination, awe, trembling and trance, to complete surrender. A diagram of this scale, as a teeter totter, may be of some help at this point in the discussion:

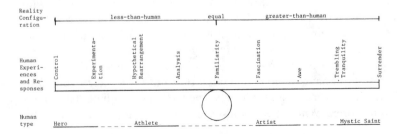

THE PERFECT HUNTER

Homo sapiens became what he now is in the process of first becoming a gatherer, a competitor of other predators, and a self-sufficient hunter. Among these activities, surely the chasing of live animals and the competition coming from more effective predators presented the greatest challenge to the budding hominid intellect. All subsequent progress in human skills and intelligence can best be understood as an amplification of predator mentality and trickery. But that evolutionary process was not without its reversals, religious retreats, and common-sense adjustments marked by moments of remorse. The complete range of activities, from heroic killings to saintly surrenders, comprises the range of options of all intelligent predators in this world. This range of possibilities is as wide for the hunting dog as it is for a hominid master hunter.

A simple stone cutting-edge, in prehistoric times, wielded by the hand of an ancestral predator-toolmaker signaled the presence of unprecedented intelligence in the creature who was carrying it. The primitive toolmaker was able to remember past encounters with animal victims, and he fully anticipated the singular purpose for which he carried the weapon and for which he had manufactured it. Physically endowed as less-than-perfect natural hunters, with short incisor teeth and flimsy fingernails, our Stone Age ancestors learned to compensate for natural deficiencies with the exercise of their progressive predator intellect. They made enlarged artificial stone substitutes for their teeth and fingernails, carried stick-extensions for their limbs, and to compensate for a deficiency in speed they discovered means of storing, using, and quickly releasing bursts of energy. By way of their experimental innovations the species homo became the most effective predator group in our world: they are surpassed as predators only by the Devil and by evil demons about whom they seem to know quite a lot.

Technologically considered, tools and weapons are modifications of objects which can be found as resources in the nearly inexhaustible realm of plants and minerals; they could therefore be enlarged and multiplied indefinitely. Because the hominid hunter was thus able to add artificial modifications—*ad infinitum*—to his natural limbs, fingernails, and teeth, many of his physical limitations could, by the dimension of his creative awareness, be gradually sidestepped.

With the horizon of physical effectiveness continually expanding beyond achieved limits, mental thresholds came to assume greater importance. Such thresholds are encountered along boundaries where the human intelligence itself collapses and where it turns against itself. That limit, anticipated and weakly prefigured in sports, and more strongly in the arts, is none other than the threshold of religion. It is a point along our experiential scale at which aggressive analysis oscillates with regressive fascination, where aggressive experimentation flips over into fearful retreat—into a feeling of dependence and of being experimented with. This threshold is the boundary line at which killer egos lose control over their victims, where they disassociate themselves from their tools, repent from aggression, and surrender to the demands of a greater-than-human trickster intelligence. They identify with their victims, and in response to their cruel acts, because of their superior intelligence, they are led to contemplate their own mortality. In the end their own sense of honor demands that, as fully rational minds capable of thinking aggressive tricks as well as mystic retreats, they find ways to surrender voluntarily; to repent and retreat with honor before they themselves are defeated.

At no point in human evolution does it seem as though man ever felt that he had full control over his artificial tool powers—even less so today as our piles of conquered and split atoms have begun to scare us. Stone Age hunters who continue to survive to this day in remote corners of the globe still tend to give credit for their weapon technology to greater-than-human inventors or culture heroes of primeval times. In spite of having in his possession today some goodly measure of modern technological advantage over natural predators, many a primitive hunter still consciously imitates in actual practice the hunting methods of some so-conceived greater-than-human predator sponsor and justifier. He may strike like Snake, stalk like Lion, or attack like Wolf. In many primitive hunting songs, where weapons are mentioned, these tend to lose their man-made status as tools and instead become bodily extensions, not of the hunters themselves, but of their divine predator sponsors; or, they tend to assume an extra-human personality of their own. In this manner, and by numerous other fascinating methods, the guilt-ridden artificial toolmaker-killer has tried to disassociate himself from his bloody deeds.

Themes of heroic killings of certain monster animals, by early anthropomorphs, continue to echo in fairy tales and in remnants of hunter mythology. They reflect the original vulnerability of early humanoid hunters. All too easily modern interpreters of prehistory overlook that the early pioneers of human progress had no traps, guns, poisons, or tranquilizers—until recently not even bow and arrows. Nowadays we can with a little foresight and preparation destroy any Kodiak bear, Siberian tiger, wolf, lion, reptile, or mighty bird of prey that might come our way. And thanks to our latest technology we can effect their destruction rather unheroically. The greatest threat to a modern un-hero is not the monster itself, but some game warden whose job it now is to protect endangered monsters against their former human victims. Formerly a human killer of such monster-babyeaters could expect to be hailed as the heroic savior or semi-divine avenger of human lives.

A hero who kills a monster to liberate his own kind may be given near-divine honors. But heroism in relation to human society is all the while burdened with a nagging discrepancy. The hero knows that he has in fact killed a being who counts for more than all those whom he has saved. On the one hand, the hero's status is defined in relation to the former greatness of his victim. The greater the monster's original threat has been, the greater the slayer will seem. But on the other hand, the acclaim for him, by people dependent upon his heroic deeds for their survival, by comparison, fall forever short of his earned status and self-perceived perfection. The fact that they ever were endangered by someone whom the hero was able to slay, implies that they will never be able to comprehend the hero's true excess in greatness nor be able to appropriately express to him their appreciation.

To the extent that primitive hunters admired naturally superior predators as their models of perfection they found themselves adopted by them into their totemic clans as religious apprentices. When for the duration of a hunt human apprentices learned to imitate their divine sponsors' nonhuman ways, they themselves became other than human. Complete participation in the ways of predator divinities subsequently explained ecstatic surrenders; in turn, their surrenderings invited these totemic sponsors and justifiers to possess, to rule, and to "devour" them.

A hunter who is intellectually capable of making tools, and thus of premeditating murder, is also able to remember failures, pain, emotions of vengeance, parental punishment, and thus also feelings of guilt. Primate intelligence, which is foremostly

adept in the art of imitation, has learnt to identify with its victims. A guilty hunter who can sympathize with his victims is
aware of the fact that for him perfection is presently out of
reach. The concept of a perfect state of survival includes balance
among equals, living harmlessly with lesser beings, as well as
surviving unharmed and in harmony under greater ones. In the
course of the history of religions a great variety of human attack and retreat postures have been rationally assimilated by
human minds and ritualized at the societal level. Sportive
gamesmanship is one of the first among these retreat
postures—inasmuch as most of it comes natural in the play of
young predators as they grow up.

While most divine tutelaries of primitive hunters appear to
have been fellow predators, some have come from among the
"game animals" side. Animal elders of herds, masters and mistresses of species, have occasionally become involved in treaty
or marriage arrangements with hungry hunter families. They
lent their animals' meat temporarily. Because hunters tried to
be considerate fellows, and tried to abstain from killing actual
animal souls (i.e. essences), they played some friendly "game"
of cyclic fun and happiness with their victims. Of course, the
norms of what constitutes perfect fun did always vary somewhat between predators and their victims. Be that as it may,
human hunters were happy for winning the animals' meat, and
the animals, supposedly, enjoyed being set up reverently by
their hunters for their next resurrection. Placing a victim's
bones (i.e. its soul essence) into bodies of water or under living
trees to assure its resurrection and to invite him formally to
another chase, seems to have been one of mankind's first steps
of sportsman's "religious" retreat. It involved the reduction of
raw conquest and heroism to treaties of fair play, game, and
sportsmanship. This essayist has always been impressed by the
intensity with which primitive hunters still love to gamble.
Their legends tend to intensify gambling episodes to where the
gambler's life itself is lost. Gambling episodes of this sort are
primitive secularized versions of mystic surrenders.

Our modern understanding of hunting as a game of sport and
our way of defining victims today as "game animals," appears
indeed tasteless and flat when compared with the ancient
dramatic rounds of facilitating an animal's death and resurrection. Indeed, modern hunters no longer have very valid reasons
for explaining their killings as "sport" or for calling their vic-

tims "game." In our modern version of hunters' "sport" only one party has a real choice in the matter. This latterday unsportsmanlike arrangement, solidly based on the religious justifications of later domesticators, trustees, and owners, has severely affected our ability to understand primitive hunters. Still searching after unspoiled human children of Nature, who supposedly have remained in harmony with their environment, many a modern ethnologist has regularly overlooked the universal presence of guilt. He has therefore also generally misunderstood the abundance of religious retreat measures which peoples all over the world have developed to alleviate their guilt. Gestures of religious retreat range all the way from self-surrender and fasting to near-egalitarian—artistic and sportive—flattery of the gods. Carried from the realm of religion into analytic philosophy, where gods are reduced to abstract principles and manageable concepts, religious retreat behavior is being transposed again into postures of persuasion and aggressiveness thus into nonreligion.

Artistic retreat from the struggle for existence, away from the ambiguities which sportsmen still leave unresolved, presents an additional step in the direction of religious surrender. What athletes try to naturalize by rules of fair play and by retreat to pre-technological chivalry, remains to artistic sensibilities nevertheless infinitely ugly and unfair. Artists, for the most part, tend to ignore the sportsman's competitiveness.

In a primitive context, the arts of image-making were far more guilt-ridden and far less egotistic than we with hindsight and forward-reaching creativity prefer to interpret them. Images of animals are being painted and figurines representing them are being fashioned to this day to reconstitute lost limbs and bodies. Sometimes such measures were undertaken to restore animals whom hunters have wounded in self-defense but toward whom initially they had no hostile intentions. Artistic representations of this kind appear to be continuations of earlier bone displays arranged by guilty killer minds to assure the continued, though "domesticated", existence of individual victims. Rock paintings of Australian aborigines are created for the propagation and the return of specific totemic lines. Since Australian totemic boundaries do cut across animal and human clans, their ceremonialism on behalf of the "spirit children's" return to a state of living-in-bodies applies to all species, including humankind. Similar artistic reconstructions are made in many parts of the world for the reconstitution of human as well as animal patients, even for the restoration of entire disrupted worlds in which patients hope to recover for living longer lives.

The verbal arts of chant, prayer, and narration (philosophy and history included), involve the entire spectrum of possible human perfections. The perfect heroic hunter is a successful killer. Moving closer to the balance point of human decency he converts to the role of an athlete or an ideal sportsman, namely, of someone who hunts by divine rules and who on account of his conforming can be trusted by his human peers. His weapons are as dangerous to the latter as to game animals.

The boundary between hunter athletics and hunter arts is as vague as the one between general heroics and athletics. A perfect hunter is a successful killer and trickster. As superior trickster he not only kills his victims but also demonstrates generosity to the delight of his peers. Delighting his peers, an artistically active hunter transforms for them their natural world into human culture. All the while an artist does not advance far beyond the realm of re-creation. Athletes re-create their own bodies; artists re-create their natural environs into culture. Their measures of self-discipline have helped them escape at least the limitations of raw heroic perfection. Re-creation, for a discerning human mind, must be more than mere heroic destruction and novel re-arrangement.

Dance rhythms relive the original deed of divine proto-hunters. With divinely intuited artistic responses they beautify and perfect the bloody version that had been performed imperfectly in the field perhaps only hours earlier. Their deadly clubs are being refined into drumsticks, and hollow-sounding trees are used as substitutes for victims' skulls. Two bows, one tickling and neutralizing another, add up to a fiddle. The communal reenactment of a timelessly divine, justified, and therefore perfect deed is what finally cancels incongruent and specific memories from the killer's conscience.

Thus, in primitive life art blends easily into religion. Killers, hunter companions, and beneficiaries at the camp who themselves cautiously avoid wielding the powers of death, become all reintegrated into a divinely reconciled and justified order. They enter into this order by way of rhythms, song, and dance, which all had been revealed to them by greater-than-human inspirers and sponsors. *Homo religiosus* retreats from awareness of sin; he has become a responsible, that is, a scientious *and* con-scientious predator-innovator. He retreats from aggression by artistically realigning himself again and again with the better order that somehow during his struggle for survival seems to have been eluding him. That better and perfect order appears as though it must always have been there and must somewhere be present now. But it must be rediscovered again and again in the future. Eating the fruit of knowledge is always a two-directional affair; a *Homo sapiens* is of necessity also a *Homo religiosus*.

Of course, ceremonial rites are not in the same degree "religious" retreats for all ceremonial participants. While rank-and-file participants may fall into private states of trance-surrender, their ceremonial leaders might remain quite aloof and may even rise a notch or two on the social scale by artistically perfecting their talents as cheerleaders. Or, as leaders they might find it more honest and easier to compete with their peers in the embellishment of personal trance experiences—of amplifying their experiences into perfect dramatic performances. Religious ceremonialism is accompanied anywhere in the world by a substantial amount of social competition and bluffing. Ceremonials therefore have a tendency of always becoming more boisterous than would actually be called for by merely meeting up humbly with the greater-than-human reality that is being encountered. From overstaged displays of glory and excitement, which as artistic performances become enjoyable and worthwhile in themselves, it is quite possible for a participant to emerge with his self-esteem and status on the rise. An intentionally beautiful performance establishes a norm—a plateau sublime enough to entice the gods to descend and to participate. After excitements and trances subside, the human ego can continue to cling to the symbolism of its own artistic plateau, and so dwell near its gods. It may also proceed to embellish its symbolism further. The more man adds to his religious responses the more he immunizes himself against the possibility of total religious surrender, and the more his so-conceived greater-than-human reality is indebted to him for his contribution to the hierophany. Singing, whistling, or running away in the dark can thus be transformed, artistically and ceremonially, into confident hope and pleasant patterns of daytime consciousness.

The inducement of trance in the rituals that primitive human hunters perform provides important clues for our understanding of their existential "teeter totter." Their lives, like ours, can be plotted at any given moment along the scale of a continuum—their teeter totter—ranging from heroic killing to mystic surrender. (See diagram above.) A primitive hunter's act of killing registers at the point of "control," but his submission to trance happens at the point of "surrender."

Over a period of several years this writer has become increasingly impressed by the nonchalant moments of disciplined humility that certain primitive hunters display right after they have killed their victims. He has reexamined their hunting methods as well as their rituals and rationales through which they endeavor (as fellow mortals) to undo their bloody deeds. At the very least their ceremonial precautions aim at warding off the post-mortem anger of their victims, or at avoiding the punishment of such gods as are concerned about the well-being of these victims. But then, when the apologetic and sometimes penitential gestures of hominid killers are examined more closely, the reciprocal relationship between their artificial trickery and their religious surrenderings comes into focus. The hunter who has stabbed his admired victims and made them collapse into transfixed immobility experiences in his own trances and religious surrenders a similar treatment to what he himself had inflicted on his victims. Some greater-than-human predator, surely some just and balancing god, now hunts and pierces human hunters. One might marvel at the reasonableness of it all. How else, in a hunters' world, should one account reasonably for human defeats, for human sufferings and death!

The imprint which surrenderings of primitive hunters have left upon our modern metaphors of sexuality still betrays this ancient religious context of surrender to divine hunters. Our experiences of "falling in love," which frequently entail a measure of trance and ego-surrender, are to this day still symbolized by a hunter's bow and arrow—by Cupid's bow and an arrow that pierces human hearts.

As long as human intelligence is capable of registering responses of fascination, awe, trembling, fear, trance, and surrender it will eventually be led by its own standards of common sense to recognize the presence of some thing greater-than-human. As the result of additional reflection a human mind will sooner or later also discover that, in order to be truly greater-than-human, the source of its fears must be a kind of personage. More specifically, in a world where potential human equals are hunter-tricksters, it follows that this greater-than-human dimension is made manifest to them by certain greater personal hunter beings, i.e. by predator and trickster gods. The eventual surrender in sickness and death of all mortal hunters remains an inescapable fate; it reduces hunters to the level of their victims and thereby also defines the nature of their hunter gods.

Of course, no primitive hunter can respond perfectly throughout his life to all possible reality configurations—neither with methods of conquest, of sports, arts, nor of religious retreat. In the course of a lifetime, mystic surrender comes easiest for infants and then again for the very old. Wise old people at all levels of culture have learned to smile knowingly with friendly twinklings of their eyes whenever they reminisce about the foolishness of youth in general; they have been *there* and have successfully decoded some of the mysteries of both youth and life. On the other hand, their facial expressions become more somber when they undertake to recast their bloody deeds as mature killers—for this they drift into the artistry of heroic boasting and epic poetry. Further along on his path of aging a wise hunter-mystic acquiesces to his fate of falling into the hands of a divine hunter. He begins to see himself transfigured, as a reconciled non-killer who lingers in peace together with all "peoples" of the living world, including gods, humans, animals, plants, and even minerals.

What does it all come to? Only situation ethics and relative sacralities? Far from it. Even young and strong hunters can afford to be somewhat philosophical, or even religiously thankful, after enough animals have been laid low. Relativity among human ideals of perfection certainly does not call for another mortal's hypocritical disdain. The mere fact that we are able to discern variations among norms of perfection, surely, does not eliminate our basic predator predicament of having to kill some kind of living creature before we are able to eat. The *Genesis* narrative, mentioned at the beginning of this essay, is thoroughly realistic in this regard. Civilized specialization, which enables citizens to hire professional killers and butchers in exchange for artistically designed and printed money, provides no unambiguous cure for a sensitized religious conscience. The "sin" which is mentioned in that story is not traced to plucking or killing—both being services which civilized people might purchase—but to basic ordinary everyperson's eating. A common gesture of religious retreat from the original sin of eating can be found practiced worldwide in the form of its undisguised opposite—in fasting. Many modified gestures of partial repentance from eating, such as food tabus related and traceable to extreme fasting, can also be found worldwide.

Young hunter-killers become more considerate, more educated and "perfected," by listening to artfully told religious old men's and old women's tales. By these they learn to hunt with restraint and to observe a great number of religiously sanctioned rules and limitations. As useless and as counterproductive as these educational subject matters might presently seem to modern one-directional critics, young hunters were indeed educated in the old men's mystic visions concerning some paradisiac prehuman/prehunter condition—they were indeed told about a time when all families of latterday predators and victims, on earth, still lived together in peace. Maturing hunters educated into these utopian visions, who in addition have learned to live under the tutelage of some greater-than-human sponsor, become more humane in the process. They have acquired the intellectual wherewithals that enable them to back away from social confrontations with their self-esteem still intact. Instead of bowing to potential equals they bow to gods; they live for a destiny which transcends present disputes, and in the process of bowing and hoping they get along better with those of their fellows who are also bowing.

Without some kind of commonsense religious retreat from exaggerated humanoid aggression, now and then, an intelligent and introspective hunter could not hope to balance his ego and to survive even among his own kind. Reasoned aggression always has necessitated, for balance and for justified existence, an equally well-reasoned pattern of retreat behavior. Human survival in the company of humankind required the perfection of "balanced coexistence." In some formulation of the Golden Rule this vision of balance had to be rediscovered—revealed and sanctioned by greater-than-human reality—for every human activity in every era of human evolution. All the while, the vision of a perfection of "balanced coexistence," in harmony with the Golden Rule, could obviously not without severe strains be applied to all the living creatures whom hunters eat. The general pathos which is highlighted in primitive hunter religions has resulted from the necessity of such compromise. Hunters cannot naturally coexist by the Golden Rule with those creatures whom they kill and eat. The perfection of harmonious or "balanced coexistence" had to be reduced by rational hunters to something that became logically unthinkable—a "perfection" of "moderation."

THE PERFECT DOMESTICATOR

Humankind awoke to the possibility of domestication in swells and waves. There was the long drawn-out domestication of the mineral world—from the utilization of bone and stone to the control of fire, and thence to metallurgy. Each step of progress in domestication, recognized as such by *Homo sapiens*, implies the lure and attainment of another level of perfection. Success in domestication efforts depends on two things—first on the degree of religious surrender which is accepted by the victims, and second on the resolve which can playfully be cultivated among the conquerors themselves. From among the animals, dogs apparently fell into their camp-follower role quite easily. A human child's playful use of hands, pushing a playful puppy down against the ground by its neck, mimics the natural playful encounters by which members of a *Canis* pack are being ranked. A mutual interest in hunting has subsequently deepened the relationships that were established between human hunter folk and infantile puppies. Later in human evolution, similar playfulness, mothering, and filial imprinting facilitated the domestication of young grazing animals whom hunters quite frequently turned into orphans. Primate imitators, imitating the parents of other animals, became functional parents for the offspring of their victims. Their foster parents roles placed them into a position from which they could dictate most subsequent terms of relational behavior.

The great leap forward in the domestication of plants and animals was taken during the past 14,000 years in the Near East, subsequently and ever since in other parts of the world. Meanwhile, the ancient domestication of minerals for the manufacture of tools has slowly crept toward degrees of greater complexity—or perfection. During the 19th century this development virtually exploded into production of complex machinery and of explosive marvels that by now are riduculously out of proportion with actual human needs. If one were to exclude from consideration the general play behavior of primates and to examine modern human behavior by principles of rationality alone, our relationships with gadgets and machines would have to remain completely incomprehensible.

The boundary between hunting and domestication in the entire animal world is rather ambiguous. The beginnings of domestication techniques can be seen already in the world of animals. Squirrels bury nuts in the ground, those which they fail to retrieve for food will grow into trees to be harvested by future generations of squirrels. Beavers build dams and by their dams keep fish. On the open ranges of Africa lionesses watch herds of grazing animals. Their cowgirl strategy and teamwork for singling out and bringing low individual herd animals is most impressive. In human evolution it took much effort and craft, including the domestication of horses and the making of ropes, before cowboys would come close to such natural performance. Far north in the arctic tundra, wolves follow and "work" herds of reindeer in a remarkably similar fashion.

The boundary between human hunting and domestication is equally ambiguous, especially in situations where human populations have not yet decimated large wild grazing herds. Take the case of the Lapps and their reindeer. They follow and work their herds of reindeer as do wolves elsewhere in the arctic circle where men are absent. Only a small number of their animals are actually tamed and used to pull sleds, the remainder of the herd is permitted to follow their accustomed migration routes. Perhaps the only reason why the Lapps do not bother to extend their control over the reindeer much beyond that of the wolves is the absence of alternate pasture lands. After they acquired Spanish horses, Plains Indians followed and preyed on buffalo herds with a similar hunter-domesticator ambiguity. And then today, the descendants of these buffalos now grazing in fenced national parks are "managed" by federal rangers so as to protect their "wildness." How small must pastures be for guarded grazing animals to be classifiable as "domesticated?" Or, for the sake of this essay, at what point are conditions suitable for human controllers to be "perfect" domesticators— "good" shepherds? Thus, at every level of human culture "perfection" is being defined in revolutionary fashion, in terms of some former greater-than-human reality that is being imitated and eventually upstaged by man.

It now appears that the era of stonetool-hunters was dominated by two kinds of divinities—representatives of predators and representatives of victims. A Master or a Mistress of Animals, or both together as a pair, represented in the late Stone Age the animals that humans hunted. The animals who lived under the tutelage of these gods were eventually classified by modern humans as "game animals." On the side of the human hunters roamed the greater-than-human animal predators, experienced by humans as divine hunter tutelaries. In due time some of these divine predator-tricksters competed with the representative animal masters of the "game animals" side. They continued to justify the lifestyle of their human protégés as fellow usurpers—as Thief-masters-of-animals and as Predator-trickster-transformers—until their human protégés became better domesticators and preferred dealing with more legitimate greater divine owners.

On the horizon of the late Stone Age art a new iconography and set of symbols appear. Male and female symbols appear in association with images of huntable animals. Such symbolization is significant, because hunters who think "male versus female" in relation to wild animals are actually thinking the thoughts, and are depicting the concerns, of divine Masters and Mistresses of Animals. When human minds reached for the thoughts of these greatest among hunter gods, they stretched and reached for another level of divine perfection. A "good" hunter—as defined by his band and his family—was one who brought home meat most of the time. By his own estimate, however, a "perfect" huntsman would have been one who has access to all the animals all the time—like the supreme Master or Mistress has access to the entire animal stock. Before these human usurpers of divine thoughts and roles had become aware of what they had wrought, their own ambitions and their new scopes of relationship with animals had already transformed them into other kinds of beings, into herders. They had become human masters of animals.

In this manner it was discovered that a "perfect hunter" had to be a "herder." With eyes thus opened by the fruit of knowledge, the "good" and "evil" in the animal world was also reevaluated and rediscovered. Good animals were those who were docile and could be easily enslaved; bad animals were those who remained monsters and insisted on roaming wild. And how were the hunter gods redefined—now that their authority as animal masters had been usurped? What kind of god occupied the next rung on the ladder of evolutionary religious perfection? The type of deity who revealed itself next, and who from that point on helped explain rationally the universal religious experiences of humans—namely fascination, awe, trembling, fear, trance, and surrender—was a size greater than the former patrons of animals of the hunter era. It was a divine lord of animals, yes, but also of human families and tribes (i.e. of human herds); and it was its presence and imitable example which, from that point onward, lured some guilty human usurpers of the Master of Animals toward the next degree of egotistic perfection.

The hiatus between hunter and domesticator religiousity can best be bridged with a historical outline of sacrifice. The history of sacrifice can be studied with profit as the backbone of the entire history of religions. Primitive hunters offered share sacrifices, portions from the bodies of their victims, as food offerings to certain greater-than-human predator sponsors. In the same manner pious herders and planters subsequently felt obligated to offer shares from their herds and fields—thus firstborn animals and firstfruits. Prepayment to divine providers for all subsequently born animals and subsequently harvested fruits was by far the safest way to forestall a deity's hungry anxiety. A god's distrust toward human sharecroppers could conceivably deteriorate into angry measures of foreclosure or greater-than-human stinginess in retaliation. On that account, an early show of appreciation by man (i.e. prepayment) was the safest and most direct way to obtain clear title for subsequently produced domesticated animals and plants.

The change in size of sacrificial offerings, from meat portions given by hunters to whole animals given by herders, reflects the obvious. Whole animals are portions of herds, and basketfuls of fruits are portions of harvested fields. In addition, hunters and gatherers who had become perfected into herders and planters felt not only obligated to adjust the size of their gifts; their methods of presentation required adjustment as well. Methods had to be adjusted to handle the magnitude of the offerings as well as the magnitude of the sacrificers' hopes—their claims to title and divine justification. By presenting whole animals and whole containerfuls, a domesticator ceremonially magnified his moments of killing, of cutting, and of giving.

The ceremonial magnification of a domesticator's sacrifice stands in direct contrast to hunter experience and practice. A primitive hunter's pursuit and excitement comes to its climax often at the height of exhaustion. Killing is done as swiftly as possible and is then frequently followed by moments of embarrassed or even guilt-ridden silence. By contrast, butchering an animal from a domesticated herd seems unheroic, unsportsmanlike, and definitely unfulfilling for masculine egos. Religious ceremonialism had to fill the void which the transition from hunter excitement to domesticator routine had left in those increasingly self-conscious predator souls. So, for example, in order to compensate for the scarcity of bears, the Ainus of Hokkaido developed their bear hunts into lengthy sacrifices of domesticated bears, into major spectacles of prolonged torture. The *via dolorosa* of the domesticator's sacrificial victims was lengthened and accented in many gruesome ways. The counterpart of a successful hunt, in the era of domestication, is a ceremonially perfected sacrifice.

By presenting whole animals and baskets of fruits, and by the ceremonial amplification of unsportsmanlike killings, the domesticators' notion of killing for the gods became separated from ordinary secular and self-serving butchering. By this process the domesticator became, on the one hand, an owner of less-than-human creatures, and on the other a justified and more perfect sacrificer. The perfection to which he attained, covering up his loss of roaming and filling the void which was left in his nostalgic predator soul, transformed him into a magnificent master of ceremonies. The hunter shaman who once ministered to professional tricksters had become a sedentary priest. Trickery, the attribute which defined perfection at the functional hunter level of evolution, became a foil for sedentary values and norms of perfection.

Domestication necessitated the development of a variety of tools, it stimulated the arts and the crafts. In this cultural context, the gods of domesticator-artisans offered a new kind of justification for the ownership of herds and fields. Being themselves enthusiastic creators and makers, they sanctioned and rewarded the steady labors of human makers and domesticators. This new right, *to own* the fruits of one's labor, contrasts strikingly with the work ethics that governed primitive and religiously sensitive hunting. The work of hunters was trickery, murder, robbery, and theft. The gods of hunters were not given credit for such an irrelevant point as creating or making a world *ex nihilo*; rather, they were respected for having been superior tricksters and transformers, for being spontaneous to do as they pleased in accordance with momentary situations.

But among watchful domesticators and keepers of animals an acquisition of property, by hunter methods, seemed no longer functional or ethical. Because sedentary planters gathered, and herders assembled and tried to hold on to as many possessions as they could, ancient trickster-transformer gods in their midst were eventually reevaluated and rediscovered as untrustworthy devils.

A realistic evaluation of life and death has further amplified the need and mode in which sacrifices were subsequently to be offered. Whereas originally hunters simply inflicted themselves on their victims, only to interrupt those individual victims' lives, domesticators took charge of their animals from the time of conception to birth, through nurture, and unto death. Domesticators of plants have discovered an additional happenstance. Seeding and harvesting, one belonging to the beginning and the other to the end of a planter's work cycle, both signified the same reality—death. Harvesting was cutting and killing, planting was burial, and germination demonstrated the fact of resurrection to new life. In addition to its own seasonal process of sacrificial death and resurrection, the cycle of plant life was producing spinoff benefits for the sustenance and re-creation of humankind.

To all these givens in a domesticator's experience one must add the fact that, after an entire era of hunting, primitive males had to be weaned from roaming and had to be retrained for a life of restrained nomadic herding or sedentary planting. One can easily see how the life-sustaining, ego-filling, deeds of our primitive hunter ancestors had to be amplified into sacrificial ceremonialism. In certain equatorial paleo-planter cultures this application of planter philosophy led to headhunting and cannibalism. In the cradle lands of Western civilization it has, with a blend of herder logic, led to the sacrifice of firstborn specimens from human herds. A good planter controls the destiny of his plants from beginning to end, and his awakened mind must explain how it is that sacrificial substances build human bodies. The domesticator's sense of rightful ownership, caught up in a mysticism of sacrificial food essences, convinces him that he must pay his dues in kind—in the form of his own life-juices and blood.

In a world where wild animals have become scarce, and with philosophical introspection of this sort of food mysticism, ingenious men who all along would rather have hunted than dug roots or gathered humble seeds in the company of women, discovered their new function and meaning of life in cosmic speculation and amplified religious ceremonialism. Former hunter-killers found their new identity as philosophical and artistic killer priests, also as heroic members of noble warrior bands. On either path they became justified killers of humankind. Men's secret societies, sacrificial priesthoods, noble warrior associations, veterans clubs and business-men's societies, have all labored diligently since domestication began to arrange a beautiful and honorable—and when possible a magnificent and glorious—retreat for the chronically artificial and guilty hunter. The new pursuit of domestication, which precipitated and institutionalized its own concommitant norms of human perfectability, was straightway exaggerated into "overdomestication." What this essayist calls "overdomestication" some historians have called "civilization." But the addition of a hyped-up new name will only serve to conceal, not to remove, the exaggeration of an aberration. Civilization is merely domestication "perfected" and overdone.

THE PERFECT OVERDOMESTICATOR

Inasmuch as the companion essays in this anthology all concern themselves with perfectionisms of the past four thousand years, this section of the present essay, and the next, can be presented more briefly. To reduce this section's thesis to the size of a nutshell: *Good* domesticators answered the tempter's challenge to become *perfect* domesticators. Thus they *imitated* and *became* the gods of less perfect fellow domesticators. They became overdomesticators.

By overdomestication we mean such assertive human activities as go beyond the mere control and exploitation of minerals, plants, or animals. Overdomesticators move beyond to where they also organize and control human herds as well as the gods of herded people. Of course, as he thinks the category "*over-domestication*," the writer implies a value judgment. Even though, throughout the history of civilizations, scribes and writers have in the service of overdomesticators fared better than most—betraying humanity by keeping track of it as possessions and by producing justificational propaganda—this writer dislikes the end product. He dislikes slavery in any form and regards the slaughter of human beings with disgust, no matter how purportedly noble the cause may be made out to be. But liked or disliked, the ambition by which civilizations have been generated—overdomestication—is an undeniable fact of history.

Efficient domesticators have surpassed themselves while usurping the roles of tribal gods, they have thus come to claim ownership of human tribes for themselves. Applying the methods of beekeepers, they have succeeded in controlling people by sponsoring the cults of regional and tribal gods. Wherever a divine "queen bee" is being kept, in a box, there her worker bees will collect honey.

Overdomesticators have organized two basic human activities, from two evolutionary epochs; they have restructured these two activities to where they could coexist side by side: the conquests of hunters and the labors of domesticators. Fighter herds of warriors were institutionalized on the strength of men's nostalgia for something resembling the hunters' moments of truth; worker herds of serfs and slaves were maintained on the basis of maker-domesticator work ethics. Both types of herds were organized under gods with whom the people were already familiar but who were installed by over-domesticators in subordinate divine ranks. The overdomesticator himself, to the extent that he was able to keep his competitors at bay, would himself answer only to the greatest God in the world. His imperial "God of gods," on the other hand, was defined and manifested physically by his own person. From the perspective of owned servants beneath them, both the royal overdomesticator and his universal God blended into a single greater-than-human reality. In many civilizations both positioned themselves in such a manner that their appearance could also be backed by the splendor of sky and sun. While the god-kings of ancient Egypt were excellent examples of such overdomestication enterprises, the claims of Roman emperors to divine status, millennia later, echo ambitions of the same sort.

Of course the overdomesticator founders of great civilizations were not originally inhumane monsters or parasites. Naturally enough, they continued the religious pattern of authority which had already been established in the predomesticator era by shamanic leaders of hunter bands. Whichever hunter of a group was possessed by the greatest divine sponsor naturally displayed the greatest intellect and rendered the most

impressive insights in the pursuit of hunter trickery and liveli-
hood. If one were to take a hypothetical hunter band with a
distinguished shaman for a leader, and if one were somehow to
force them together to become sedentary planters—what
emerges at the top would still be a divinely predator-possessed
chief. Give his ambitions sufficient generations of time for
growth, and the end product will be some sort of divine emperor of the kind of which Near Eastern civilizations have produced quite many. Their totemic crests of divine falcon- eagle-
lion- and wolf-tutelaries still reveal their roots in hunter religion.

In spite of their preference for divine predator sponsors,
many kings have added to their regalia the staff of not only
"some great domesticator" but also of "the good shepherd."
Their divine hold on herds of human individuals of lesser status
was often experienced and celebrated by both high and low as
a divine gift and blessing. This drama of stratification began to
unfold, innocently enough, in the wake of learning domesticator
tricks—when successful patriarchs among domesticators began
to command the respect of their less successful fellow domesticators. The same dynamic that had earlier showed off natural
predators as man's hunter gods also lifted the most successful
human domesticators to the height of a model in the art of
domestication. Beyond the vague point where apprentices became willing to learn more than domesticator methods, where
they also learned how to defer to and to flatter superiors to
their own advantage, they themselves became the subject matter about which they had hoped to learn more. The courage of
a very successful domesticator, such as that demonstrated in
our time by trainers of lions and tigers, appears heroic and godlike to most others. Snake charmers, too, still earn their awesome respect in direct proportion to the fearsomeness of the
reptiles that they control. All these responses to awesome animal gods can easily be mobilized for religious and political purposes.

Once begun, the fears which are generated by an overdomesticator's performance and charisma are transferred and attached symbolically to the religio-political edifice which he
builds. Fears toward so-conceived greater-than-human configurations of reality, toward divinities and god-kings, and fears
toward neighboring and hostile overdomestication systems become, when they are mobilized by overdomesticators, practi-

cally indistinguishable. The mixture of fear from religious as well as political sources of conceptualization serves as the glue which holds individual overdomestication systems together. Human frailty and mortality underscore the significance of all religious fears, and vulnerability to attack from neighboring overdomestication systems establishes the necessity of deference to one's own leaders and the necessity of cooperation for defense. Beyond these predicaments of existential and societal survival, prudence often dictates the less costly approach of arranging confrontations at one's own terms. On the side of religious surrender this means initiation into a less scary death process, and on the side of societal aggression the solution is found by organizing a war campaign.

The most successful overdomesticators have always tried to view war as their kind of sport, with nothing more than their personal "possessions" at stake. When their contests were over, when it was time to count what could be held, they covenanted and intermarried with their opponents. Former enemies were flattered and celebrated as brethren, that is, as potential equals who happen to control other overdomestication systems. Each "great" or "good shepherd" may have lost some specimens from his herd, but the fight usually was well worth its price. His herd of thinking animals had again been purged by the fear of death. It had been consolidated by the brotherhood of battle, by the sorrow of loss, and it had been reborn by the mobilized reconstruction which followed.

At the religious level, where human beings respond to greater-than-human configurations of reality, the overdomestication of human societies requires the domiciling of their gods. Indeed, the civilizing methods of overdomesticators are surprisingly ordinary schemes of domestication, merely amplified.

By the same methods of building pens and stables with which domesticators control the domicile of their animals, overdomesticators build somewhat more elaborate temples—to correspond to the glory of those who will be kept there. Ordinary domesticators establish boundaries and build fences; overdomesticators map out sacred territories. Domesticators control pastures and food supply; overdomesticators set up altars on which to offer sacrificial food. But how are gods brought into stables like animals? Many gods, since hunter days, were already known in their form as animals; then, beginning with the last great hunter gods, of the Master of Animals type, anthropomorphic hierophanies have been envisioned. In the forms of many animals, of anthropomorphs, and of beings caught in a twilight existence between those two, early overdomesticators invited their people's gods into the magnificent pens which they had built for them. With the proper pomp and glory, heroics and athletics were sublimated into heroic arts. And wonder of wonders! The sculpted divine anthropomorphs entered their magnificent temples with less resistance than domesticators formerly encountered when they tamed their first theriomorphic live specimens. Human overdomesticators promptly prescribed visiting hours for their divine captives—to protect their privacy and their exclusive status, of course. Festivals during which the people could joyously approach their gods, days of rest prescribed by sacred calendars, would graciously interrupt the people's work and fighting schedules. By some kind of divine providence they also just happened to coincide with some officials' deadlines for census taking, conscription, or the collection of taxes.

And what happened during all this in the world of theology? What happened to the god, who as theriomorph or anthropomorph stood in a lifeless temple, immoveably transfixed to impersonate the forces of life outside? Being housed, entertained, fed, bathed, and pampered by his chosen human overdomesticator—the god became dependent on the latter. Any god who for the management of his cult and for the manifestation of his presence depends on a human overdomesticator, reveals himself necessarily as a second-greatest power in the world, next to his human sponsor. At the same time, in relation to a god thus maintained and kept by him, no sanctions, no checks or balances, remain intact to obligate the human overdomesticator. In the wake of extended tyrannical abuse of divine authority, and insofar as daily toil has failed to stupify all human minds permanently, herds of *Homines sapientes* eventually reasoned and hoped themselves into becoming receptive to a new revelation of divinity—one which reduced previous overdomesticators again to the status of potential equals or, while the going was good, threw them below that level into hell. Rejected overdomestication systems are weighed on the scales of new divinities, of new soteriologies and revelations. They are found wanting, are consequently judged and defeated.

When an overdomesticator sacrifices to his imperial deity, or to lesser gods whom he and his personal deity together patronize, his status is not served best by presenting only the same kind of animal specimens which ordinary domesticators could afford and present equally well. The firstborn victims from his choicest herds are not animals but human specimens. Moreover, the higher-born his sacrificial victims are the nobler will appear his intentions and the more awesome his power and wealth. Inasmuch as human sacrifices are understood as share payments to gods who collaborate with overdomesticators—as amplifications of hunters' and domesticators' share offerings—ownership of human herds becomes divinely legitimized. Upwards of fifty thousand human victims were sacrificed to dedicate a late Aztec pyramid and to provide a divine Earth Serpent manifestation with its first feeding. Slaughters which redeem and valorize modern politico-ideological systems necessitate counting their human victims by the millions.

Once it is viewed as a divine quality and identified with a greatest conceivable reality configuration, the power of over-domesticators knows no upward limit of perfectability. The pool from which an overdomesticator draws his authority and power is as unfathomable as the appetite of his God of gods might prove to be insatiable. The only delimiting factors appear to be the availability of sacrificial victims and the symbolic scope of a god's manifestation. As a rule, lions devour more victims than lambs, and eagles destroy more lives than turkeys. The symbolic scope of a god's manifestation must be humanized in a perpetual competition among priestly storytellers, prophets and reformers; the supply of sacrificial victims becomes a matter of economics, and it concerns the ability of groups to free themselves from the symbols of herd mentality.

As the supply of human victims dwindles, and as potential victims begin to think and to resist the patriotism of herds, to reject the greatness and glory of sacrificer priests, or to drop out from the power configurations of divine kings and imperial high gods, the overdomesticator's attempt at civilization crumbles. Restless herds of potential victims, those who have been awakened to the democratized invitation to come and eat from the tree of knowledge *together*, then reexamine the apparent universality of their master's God of gods. Sooner or later a tyrannical overdomesticator provokes the discovery of a new gospel, the good news, that the real God of gods loves and cares for victims, or that he is greater than the one who merely collaborates with overdomesticators. On this crucial insight turns the next period of religious evolution. Desperate human minds have been readied for a new theophany. And human imitators being what they are, they will, in turn, by their encounter with this new theophany, discover and project a newer and still higher norm of human perfectability.

PERFECTION AMONG THE SAVED

The ferment of universal salvation religion was already bubbling in India at full-strength several centuries before the Christian movement began in the Near East. Hippie-monks, in great numbers, emerged from the castles and schools where India's best were being reared. Displaying immense collages of sacrificial rites, the Brahmanic overdomestication cult had been building up its strength for nearly a millennium before it finally crested and collapsed into more inwardly oriented ways of spiritualized retreat. Mahavira, the founder of Jainism, and Gotama, the founder of Buddhism, were aristocrats who during their younger years were prime candidates for overdomesticator roles. But they and their numerous followers, together with a host of nonaligned seekers, preferred a life of poverty, nonviolence and celibacy, to overdomesticator status and kingship.

Reverberations from this largest hippie walkout in human history, in India, two and a half millennia ago, reached during successive centuries the Hellenistic Near East. The spiritual and philosophical ferment in the Near East reflects strong traces of influence from this change of mood in Eastern religiosity. As in India, spiritual seekers and mystics in Near Eastern desert lands withdrew into solitude and poverty.

Nevertheless, protests against overdomesticators in the history of Near Eastern religions two millennia ago were nothing new. The history of religious protests in Near Eastern civilizations merits attention by itself. Three millennia ago · King David, an Israelite rebel leader gone royal, began to sponsor the recording of religious traditions of certain patriarchal families. Abraham, a personage who might have lived almost another millennium earlier, is identified in those records as the first patriarch who reverted back from overdomesticator sacrifice of human firstborns to the simple animal sacrifices of domesticators.

This backing away from overdomestication by a patriarch, nearly four millennia ago, matched nicely the later obvious flight away from Egyptian civilization by Israelite slaves under the leadership of Moses. All of it together harmonizes again, of course, with the aspirations of David's people three millennia ago—with their escapings from Philistine city authorities along the weakening frontier of Egyptian civilization.

In Egypt, under the monotheistic and increasingly popular priesthood of Amon, god-kings were challenged by wise men to rule as better and more righteous shepherds over their entrusted people. Monarchy and priesthood could, indeed, supplement each other as "checks and balances." The Exodus of the Israelites from Egyptian bondage, however, illustrates the new protestant mood with considerably sharper theological contrasts. Yahweh, a god who would not tell his name to Moses, defeated in the end the Egyptian nameless God of gods, Amon. "Yahweh" is not a name, and "Amon" is not the Egyptian God's real name either. Because Moses must surely have studied Amon theology in Egypt during his early years, many years before he heard Yahweh speak, the story's insistence on the namelessness of Yahweh in his contest for the title "God of gods" holds no surprises. Like Yahweh, so to some extent already the Egyptian Amon showed concern for the well-being of ordinary citizens—which in the Egyptian context stands in sharp contrast, for instance, with Aton's exclusive care for his pretentious chosen son, Akhenaton.

But there is one immense and practical difference between these two theologies, namely, the manner in which each is anchored in real life. Amon was the God of gods for members of the Egyptian empire, and Yahweh appeared as the God of gods who sponsored tribes of runaway *habiru* (the Egyptian word for outlaws), who, in turn, came to think of themselves as *yisrahel* (a term suggesting fighters of God). While on many subsequent occasions the religious outlook of these *yisrahel* tribes relapsed into postures of ethnic defensiveness and nationalistic overreaction and aggression, and while outsiders often were excluded from the special ethnic covenant which they contracted with their "God of gods," one universalistic kernel of conviction nevertheless preserved their tradition as a seedbed for subsequent universalisms. The God of gods, God of heaven and earth, had chosen an insignificant group of slaves, who for generations had been victims to mighty overdomesticators. Their God, identified simply as "One who is," has triumphed on their behalf against the greatest Near Eastern contender for the title of God of gods. The unthinkable in an overdomesticator's world has happened. The divine winner in a liberation contest of surviving underdogs has come to be hailed as the real God of gods.

Jesus, the Christian savior-surrenderer, stands in a long line of Israelite prophetic protesters. As his prophetic predecessors, he, likewise, ignored overdomesticator claims and maintained personal contact directly with the God of gods. As did many Jews in his day, Jesus spoke to God directly as to his personal heavenly Father—his "heavenly Daddy," to be more precise. He counselled his followers to become as perfect as their heavenly Father happens to be.

"Now watch this!" Such will surely be the response of my attentive readers. This invitation by Jesus sounds exactly like another round of familiar temptations to imitation of divine perfection. However, for the time being, the remainder of the life and teachings of this Jesus points unmistakeably in the opposite direction. By the heavenly and fatherly perfection, which Jesus tried to communicate, the traditional lordly perfection of the typical Near Eastern God of gods was thoroughly inverted and challenged.

Playing the role of a beggar king, in a "kingdom" that features no superiors and no inferiors and which, thus, obviously was "not of this world," Jesus rejected the values and claims of overdomesticator kings; he also rejected their notions of world improvement through civilization by increase of overdomestication. He hung on a cross, while they preferred to sit on thrones. He wore a wreath of thorns, while they gloried under crowns of gold. He chose death over conquest, preferred human love to authority and territory. Regardless of where a modern observer now might stand in his herd affiliations and in his personal attitudes toward this Jesus, the historical record speaks for itself. A multitude of poor folks heard his teachings gladly, and they celebrated his resurrection to spite the overdomesticator authorities that had sentenced him to death. They proclaimed him to the world as being both God of gods and King of kings.

Jesus and his cross became the symbol of a mass movement that defiantly and nonviolently redefined divinity and kingship, with the result that the bottom dropped out from under Near Eastern and Mediterranean overdomestication systems. Followers of this Jesus ignored not only the civilized commanders of armed hosts and their claims to divine-royal status, they also repudiated ancient temple cults as vestiges of sacrificial over-domestication. Not even sacrificial methods from the domesticator epoch, being still cruel and bloody, could be maintained. The curtain which concealed a temple's "holy of holies" is said to have been rent in two when this Jesus died. This asserts that the temple cult, with its mystery indecently exposed and no longer maintained, has been rendered ineffectual and obsolete.

The reader who with a measure of compassion for our evolving humankind has followed this essay from its beginning will have found few real surprises. Human aggression and religious repentance have been remarkably consistent through eras and epochs. When our hunter ancestors made their first killer tool, and when they intellectually premeditated and prepared their artificial predator tricks, they were already faced with an imponderable paradox. As hunters they were confronted by the greater-than-human reality of two major dimensions. Master of Animals types of gods maintained a covenant relationship with the victims of humanoid hunters while, on the other hand, human hunters were sponsored and claimed by greater-than-human predators as their chosen and adopted imitator children. Thus, one kind of deity restricted and another encouraged their lifestyles as artificial killers.

Three centuries after Jesus of Nazareth had been gathering a following for his alternative to overdomestication systems, the Kingdom of Heaven, his followers had drifted to the verge of becoming again overdomesticated. Their new place in the Roman Empire was being arranged in the name of that very divine victim, that Lamb of God, by whom they had discovered salvation in the first place. Not all was lost, however. Enshrined in the ritual of this re-overdomesticated Lamb of God, in the Christian mass, there remained institutionalized a check and balance rhythm for life in Western civilization. A sacramental universe demands human reverence and stifles arrogant experimentation. While the mass remained a constant source of temptation to subsequent overdomesticators, it never-theless preserved a measure of unified retreat from raw aggres-siveness. A thousand years later with the Renaissance and Ref-ormation periods that check-and-balance ritualism was analyzed and destroyed to prepare the way for more aggressive liberation movements—namely, "enlightenment" away from the overdomesticated ruler-savior deity of Christendom. When the divine Savior was perceived as favoring the ranks of mod-ern exploiters, the exploited masses had no other choice but to look for help to themselves. An age of democratic revolts began to dawn.

Nationalistic and trans-nationalistic ideals and their slogans have since vied for world attention and supremacy; they have scared masses of human camp-followers into conformity. While in post-Enlightenment days individual overdomesticators can no longer maintain an apparent identity with some nameable ontology—as with some God of gods—they now manage their human herds in the name of certain greater-than-human, imper-sonal, cosmic or temporal processes—or by whatever slogan which might the last time around have brought them a measure of freedom. Providential destinies, divine orders and processes, natural orders and processes, historical processes, and legal traditions, have all by now become the sheepskins in which subsequent overdomesticator-wolves have learned to disguise themselves. In spite of claims to the contrary, democratically secular systems of government, humanistically conceived and supposedly balanced systems, also can fall prey to ruling par-ties and elites. Such systems now face each other in global con-frontation. Each makes it its primary business to scare all others with highly developed tools of space science and terror. The ancient bloody sacrificial cult—largely rejected by univer-sal salvation has gone secular, global, and beserk as it now threatens controllers as well as their victims with extinction.

During the century-old upswing in the domestication of min-erals, combined with the overdomestication of immense human worker and fighter herds, the sacrificial daggers of old have been both enlarged and perfected. The pressing of a pea-sized button safely entrusted to the imagined restraint of scientific tempers—precisely such folk as have been schooled in the love of analysis and experimentation—can now throw self-propelled missile daggers halfway around the globe. These missiles can sacrifice an entire competitor's overdomestication system to the mighty truth of whatever slogan happens to have justified or financed their manufacture. All sides have readied themselves for their final defense, yes, for the grand sacrifice of the human species. The ceremony may last less than a single day. All rational and not-so-perfect animals on the earth surface will be included in this great sacrifice, and most gophers. Truly, the overdomesticator's science of sacrifice—the queen of all human sciences of which all other sciences are branches—has been perfected to a degree that has never even been imagined before. What individual tyrants, high priests, and god-kings in the past were unable to attain, this a host of liberated offspring from among their potential but saved victims—liberated minds who have learned to imitate and to outdo the ancient threats of predators and overdomesticators—are now on the verge of achieving. Their collective scientific endeavors, together with their democratized statecraft, promise to orchestrate the most magnificent, the mightiest, most beautiful, most efficient, and most perfect sacrificial rite ever performed in our corner of the Milky Way galaxy. Of such moments and achievements of glory and death, the pathos of human perfection is wrought.

Mark D. McLean

Mark David McLean earned his B.A. from Southern California College, and his S.T.M. and Ph.D. from Harvard University. At present he is an Assistant Professor in the Department of Biblical Studies and Philosophy, Evangel College, Springfield, Missouri. Since 1979 he has been Keeper of the Coins, Harvard Semitic Museum. The results of his dissertation, *The Development and Use of Paleo-Hebrew in the Hellenistic and Roman Periods*, were published in *American Numismatic Society Museum 26* (1981). His research interests include the articulation of a hermeneutic appropriate for Pentecostal theology.

In his essay, "Perfectionism in the Old Testament," McLean examines three communities which adopted perfectionist lifestyles—the Nazirites, the Rechabites and the prophets. He also identifies expressions of perfectionism in a number of other exilic and post-exilic groups mentioned in the Old Testament, including the Samaritans.

2

PERFECTIONISM IN THE OLD TESTAMENT

Mark McLean

COMMUNITY IDEALS OF PERFECTION

IN CHAPTERS two and three of his work *Perfection and Perfectionism*, LaRondelle deals with the conception of both divine perfection and human perfection in the Old Testament. However, his work interests itself mainly in the background of the ideals suggestive of perfection, rather than any specific embodiment of those ideals by members of the Israelite community. Our task in this particular chapter is to go beyond the ideals of perfection and to examine the ways in which perfectionism manifested itself among the Israelites in both the pre-Exilic and post-Exilic communities.[1]

The goal of perfection is clearly stated, indeed, commanded in Lev 19:2: "Say to all the congregation of the people of Israel, You shall be holy; for I the LORD your God am holy." The question then is how was this "holiness" defined, and how might it be achieved?

A common understanding of "holiness" found throughout the Ancient Near East is one of an impersonal and material entity which had something of its own existence and which could be transferred from one object to another. The term was frequently used to designate objects, actions, or personnel of the cultus.[2] This same conception is evident throughout Israel's history. A late example of this conception is found in the struggle to define "normative Judaism" in the first through the third centuries A.D. *Yadavum* 4.5 and 4.6 state that scriptures written in any other form than the *'sryt* script, in the Hebrew language, and on parchment with ink are not "holy" and therefore do not make the hands of one handling such texts unclean.[3]

Yet, in Israel, it is the designation of Yahweh as "holy" which shapes the community's understanding of the term.

Yahweh is the source of all that is holy; it is relationship with Him that makes objects, actions, places, times, and people holy, not some impersonal force. Holiness speaks of a relationship rather than a quality.[4] The same is true for the idea of the perfection of God. While the word *tmm* (complete, sound, perfect) is not used directly of Yahweh, it is employed to describe His work, His way, and His covenant promise to Israel.[5] Yahweh's relationship with His creation is the standard of perfection.[6] Deuteronomy 32:4 illustrates this standard: "The Rock, his work is perfect; for all his ways are justice. A God of faithfulness and without iniquity, just and right is he."

If then, Yahweh is the standard of all that is holy, righteous, and just, what is required of His people? As LaRondelle asks, is human perfection to be equated with some quality such as sinlessness?[7] Once again, the answer is tied up in right relationship with Yahweh rather than any specific human achievement. Thus Noah is called "blameless" (*tmm*), "he walked with God" (Gen 6:9). Abraham is told, "I am God Almighty; walk before me and be blameless" (Gen 17:1). The writer of Psalm 19 speaks of having God clear him of hidden faults and restraining him from presumptuous sins: "Then shall I be blameless, and innocent of great transgression" (19:13).[8]

Yahweh, then, is the source of all holiness, righteousness and justice. His people are called to perfection by "walking" before their God in a right relationship with Him rather than according to any objective or external standard. This relationship is defined as loving and seeking God with all of one's being.[9] Yet, how does one define the outward expression of that "walk" so as to have an assurance that one is indeed in fellowship with Yahweh, or sometimes seemingly more important, the assurance that one's fellows are "walking" with God?

PERFECTIONISM WITHIN THE COMMUNITY AND IN RELATION TO OTHER PEOPLES

Perfectionism is a response to a real or perceived lack of commitment on the part of oneself and/or one's fellow members of any particular religious faith. Within the community itself there are always those members whose religious zeal is so vital to their self-understanding of their relationship with the Diety, that they find it necessary to admonish their fellows to "know the LORD" (Jer 31:34). This zeal may result in the creation of a separatist sect which may have little or no desire to convert others in the community, but rather it consigns them to perdition. Another response is to take on an outward asceticism as a sign of one's own zeal and thus as a badge of authority, but with no real desire to demand this self-imposed asceticism on others in the community. This form of perfectionism sees as its goal the calling of others into a deeper personal relationship with Yahweh. It is the achievement this goal Jeremiah envisions in 31:33-34. No longer would it be necessary for anyone to say to one's neighbor "know the LORD" for all would know Him already.[10]

The people of Yahweh, however, face an even greater problem than "perfectionism within the community" even when it may result in division and intolerance among fellow Yahwists. The people of Yahweh have been called to perfection in terms of a singular "walk" with their God that allows for no religious tolerance of non-Yahwistic faiths. We see, then, in Israel a perfectionism of the nation as a whole, which sets her apart from all the peoples around her, as well as internal manifestations of perfectionism which cause division within the nation.

INTRA-COMMUNITY EXPRESSIONS OF PERFECTIONISM IN THE PRE-EXILIC PERIOD

The Nazirites

Amos 2:11 lists both the prophets and the Nazirites as individuals provided by Yahweh for the well-being of Israel.[11] This simple connection of the prophets and the Nazirites indicates the importance of the Nazirites as a counterbalance to the "Canaanisation of the cult of Jahweh" as von Rad puts it.[12] The Nazirites, as well as the prophets and the Rechabites, seem to hark back to a "desert" or "wilderness" ideal such as found in Deut 29:5-6:

> I have led you forty years in the wilderness; your clothes have not worn out upon you, and your sandals have not worn off your feet; you have not eaten bread, and you have not drunk wine or strong drink; that you may know that I am the LORD your God.[13]

One of the major difficulties in determining how the Nazirites functioned in Israelite society is that the two Nazirites we know by name and deed, Samson and Samuel, as well as the Nazirites mentioned in Amos 2:10-12, do not fit into the "law of the Nazirite" in Numbers 6:1-21 nor the discussions in the Tractate *Nazir*.[14] Numbers 6 envisions a temporary Nazirite vow for either a man or a woman. This included total abstinence from any product of the vine and dedication of one's hair. At the end of the period of separation the hair was shaved. After presenting the hair and the proper sacrifice at the Tent of Meeting, the "former" Nazirite could drink wine (Num 6:20). We have no indication whether the lifelong vows imposed upon their children prior to conception by the unnamed mother of Samson or Hannah included a lifelong dedication of the women themselves (Judg 13:2-7; 1 Sam 1:11). It seems possible then that even in the earlier period temporary Nazirite vows were possible.[15] However, it is also possible that it is this very innovation of a temporary vow that allows "former Nazirites" to drink wine that Amos is railing against in 2:12.

From what is known of Samson and Samuel the other major difficulty is the matter of a Nazirite's contact (even accident l) with a dead person. Eichrodt has asserted, on the basis of the Samson cycle, that the early Nazirites were "battle beserkers" who served Yahweh by going to war.[16] The provisions of Numbers 6:9-12 would seem to have been quite troublesome for any Nazirite warrior worth remembering:

> And if any man dies very suddenly beside him, and he defiles his consecrated head, then he shall shave his head, on the day of his cleansing (Num 6:9).

Nazir, I, 4b discusses the question of how Samson maintained his Nazirite vow in light of the numbers of Philistines he is credited with having had die suddenly in his presence. One suggestion is that he never touched any of those he slew with anything other than his weapon (Judg 15:14-20). Another point of discussion revolves around how Samson could strip the garments of the thirty men he slew in Ashkelon without defiling himself (Judg 14:19). While we have no tradition depicting Samuel as having any personal role in battle as a warrior, 1 Sam 7:13 states, "And the hand of the LORD was against the Philistines all the days of Samuel." And 1 Sam 15:33 relates that "Samuel hewed Agag to pieces before the LORD in Gilgal." Therefore, it seems likely that the contact with the dead, like the possibility of a temporary vow, may reflect the later formulation of Nazirite obligations.

The full effect of the Nazirites other than Samson and Samuel is hard to delineate. The present form of the vow in Numbers 6 and the discussion of the vow in *Nazir* indicates it had become primarily a form of religious asceticism patterned after the priestly regulations for personal holiness.[17] Even though the continued presence of Nazirites is found within the New Testament (Acts 21:23ff), Amos judged their effect on the nation in his day as a failure: "But you made the Nazirites to drink wine" (Amos 2:12a).

Rechabites

Perhaps the most telling critique of the impact of the perfectionism of the Rechabites on the people of Yahweh is that had Jeremiah not used them as an example of faithfulness to a principle in contrast to the faithlessness of the people of Yahweh as a whole, we would know nothing of their perfectionism or even their existence other than from the cryptic references found in 2 Kgs 10:15-24 and the genealogical note of 1 Chron 2:55.[18]

Jeremiah brought the Rechabites to the temple and offered them wine. They refused saying:

> We will drink no wine, for Jon'adab the son of Rechab, our father, commanded us, "You shall not drink wine, neither you nor your sons for ever; you shall not build a house; you shall not sow seed; you shall not plant or have a vineyard; but you shall live in tents all your days, that you may live many days in the land where you sojourn." (Jer 35:6-7)

Whether one sees the Rechabites as a "puritan sect"[19] or a "clan-like association"[20] they were certainly at the fore in the battle against syncretism with the Canaanite culture. Ironically the Rechabites are linked by genealogy to the Kenites, a people listed in Genesis 15:18-21 as one of the groups whose land Abraham's descendants were to possess, and yet, who became a prophetic model of fidelity to Yahweh. Through Jeremiah's use of this group to make a prophetic point, the passage in 2 Kgs 10:15-24 takes on new meaning. We know nothing of their numbers, but the group was large enough that Jehu found it expedient to ally himself with Jon'adab. Yet, despite their zeal for Yahweh, they left no discernible mark on the community that we would have recognized aside from Jeremiah's prophetic point.[21]

Prophets

Amos declares that the prophets like the Nazirites were a gift of Yahweh to His people given for their welfare (2:11-12). We find that the prophets, the Nazirites and the Rechabites all hark back to that "desert" or "wilderness" ideal of Israel's childhood.[22] Yet, there is a distinction to be made here. In contradistinction to the asceticism of the Nazirites and Rechabites, the prophets do not call for a return to a literal nomadic ideal, but rather by their lifestyle and preaching they castigate the misuse of the good gifts of the land provided by Yahweh.[23] Their opposition is directed against the Canaanite cultural and religious influence which threatens to overwhelm the prophetic view of "normative" Yahwism.[24] The prophets were the religious watchmen of Israel. Their concern was for the state of God's people in the here and now, not the distant future. Their purpose was to critique the present and to announce to God's people the inevitable consequence of both obedience to and rebellion against Him. The prophets were teachers, preachers, and intecessors given by Yahweh to His people.[25] While not condemning the goods of the earth, which are Yahweh's gift to His people, by their lifestyle and dedication to Yahweh, they made clear that right relationship with Yahweh takes full precedence over the concerns of earthly life.[26]

One must realize, however, that the above description fits only one strand of the prophetic presence in Israel.[27] There was no monolithic block of prophetic opinion. Not only must one distinguish between the various periods of Israel's religious life, one must also take into account the various types of "prophets" found in the biblical records.[28] The prophetic types have been characterized by titles such as coenobitic (monastic), court, sanctuary, cultic, shamanistic, free and mixed-type.[29] Naturally there is some overlap in these definitions. For instance, the court sanctuary and cultic prophets have a similar station. One could say that the court prophets could also be cultic prophets, given a stipend by the king in the king's sanctuary (Bethel and Jerusalem).[30] This leads to another distinction. The prophets associated with the local Yahwistic shrines throughout Israel could be termed cultic prophets, but unlike those serving the national shrines of the kings, they seem to be associated with the prophetic guilds which Aune describes as "shamanistic."[31] Therefore, while one can say that the distinctive dress of the prophets—life in communal prophetic colonies, the possible physical stigma and tonsure, and their ecstatic behavior—becomes traits by which "prophets" assert their identity and authority, one doubts that these "distinctives" ought to be associated with all of the prophets known to us from the biblical record.[32]

The same may be said about the question of "ecstatic" behavior in particular. The discussion concerning the occurrence of this behavior centers on whether the classical prophets participated in such behavior or if this ecstasy was limited to the early prophetic movement. Certainly, the biblical record regards "ecstasy" as part of the credentials which marked one as a prophet.[33] This behavior is often associated with music, dancing, singing and trance-like behavior (1 Sam 10:10–13 and 19:18–24). There is even evidence of self-mutilation in the prophetic trance or in the attempt to induce the trance. This is specifically mentioned in the case of the prophets of Baal during the contest arranged by Elijah (1 Kgs 18:28). However, the same type of behavior is also suggested in the anti-prophetical polemic found in Zech 13:2-6. Here the wearing of the distinctive "rough garment" as a badge of one's prophetic authority is in parallel with the "wounds" found on the bodies of prophets.

> On that day every prophet will be ashamed of his vision when he prophesies; he will not put on a hairy mantle in order to deceive, but he will say, "I am no prophet, I am a tiller of the soil; for the land has been my possession since my youth." And if one asks him, "what are these wounds on your back?" he will say, "The wounds I received in the house of my friends." (Zech 13:4-6)

The reaction of the people and the leaders to the prophets and their distinctive way of life ranged from that of honor: "And behold a man of God came out of Judah by the word of the LORD to Bethel" (1 Kgs 13:1), to that of derision: "When Jehu came out to the servants of his master, they said to him, 'Is all well? Why did this mad fellow come to you?' " (2 Kgs 9:11). Still one must note that while Jehu's officers referred to the prophet as a madman, once they knew the content of this madman's message they wasted no time in proclaiming Jehu king. The confrontation between Ahab and Micai'ah ben Imlah shows the same tension. Though Ahab preferred not to consult Micai'ah ben Imlah because "he never prophesies good concerning me, but evil" (1 Kgs 22:8), Ahab recognized him as a prophet of God. In spite of the uniformly favorable oracles of the other Yahwistic prophets consulted concerning the battle of Ramoth-Gilead, Ahab tries to disguise himself in order to foil the prophecy of Micai'ah concerning Ahab's death, but in vain.[34]

The very distinctives by which a person proclaims himself to be a prophet lead to confusion among the people receiving the word of the LORD. For while these prophetic trademarks identified the prophet, the words of the LORD obtained from these prophets were certainly not distinguished by their uniformity. Perhaps we need to rephrase the lament of Amos concerning the response of the people to God's prophets: "You commanded to true prophets to remain silent, while encouraging those who tickled your ears with glad tidings to 'say on, say on.' "[35]

The Fruits of Perfection

There is a sense in which one must judge the attempts of the Nazirites, the prophets and the Rechabites a success in that their memory has been preserved. They are the ones who remain as models of that principle, "right relationship with God should supersede every other consideration in one's life." Yet, in terms of their own generations, their efforts failed to make any substantial impact on the people until their vindication by the destruction and exile of both Israel and Judah. If this seems to be an overly harsh judgment, consider the following evidence. The reforms of both Hezekiah and Josiah at the behest of the radical Yahwistic prophets[36] was an administrative reform imposed from above, not a popular reform desired by the population as a whole. The speech of Rab'shakeh outside the walls of Jerusalem struck a raw nerve among the people:

> But if you say to me, "We rely on the LORD our God," is it not he whose high places and altars Hezekiah has removed, saying to Judah and to Jerusalem, "You shall worship before this altar in Jerusalem. (2 Kgs 18:22)

An identical response is found in the rejection of a word from the LORD through Jeremiah found in Jeremiah 44:16-19:

> As for the word which you have spoken to us in the name of the LORD, we will not listen to you. But we will do everything that we have vowed, burn

incense to the queen of heaven and pour out libations to her as we did, both we and our fathers, our kings and our princes, in the cities of Judah and in the streets of Jerusalem; for then we had plenty of food, and prospered, and saw no evil. But since we left off burning incense to the queen of heaven and pouring out libations to her, we have lacked everything and have been consumed by the sword and by famine.

However, it is the words of Isaiah and Jeremiah and the remaining canonical prophets which the course of events confirmed. The Exile forced a redefinition of the covenant community which planted the seeds of factionalism that began to sprout during the Exile itself. After the judgment, God will restore the faithful remnant. But who is it that makes up that remnant—those who remain in the land or those who have been carried off to exile?[37] This doctrine of the "remnant" will be central to the expression of perfectionism in the post-Exilic community.

EXTRA-COMMUNITY EXPRESSIONS OF PERFECTIONISM IN THE PRE-EXILIC PERIOD

The "normative" viewpoint of what the extra-community relations of Israel should have been with the peoples whose land she was to possess is clearly seen in such passages as Exodus 34:11-16:

Observe what I command you this day. Behold, I will drive out before you the Amorites, the Canaanites, the Hittites, the Perizzites, the Hivites, and the Jebusites. Take heed to yourself, lest you make a covenant with the inhabitants of the land whither you go, lest it become a snare in the midst of you. You shall tear down their altars, and break down their Ashe'rim (for you shall worship no other god, for the LORD, whose name is Jealous, is a jealous God), lest you make a covenant with the inhabitants of the land, and when they play the harlot after their gods and sacrifice to their gods and one invites you, you eat of his sacrifice, and you take their daughters for your sons, and their daughters play the harlot after their gods and make your sons play the harlot after their gods.[38]

Yet, one must note that there are provisions, indeed clear commands concerning the incorporation of non-Israelites into the nation and Yahwistic faith. Not only is it possible for slaves to participate in the Passover, but resident aliens, who are willing to take on the full obligations of the Law as evidence in accepting circumcision are to be integrated into the community (cf. Num 15:14, 15, 29f). Even more forthright are the provisions of Deut 23:15-16:[39]

You shall not give up to his master a slave who escaped from his master to you; he shall dwell with you, in your midst, in the place which he shall choose within one of your towns, where it pleases him best; you shall not oppress him.

It is clear from the biblical record both in terms of the description of the conquest in Judges 1 and the denunciation in 2:1-5 that there was much more integration than outright slaughter in the conquest.[40] Still there are a number of incidents which record the clash of Yahwistic ideals with neighboring nations and peoples. The contest between Yahweh and Baal so vividly pictured in the books of Kings reveals reciprocal enmity on the part of Jezebel and her Tyrian and Israelite subjects and the Yahwistic Israelites. Resistance from the Yahwistic element led Jezebel to a campaign of active persecution against the Yahwistic prophets. Elijah countered with the well-known contest between Yahweh and Baal on Mt. Carmel. Yahweh wins the contest. In the aftermath, Elijah has the 400 prophets of Baal slain at the Kishon (1 Kgs 18:7-19:3). As Elijah notes, "I have been very jealous for the LORD, the God of hosts" (1 Kgs 18:10a).[41]

A similar clash of ideals is shown in Ahab's treatment of the vanquished Ben-Ha'dad. After a battle provoked by Ben-Ha'dad, Ahab received his entreaty to spare his life by saying, "Does he still live? He is my brother?" (1 Kgs 20:32). as when Saul before him spared Agag (1 Sam 15), Ahab received a prophetic rebuke announcing

> Thus says the LORD, "Because you have let go out of your hand the man whom I had devoted to destruction, therefore your life will go for his life, and your people for his people." (1 Kgs 20:42)

Jehu's bloody purge of the Omrides and his slaughter of Baal worshippers is a further confirmation of the seeds of religious intolerance which were nourished in the pursuit of right relationship with Yahweh and Yahweh's demand for exclusivity.[42] The seeds will bear bitter fruit in the Exilic and post-Exilic period, both in terms of intra-community and extra-community relationships.

INTRA-COMMUNITY EXPRESSIONS OF PERFECTIONISM IN THE EXILIC AND POST-EXILIC PERIODS

The message of the canonical prophets to the people of Yahweh was not merely one of judgment and destruction. The message always included the promise of restoration and salvation for a righteous remnant preserved by Yahweh.[43] The definition of that remnant was outlined by the exiles in Babylon. At its core was a pure monotheism and complete exclusivity in the worship of Yahweh. Its attitude towards foreign gods is forcefully presented in the scathing caricatures of idols and idolaters found in Isaiah directed at both the idolatry of the nations as well as Israel's idolatrous past.[44] The Torah becomes the rule by which all of life is measured.[45] Though this reformed remnant would become an evangelistic faith which would be quite successful in gaining proselytes, in the early post-Exilic period, purity before God was so vital that wives whose bloodlines could not be traced to the Babylonian genealogical records which defined that "holy remnant" were put away.[46]

As noted above, the Exile forced the adherents of Yahweh to define the righteous remnant. Those fleeing from Judah to Egypt were told by Jeremiah that they faced destruction because of their continued syncretistic worship of Yahweh and His court. The vow of the people to continue to "burn incense to the queen of heaven and pour out libations to her, as we did, both we and our fathers, our kings and our princes" (Jer 44:17) was not a repudiation of their Yahwistic faith, but of Jeremiah's definition of that faith. They considered themselves the righteous remnant who would now return to the traditional faith. Those who remained in Judah also claimed to be the remnant. The aristocracy, who came under the scathing judgment of the prophets, had been carried off into exile. Was it not a logical move to assume that those who remained had been given a now purified promised land and that it was they who constituted the righteous remnant? Yet, the words of Jeremiah and Ezekiel make it clear that the good figs, the righteous remnant, are indeed those in Babylon.[47]

Though Lamentations 2:9 weeps that "the law is no more," it was in the Babylonian exilic community that the Law was becoming the center of communal and personal existence. It was the genius of the Babylonian exiles in focusing on the Law as the objective standard by which one could judge right relationship with Yahweh and one's place in the righteous remnant that preserved the identity of people of God in the face of the historical, religious, and personal anomie caused by the destruction of the Temple and Jerusalem. Yet, it was this very solution which carried the seeds of religious intolerance that would rack the fledgling post-Exilic community and continue to threaten the community with the dead weight of legalism.[48]

Ezekiel 40-48 envision a return to a purified Jerusalem and Temple and the reinstitution of a purified cult.[49] Isaiah 40:3-6 announce a smooth and level highway prepared for the returning exiles. Yet, the road home was as rocky, dusty, and dirty, and as hilly as had been the road to exile. The people, both those returning and those who had remained in the land, were just as human as their fathers and just as sure of what the LORD's will for His people was. Ezra 4:1-3 indicate the tension began almost immediately:

> Now when the adversaries of Judah and Benjamin heard that the returned exiles were building a temple to the LORD, the God of Israel, they approached Zerub'babel and the heads of the fathers' houses and said to them, "Let us build with you; for we worship your God as you do, and we have been sacrificing to him ever since the days of E'sar-had'-don king of Assyria who brought us here." But Zerub'babel, Joshua, and the rest of the fathers' houses in Israel said to them, "You have nothing to do with us in building a house to our God; but we alone will build to the LORD, the God of Israel, as King Cyrus the king of Persia has commanded us."

The source of the tension was the assumption on the part of the returning exiles that they alone represented the true Israel. Only those who could show a connection with the "fathers' houses in Israel" as delineated in the Babylonian genealogical lists could participate in the promised restoration of the LORD.[50] Still it seems the deportation did not strip the land of its whole population, but rather its upper classes and artisans.[51] One does not want to paint an overly rosy picture, however, of the conditions in Palestine. Though only about 20,000 to 30,000 may have actually been deported, Bright suggests the loss of population by war, famine, disease, exile, and immigration probably reduced the population from ca. 250,000 to 20,000 at the time of the first return in 538 B.C.[52] Still Noth feels enough talent was left in the land so that "the tribes left behind in the old country continued to be the centre of Israelite history and life."[53] Indeed, many suggest that besides Lamentations, the Deuteronomistic History was written in Palestine after 587 B.C.[54] As is portrayed in Neh 1:1-3, the exiles were aware that there were those who escaped both the destruction and the Exile and were living in the land. Nehemiah does not ask, "how are those who have returned from exile faring?" but, "how are those who survived, escaped exile, and are even now living in the province?" Further complicating the issue was the tendency of the returned Babylonian exiles to intermarry with the "people of the land" whom their Babylonian brethren considered to be foreigners. This Babylonian elitism is evidenced by the accusations of racial pollution found in Ezra 9:1-10:44 and Nehemiah 13 and the Talmudic assertion that three times Babylonian returnees had to save the Torah, or at least parts of it, from oblivion in Judah: Ezra, Hillel and R. Hiyya and his sons performed these rescue operation (*Sukk* 20a-b).

Another source of tension was the continued friction between the Mushite and Zadokite priestly families.[55] The Mushite/Levitical priests had superintended the religious life of the Judahites who had remained in the land during the Exile. Now they found themselves thrust from any connection with the cult on the basis of their alleged racial impurity. It was out of this rivalry that apocalyptic writings and groups including the Samaritan sect arose.[56]

The study of J. D. Purvis has fully confirmed the earlier judgment of Albright and Cross that the beginning of the Samaritan script, and thus the final schism of the Samaritan community, is to be dated to the first century B.C. rather than the fifth century B.C.[57] Cultural and political differences between the north and sourth are documented from the period of the Judges onward. Certainly the elitist attitude of the returning Babylonian exiles under Ezra and Nehemiah combined with the ethnic and religious discrimination of that elitism added to the continuing estrangement of these two Yahwistic communities. This continued tension was heightened by divergences in the political allegiances and policies of the rival Gerizim cultus. It did not, however, cause a complete and irrevocable estrangement of the two communities until the Hasmonaean usurpation of the high priestly office ended the familial ties—however limited or strained they might have been—of the Samaritan Zadokites with the Jerusalem Zadokites who had held internal control in Judaea from the beginning of the post-Exilic community. The final break was the result of the military attempts of John Hyrcanus I to establish a single orthodoxy under his control which led to the destruction of Shechem and the temple on Gerizim.[58]

The Jerusalem Zadokites, finding themselves thrust out of the priesthood by the Maccabeans, retired to Qumran to form the one true community of Israel, the righteous remnant, the ideal congregation of Yahweh. This ascetic community was

priestly and scribal in nature. Their sectarian writings preserve
the rules and manner of life this separatist sect imposed upon
itself by embracing the laws of purity for Holy War in preparation for that cataclysmic apocalyptic end when they would join
with the hosts of Heaven in destroying the wicked who now
held sway in all the world, including Jerusalem.[59] For both the
Samaritan and Qumran communities, it was the usurpation of
the high priestly office and political power which forced these
collateral Zadokite branches either to redefine their *raison
d'être* in face of their loss of political, social, and religious
status or to be absorbed into the new "normative" Judaism established by the Hasmonaeans.[60] The Samaritans retained their
loyalty to Gerizim as the mountain of God, the Essenes of
Qumran their loyalty to Mount Zion, but otherwise these two
communities had a number of common features and possibly
some limited contacts.[61]

The Samaritans had adopted Palaeo-Hebrew as their official
script and as part of their contention that they represented the
true line of tradition of the ancestoral faith. The Essene community and its adherents were destroyed and scattered as a result of the inevitable loss of the First Jewish War against
Rome. The "normative" community at that time found itself
faced with the same questions Israel had faced in 587/86 B.C.
and which the Samaritans and Essenes had faced under the
early Hasmonaean rulers: how to define the community in such
a way as to preserve its identity in face of the loss of its political identity and its religious and cultural center. The questions
of perfectionism, "who represents the remnant, who has possession of God's Word, who has the authoritative interpretation
which defines right relationship with Yahweh?" had to have
fresh answers, for more than perfectionism was at stake here.
Rather, the continued existence of the people of God hung in
the balances. In the Hasmonaean era, the Hasidim were the
expression of an extraordinary zeal for the Law and the
forebears of the Pharisees.[62] The Pharisaic movement under the
guidance of the *hakhamim* (sages) stressed strict faithfulness to
the Torah and the laws of ritual purity. It was these sages who
defined right relationship with God and one's fellows. Their
words and memory became sacred. Thus b*Kiddushin* 66a could
boast, "The world was desolate until Simeon ben Shetah came
and restored the Torah."[63] The Sadducees, technically "scriptural conservatives" who held that the Torah alone was the

Word of God, were actually more liberal in lifestyle being free from the demands of the oral tradition and the imperatives of the Prophets and Writings which formed the center of the Pharisaic movement.[64]

Under the pressures brought about by the destruction of the Temple and Jerusalem in A.D. 70, the "normative" community under the firm guidance of the *hakhamim*, pressed by both the claims of the Samaritans and by the growing Christian community, responded with the promulgation of an official recension of the biblical text in a specific script, the *sryt* or Jewish script.[65] This move toward an official recension began before the First Jewish War, but as the evidence from Masada and Murabba at suggests, it was complete in the normative community by the beginning of the Second Jewish War against Rome.[66]

EXTRA-COMMUNITY RELATIONSHIPS
IN THE EXILIC AND POST-EXILIC PERIODS

It is hard to separate the divisions caused by the desire for religious purity from political, social, and economic concerns, because the intra-community debate over what it means to be a Jew and the seductiveness of Hellenism intertwine these factors so completely, both in terms of intra-community and extra-community relationships. From the time of Alexander the Great through the Roman era, the Jews found themselves amidst the *oikoumenē*.

> The *oikoumenē* [the "known inhabited world"] was as far as the mind could reach, a Greek mind thinking Greek thoughts, elastic enough to recognize, salute and co-opt what lay outside its pale. It differed from the then forming Jewish Diaspora, which saw itself as a community in the form of a network within a larger alien body.[67]

The Greek city-state or *polis* was the ideal around which Hellenism centered. This involved more than the construction of a physical city; it required a citizenship with the needed political institutions including a constitution, a city council, a gymnasium, temples, and courts. Intellectual, religious, and civic duties all intertwined to make individuals *politeis*.[68] But as Peters points out,

> Some Jews were either unwilling or unable to share in that *polis* life, because of their attachment to a different competing ideal, the Mosaic Law. Their refusal, which had no real parallel in the *oikoumenē*, was noted but never really understood.[69]

The scandal of a Jewish Hellenistic *gymnasium* in Jerusalem

and the open sale of the high priest's office to the highest bid-
der embittered inter-community relations, which, when combined with the hellenizing pressures of Antiochus IV, led to the
Maccabean revolt.[70] The demands for ritual purity growing out
of the Pharisaic movement required not only separation for
less-observant Jews, but they demanded as much separation as
possible from Gentiles. It is out of the caldron of inter-
community strife that perfectionism spills over into the extra-
community relationships.

Religious and cultural toleration was the standard policy of
the imperialism of the ancient world. The status of the Jewish
Diaspora in the empire was similar to that of the other national
groups residing in a country or *polis* other than their own. They
were recognized as a *politeuma*, an ethnic group living outside
their country of origin. As such, they had certain rights which
protected their religious and cultural customs.[71] However, for
the Jews this toleration was stretched beyond its usual limits,
for certain aspects of Judaism could not be practiced without
the violation of existing laws, such as refusing a court sum-
mons on the Sabbath. Therefore, while the requirements of
Judaism resulted in several unparalleled privileges, one cannot
say that Judaism was the only foreign creed tolerated by the
empires.[72]

The privileges granted to the Jews, both in the homeland by
their suzerains and in the Diaspora, were not the only source of
friction, however. For while the pagans were religiously
tolerant, the Jews were most certainly not. They were often
openly contemptuous of the polytheism of their neighbors.[73]
The Jewish belief in their divine election—their eternality as a
people, and their intolerance toward others, combined with
their self-maintained separatism to create some of the factors
which led those around them to contempt, then anger and finally hatred.[74]

CONCLUSIONS

This survey of the embodiment of the ideals of perfectionism
has focused on the negative aspects that all too often result
when an individual or a group takes that "step beyond." However, I do not want to end on that negative note. Experiential
religion (some would say fanaticism) has always been a minority affair. Yet, it is the Nazirites, the Rechabites, the prophets
and the sages among us who call us back to what it means to

be truly and fully human. It is they who summon us back from a mindless, though seductive, materialism. Though religious commitment misused is one of the most destructive forces humans can wield, there is nothing that can replace "right relationship with God and one's fellow human beings."

NOTES

1. H. K. LaRondelle, *Perfection and Perfectionism* (Berrien Springs, MI: Andrews University, 1971), 35-158.

2. J. Pedersen, *Israel, Its Life and Culture*, 4 vols. (London: Oxford University Press, 1962), 3-4: 270, 281. Cf. Gerhard von Rad, *Old Testament Theology*, 2 vols. (New York: Harper & Row, 1962), 1:206. Walther Eichrodt, *Theology of the Old Testament*, 2 vols. (Philadelphia: Westminster, 1961), 1:271-272.

3. I. Epstein, ed. *The Babylonian Talmud* (London: Soncino, 1938). The problems involved with the definition of "normative" Judaism will be discussed below.

4. LaRondelle, *Perfection*, 47-48. Cf. von Rad, 1:205, 242; and A. B. Davidson, *The Theology of the Old Testament* (Edinburgh: T. & T. Clark, 1904), 145. Eichrodt, *Theology* 1:136, writes "For here the norm resides in the all-controlling concept of Yahweh himself and has as its goal the setting of a personal relationship with God."

5. LaRondelle, *Perfection*, 45.

6. Ibid., 39-40.

7. Ibid., 109.

8. See LaRondelle, *Perfection*, 109-158, for a detailed discussion of this topic.

9. Deut 6:4-5: "Hear, O Israel: The LORD our God is one LORD; and you shall love the LORD your God with all your heart, and with all your soul, and with all your might." Jer 29:13-14a: "You will seek me and find me; when you seek me with all your heart, I will be found by you, says the LORD. . . ."

10. The root *yd'* carries more than the idea of cognitive knowledge. It stresses relationship, the experience of right relationship with Yahweh.

11. W. F. Albright, "Samuel and the Beginnings of the Prophetic Moveme ," in H. Orlinsky, ed., *Interpreting the Prophetic Tradition* (New York: K V Publishing Co., 1969), 161. Albright traces the root *nzr* (to vow) to West Semitic noting that it is identical to Ugaritic, Aramaic and Hebrew *ndr*, originally *ndr*. Cf. von Rad, *Old Testament Theology*, 1:241; and Roland de Vaux, *Ancient Israel* (New York: McGraw-Hill, 1961), 465.

12. von Rad., *Old Testament Theology*, 1:62. Cf. Eichrodt, *Theology*, 1:306; Georg Fohrer, *History of Israelite Religion* (New York: Abingdon, 1972), 153; and Pedersen, *Life and Culture*, 3-4, 264 ff.

13. Cf. Jer 2:2-3 and Hosea 2:14-15.

14. Albright, "Beginnings," 160, points out that the *Mishnah* in the tractate *Nazir* has always noted that Samuel was indeed a Nazirite. This has been further confirmed by F. M. Cross's publication of a fragment of Samuel from Qumran which reads "he shall become a *nazir* forever." ("A New Qumran Fragment Related to the original Hebrew Underlying the Septuagint," *BASOR* 132 [December 1953]: 15-16).

15. Eichrodt, *Theology*, 1:304, contends that the Nazirite vow as preserved in Numbers 6 reflects a radical change in the character of the vow during the monarchical era. The Babylonian tractate *Nazir* for the most part concerns it-

self with defining when a Nazirite vow has actually been made and the circumstances involving defilement and the polling of one's head. The discussion presumes the canonical form of Numbers 6. See below the discussion of a Nazirite's contact with the dead. Cf. von Rad, *Old Testament Theology*, 1:62; Fohrer, *History*, 153; James Luther Mays, *Amos* (Philadelphia: Westminster, 1969), 52.

16. Eichrodt, *Theology* 1:304. Cf. Fohrer, *History*, 153. Cf. Patrick D. Miller, Jr., *The Divine Warrior in Early Israel* (Harvard Semitic Monographs 5, Cambridge, MA: Harvard University, 1973), 88-89.

17. *Nazir*, 1:3a, questions whether the taking of a Nazirite vow is in a way a sin, seeing as the Nazirite denies him or herself something allowed by the Torah. Cf. Eichrodt, *Theology*, 1:303-304; Foher, *History*, 153; Mays, *Amos*, 52; von Rad, 1:272. Von Rad (2:137), suggests that any kind of asceticism or rejection of material goods was alien to Yahwism. Rather the gifts of God's good creation were to be received with "simple thankfulness from Jahweh's hand."

18. For a discussion of Kenite genealogy see Y. Aharoni, "The Settlement of Canaan," in *Judges, The World History of the Jewish People*, Benjamin Mazar, gen. ed. (New York: Rutger University Press, 1971), 3:104.

19. Eichrodt, *Theology*, 1:106, n. 1; and 355. Cf. de Vaux, *Ancient Israel*, 14-15. He points out that all the Rechabite names we know are Yahwistic.

20. von Rad, *Old Testament Theology* 1:63. Cf. Fohrer, *History*, 154. Fohrer takes a negative view of the Rechabites as trying to associate Yahwism with a specific cultural context, rather than accepting the inevitable change every religion goes through as the cultural envelope of the society changes, bringing new questions which demand new answers.

21. Another possible reflection of the Rechabites nomadic ideal might be the "Wilderness as the time of Israel's perfection" found in Jer 2:2-3 and Hosea 2:14. The *History of the Rechabites* (first to sixth centuries A.D.) is clearly dependent on Jeremiah 35 and does not represent an independent tradition handed down by a "Rechabite" community. See James H. Charlesworth, "The History of the Rechabites, A New Translation and Introduction," in *The Old Testament Pseudepigrapha*, Vol. 2, edited by James H. Charlesworth, (Garden City, New York: Doubleday and Company, Inc., 1985), 443-461.

22. See note 13 above.

23. Eichrodt, *Theology*, 2:245. Cf. note 17.

24. Eichrodt, *Theology*, 1:317, 355; 2:354. Cf. von Rad, *Old Testament Theology*, 2:142; and Salo W. Baron. *A Social and Religious History of the Jews*, 15 vols. (New York: Columbia University Press, 1960), 1:89. J. Lindblom, *Prophecy in Ancient Israel* (Philadelphia: Fortress Press, 1962), 293.

25. Ezek 3:17-21; 33:7-20. Lindblom, *Ancient Israel*, 29, 204; Fohrer, *History*, 272.

26. Eichrodt, *Theology*, 1:326.

27. See note 32 below.

28. The three main divisions are pre-Exilic, Exilic, and post-Exilic. Cf. Lindblom, *Ancient Israel*, 292.

29. David Aune, *Prophecy in Early Christianity and the Ancient Mediterranean World* (Grand Rapids: Eerdmans, 1983), 83-85; Lindblom, *Ancient Israel*, 76, 83, 206-210. Lindblom defines the free prophet as an individual connected with neither a guild nor a shrine. Amos would be the primary example of this type.

30. Amos 7:12-13. For a discussion of David's selection of Jerusalem as a neutral city and center for the Tent Shrine, see F. M. Cross, *Canaanite Myth and Hebrew Epic* (Cambridge, MA: Harvard University Press, 1973), 202-213, 229-237.

31. Aune, *Prophecy*, 83.

32. Lindblom, *Ancient Israel*, 66-69. Lindblom (p. 66), suggests that the hairy mantle and leather loincloths are other evidence of the nomadic ideal. Cf. Eichrodt, *Theology*, 1:310, 316; for the discussion of the various external signs used by those who wished to assert their identity as a prophet. See also 2 Kgs 1:8; Zech 13:2-6; 1 Kgs 20:35ff; Amos 7:14; 1 Sam 10:5.

33. For an excellent survey of the range of opinions on the matter of prophetic ecstasy see Robert R. Wilson, "Prophecy and Ecstacy: A Reexamination," *JBL* 98.3 (Sept 1979): 321-337. Cf. Eichrodt, *Theology*, 1:309-312; von Rad, *Old Testament Theology*, 2:26-27. One must note in regard to prophetic ecstasy, nowhere in the biblical records do we find any suggestion that the prophets presented the ecstatic behavior as something to be imitated by "laypersons." See Lindblom, *Ancient Israel*, 307, 309; cf. Eichrodt 1:317-318.

34. Robert R. Wilson, *Prophecy and Society in Ancient Israel* (Philadelphia: Fortress Press, 1980), 205, suggests that those who termed the prophets "madmen" (2 Kgs 9:11) felt their messages could safely be ignored. However, both 2 Kgs 9 and 1 Kgs 22:30 suggest a bit more credence given to these "madmen" than one might expect.

35. Cf. Jer 27:9-10, 14-15: "So do not listen to your prophets, your diviners, your dreamers, your soothsayers, or your sorcerers, who are saying to you, 'You shall not serve the king of Babylon.' For it is a lie which they are prophesying to you, . . . I have not sent them saith the LORD, but they are prophesying falsely in my name. . . ." Both Aune, *Prophecy*, 87-88 and J. L. Crenshaw, *Prophetic Conflict* (Berlin: Walter de Gruyter, 1971), 39-61, deal with the problem—or better, the impossibility—of distinguishing true versus false prophecy. One must simply observe that whatever the criteria used, the post-Exilic community saw the "canonical prophets" as the true prophets whose writings were to be preserved and revered despite problems such as those posed by Ezek 26:1-28:19 and 29:17-21. Cf. Lindblom, *Ancient Israel*, 210-213, particularly p. 212, n. 183.

36. The "radical Yahwistic prophets" may be defined as those who insisted on the worship of Yahweh alone. It is these prophets, whose writings alone have been preserved, who have defined what normative Yahwism ought to be. The popular religion to which they stood unalterably opposed is seen only through the eyes of these "true" prophets of Yahweh whose words were vindicated in the course of events. Wilson, *Prophecy and Society*, 299, says "In spite of the fact that pre-exilic Ephraimite prophecy played a peripheral role in Israelite society, the Ephraimite view of prophecy now dominates the biblical material." J. Wiener, "The Religious Culture of the Jewish People in its Beginnings: The Faith and the Cult," in *Judges, The World History of the Jewish People* (New York: Rutgers, 1971), 3:212, discusses the question of whether the biblical picture of the Yahwistic faith was the legitimate religion of the people or one imposed on Israel after a protracted struggle.

37. Jer 24; Ezek 10-11, particularly 11:15-16.

38. Cf. Num 25; Deut 7:1-11; 12:2-3, 29-31.

39. Cf. Exod 12:43-49.

40. As John Bright, (*A History of Israel*, 3rd ed. [Philadelphia: Westminster, 1981], 137) points out "whatever may be said on the subject [of the conquest] remains to some degree hypothetical and subject to correction in the light of further information." See his survey of the formation of the people of Israel, 133-143, for more information and bibliography.

41. See Bright, *Israel*, 240-253, for his discussion of the Omride dynasty and bibliography.

42. 2 Kgs 9-10.

43. Isa 10:20-27 is typical of remnant passages: "In that day the remnant of

Israel and the survivors of the house of Jacob will no more lean upon him that smote them, but will lean upon the LORD, the Holy One of Israel, in truth. A remnant will return, the remnant of Jacob, to the mighty God" (vv. 20-21). Cf. Jer 31:7-9; Ezek 11:13-21; etc.

44. Isa 40:18-20; 41:6-7; 42:17; 44:9-20; 46:1-7.

45. von Rad, *Old Testament Theology*, 2:90-92; and Eichrodt, *Theology*, 2:342, 344.

46. Ezra 10 and Neh 13:23-31.

47. See Jer 24:4-7; 44; Ezek 11:13-16. Cf. Bright, *Israel*, 345.

48. See Bright, *Israel*, 349; Eichrodt, *Theology*, 2:342, 344; Fohrer, *History*, 313, 378; and von Rad, *Old Testament Theology* 1:90, 91.

49. Bright, *Israel*, 351.

50. See F. M. Cross, "A Reconstruction of the Judean Restoration," *JBL* 94 (March 1975): 1-18.

51. 2 Kgs 25:12; Jer 39:10. Cf. Peter R. Ackroyd, *Exile and Restoration* (London: SCM, 1968), 22-2; Bright, *Israel*, 327; John L. McKenzie, *Second Isaiah* (Garden City: Doubleday, 1968), 24; W. Stewart McCullough, *The History and Literature of the Palestinian Jews from Cyrus to Herod* (Toronto: Univ. of Toronto, 1975), 11; C. C. Torrey, *Pseudo-Ezekiel and the Original* (with prolegomenon by M. Greenberg; New York: KTAV, 1970), 23; and Claus Westermann, *Isaiah 40-66* (London: SCM, 1969), 5.

52. Bright, *Israel*, 327. Cf. McCullough, *Literature*, 4-6 for a list of publications bearing on the archaeological evidence for this period presented by such sites as Beth-Zur, Gibeah of Saul, Gibeon, Bethel, etc. Cf. McKenzie, 24; and Christopher R. North, *The Second Isaiah* (Oxford: Clarendon, 1964), 18-19.

53. Martin Noth, *The History of Israel* (New York: Harper & Row, 1958), 291.

54. See Noth, *The History of Israel*, 291; Ackroyd, *Exile*, 29; von Rad, *Old Testament Theology*, 1:81-82; Otto Eissfeldt, *The Old Testament: An Introduction* (New York: Harper & Row, 1965), 504 for a discussion of various theories.

55. See Cross' discussion (*CHME*, pp. 195-207, 326-342) on the tensions between the Mushite and Zadokite priests. Cf. Paul Hanson, *The Dawn of Apocalyptic* (Philadelphia: Fortress, 1975), particularly "The Origins of the Post-Exilic Hierocracy," 209-279.

56. Hanson, *Dawn*, 29, concludes "(1) the sources of apocalyptic eschatology lie solidly within the prophetic tradition of Israel; (2) the period of origin is in the sixth to the fifth centuries; (3) the essential nature of apocalyptic is found in the abandonment of the prophetic task of translating the vision of the divine council into historical terms; (4) the historical and sociological matrix of apocalyptic is found in an inner-community struggle in the period of the Second Temple between visionary and hierocratic elements." While this indeed involves social, econonic, and political factors, the question of who should define the will of Yahweh for the nation and who represents the "holy restored remnant, the true Israel" remains in the forefront of the polemic. See also Hanson, *Dawn*, 96-97, and particularly 161-186 for the discussion of Isa 66:1-16.

57. J. D. Purvis, *The Samaritan Pentateuch and the Origin of the Samaritan Sect*, (Harvard Semitic Monographs 2; Cambridge, MA: Harvard, 1968), 18-52; cf. W. F. Albright, *From the Stone Age to Christianity*, 2nd ed. (Baltimore: John Hopkins, 1946), 336, n. 12; and F. M. Cross, *The Ancient Library of Qumran*, 2nd ed., (New York: Anchor, 1961), 34, n. 46 and 172 ff.

58. Purvis, *Samaritan Pentateuch*, 1-15, 88-118. Cf. F. M. Cross, "The Papyri and Their Historical Implications," in *Discoveries in the Wadi Ed-Daliyeh*, eds. Paul and Nancy Lapp, *AASOR* 41 (Cambridge, MA: ASOR, 1974), 22.

59. See Cross (*CHME*, 326-343), for his discussion of the origins of the Essene community of Qumran. Cf. Eichrodt, *Theology*, 2:262-263 and F. E. Peters, *The Harvest of Hellenism* (New York: Simon & Schuster, 1970), 329-330. See Theodor H. Gaster, *The Dead Sea Scriptures* (Garden City: Anchor Books, 1964), for an English translation of the sectarian documents. One must keep in mind, the scriptures used and copied by the Essenes were *not* sectarian, but represented the several textual types available and in use within the wider Jewish community. Cf. below, note 66.

60. Cf. the remarks of Purvis, *Samaritan Pentateuch*, (116-118), on this point in regard to the Samaritans. The term "Normative" is used here to designate that wider community, which despite the existence of different religious and political parties did not splinter into separatist groups representing the one and only "True Israel." Rather, this wider community retained its loyalty to the High Priest in Jerusalem and allied itself with the ruling party to maintain the Jewish commonwealth and the ancestral faith. It does not refer to the Pharisaic party which ultimately won power and whose religious belief became "normative" for the Jewish community. Nor can it be limited to association with the "ruling party" in power at any specific time.

61. Ibid., 116. Cf. J. Bowman, *The Samaritan Problem* (Pittsburg: Pickwick, 1975), 91-92. Any such contacts must have been limited by more than the geographic isolation. No matter how many common features might be shared, tolerance for a rival "True Israel" must have been limited in both sects.

62. Fohrer, *History*, 369. Cf. Peters, *Harvest*, 289.

63. M. Stern, "The Period of the Second Temple," in *A History of the Jewish People*, ed. by H. H. Ben-Sasson (Cambridge, MA: Harvard, 1976), 234-236. Simeon ben Shetah flourished at the beginning of the last century B.C. The wisdom and importance of these sages is easily seen in *Pirke Aboth*. See R. Travers Heford, *The Ethnics of the Talmud: Sayings of the Fathers* (New York: Schocken Books, 1962), for his translation and commentary of the sayings of these sages who defined the Faith for their time and subsequent generations.

64. Peters, *Harvest*, 289.

65. F. M. Cross has proposed the following technical paleographic definitions to prevent confusion and to establish a common terminology: the term "Hebrew script" refers to the original Hebrew letter forms derived from the Phoenician letter forms and used throughout the monarchical period. The term "Palaeo-Hebrew script" refers to the continued use of the Hebrew script after the loss of national sovereignty and in particular to the revived official use of the Palaeo-Hebrew script first noted in the late Persian period and last documented on the coins of the Bar-Kokhba Revolt or the Second Jewish War against Rome (A.D. 132-135). However, Palaeo-Hebrew script survives until this day in the collateral branch known as the Samaritan script. The term "Jewish script" refers to the national script which developed from the Persian Aramaic script employed for official use throughout the Persian empire. See "The Development of the Jewish Scripts," *The Bible and the Ancient Near East* (London: Routledge and Kegan Paul, 1961), 189-190, n.n. 4-5.

66. See F. M. Cross, "The Contributions of the Qumran Discoveries to the Study of the Biblical Text," 291; "The Evolution of a Theory of Local Texts," 314; and "The History of the Biblical Text in Light of Discoveries in the Judaean Desert," all three in *Qumran and the History of the Biblical Text*, edited by F. M. Cross and S. Talmon (Cambridge, MA: Harvard, 1975).

67. Peters, *Harvest*, 63.

68. Ibid., 61-62.

69. Ibid., 261-262.

70. Bright, *Israel*, 419-420; cf. Peters, *Harvest*, 261-261, 265.

71. J. P. V. D. Balsdon, *The Emperor Gaius* (Oxford: Clarendon Press, 1934), 121-122. Cf. Victor A. Tcherikover and Alexander Fuks, eds., *Corpus Papyrorum Judaicarium*, 3 vols. (Cambridge, MA: Harvard University Press, 1957), 1:6.

72. Balsdon, *Emperor*, 121-122. Cf. Jules Isaac, *The Teachings of Contempt* (New York: Holt, Rinehart and Winston, 1964), p. 31; and Edward H. Flannery, *The Anguish of the Jews* (New York: Macmillan, 1965), 18. Both Isaac and Flannery suggest the Jews had something of a special imperial status of "alien" character. But, cf. Josephus, *Against Apion*, trans. by H. St. J. Thackeray (Cambridge, MA: Harvard University Press, 1926), 2:73-75, Josephus indicates the policy of general toleration in one of his answers to Apion's charges by saying that rather than complaining about Jewish privileges, Apion should admire the wisdom and tolerance of the Romans in not requiring their subjects to violate their national laws.

73. Flannery, *Anguish*, 23. Cf. Balsdon, *Emperor*, 122-123. This is generally true despite the efforts of certain Hellenized Jews, such as Philo or Josephus, to picture the Jews as religiously tolerant. See *Against Apion*, 2:237-238 (Loeb). "Our legislator has expressedly forbidden us to deride or blaspheme the gods recognized by others out of respect for the very word 'God.' " This is Josephus' exegesis of the septuagintal reading of Exodus 22:28. Cf. Tcherikover, *Corpus Papyrorum*, 1:124, 41, 47. By contrast, the Green translations of Esther, the books of Second and Third Maccabees and the Wisdom of Solomon all evidence a strong hatred for Greeks by the Jews.

74. Flannery, *Anguish*, 23, 269. Cf. Baron, *Social and Religious History*, 1:188, 209. Baron suggests that Jewish separatism was one of the fundamental factors in the growth of anti-semitism in the ancient world.

Robert Hodgson, Jr.

Robert Hodgson, Jr., is an Associate Professor of Religious Studies at Southwest Missouri State University. He holds degrees from Heidelberg (Th.D. 1976), Marquette (M.A. 1970), and Gonzaga (B.A. 1965). A frequent contributor to scholarly and popular journals and encyclopedias, Dr. Hodgon's first monograph, *Superstition and Politics in Julio-Claudian Rome,* will appear in 1987. From 1976 to 1980 he served as an appointed missionary to the Philippine Episcopal Church, teaching at St. Andrew's Seminary, Manila, and in the Southwest Asia Graduate School of Theology, Manila. Currently, he serves on the steering committee for the Assemblies of God-Roman Catholic dialogue.

This essay traces the literary and social influences of the Levitical Holiness Code from its Hebrew text in Leviticus 17-26 through intertestamental Judaism to early Christianity. The milestones along the way are the Septuagint rendering of Leviticus 17-26, Pseudo-Phocylides, the Damascus Document, and 1 Thessalonians 4:1-12. The Holiness Code proves to be a source of religious as well as social identity, allowing groups as diverse as sectarian Essene monks and Hellenistic Christian apocalyptists to define their status before God and man.

3

HOLINESS TRADITION AND
SOCIAL DESCRIPTION:
INTERTESTAMENTAL JUDAISM
AND EARLY CHRISTIANITY

Robert Hodgson Jr.

NEW TESTAMENT scholars in growing numbers are turning
their attention to the social and cultural history of biblical
texts.[1] One should wholeheartedly welcome this renewed interest in the ancient world out of which the New Testament has
emerged. Detecting the social and cultural history of any ancient text inevitably leads to a clearer understanding of the text
in its own time and helps the modern reader gain insight into
contemporary social and cultural issues. Without a clear understanding of the social and cultural history of a biblical text one
always runs the risk of missing its original sense and champion-
ing wrongheaded applications.

Romans 13:1-7, for example, is a biblical text which has
caused much mischief in Western Christendom chiefly because
no one fully understands the social history of Christians in
Rome during the first century A.D. In this text Paul calls upon
everyone to be submissive to existing authority, because, in
Paul's words, all authority comes from God and all authorities
are God's servants. When one bears in mind that the authority
under whom Paul and the Roman church lived was that of the
Emperor Nero, it is apparent that the text requires careful
analysis of the historical situation then obtaining in Rome to
determine what Paul is driving at. Three potentially explosive
events appear to have led Paul to counsel complete submission
to Roman authority: tax revolts among shopkeepers and land
owners, riots inspired by Jewish Messianists,[2] and death warrants issued for people found guilty of superstition.[3] Against
such a backdrop Paul advises the church in Rome to keep a
low profile in order to avoid calling the attention of the Roman

authorities to a group already guilty of superstition in Roman eyes.[4]

A second example of how the reconstruction of early Christian social history helps illumine traditions embodied in biblical texts is provided by the lists of domestic duties found in Ephesians, Colossians, and 1 Peter. While one has known for a long while that these lists bear striking resemblance to similar lists in the writings of Hellenistic Judaism and Greek popular philosophy, it is only recently that attention has turned to the question of the social history of these catalogs of domestic duties within early Christianity. Two explanations will illustrate the progress made in responding to this question. On the one hand, it is said that Col 3:18-4:1; Eph 5:21-6:9 and 1 Pet 2:18-3:7 wish to instill a sense of order and discipline into Christian homes in order to facilitate their withdrawal from a hostile world into the surer refuge of a network of closely knit and tightly managed Christian house-churches.[5] On the other hand, it is said that the author of these texts hoped to achieve exactly the opposite: he hoped to solidify Christian family life in order to brace it and arm it with sound management and discipline for its entry into the larger Mediterranean world.[6] However one assesses these two options, it is clear that they both offer a lucid explanation of the social and cultural forces that might encourage an early Christian writer to borrow the domestic duty tradition from contemporary Hellenistic Judaism (or Greek popular philosophy).

THE HOLINESS TRADITION (HT) AND EARLY CHRISTIANITY

Recent research into the HT of intertestamental Judaism and early Christianity has broadened our understanding of the role and function of holiness.[7] One understands it now not only as a theological claim about the sacredness of a people, of animals, of land, or of a diet, but also as having a social dimension as well. It aids in self-definition, group identity, boundary maintenance, and assimilation and rejection of alien ideas, values, peoples, and ritual acts.

Before talking about the social setting of the HT one must first uncover that tradition[8] in the texts of early Christianity and intertestamental Judaism. To this end the following method is used. First, one looks at some external evidence for the view that 1 Thess 4:1-12 is a traditional pattern of ethical exposition on the theme of holiness. A comparison with 1 Pet 1:1-2:3, 11-12 supplies such evidence. Second, one examines the internal evidence for such a view, and points out features of 1 Thess 4:1-12 that qualify as such evidence. Third, one looks at the origin of the HT in Leviticus 17-26 in order to gain a sense of how the tradition looked in its earliest form.

For the sake of the argument, the HT is determined to have three formal or structural parts: foundational statements, concrete demands, and motivations. Each witness to the tradition will be examined, first, in terms of its foundational statements, next, in terms of its concrete demands, and finally in terms of its motives. The foundational statements are assumptions or assertions about God and his people, and generally take the form "God is holy," "God's people are holy," "God's abode is holy," and so forth. These foundational statements serve to establish the condition for the possibility of fulfilling the concrete demand. The only witness to the HT not having such foundational statements is Pseudo-Phocylides, an omission that will be discussed on page 77. The chief metaphor for depicting the behavior of this holy God and his holy people is "walking with his people" or "walking in the precepts." The concrete demands comprise the prescriptions and proscriptions regulating sexual, business, and social affairs. And, while strict philological parallels exist only now and then among the witnesses to the HT, the substance of the demands and the grammatical form overlap to a considerable degree within the broad categories of sexual, business, and social affairs. With respect to the grammatical form of some of the demands, attention is drawn to the use of the infinitive in Hebrew law codes generally, and to the use of imperative infinitives in intertestamental Jewish literature and 1 Thess 4:1-12 as possible indicators of the HT. The motives include God's vengeance or justice, concern for the outsider, and polemic against the heathen.

External Evidence: 1 Thess 4:.-12 and 1 Pet 1:13-2:3, 11-12

The comparison of 1 Thessalonians with 1 Peter offered by E.G. Selwyn shows a common pattern of ethical exposition at 1 Thess 4:1-12 and 1 Pet 1:13-2:3, 11-12, which Selwyn attributed to a pre-Pauline catechetical tradition.[9] Though it is by no means clear that the agreements between 1 Thess 4:1-12 and 1 Pet 1:13-2:3, 11-12 confirm the existence of a pre-Pauline catechism, they do make a case for a pre-Pauline HT. The chart summarizes seven points of contact:

	1 Thessalonians	1 Peter
Foundational statements	holiness (4:3, 4, 7)	holy (1:15, 16)
Material Demands: sexual life	fornication (4:3)	desires (1:14; 2:11)
Material Demands: business life	business	[lacking]
Material Demands: social life	brotherly love (4:9a) love (4:9b) nations	brotherly love (1:22a) love (1:22b)
Motivations	ethne (4:5) God is judge (4:6) outsiders (4:12a)	(cf. 1:18) Father who judges (1:17) (cf. 2:12a)

The pattern of exhortation in 1 Thess 4:1-12 breaks down in the following way:

1. Vv. 1-2 introduce the foundational statement in v. 3a that God's will is the sanctification (*hagiasmos*) of the church.

2. Vv. 3b-6a reproduce three concrete demands from the world of sexual and business affairs:

   a. on fornication (*porneia*)

   b. on taking a wife (*skeuos ktasthai*)

   c. and on transgressing and defrauding one's brother in business (*pragma*).[10]

3. Vv. 5 and 6b motivate these three counsels by reminding the church that unbridled lust belongs to the life of the heathen, and that God avenges all transgressions.

4. V. 6c underlines again the consistency of Paul's earlier preaching with what he now writes.[11]

5. V. 7[12] repeats the foundational statement, while v. 8 concludes that disobedience to this program of ethical behavior amounts to a denial of God.[13]

6. Vv. 9-10a begin a second round of exhortation dealing with social affairs by disclaiming the need to address the theme of *philadelphia* ("brotherly love") since the church's *agapē*

("love") is well demonstrated.

7. Vv. 10b-11 urge more progress[14] and an aspiring to three things:

    a. living quietly[15]
    b. minding one's own business
    c. and working.

8. V. 12 motivates this final set of counsels by recalling the need to walk in such a way that wins the respect of outsiders[16] and promotes self-reliance.

A similar pattern of ethical exhortation appears in 1 Pet 1:13-2:3, 11-12, although it is diffused throughout this section of the baptismal homily constituting 1 Peter.[17] The most striking features of the pattern in 1 Peter are its material and functional parallels with 1 Thess 4:1-12 as well as the common sequence of ideas. After the salutation in 1:1-2[18] and the panegyric on regeneration in 1:3-12,[19] the pattern begins to emerge, and insofar as it preserves the sequence of 1 Thess 4:1-12 it runs as follows:

1. 1:15-16 provide a foundational statement to the effect that, just as the God who called the believers is holy, so, too, they must be holy, an assertion for which Lev 19:2 LXX is the proof text.

2. 2:11 (cf. 1:14) regulates sexual affairs (*sarkikai epithymiai*).

3. 2:12 motivates the entire exhortation with a call for right behavior among Gentiles and for a conscience so clear that it will not only disprove gentile calumny but lead to their praising of God as well.

Within this broad framework 1 Peter includes additional demands and motivations that recall the pattern of 1 Thess 4:1-12. Some of the most apparent are:[20] the exhortation in 1:14 to resist the passions (*epithymiai*) of their former life in ignorance (*agnoia*: cf. 1 Thess 4:5); the exhortation in 1:22 to move beyond *philadelphia* to *agapē* (cf. 1 Thess 4:9); the motivating circumstance that God is both father and judge (*krinōn*; cf. 1 Thess 4:6c); and the polemic against the Gentile in 1:14, 18 (cf. 1 Thess 4:5).

Internal Evidence

Certain features of 1 Thess 4:1-12 betray the presence of traditional material insofar as they either correspond to how Paul edits traditions elsewhere or, by their awkwardness and opaqueness, suggest that the present context may not be the original one.

In its present position 1 Thess 4:1-12 stands out in its narrower context. The first three chapters applaud fully the Thessalonian faith and life, and whatever concerns Paul in 1 Thessalonians 1-3 originates in local harassment of the community (2:14) and possibly in charges raised against him (2:3). In 4:1, however, Paul shifts to exhortation whose directness in view of chapters 1-3 catches the reader by surprise. The assumption of actual moral lapses raises more questions than it answers, and one is on firmer ground to treat the text as conventional and prophylactic instruction.[21] With 4:13, however, the exhortation turns to what is clearly an actual problem, namely the untimely demise of certain Thessalonians and Paul's assurance that they, too, will be raised.[22] In sum, the exhortations in 1 Thess 4:1-12 cut across the grain of chapters 1-3 and, assuming the conventionality of 1 Thess 4:1-12, the text fits awkwardly into the parenesis that follows in 4:13-5:22 with its clear application to the Thessalonian situation.

1 Thessalonians 4:1 opens with the particle *loipon* "finally" which elsewhere signals Paul's transition to inherited material (Phil 3:1; 4:8, *to loipon*).[23] Despite the ragged syntax, v. 1 provides a coherent heading for the exhortations that follow, exhortations which collectively describe the correct *peripatein* "walking" and *areskein theou* "pleasing God."[24] In writing that the Thessalonians have already received (*paralambanein*) these instructions, Paul uses a word that has the restrictive sense of receiving traditional material.[25] Paul says this again in v. 2 and a third time in v. 6, although the emphasis of v. 1 upon Paul's reception of the material is replaced by the assurance that the Thessalonians are acquainted with this body of instruction.[26]

1 Thessalonians 4:3-6 have the distinction of pressing more infinitives into service as imperatives than all other NT texts combined.[27] There are five such infinitives (matched by five in vv. 10-11!), the first three anarthrous, the last two with article and negation. While it may be simply a coincidence, it is

nonetheless a curious one that the great law codes of the Hebrew OT have a fondness for infinitive constructions that is
really without parallel in the rest of the OT.[28] In two instances,
Exod 20:8 and Deut 5:12, the infinitive serves as an imperative.[29] If this observation is of any relevance it would be that
the extraordinary number of infinitives in 1 Thess 4:3-6 (and
10-11) may betray a semitism.[30]

Five more infinitives appear in 1 Thess 4:10b-11, although in
this case they depend syntactically upon *parakalein*. The formal symmetry with vv. 3-6 is striking, and the possibility of a
semitism may be raised here, too, especially if Paul or the puta-
tive tradition has consciously preserved the number ten.[31]

Because the material demands of vv. 3-6 are not only surprising but obscure as well, they may have originally had a different context. The assumption of a HT behind 1 Thess 4:1-12 has
the advantage of offering a single tradition on the strength of
which the sense of vessel (*skeuos*), fornication (*porneia*), to
know (*eidenai*), and defraud (*pleonektein*) can be at least partially determined.[32]

Summary. The comparison with 1 Peter and the pointing
out of four features within 1 Thess 4:1-12 as possible signs of a
supporting tradition lead to the following question: Is there an
identifiable tradition combining foundational statements about
the holiness of God and his call to holiness with concrete
exhortations in the areas of sexual, business, and social ethics,
which motivates such behavior with references to God's vengeance, a concern for outsiders, and a polemic against the heathen? In the following section the thesis is developed that the
ethical exposition of the Holiness Code of Leviticus 17-26
which appears in various forms in intertestamental Judaism
provides such a tradition.

The Holiness Code (HC) of Leviticus 17-26[33]

The relevant features of the HC may be summarized under
the headings of its foundational statements or assertions about
God, its concrete injunctions, and the motivations. With respect to foundational statements the most characteristic of
these is the repeated assertion that God is holy; indeed "holy"
and its derivatives appear nowhere in the OT more consistently
as an attribute of God than in the HC. Typical is the refrain

"Do this or that—because I the Lord your God am holy,"[34] while references to God's sanctuary,[35] God's holy name,[36] and God's sanctification of people and objects[37] abound. Conversely, the HC warns against the danger of profaning God's holiness and holy things (Lev 20:3; 21:6, 12 passim).[38]

A corollary of God's holiness is that God has called his people to holiness, so that at least five times in the course of the HC one reads something like "you shall be holy; for I the Lord your God am holy."[39] In one instance (Lev 19:2) the call to holiness introduces a levitical decalog, in another (Lev 20:7) it rounds out preceding legislation (Lev 20:1-6), while in a third (Lev 20:26) the call concludes a series of injunctions (cf. Lev 20:10-25). It should be noted that Lev 20:7 and 20:26 serve as foundational statements for proscriptions of sexual offenses, so that already here the pattern observed in 1 Thessalonians and 1 Peter begins to emerge. A further refinement of this statement constitutes an entire chapter in the HC, namely Leviticus 23, the catalog of feasts of the Lord. These are those days on the festal calendar when God calls his people together as a holy convocation,[40] an expression that materially and philologically stands close to 1 Thess 4:7 and 1 Pet 1:15a.

In the sermonic conclusion to the HC, Leviticus 26, the figure of walking in the precepts of the Lord describes the anticipated response to God's call,[41] and this metaphor, though not peculiar to the HC, does provide another parallel for investigation. The same may be said about the assertion, found in the sacrificial legislation of Leviticus 19 and 22, that certain forms of sacrifice are not pleasing to God.[42]

The relevant injunctions of the HC fall into three groups: exhortations dealing with sexual behavior, business affairs and social obligations. Naturally, the HC embraces far more material than can be conveniently included here, so that only a representative selection will be offered. The selection is representative, too, insofar as different witnesses to the HT will draw upon different concrete injunctions from the code.

The sexual delicts against which Leviticus 18 and 20 militate may, broadly speaking, be summarized under the rubric of incest, that is, in the view of the HC certain degrees of blood and marriage kinship preclude sexual intercourse. The list of forbidden unions in Lev 18:6-18 reads like a litany, repeating again and again its proscription of "uncovering the nakedness" of one's father, mother, mother-in-law, and so forth,[43] concluding that such a practice is a wickedness. Verses 19-23 continue, however, with injunctions against intercourse with a woman in menstruation, the worship of Molech, adultery, homosexuality, and sodomy, summing them up in vv. 22-23 as abominations and perversions.

Leviticus 20 recapitulates the legislation of Leviticus 18 and supplements it with provisions against wizardry, cursing parents, and the insertion of the call to holiness at vv. 7 and 26. Verse 5 brands the worship of Molech as whoring; v. 13 calls homosexuality an abomination; and v. 21 sets incest off as impurity.

Under the heading of fair and unfair business practices one may subsume the legislation of the HC regulating the buying and selling of slaves and property during the jubilee year (Lev 25:13-17, 39-49), the timely distribution of wages (Lev 19:13), and the fairness of weights and measures (Lev 19:35). Lev 25:36 also forbids taking interest from an impoverished brother.

The interest of the HC in social conduct is well known and may be treated summarily. Leviticus 19:17-18 contains the familiar injunctions against hating one's brother and taking vengeance as well as the positive counsels for reasoning with and loving one's brother. Legislation regulating the indenturing of slaves (Lev 25:43), stealing and lying (Lev 19:11), impartiality in justice (Lev 19:15), and so forth all belong here.

The HC motivates its legislation with warnings about God's vengeance, comparisons with the wickedness of the heathen, and a concern for the well-being of the sojourner. The sermonic conclusion to the HC warns of the consequences should the people not walk in the precepts given them. Leviticus 26:14-22 lists with an apocalyptic fervor the terrors, consumptions, fevers, plagues, and famines that God holds ready, a catalog of destruction that v. 24 summarizes as God's punitive walking with his people.[44] Although Leviticus 26 only obliquely refers to the wickedness of the nations by threatening to consign the people over to them (26:33, 38), the theme is most apparent in Leviticus 18 and 20, the sections of the HC dealing with sexual matters.[45] There the comparison is drawn between the ways in which God's people walk and the ways of the nations with a view to motivating right conduct. And, finally, a concern for the sojourner is evident in much of the legislation of the HC to the extent that the code strives to attract outsiders by including them in as many provisions as practicable.[46] This attention of the HC to the sojourner corresponds materially to 1 Thess 4:12a and 1 Pet 2:12.[47]

Summary. This survey of the HC indicates that at a number of important points the legislation of Leviticus 17-26 converges with what is presumed to be a traditional pattern of ethical exhortation behind 1 Thess 4:1-12 and 1 Pet 1:13-2:3, 11-12. With the HC as a *terminus a quo* the mediating stations along the way to the NT in intertestamental Judaism may now be examined.

THE HOLINESS TRADITION IN INTERTESTAMENTAL JUDAISM

In this penultimate section one turns to the literature of inter-testamental Judaism in order to identify the stages through which the HT passed on its way from Leviticus 17-26 to 1 Thessalonians 4:1-12. The intertestamental witnesses germane to our discussion include: the Septuagint, Pseudo-Phocylides, and the Damascus Document.

The Septuagint (LXX)[48]

The Greek translation of Leviticus in the LXX provides an early, if not the earliest witness to the HC. Its importance reposes in a special way in providing, for a body of Hebrew legislation, semantic equivalents in Greek which help guide all Hellenistic Jewish exposition of the HC. As in the case of the Hebrew text, relevant foundational statements, demands, and motivations will be highlighted, although in summary fashion to avoid repetition.

The foundational statement that God is holy translates in the LXX as "I am holy, the Lord, your God."[49] Similarly, God abides in a sanctuary;[50] his name is holy;[51] and God sanctifies his priests.[52] The call of the people at large to holiness is then "be holy" or a variation of this formula,[53] while the legislation providing for the feasts of the Lord calls the assemblies of the people "holy convocations," an expression which presupposes a God who calls to holiness and suggests a tradition out of which the two NT witnesses may have emerged.[54] Opposed to God's holiness and his holy things is, for example, the eating of a carcass or torn animal,[55] for that renders one *akathartos* "unclean" (Lev 17:15); intercourse with a woman in menstruation, for she has an *akatharsia* "uncleanliness" (Lev 18:19); and uncovering the nakedness of a brother's wife (Lev 20:21), for that, too, is *akatharsia*. Lev 22:3 provides that any priest who enters the sanctuary with an *akatharsia* will be cut off from his people.

The metaphor "to walk in the precepts" or simply "to walk"[56] describes the anticipated response to God's call, and is the material equivalent to the *anastrophē* and *peripatein* "living" and "walking" of 1 Pet 1:15; 2:12 and 1 Thess 4:1, 12.

The relevant injunctions in the LXX are those regulating sexual, business, and social ethics. Incestuous unions are by definition those in which an "uncovering of nakedness" occurs among certain blood and marriage kin (cf. Lev 18:6-18; 20:11-21), and these alliances are branded as "wickedness" (Lev 18:17) and "uncleanliness" (Lev 20:21). The injunctions against adultery, homosexuality, and sodomy (Lev 18:19-23) define these actions as "abominations," while the worship of Molech is "whoring" (cf. Lev 20:6).

The legislation in Leviticus which aims at business practices regulates the fair buying (*ktasthai*) and selling (*apodidosthai*) of property (25:13-17) and slaves (25:39-46), stipulates a timely payment of wages (19:13), and orders correct weights and measurements (19:35). The injunction against interest and profit-taking (*pleonasmos*) in Lev 25:37 is of special interest in light of 1 Thess 4:6a (*pleonektein*).

The Greek expressions given to the motivations for holy behavior correspond both materially and, to some extent, philologically to the motivations of the HT assumed for 1 Thess 4:1-12 and 1 Pet 1:13-2:3, 11-12. God blesses his people when they walk in his precepts, but when they treat his judgments with contempt and reject his covenant, he will walk against them in anger.[57] The blessings and curses of Leviticus 26 motivate right conduct with threats of punishment and promise of reward in a manner similar to 1 Pet 1:17 and 1 Thess 4:6b with their references to God as judge and avenger, respectively. The negative example of the nations reinforces continually the concrete injunctions of the HC, especially those regulating sexual behavior in Leviticus 18 and 20. Rounding out the proscription of incest, sodomy, worship of Molech, and so forth, Lev 18:24

warns against polluting one's self in this manner, because this is the way of the nations.[58] Concern to include the proselyte in the legislation is evident throughout the Greek text, appearing at least once as an expansion of the Hebrew text.[59] This deference may be the equivalent of what appears as a concern to generate good will among outsiders in 1 Pet 2:12a and 1 Thess 4:12a.

Summary. The exposition of the HC in the LXX includes foundational statements, concrete exhortation, and motivations, various combinations of which constitute the HT in intertestamental Judaism. It is not so, however, that every *topos* is represented in the subsequent witnesses; indeed, as the hortatory poem of Pseudo-Phocylides shows, it is possible to cull ethical demands from the HC without even referring to the concept of holiness, or to advance texts from the HC not included in the summaries above.

Pseudo-Phocylides[60]

Pseudo-Phocylides is a poem of some 230 lines of dactylic hexameter allegedly written by the sixth century B.C. Ionic sage Phocylides. Its literary genre combines features of the wisdom poem and sentence collection or anthology. The poem's actual date is uncertain, but estimates range from 150 B.C. to A.D. 40. Its provenance is generally given as Alexandria, although the demonstration is a fragile one, resting on a single injunction against the dissection of a human body, a custom associated with the practice of medicine in Alexandria. The poem is a manual for correct living, the bulk of whose injunctions stem from the LXX and Greek wisdom literature. Because it is written in a deliberately archaic Ionic style, its exposition of the HC is reflected more in material parallels than in philological ones, although the latter are not completely lacking. The Pentateuch (especially the great law codes) is mined extensively, so that van der Horst detects around thirty-five references and allusions to the HC alone.[61] If the author is a Hellenistic Jew, he is writing for a pagan audience with a view to winning it to a life that, at least ethically, conforms to Judaism.[62] His chief interests are justice, honesty, moderation, faithfulness, concern for the poor, the well-being of the household, and moderation in sexual affairs. The principle of the collection is given at the end (228) when the author concludes his anthology with "Purifications are for the purity of the soul, not of the body," a sentiment which amounts to saying that his *dicta*, originally cultic, are now spiritualized and universalized.

The HT is diffused throughout Pseudo-Phocylides in such a way that any reconstruction necessarily pulls together texts that vary widely in position and function in the poem. Nonetheless, a recognizable pattern emerges, if one uses the threefold schema of foundational statements, material demands, and motivations. Especially prominent is the exposition of Leviticus 19—that part of the HC containing legislation regulating business and social obligations.[63]

Foundational statements deriving unambiguously from the HC do not appear in Pseudo-Phocylides, because the poem as a whole scrupulously avoids mention of peculiarly Jewish cultic practices and concepts. Thus, references to Sabbath, circumcision, temple sacrifice, covenant, holiness, and so forth are conspicuously missing.[64] What foundational statements there are turn out to be, broadly speaking, sapiential: God is one, wise, and mighty (54); God rules over souls (111); God is the source of all prosperity (29). The writer of Pseudo-Phocylides has, in fact, gone to such lengths to excise or camouflage specifically Jewish foundational statements that on at least four occasions (75, 98, 104, 163) he makes assertions about the gods!

If foundational statements derived from the HC are wanting in Pseudo-Phocylides, material demands regulating business, social, and sexual life do appear. The four clearest instances of an ethical exposition of the HC are lines 10 (Lev 19:15), 14 (Lev 19:35), 19-24 (Lev 19:13), and 179-185 (Lev 18:8, 9, 16). In lines 9-21 Pseudo-Phocylides has gathered sentences dealing with the themes of social justice and fair business practices, so that in line 10 one reads "Cast the poor not down unjustly, judge not partially" as an abridgement and exposition of "Do not deal unjustly in judgment; do not show partiality to the poor; do not defer to the great." The most obvious modification of the LXX is the elimination of the great or powerful as one special focus of the injunction and the concentration on the plight of the poor. This refinement may reflect theological, social or economic forces in Alexandrian Judaism, although this cannot be discussed in detail here. In the same section (line 14) the poem calls for fair business practices with "Give a just measure, good is an extra full measure of all things," an injunction which appears to be an exposition of the LXX "Do not deal unjustly in (business) judgments in length, weight or quantity." That Pseudo-Phocylides has the LXX text of the HC in mind seems clear, since line 15 plays on the so-called Kil'ayim law of Lev 19:19 (*heterozygos*).[65] Again, in line 19, the theme is fair business practices, and Pseudo-Phocylides has taken the levitical injunction against withholding a laborer's wages "Do not keep the wages of your worker overnight" and versified it with "To the laborer give his pay!" One of the striking features of line 19 is that it concludes a series of injunctions dealing with perjury, stealing, and payment of wages, a series that corresponds almost exactly to the sequence in Lev 19:11-13.

Toward the end of the poem (lines 179-185), in a section of counsels on marriage, chastity, and family life, Lev 18:8, 9, 16 are reworked into appropriate maxims, although there is no interest at all in the levitical notion that incest is forbidden because it involves an uncovering of the nakedness of a kinswoman. Line 179 runs "Touch not your stepmother, your father's second wife," and in so doing transposes the semitic idiom of the LXX to Lev 18:8 into proper Ionic Greek. Likewise, line 182 forbids intercourse with a sister, as does Lev 18:9. And, finally, the injunction in line 183 forbids intercourse with a sister-in-law, as does Lev 18:16. It should be noted, too, that the sequence of mother-in-law, sister, and sister-in-law is also the sequence in Leviticus, although the latter has included other degrees of kinship in the series as well.

While the four texts treated above represent the clearest cases of Pseudo-Phocylides' exposition of the HC, there are many other verses in which the poem may be reworking and versifying injunctions of the HC. Some of the more conspicuous are the injunctions against eating blood and food sacrificed to idols (31),[66] against compelling a wife to earn a living as a prostitute (177),[67] and against eating meat torn by animals (147-48).[68]

Before passing on to the motivations that Pseudo-Phocylides may have drawn from the HC, a word about the infinitive form of many of the poem's injunctions is called for. Above, it was noted that the ten infinitives that bulk so large in 1 Thess 4:1-12 may represent a semitism, going back to the use of the Hebrew infinitive construct in the law codes of the OT. Küchler is correct in calling the imperative infinitives archaic but too quick to assume that they are Ionicisms. They may well be an expression of the poet's carefully shrouded yet real interest in reworking Jewish legal traditions for his day.

The motivations which Pseudo-Phocylides may owe to the HC are only two, for the poem has scrupulously avoided motivating right conduct with specifically Jewish ideas, just as it avoided grounding right conduct in such Jewish concepts as covenant and holiness. Thus, there is no polemic against the nations. What one does find is the concern to incorporate the outsider into its legislation and reference to God's judgment. In the first place, the poem concludes its section on mercy (lines 22-41) with the statement that "Strangers should be held in equal honor with citizens." Van der Horst suggests that the poem has reworked a text such as Lev 19:34 with the intention of extending Jewish law to proselytes in Alexandria or, as appears more likely to him, with a view to moving the civic authorities in Alexandria to protect (Jewish?) peasants who have migrated to the city.[70] In the second place, Pseudo-Phocylides warns that "If you judge evilly, God will judge you thereafter" (11).[71]

Summary. Pseudo-Phocylides comprises, among other material, a series of injunctions that originates in ethical exposition of the HC. As such, the poem constitutes another link between the earliest formulation of the code in the Hebrew text of Leviticus 17-26 and the NT witnesses. The final stage of the tradition with which this paper is concerned comes from the Damascus Document.

The Damascus Document (CD)[72]

The CD is a manual of theological exhortation and practical ordinances designed to animate, organize, and guide the life of the Essene community at Qumran. Originally discovered by Schechter in 1896-97 in a Cairo synagogue's geniza, later supplemented by finds from caves IV and VI at Qumran, the reconstructed document runs to eight pages of exhortation and eight of ordinances. The exhortation centers on the themes of obedience to the laws of the community, the holiness of the

sect, the wickedness of outsiders, and the nearness of judgment, while the ordinances provide Essene halakah of the
mosaic law. Not unexpectedly, exposition of the HC plays a
role in the ordinances at key points, not to mention its influence in the exhortation itself. Dupont-Sommer dates the final
redaction of CD to 63-48 B.C. principally because of the allusion
to Pompei's capture of Jerusalem in 63 B.C. in CD VIII, 1-13.

Direct foundational statements of the sort "I the Lord your
God am holy" do not appear in CD, but since there are in fact
only four direct quotations from Leviticus in the whole document to begin with, such a finding is not surprising. If one,
however, collects the assertions that are made about holiness in
the document, then the presence of the HT in the form of a
basic assumption about God, his people, and the things set
apart for them is evident. Statements about holiness occur both
in the exhortation and in the ordinances, although predomi-
nately in the former. CD's opening reviews the circumstances
which called the Essene community into being: God turned
away from Israel and from his holy place,[73] leaving only a
remnant from among those whom he delivered over to the
sword (i.e. Nebuchadnezzar). From this remnant some 390
years later a "root of planting" (i.e. the Essenes) sprang forth
when God revealed to them his holy Sabbaths and glorious
feasts, his testimony of righteousness, his ways of truth, and
the desires of his will (cf. 1 Thess 4:3a). All this is done so that
each man might perform the commandments and live through
them,[74] an expression which Lev 18:5 has possibly inspired. To
this remnant falls the duty of setting apart "holy things"[75] and
of distinguishing between the holy and the profane.[76] The sect's
earliest members are designated men of holiness,[77] while the
present members have each a holy spirit.[78] Appropriately, the
members walk in God's precepts in holy perfection.[79]

Both in the exhortations and the ordinances CD raises material demands that derive from ethical exposition of the HC. Following the outline of the earlier sections, injunctions regulating
sexual, business, and social affairs are collected and briefly
discussed. Describing the present distress and affliction of the
sect, CD determines that the grounds for God's chastisement
include, among other things, past sexual sin. Specifically, CD
charges the defilement of the holy place to nonobservance of
the law proscribing intercourse with a woman in menstruation,

an application of Lev 18:19. The text continues with the observation that violation of the law of nakedness, that is, incest, also accounts for the holy place's defilement. While the HC does not specifically address women in its provisions against incest, CD does here: "This law is for men and women."[80] The two specific cases which CD addresses are intercourse with the sister of one's mother (Lev 18:13) and with the brother of one's father (Lev 18:14). The ordinances also provide that sexual relations of any sort are forbidden within the city of the holy place, i.e. Jerusalem, an injunction which may be an application of Lev 15:18 to the life of the sectarians.[81]

Ordinances that apply strictly to business affairs include provisions against work on the Sabbath, none of which are directly derivable from the HC (cf. X.14-XI.18), although interestingly enough this whole section ends with a wordplay on Lev 23:38.[82] The selling of clean birds and animals, slaves and grain to Gentiles is forbidden by CD XII. 8-11, a series of ordinances which is introduced by a warning against doing violence to Gentiles in business affairs. That, by and large, CD comprises relatively little legislation pertaining to business may be due to the monastic and self-sufficient character of the community.

The ordinances regulating social affairs include one direct quotation from the HC (CD IX.2), a text which is the beginning of the entire ordinance section as well as the beginning of a subsection on community discipline. Quoting from Lev 19:18, it reads: "You shall not take vengeance or bear a grudge against the sons of your own people." The same section (CD IX.7-8) quotes Lev 19:17 b-c: "but you shall reason with your neighbor, lest you bear sin because of him," interpreting it to mean that failure to rebuke a brother amounts to sin itself.

In the exhortation section of CD, Lev 19 has provided injunctions for the list of obligations incumbent upon the sect's membership (VI. 11-VII.6). This is a section already observed to share the emphasis of the HC on "walking in the holy precepts." Dupont-Sommer translates:[83]

To separate themselves from the sons of the Pit, and to keep themselves from the unclean riches of iniquity. . . . to distinguish between the unclean and the clean (Lev 20:25 passim). and to make known (the distinction) between sacred and profane, and to observe the Sabbath. . . . to set holy things apart. . . . to love each man his brother (Lev 19:18), and to support the hand of the needy, the poor, and the stranger, and to seek each man the well-being of his brother, and not to betray . . . to keep from lust . . . to re-

prove each man his brother according to the commandment (Lev 19:17) . . .
and to bear no malice (Lev 19:18) . . . and to be separated from all uncleanliness. . . . For all who walk in these (precepts) in holy perfection. . . . the
Covenant of God is assurance that they will live (Lev 18:5). . . . (CD
VI.14b-VII.6a)

Apart from material points of contact with the HC and the
NT witnesses, another feature of this text stands out. The demands are almost all infinitives with the preposition "to," so
that once again the fortuitous (?) combination of infinitives as
imperatives with ethical exposition of the HC is noted.

The ways in which CD motivates right behavior may be
summarized briefly under the usual headings of the vengeance
and justice of God, concern for the outsider, and polemic
against the heathen. CD opens with a reminder of divine judgment, so that in one sense this motivation overshadows the
whole document: "Therefore hear now, all you who know justice, and comprehend the words of God! For He tries all flesh
and will judge all those who scorn Him."[84] Concern for winning the support of the outsider may be present in the passage
quoted at length above insofar as the community is called not
only to support the needy and the poor but the stranger as
well. Similarly, the ordinances proscribe the sending forth of
strangers to do a job on the Sabbath (CD XI.2) and call for the
protection of Gentiles in business transactions (CD XII. 6).
Polemic is reserved in CD not for the Gentiles, (i.e. Romans),
to whom a certain deference is shown (cf. CD IX. 1), but for
fallen away sectarians and the sect's enemies in Jerusalem,
presumably members of the Sadducean and Pharisaic parties.[85]

THE SOCIAL SETTING OF THE HT IN
INTERTESTAMENTAL JUDAISM AND EARLY CHRISTIANITY

The literary witnesses for the HT share not only a common
content and structure but a similar social setting as well. This
becomes apparent if one looks at the support groups or advocates out of which the literary witnesses come and which they
serve. Each of the groups is separatist, determined to construct
its own self-identity and status, and concerned to establish and
maintain boundaries between itself and outsiders. In short, the
advocates of the HT use "holiness" as a rationale for con-
structing and maintaining a cosmos that is set over against a
hostile outside world. Holiness is thus not just ethical perfection; it is social reality.

Early advocates of the HC are the levitical priests responsible for the preservation of the Code in the Book of Leviticus. Already in ancient Israel the Levites were accorded a special status insofar as certain cities belonged to them as Levitical cities (cf. Numbers 35; Joshua 21). Moreover, the Levites could not be dispossessed of their city plots (Lev 25:29-34):[86]

> From the time of the return to Zion the boundaries between priests and Levites were firmly established. The Levites acquired an honored status, and even their small number in comparison with that of priests (Ezra 2:40-42) added to their importance in the eyes of the people. In the time of Ezra and Nehemiah it was necessary to bring Levites to Jerusalem from the Exile and from rural towns. From this time on the division between priests and Levites remained permanent.

Read against this social background the HC in Leviticus 17-26 becomes a sort of constitution and policy statement for a minority group seeking to define and safeguard its status and identity. Thus the Levitical priesthood lives separately, marries separately (Lev 21:7, 13) and even grieves separately (Lev 21:1-2) from other Jews. Identity and status are defined, for example, by regulations controlling physical appearance (Lev 2:16-21), shaving (Lev 21:5), hair style (Lev 21:10), and tattooing (Lev 21:5). Provisions such as "You shall not do as they do in the land of Egypt . . . and you shall not do as they do in the land of Canaan" (Lev 18:3) spell out the importance of boundary maintenance: Levites are not like Egyptians and Canaanites and may not be like them.

In a more general way, the HT of the LXX reflects the separation, self-identity, and determination to establish and maintain boundaries of Alexandrian Judaism. The best known Jew of Alexandria, the cosmopolitan and learned Philo, cannot be taken as typical of Jewish life in this second largest of all cities in the Roman Empire of the first century A.D. His attempt to merge Greek philosophy and Jewish law and tradition, while no doubt typical of the intellectual life in a city that once held the largest library in the ancient world and that will later produce in the person of Clement of Alexandria the first Christian philosopher, must have seemed a curiosity to the average pious Jew. It is, of course, true that leaders of Alexandrian Jewry occasionally sought full citizenship for their constituents, but in the end the price of accommodating fully to Hellenistic city life and civic duties proved too high, and the Jews of Alexandria made do with their status as resident aliens, living apart in the so-called Delta section of the city with their own corporation laws, popular assembly, archives, and law-court.[87]

The temptation to conform to Hellenistic city life by training in the *gymnasia*, attending festal meals in the city's temples, joining the guilds and clubs, or by marching in the grand processions honoring a god or an emperor was both powerful and profitable. Contact with civic, religious, and political leaders in a Hellenistic city like Alexandria inevitably led to increased influence, wealth, and social status. Over against this tendency to assimilate stands the HT. Its foundational statement "I am holy, the Lord, your God" may, in this setting, mean simply that the God of the Jews claims a holiness for himself which the Hellenistic deities do not share. The imperative "you shall be holy" then limits the source from which the holiness of the people derives. The competition between Jewish Lord and Hellenistic deity for the loyalty of the Alexandrine Jew certainly lies in the background. The emphasis on the holy congregations of Jews gathered together on the appointed feasts may be seen as the Jewish response to the ever present invitations to participate in Hellenistic religious life. That the HT calls unclean the eating of a carcass or of a torn animal, having intercourse with a woman in menstruation, and the marrying of a brother's wife reflects the strongest possible appeal to the ancient but still powerful value system centered on ritual and ethical purity. Behind such an appeal may well stand such features of Hellenistic city life as eating meat offered to idols (cf. 1 Cor 8-10), temple prostitution, and marriage contracts such as Herod Antipas and his sister-in-law Herodias executed. Assimilation to the profit-oriented and expansionist economic system of Hellenism as well as membership in the professional guilds threatened an older Jewish mercantile system based on individual ownership, fair business practices, and the proscription of interest taking. Thus the injunctions of the HT regulating fair buying and selling, payment of wages, treatment of slaves, and the taking of interest function in the context of a Hellenistic city as boundaries marking off the limits beyond which one may not go without violating Jewish law and custom.

Over against the Holiness Code of the Hebrew text the HT of the LXX makes one concession with respect to outsiders: it invites them into the community as proselytes (Lev 17:3). This should not be interpreted as a crumbling of the walls of exclusivism or a lack of confidence in the traditional self-identity. Rather, such an invitation suggests a confidence in the traditional boundaries that is so firm that the community has

developed a sense of mission based on its ability to absorb outsiders into its powerful system of belief. It is this complex type
of Judaism, which is both inward-looking and prepared to do
mission work, that meets the reader in Pseudo-Phocylides. The
deliberate suppression of all the references to holiness, Sabbath, circumcision, and the covenant may be interpreted as an
effort to simplify what to the outsider must have appeared as a
vast and complex religious sytem, an accommodation to outsiders much in the vein of the reduced vision of Judaism that
appears in the so-called Apostolic Decree of Acts 15. If the issues of exclusiveness, identity, and boundaries do not arise for
Pseudo-Phocylides in terms of theological belief or ritual practice, they do arise in terms of ethics. The outsider is told on
the basis of injunctions drawn from the HT and elsewhere how
he shall differ from others in matters of business, social, and
sexual life. Of special interest here is Pseudo-Phocylides play
on the Kil'ayim law of Lev 19:19 ("You shall not let your cat-
tle breed with a different kind; you shall not sow your field
with two kinds of seed. . . ."). It would seem that for Pseudo-
Phocylides the exclusiveness, self-identity, and boundaries
which result from not mixing things of a different kind (the
sense in which Pseudo-Phocylides understands Lev 19:19)
emerge from conformity to a set of ethical standards defining
responsible behavior.

The exclusiveness, self-identity, and concern for boundary
maintenance of the Essenes repose in a special way in their
selection of a site for a monastery. Qumran, the name of the
site, lies on the fringe of the Judean wilderness on the north-
west shore of the Dead Sea. Even if one had no literature from
this sect of monastic Jews, this mountain retreat would amply
document the mind set of a group for whom the HT is but one
expression of its withdrawal from the world of day-to-day affairs. Recent studies report that the Essenes withdrew from
Jerusalem during the reign of Jonathan (160-142 B.C.) as a protest of his seizure of the high priest's office.[88] Against this
background one must read the language of separation: the
Jerusalem religious community includes the "sons of the Pit,"
while the Essenes are the "sons of light." The CD's emphasis
on obedience to the laws of the community, the holiness of the
sect and all that pertains to it, the round condemnation of outsiders and all constitute an effort to forge self-identity and erect
boundaries. Even history can be interpreted and made to serve

these social goals, for to paraphrase CD's opening statement, "God has turned away from Israel and its holy place leaving only the Essene remnant as his people."

How does all of this help one to understand the social setting of the HT in 1 Thess 4:1-12? Three points may serve as an introduction to the answer to this question. First, Christians, like Jews, settled almost exclusively in the cities of the empire. The same economic, social, and religious forces that played upon Jews played upon Christians. Second, Christians, like Jews, formed communities. In the case of Jews the communities became identified with specific locations and structures called synagogues (Roman law classified the synagogues as *collegia* or associations). In the case of the Christians the community became identified with house-churches (cf. Phlm 2; Rom 16:5; 1 Cor 16:19; Col 4:15). Third, Christians, like Jews, lived as a minority among a pagan majority in what was at best a suspicious, at worst an openly hostile environment.

Thessaly in Macedonia had since at least the first century B.C. a Jewish population, though probably a small one; and presumably the chief city of this district, Thessalonica, numbered Jews among its citizens, too. Probably the Christian community which Paul founded in Thessalonica (Acts 17:1-9) began among the Hellenized Jews and grew to include Gentiles as well. Whatever the origins and sociology of Thessalonian Christianity might have been, it is beyond doubt that its advocates lived as a minority and suffered harassment and persecution from their fellow countrymen (1 Thess 2:14).

To this beleaguered congregation Paul has written a letter of thanksgiving, comfort, and advice; thanksgiving because of their steadfastness and service; comfort because of persecution and the untimely death of some faithful; and advice because of the need to repeat earlier teaching and reinforce their self-identity and preparation for the Second Coming. Against this background one reads 1 Thess 4:1-12 as a sort of constitution and policy statement designed to articulate the deepest truths of the communal life and spell out its practical consequences. But beyond that 1 Thess 4:1-12 also serves an important social function. Its foundation statement ("God's will is your holiness") explains in theological terms why the Thessalonian Christians have been set apart, i.e. are holy: it is God's will. Thus a minority social status is made transparent by a religious belief. Likewise, the instructions of 1 Thess 4:1-12 on sexual, social, and business life—whatever they may specifically have in view—set up boundaries by means of which the Thessalonian Christians can recognize and define their common life. That this exclusiveness, self-identity, and boundary maintenance has the non-believer, i.e. the outsider in mind is apparent from 1 Thess 4:12 "so that you may command the respect of outsiders."

CONCLUSION

In intertestamental Judaism and early Christianity the idea of holiness is a religious force of supreme importance. Holiness is, however, all too often limited to being a quality of God's life or of the life of the believer. Such a limitation overlooks an important role that holiness has played in the history of Judaism and Christianity, namely its ability to construct identity, explain exclusiveness, and maintain boundaries.

NOTES

1. Representative are: W.A. Meeks, *The First Urban Christians. The Social World of the Apostle Paul* (New Haven: Yale University, 1983); R.E. Brown, SS. and J.P. Meier, *Antioch and Rome. New Testament Cradles of Christianity* (Ramsey, NY: Paulist, 1983); J. Murphy-O'Connor, *St. Paul's Corinth* (Wilmington, DE; Glazier, 1983); B.J. Malina, *The New Testament World: Insights from Cultural Anthropology* (Atlanta: Knox, 1981); A. Malherbe, *Social Aspects of Early Christianity* (Baton Rouge: Louisiana State University, 1977). G. Theissen, *Sociology of Early Palestinian Christianity*, (trans. J. Bowden; Philadelphia: Fortress, 1978); E.A. Judge, *The Social Pattern of the Christian Groups in the First Century. Some Prolegomena to the Study of New Testament Ideas of Social Obligation* (London: Tyndale, 1960).

2. Cf. V. Riekkinen, *Römer 13: Aufzeichnung und Weiterführung der exegetischen Diskussion* (Annales Academiae Scientiarum Fennicae 23; Helsinki: Suomalainen Tiedeakatemia, 1980), pp. 217-8. Riekkinen's book has, among other things, put to rest the thesis defended by Kallas and others that Rom 13:1-7 is an interpolation.

3. Cf. Tacitus, *Annals* 12.59 and 6.29.

4. Interpreters of Romans 13 have not always troubled to uncover the social history of this text in their effort to apply it to contemporary issues. When the German peasants revolted in 1524 and asked Martin Luther to join in their cause, the reformer's reply was the *Ermahnung zum Frieden auf die 12 Artikel der Bauernschaft in Schwaben (Exhortation to Peace with Respect to the Twelve Articles of the Schwabian Farmers)*, a tract in which Luther condemned the revolt by appealing to Romans 13 and the need to submit to worldly authority. The result of Luther's stand was, of course, the alienation of a large proportion of the German peasantry from the spirit of the Reformation.

In our own time one can point to the use of Romans 13 by the propaganda machine of the National Socialists in Germany of the 1930s. Sensing a certain reluctance of the German state churches to endorse the political platform of Hitler and his minions, the National Socialists turned to Romans 13 and argued persuasively that the sacred scripture of the churches themselves called for obedience to whatever government reigned in the land. Although the German state churches were inextricably caught up in the fateful events that were to follow in Germany of the 1930s and 1940s, a small group of church leaders gathered in Barmen to issue the Statement of 1934 repudiating this bogus appeal to Romans 13 and to found the Confessing Church.

Such a text as Rom 13:1-7 serves to remind us that Paul's letters are written to Christians living in major cities of the Roman Empire. These cities had well defined governments and constitutions, citizens that voted, went into exile, revolted, married, wrote contracts; they had guilds and clubs, schools, libraries, theaters, markets, temples, and law courts. To what extent did city life in all its color and variety contribute to the issues that Paul addressed? What, for example, should one know about the design, cost, and function of a house in a city like Corinth as a basis for understanding Paul's references to house-churches (Phlm 2; 1 Cor 16:19; Rom 16:5). Or, what social convention could Paul assume, when he called for hospitality (Rom 12:13) or for the veiling and silence of women (1 Cor 11:6)? Did urban hospitality embrace strangers as well as family? Did persecution increase or decrease the need for hospitality?

5. J.H. Elliott, *A Home for the Homeless. A Sociological Exegesis of 1 Peter, Its Situation and Strategy* (Philadelphia: Frotress, 1981).

6. D. Balch, *Let Wives Be Submissive: The Domestic Code in 1 Peter* (SBLMS 26; Chico: Scholars, 1981).

7. Cf. R. Hodgson, "1 Thess 4:1-12 and the Holiness Tradition," *SBL Seminar Papers, 1981* (Chico: Scholars, 1981).

8. A tradition is a set of assumptions, values, attitudes, ethical demands, motives, and goals that occur repeatedly in the literature of intertestamental Judaism or early Christianity. It is a pattern for expressing a thought. In the case of the HT one means a recurring set of assumptions, values, attitudes, motives, goals, and ethical demands, designed to explain what holiness is, whence it derives, why one should seek it, and how one lives it out.

9. E.G. Selwyn, *The First Epistle of St. Peter* (London: Macmillan, 1946) 370; Cf. Ph. Carrington, *The Primitive Christian Catechism* (Cambridge: University Press, 1940); A.M. Hunter, *Paul and His Predecessors* (Philadelphia: Westminster, 1961). F.W. Beare, (*The First Epistle of Peter* [Oxford: Blackwell, 1970], 216-220) surveys recent literature on traditional material in 1 Peter. For the sake of the argument I am assuming that 1 Peter is not dependent upon 1 Thessalonians, but that whatever material they share derives from common pre-Pauline traditions.

10. RSV: "that no man transgress and wrong his brother in this matter." If 1 Thess 4:1-12 does stem from the Holiness Tradition, then a proscription of unfair business practices is possibly meant.

11. Does *diamartyresthai* "to testify" refer to Paul's use of a testimony tradition? Cf. Acts 2:40; 28:23; LXX: Exod 18:20; 19:10, 21; 1 Sam 8:9.

12. V. 7 forms an inclusion with v. 2a.

13. Paul is possibly playing on a logion of Jesus (Luke 10:16) from Q.

14. *Perisseuein* "to excel" builds an inclusion with v. 1.

15. Malherbe's observation (*Social Aspects*, 25-26) that Paul is encouraging an Epicurean-like quietism in 1 Thess 4:11 suggests that Paul is redacting the Holiness Tradition at this point by supplementing it with Graeco-Roman hortatory motifs.

16. *Peripatein* "to walk" forms another inclusion with v. 1.

17. Cf. Beare, *Peter*, 220-226.

18. Note already the appearance of *hagiasmos* "holiness" here. Apart from 8 occurrences in the traditional corpus Paulinum (Rom 6:19; 1 Cor 1:30; 1 Thess 4:3, 4, 7; 2 Thess 2:13; 1 Tim 2:15; Hebr 12:14) it only appears at 1 Peter 1:2.

19. 1 Pet 2:4-10 may be left out of the discussion, since it is a tradition in its own right and does not directly derive from the ethical exposition of Leviticus 17-26. Cf.

J.H. Elliot, *The Elect and the Holy* (Leiden: Brill, 1966); K.R. Snodgrass, "1 Peter 1:2-10: Its Formation and Literary Affinities," *NTS* 24(1977/78): 97-106.

20. In the larger context of 1 Peter 2-3, cf. 1 Thess 4:3 with 1 Pet 2:15 (will of God); 1 Thess 4:4 with 1 Pet 3:7 (wife).

21. So B. Rigaux, *Les épîtres aux Thessaloniciens* (Paris: LeCoffre, 1956), 493; E. Best, *A Commentary on the First and Second Epistles to the Thessalonians* (London: Harper & Row, 1972), 178-179; and M. Dibelius, *An die Thessalonicher* (HNT 11; Tübingen: Mohr, 1937), 19-20 are typical. H. Baltensweiler ("Erwägungen zu 1 Thess. 4:3-8," *TZ* 19 [1963]: 1) and C.H. Giblin (Analecta Biblica 31; *The Threat to Faith. An Exegetical and Theological Re-examination of 2 Thessalonians 2* [Rome: Pontifical Biblical Institute, 1967]. 140) infer actual moral lapses among the Thessalonians.

22. Cf. C. Roetzel, *The Letters of Paul* (Atlanta: Knox, 1975), 28 for the overall literary structure of 1 Thessalonians. If, however, one follows W. Meeks (*Writings of St. Paul* [New York: Norton, 1972], 3), who provides for a thanksgiving running through 3:13, then the position of 1 Thess 4:1-12, immediately after the thanksgiving, is unusual. Prof. Wm. Baird first called my attention to this issue.

23. Cf. Best, *Commentary*, 154, and W. Klassen, "Foundations for Pauline Sexual Ethics," *SBL Seminar Papers* (Missoula: Scholars Press, 1978), 160.

24. The HC summarizes its exhortations in materially the same way.

25. 1 Cor 11:23 and 15:1, 3 are the two most familiar instances of this narrower meaning. Gal 1:9, 12; Phil 4:9 and 1 Thess 2:13 probably belong here, too. Cf. G. Delling, "*Paralambanō*," *TDNT* 4 (1967); 13-14.

26. Cf. B. Rigaux, "Vocabulaire chétien antérieur à la première épître aux Thessaloniciens," *Sacra Pagina* (2 vols.; Paris: LeCoffre), 2:380-389.

27. F. Blass-A. Debrunner-F. Rehkopf, *(Grammatik des neutestamentlichen Griechisch* [14th ed.; Göttingen: Vandenhoeck und Ruprecht, 1974], 315) restrict imperative infinitives in the NT to Rom 12:15 and Phil 3:16. C.F.D. Moule (*An Idiom Book of NT Greek* [Cambridge: University Press, 1953], 126-127) includes Luke 9:3; Acts 23:23; Tit 2:2.

28. C.H. Miller, "The Infinitive Construct in the Lawbooks of the OT," *CBQ* 32 (1970): 222-226.

29. Cf. Hosea 4:2; Jer 7:9 MT.

30. This is a precarious point and I do not wish to press it. On the other hand, the imperative use of the infinitive gradually diminishes in Attic Greek (and in Hellenistic, too?) so that there is some justification in suspecting a semitism here. Cf. Blass-Debrunner-Rehkopf, *Grammatik*, 315-316.

31. Again, one does not want to press a coincidence, but on sequences of ten and twelve commandments in the OT cf. M. Noth, *Exodus* (OTL; Philadelphia: Westminster, 1960), 160.

32. Cf. the relevant entries in *TDNT*, the commentaries of Dibelius and Best, and W. Klassen, "Foundations," 165-168 for the alternatives.

33. I have somewhat arbitrarily identified Leviticus 17-26 as the *terminus a quo* of the HT. There is some evidence that Ezekiel ought to be so designated. On the relationship between Ezekiel and Leviticus 17-26 cf. W. Zimmerli, *Ezekiel* (BKAT) 13:1; Neukirchen-Vluyn: Neukirchener, 1969), 1:70-72.

34. Cf. Lev. 19:2; 20:7, 26; 21:6, 8. Cf. W. Zimmerli, "Heiligkeit nach dem sogenannten Heiligkeitsgesetz," *VT* 33 (1980), 495, who points to the schema of indicative-imperative as one feature of the HC.

35. Cf. 19:30; 21:12; 26:2.

36. Cf. 22:2, 32.

37. Cf. 21:8, 15, 23; 22:9.

39. Cf. 19:8, 12; 20:3.

39. 19:2. Cf. note 34.

40. Cf. 23:2, 3, 4, 7 passim.

41. Cf. 26:3, 21, 23, 27; also 20:23.

42. Cf. 19:7; 22:20, 25; positively 22:27.
43. Cf. K. Ellinger, "Das Gestez Leviticus," *ZNW* 67(1955): 1-26. Apart from chapters 18 and 20 the HC treats sexual issues also at Lev 19:20, 29; 21:7-9. The last passage is an especially interesting one since it regulates the type of wife the Aaronic priest might choose.
44. Cf. Lev 26:11-12, a text which along with Lev 19:19 has affinities with the so-called interpolated paragraph of 2 Cor 6:14-7:1. Cf. J. Fitzmyer, "Qumran and the Interpolated Paragraph in 2 Cor 6:14-17:1," *CBQ* 23(1961): 271-280.
45. Lev. 18:24-30; 20:22-26.
46. Cf. Lev 17:13, 15; 19:10, 33-34; 23:22; 24:22.
47. In general cf. W.C. van Unnik, "Die Rücksicht auf die Reaktion der Nicht-Christen als Motiv in der altchristlichen Paränese," *Judentum, Urchristentum, Kirche* (Berlin: Akademie, 1964), 221-233, for a fuller discussion of a *topos* which is of course not limited to the HC.
48. For the purpose of the paper the complicated textual history of the LXX is bracketed, and it is determined to be a late second or early third-century B.C. Alexandrian translation of the MT. Cf. F. Cross, *The Ancient Library of Qumran and Modern Biblical Studies* (Garden City: Doubleday, 1958), 128–140.
49. Cf. Lev 19:2. The root word is *hagios* "holy."
50. Cf. Lev 19:30.
51. Cf. Lev 22:2, 32.
52. Cf. Lev 21:8.
53. Cf. Lev 20:7.
54. Cf. Lev 23:4. The *hagiasmos* "holiness" of 1 Thess 4:3, 4, 7 does not appear in the LXX text of Leviticus 17-26, although *hagiasma* "the holy place" does occur at Lev. 25:5. It is otherwise rare in the LXX.
55. On the relationship of the so-called Apostolic Decree of Acts 15 to this legislation cf. E. Haenchen, *The Acts of the Apostles* (Philadelphia: Westminster, 1971), 469.
56. Cf. Lev 26:3, 21 and note 41: *poreuesthai tois prostagmasin*. Paul's use of *peripatein* derives from the popular philosophical tradition. Cf. K.O. Brink, "Peripatos," *PW* Supplementary Volume 8 (1940): 899-949. In the LXX *peripatein* appears some forty times in either a literal or metaphorical sense, though not in Leviticus 17-26.
57. Cf. note 41.
58. Lev. 18:24; cf. 18:1-3; 20:23.
59. Lev 17:3; cf. note 46 for relevant texts of proselyte law.
60. The treatment of Pseudo-Phocylides is indebted to P.W. van der Horst, *The Sentences of Pseudo-Phocylides* (Leiden: Brill, 1978), and M. Küchler, *Fruhjüdische Weisheitstraditionen* (Göttingen: Vandenhoeck und Ruprecht, 1979), 261-302. References are to lines of the poem in van der Horst.
61. Küchler, *Fruhjüdische,* 280-281 reduces this to four, so that the actual number will be somewhere in between. The following discussion will include only the more certain references to the HC.
62. Whatever pertains to Jewish cultic life is carefully omitted from this poem: sacrifice, Sabbath, circumcision, and so forth.
63. Cf. van der Horst, *Sentences,* 66.
64. Van der Horst's use of holy to translate *hosios* and derivatives at 1, 5, 37, 132, 219 is a *faux ami* and of no relevance to this study, unless one wanted to argue that Pseudo-Phocylides has translated the more OT and Jewish sounding *hagios* into the more Hellenistic *hosios*.
65. Van der Horst, *Sentences,* 122; for the influence of the Kil'ayim law of Lev 19:19 on the interpolated paragraph of 2 Cor 6:14-7:1 cf. Fitzmyer "Qumran."
66. Cf. Lev 19:26a (MT only). The LXX reads differently. Van der Horst considers line 31 a Christian interpolation from Acts 15:29.

67. Cf. Lev 19:29.
68. Cf. Lev 17:15.
69. Küchler, *Fruhjüdisch*, 266-270.
70. Van der Horst, *Sentences,* 139-140.
71. Cf. lines 16-17 on God who hates the perjurer.
72. For the following section on CD I am indebted to A. Dupont-Sommer, *The Essene Writings from Qumran* (Cleveland: World, 1967), 114-163, and C. Rabin, *The Zadokite Documents* (Oxford: Clarendon, 1958). Text: E. Lohse, *Die Texte aus Qumran* (Darmstadt: Wissentschaftliche Buchgesellschaft, 1971), 63-107. References are to column and line numbers in Lohse.
73. Cf. CD I. 3-7 On the importance of the holy place (presumably the temple) cf. IV. 1 (=Ezek 44:15), 18; V. 6; VI. 12.16.
74. CD III. 14-16.
75. CD VI. 20.
76. CD VI. 17-18.
77. CD IV. 6. The text has a lacuna here. Presumably a list of names preceded this honorific title. Cf. Dupont-Sommer, *Qumran*, 127 n. 3.
78. CD VII. 4; Cf. V. 11.
79. CD VII. 4-5; Cf. II. 15-16; VI. 10; XII. 20-21.
80. Cf. CD V. 6-11.
81. Cf. Dupont-Sommer, *Qumran*, 154 n. 4.
82. Ibid., 153 n. 6.
83. Ibid., 132.
84. Cf. CD II. 20; VII. 9-10, VIII. 18.
85. Cf. CD I. 13-II.1; II. 5-8; IV. 13-19g; VII. 9-14; passim.
86. S. Abramsky, "Levites," *JE* 11 (1971): cols 73-74.
87. Cf. E. Mary Smallwood, *The Jews under Roman Rule* (Studies in Judaism in Late Antiquity 20; Leiden: Brill, 1976), 220-225.
88. For discussion and literature cf. B.Z. Wacholder, *The Dawn of Qumran. The Sectarian Torah and the Teacher of Righteousness* (Cincinnati: Hebrew Union College, 1983) and the (unfriendly) review by P.R. Davies *ET* 95 (1984): 155-6.

Charles W. Hedrick

Charles W. Hedrick, Associate Professor of Religious Studies at Southwest Missouri State University, holds an M.A. from the University of Southern California and a Ph.D. from the Claremont Graduate School. He is a B.D. graduate of Golden Gate Southern Baptist Theological Seminary and has served as pastor of churches in Mississippi, California and New York City. In addition, he was a Deputy Probation Officer (Juvenile) for fifteen years in the Los Angeles County Probation Department. His major research areas are Christian origins and Gnosticism.

In the light of the contemporary historical/literary understanding of early Christianity as a pluralistic and diverse phenomenon, this essay raises the question: Is there a common ethical foundation to be found among the diverse ethical stances of New Testament literature? Hedrick surveys this material, focusing on those foundations which served as the bases for the canonical writers to argue for particular lifestyles, rather than on the recommended lifestyles themselves. The results of the study present a challenge to contemporary expressions of normative Christian values.

4

PAST AND FUTURE AS ETHICAL EXORDIUM: A SURVEY OF FOUNDATIONS FOR CHRISTIAN BEHAVIOR IN THE NEW TESTAMENT

Charles W. Hedrick

INTRODUCTION

THE OBJECTIVE of this chapter is to survey, within the context of the insights of contemporary New Testament scholarship, foundations for ideal behavior in early Christianity. It does not purport to describe the ideal standards of behavior, i.e., how early Christians should have acted, nor does it intend to describe early Christian behavior, i.e., how they actually acted; rather, it intends to describe the foundation(s) or authority(ies) on the basis of which New Testament writers argued for a particular lifestyle.

Since the turn of the century, historical/literary study of the New Testament has proceeded on the basis of a history-of-religions model to explain the development of early Christianity.[1] On the basis of such a model, Christianity is one of many religions in late antiquity competing for ascendancy in the ancient world. This development is either furthered or hindered by historical circumstance and cultural context. This approach to the literature does not assume, as do many confessional communities, that the Jesus tradition rests on a common apostolic witness that insures the reliability and "purity" of the teachings of Jesus and the early church; that is to say, it does not assume an initially correct and true tradition that was later corrupted when diverse theological speculation crept into the church under the influence of Greek philosophy and gnosticism. Rather, by applying the insights and methods of historical and literary analysis, it can be shown that there existed at the very earliest period of Christian development an amazing diversity of conflicting theological stances and community practice in the early Christian literature, both canonical New Testament and extra-canonical Christian literature.[2] On the basis of this model, "orthodoxy" (i.e., the "correct" theology) must be understood as the successful and surviving strand of all these diverse theological stances; its widespread dominance appears to be a late phenomenon and its New Testament canon reflects a self-serving selection of texts that promote its own community survival. Hence, on the basis of such an approach one may expect to find a diversity of foundations in the early Christian literature on which arguments for certain types of Christian behavior are based. The question then arises, is there a *common* ethical exordium or foundation in the midst of the diversity to be found in early Christian literature? Or to put the question somewhat more specifically: Does one find common ethical foundation(s) in the canonical New Testament texts, whose provenance for the most part is regarded as uncertain, whose authorship with few exceptions is generally regarded as anonymous and whose dates are usually given as A.D. 40-140?[3]

JESUS OF NAZARETH

The primary sources for studying Jesus of Nazareth are the New Testament Gospels,[4] although some additional source material has been identified in early Christian literature apart from the New Testament.[5] Such "new" source material for Jesus of Nazareth is identified and validated on the basis of its coherence with the Jesus tradition as presented in the Synoptic Gospels. Consequently, beyond the addition of some new sayings and parables to the Jesus tradition, one would expect no radically different understanding of Jesus to emerge.[6] The non-canonical material is extremely important, however, for writing the histories of early Christianity and early Christian literature.

Since the work of Albert Schweitzer[7] and Wilhelm Wrede[8] at the beginning of this century, critical scholarship has realized that the New Testament Gospels are simply not biographical statements of the life of Jesus, rather they must be understood to be individualized and highly theological portraits or interpretations of Jesus, written for the purpose of addressing the authors' own communities of faith.

Mark is generally accepted as the first of these remarkable portraits to be written and it forms the basis for the portraits of Matthew and Luke.[9] Mark's Gospel in chapters 1-13 has been structured out of a few sayings of Jesus and narratives about Jesus (mostly descriptive of his mighty deeds) and a Passion

Narrative (chapters 14-16), whose structure and organization preceeded Mark.[10] The sayings and narratives were not created by Mark, who wrote some distance from the events he describes, but they were drawn by Mark from a body of oral tradition that had been preserved in the church.[11]

Because responsible people are compelled to raise questions about the reliability of the Jesus traditions when they observe the frequently radical differences among the Synoptic Gospels in their reporting of the same saying in the same contexts, scholars have developed certain criteria to validate a saying as being more or less probably "original."[12] To insure that diverse sayings have not crept into the tradition from Judaism or early Christianity, one eliminates all sayings that reflect *characteristic* Jewish or early Christian emphases. Of course, by using these criteria to evaluate sayings in the New Testament, one has reduced the Jesus of the Gospels to his most radical dimension because one has eliminated everything that he would have had in common with distinctive first-century Judaism and early Christianity. Such an exercise does, however, enable the scholar to speak with a strong degree of probability about the "historical" Jesus. Naturally, the church today derives its message from the distinctive faith of the early New Testament Gospel writers, on whose interpretations they rely. But the historian operates with a different set of questions and mandates. Because I do not wish to leave this study open to the charge that I have based my description of the ethical foundation(s) of Jesus on what some would regard as unoriginal sayings (i.e., attributing to Jesus things he *may not* have said), I choose to eliminate all such sayings from consideration accepting the criticism that I am not reconstructing Jesus "as he actually was" but a Jesus from the perspective of his most radical dimensions. The latter failing is more tolerable to me as an historian than the former.

The Jesus materials with which I am working have been reduced to an absolute minimum. For the purposes of this essay I have admitted as sayings of Jesus only those sayings which the most rigorous scholarship agrees derive from Jesus of Nazareth.[13] Hence my sample is sharply reduced but I am working with traditions whose originality few, if any, would question.

It is clear from the sayings of Jesus that he believed in the imminence of the Kingdom of God. He endorsed the preaching

of John the Baptist (Matt 11:7-11a, 16-19) and John also proclaimed the *near* presence of the Kingdom (Matt 3:2). Jesus
himself preached that the Kingdom was near and/or present in his
own day (Matt 11:12-13; Luke 10:18; 16:16; Mark 9:43-47; 10:15;
13:28-29). He did not stress, however, the destruction of the cosmos
with elaborate descriptions of the end as did other apocalyptists, nor
did his preaching contain the wild and bizzare imagery so descriptive
of apocalyptists elsewhere. In that sense it is probably correct to say
that the preaching of Jesus stressed the immediacy of the God of the
end-time,[14] rather than the cosmic events usually associated with the
end-time. But on the other hand, it does seem clear that his ministry
signaled the beginning of the end of the created order (Luke 11:20).

Although there is an almost total lack of bizarre apocalyptic
features in his preaching, Jesus seems to draw upon the approaching end, an appearing of God's Kingdom in the immediate future, as a foundation for governing behavior in the
present. A number of his sayings are only understandable
against the background of an immediate end of the world (Matt
5:38-42; 8:22; 19:12), and others should also probably be understood as having an eschatological backdrop (Matt 10:17-22).

It is his belief in the near end of the world that takes some of
the sting out of his "hard sayings." As an example consider
Matt 5:38-42. The sort of world that would inevitably result
from this kind of advice presents an indeed frightening vision.
To conceive of a world where evil goes unresisted, where men
and women are mistreated and abused, where one's human and
civil rights are freely abridged, where justice is unknown, is indeed a frightening prospect. Pacifists would quite simply not
survive in such a world! Nor does it appear that even Jesus
would have been happy with the kind of world that a faithful
following of his advice would have produced. Such sayings are,
however, at least tolerable against a background of the approaching end of the world: "Because the end of the world is
near, leave vengeance and justice to God. You have no time
for such social concerns; follow me and proclaim the dawning
of God's Kingdom!" It is useless to speculate on what Jesus
might have said had he known the world would have continued
for 1900 years after his ministry. It nevertheless seems clear,
that the imminent end of the world was a principal foundation
on which Jesus based his ethical teaching.

More prominent, however, is the influence of Tanak (i.e.,

Old Testament).[15] The Judaism of Jesus' day is the primary context in which his teachings must be approached. Indeed, the Torah (the books of Moses—the Law) formed the basis of his ethical instructions and he understood it to have an eternal value (Matt 5:17). As a first-century Jew who wanted to be understood by his contemporaries, he was forced to formulate his ethical teachings within the context of his first-century Judaism, its legalism and its ideals.

Yet he did not simply repeat the words of the Torah; he also assumed a certain clear personal authority in interpreting it. While the Torah had abiding value, it took *its* authority from the original will of God in granting Torah. In other words, the will of God was the real authority. Hence, on the basis of this *real* authority Jesus intensified and in some cases demanded more than the Torah required:

On killing and anger: Cf. Matt 5:21-22 to Exod 20:13; 21:12; Deut 5:17; 17:8-13; Lev 24:17.

On adultry and lust: Cf. Matt 5:27-28 to Exod 20:14-17; Deut 5:18; Job 31:1; Sirach 9:8.

On swearing: Cf. Matt 5:33-37 to Lev 19:12; Num 30:2-15; Deut 23:21-23; Zech 8:17; Exod 20:7; Mark 7:11-13; Ps 50:14.

On retaliation: Cf. Matt 5:38-39 to Exod 21:23-25; Deut 19:21; Lev 24:19-20.

On loving enemies: Cf. Matt 5:43-48 (Matt 22:39) to Lev 19:18; Deut 23:3-8.

In the above sayings of Jesus one finds a marked emphasis on inner attitudes. One is led to conclude that in the teaching of Jesus true religion is not to be identified with a ritualistic/legalistic rote performance of certain prescribed acts. Rather, it appears that it matters to God what one thinks and feels, for it is out of *that* wellspring that the true character of life is to be determined (Matt 5:43-48; 6:22-23; 7:16-18).

One also finds in the teaching of Jesus a marked emphasis on the limitation or suspension of one's rights in the interest of other human beings (Matt 5:21-24, 43-48; 18:21-22; Luke 10:30-35). It is probably at least partially in this context that one should try to understand the hard saying of Jesus about not resisting evil (Matt 5:38-41). It is at least understandable in that context, if one does not press such a concept to its universal and inevitable conclusion. He demands radical obedience and warns of the dangers of wealth (Mark 10:17-22, 25; Matt 6:19-21, 24; Mark 10:42-44; Matt 8:22; 19:12; Luke 12:16-20). He is severly critical of legalism and hypocrisy (Matt 6:5-6, 16-18). He promised rewards and warned of punishment (Mark 10:21; Matt 6:4, 6, 18, 20; 7:18). Through all of his sayings runs an unusual humanistic quality that links human behavior to the needs of the neighbor. One does find such a tendency inherent in the Torah; what is unusual about Jesus is the emphasis he gives it in interpreting Torah. This, in turn, sets him in tension with rabbinic Judaism of the first century.

The ethics of Jesus are not really practical. They involve a radical obedience to certain intensely idealistic principles of behavior. Even allowing for the imminent apocalyptic context in which Jesus lived and taught, his ethical teachings are offensive to rather practically minded modern human beings. Through the centuries the church has tried to tame his radicality, to make his sayings more appropriate to life in the world; it does the best it can with the rather noble ethical ideals that Jesus held forth in the first century.

PAUL

Traditionally thirteen letters have been attributed to Pauline authorship; however, for various reasons critical scholarship universally affirms only seven of these. Those letters that all scholars include in the Pauline corpus are: Romans, 1 and 2 Corinthians, Galatians, Philippians, 1 Thessalonians, and Philemon.[16] I will follow the consensus of scholarship and use the lower number of books as the block of Pauline material to be analyzed. The rationale for using the lower number is as follows: Since we are dealing with the foundation of Pauline ethics, seven letters should give a fair sampling of Paul's basis for human behavior, but the inclusion of a letter or letters that *may not* be Pauline could attribute foundations to the apostle that were not actually his.

Paul was a busy missionary whose first-century letters were conditioned by the individual particular historical context of those churches and individuals to whom he wrote. One should not conceive of him as an "ivory tower" systematic theologian who had worked out a monolithic systematic theology to accommodate the ethical problems of Christendom for 1,900 years plus.

With respect to his ethical foundations it appears that Paul was basically a situationist: How you behave depends on the situation in which you find yourself! For example, on the issue of eating meat that had been sacrificed to idols, depending on the context, the Christian could or should not eat such meat. The Christian should never attend a banquet in a pagan temple. Eating meat in such a context was strictly forbidden by Paul (1 Cor 8). However, the Christian could purchase such meat from the meat market for eating at home or could even attend a dinner party at the home of a pagan and eat the meat, unless the Christians' eating of meat became a matter of conscience for someone else (1 Cor 10:14-11:1).

Like Jesus, one primary authority for Paul was the nearness of the end of the world. Paul clearly believed that the world was going to end in his own lifetime (1 Cor 7:25-31). It was that eschatological context, i.e., his expectation of the immediate appearing of Jesus, that radically informed his ethical sensitivities. It was a major foundation for his teaching on Christian behavior in the human community. His teaching on sexual activity and marriage was based upon it (1 Cor 7; see in particular 1 Cor 7:25-31). His judgment about the institution of slavery was made in that light (1 Cor 7:20-24; cf. Philemon). Quite possibly, Paul allowed himself to be influenced by the nearness of the end in his teaching on the status of women in the Christian community. In Gal 3:28 Paul asserts that life in faith had eradicated the former social distinctions between Jew and Gentile, the status of slaves and masters and those social distinctions between male and female. Nevertheless, when it becomes clear that even in the short time before the end that the church's essential anti-cultural stance in this regard could produce negative community attitudes toward the church and hinder its effectiveness, he modified his teaching in 1 Corinthians (cf. 1 Cor 12:13). He argued that slaves (1 Cor 7:20-24) and women (1 Cor 11:2-16) should remember their subordinate status in the community.[17]

Paul actually based his ethical teaching on many foundations. Aside from the near end of the world, many other foundations for behavior emerge in the context of Paul's debates with his opponents in the churches he established. If we take his view of the near end of the world seriously then we must assume that Paul saw himself as accommodating immediate needs for the "short haul" of history; and not eternal ethical ideals for the "long haul." Indeed, it is possible that one does find already in Paul's letters, a sense of the delay of the end. Compare for example, 1 Thess 4:13-5:10, where the real problem appears to be the delay of the appearing of Jesus, as well as Rom 11:11, 25-26, which certainly imply at least a short period of time preceding the end so as to allow for the conversion of Israel.

Paul clearly drew upon Torah as providing a foundation for proper human behavior (to 1 Cor 5:1 cf. Lev 18:7-8; to 1 Cor 6:16 cf. Gen 2:24; to 1 Cor 11:8-9 cf. Gen 2:18-23; to 1 Cor 14:34 cf. Gen 3:16), but he also relied upon the standards of general Hellenistic morality as well (1 Cor 5:1).[16] He could also base his arguments on accepted social custom as when he argued that women should have their heads covered during prayer while men should have their heads uncovered, because this was the natural way (1 Cor 11:5, 14-15). In 1 Cor 11:10 he employed a Jewish tradition that does not appear in Tanak.[18] He also relied on "accepted" early Christian practice and tradition (1 Cor 11:16). He also drew upon the words of Jesus as an authority (to 1 Cor 7:10-11 cf. Mark 10:2-12) and when the tradition had preserved no specific teaching about a matter he was addressing, he gave his own opinion as authority (1 Cor 7:12-16, 25-40). And in some cases he *allowed* certain behavior because of the tendencies of human nature, even though he did not think it was best (1 Cor 7:6-9, 36-38).

Again in Paul's letters we find an unusual humanistic argument that involves both the needs of the Christian brother and the neighbor. If one could not settle an issue in the church, one should simply permit oneself to be defrauded rather than to take a brother into the Roman courts (1 Cor 6:7-8); one should comport oneself so that one's actions would not "wound the conscience" of another human being (1 Cor 8:9-13; 10:23-33; Rom 13:8-10; Gal 5:13-15). Indeed one's total human activity is subordinated to others (1 Cor 9:19-23; Rom 14:1-15:6). Paul argued that one fulfills all the demands of the law by simply "loving one's neighbor as one loves oneself" (Rom 13:8-10; Gal 5:13-15).

The Gospels

In their final form the Gospels reflect the faith and practice of the church in the latter half of the first century. The primary basis for ethical behavior in the Gospels is quite clearly the word and the example of Jesus, as understood in the community of each evangelist. As the basis on which ethical decisions are made, each writer looks to the past to the Jesus of the community's faith, rather than to a future end of the world. Each writer has followed the remarkable practice of casting the community tradition into a context in the life of Jesus rather than simply presenting a collection of sayings by Jesus and/or stories about Jesus. Each community understanding is somewhat different and each evangelist is true to a particular faith, each presenting unique portraits of Jesus. For example, all four Gospels contain narratives of the baptism of Jesus but each tradition presents a somewhat different picture. For example, Mark (1:9-11) has Jesus baptized at the hands of John who had preached a baptism of repentance for the forgiveness of sin (Mark 1:4-5). It is never really clear in Mark why Jesus is baptized. The *implication* of the passage (Mark 1:4-11)—that Jesus too was baptized upon His own "confession"—would have been intolerable to first-century Christians holding to a more sophisticated Christology than Mark. Matthew acknowledges the baptism of Jesus at the hands of John (Matt 3:13-17) but he includes the explanation that although John was unworthy to baptize Jesus, it was the Lord that insisted on being baptized by John to "fulfill all righteousness" (Matt 3:13-15). Luke, on the other hand, notes that John was put in prison *before* Jesus was baptized and then drops all reference to the baptism of Jesus by John (Luke 3:18-22). By contrast, John drops all reference to a *water* baptism and *alludes* to a baptism of the Spirit that had happened in the past and which John had apparently only *observed* (John 1:24-34). In opposition to the tradition reflected in Mark (John was arrested *before* Jesus began his public ministry, Mark 1:14-15) and Luke (John was arrested *before* Jesus was baptized, Luke 3:20-21), John indicates that Jesus and John were preaching and baptizing *simultaneously* (John 3:22-24).

The special understanding of each respective evangelist can be seen by comparing how each of the Synoptic Gospels reports the tradition. In doing this one senses something of the individual character and theological distinctives of each writer. Compare, for example, the reason given for why Jesus spoke to the crowds in parables. In Mark (4:10-12) Jesus speaks to the crowds in "parables" that really seem designed to keep the outsider from understanding, because if they understood, they might "turn again and be forgiven." Luke (8:9-10) follows Mark but omits this offensive last phrase. Matthew (13:10-15), on the other hand, gives the entire quotation from Isaiah (6:9-10 = Matt 13:14-15) on which the offensive expression in Mark 4:12 is based and thereby Matthew effectively makes the *people* responsible for their failure to understand because of their hardness of heart (Matt 13:15).

Hence, it would appear that the Gospels reflect a community or "church" ethic based on the words of Jesus. These words have, in a sense, become a "new law" and constitute a type of Christian legalism. By recording and documenting the official "words of Jesus" for their communities, each evangelist effectively excluded other competing traditions, as are reflected in the apocryphal gospel literature.[19] In the case of Matthew and Luke, their Gospels were apparently intended to replace Mark and the hypothetical source Q.

Matthew added large blocks of teaching material which he arranged in six lengthy discourses compiled out of discrete sayings of Jesus (Matt 5-7; 10:1-11:1; 13:1-53; 18:1-19:1; 23:1-39; 24:1-26:1), three of which deal with general Christian behavior: The Sermon on the Mount (Matt 5-7), Christian Community Regulations (Matt 18:1-19:1), and Guidance for Ministry (Matt 10:5-11:1). Matthew has also organized a cluster of sayings on discipleship and miracle stories into chapters 8-9 of his Gospel: he thereby implies the close association between the miracles tradition and what it means to be a follower of Jesus.

One does find an emphasis on the imminent end of the world in the teaching of Jesus in Matt 24-25 and Mark 13, but the immediacy of the end is somewhat toned down in Luke 21, as a close attention to the text will show.[20] But in none of these Gospels does the end expectation become a standard for behavior in and of itself. The words and deeds of Jesus are still the authority. It is not the near end of the world that governs the life of the community rather it is the *words of Jesus that describe* the end.

In Matthew one does find a subtle practical shift from the words of Jesus as authority to the judgment of Matthew's church as providing a foundation for authority. Only in Matthew is the establishment of the church given (16:18-19), and to the "church" is passed the authority of its Lord (cf. Matt 18:15-19), because the Lord is in the midst of the church (18:20).

In John the stress is also placed upon the words of Jesus as the foundation of the community and of Christian behavior in the present. Compare the dialogs and discourses of Jesus that make up the first half of the Gospel (the "ministry of signs" 2:1-12:50) and the extension of the Passion Narrative by lengthy discourse material (13:1-20:10).

There is also in John an interesting series of explanatory comments, usually understood as "asides" or "digressions" from the main action of the narrative.[21] These "digressions" seem to place the real authority for interpreting the Jesus tradition in the community itself which would understand itself in the writer's day to be under the leadership of the Holy Spirit (16:12-15). In at least several of these "asides" the Johannine author is interpreting the received tradition out of his own theological understanding. For example, John 2:21-22 offers an explanation as a conscious reflection on the word of Jesus in John 2:19, where Jesus says he will raise up "this temple" in three days if it is destroyed. John's explanation (2:21-22) does not arise naturally from the text (2:19), since there Jesus *could* have been speaking of the temple as a building.[22] John 2:21-22 is a midrash on 2:19 that treats the saying as an allegorical figure (cf. John 16:25-30), a mysterious saying on the body.

Another instance is found in 13:11 where the Johannine author "interprets" the logion in 13:10, where Jesus is talking about the necessity of washing the disciples' feet. The author understands the word "clean" to have a latent theological meaning as "pure before God" and explains it as an obscure reference to Judas. The theological implication of religious purity may be drawn from the text, as 13:8 shows (i.e., the washing brought union with Jesus), but there is no necessity to understand it as a reference to Judas in particular, since 13:8 acknowledges even Peter to be "unclean." In any case the text affirms that all disciples including Judas were present (13:12-14, 26-30) and were washed. If the washing cleansed them then one must assume Judas was also cleansed—which conflicts with John's spiritualizing interpretation of 13:10b. The authority for these kinds of exegetical clarifications of the text appears to be the community exegetical tradition rather than the words of the Lord themselves.[23]

The conclusion to Matthew's Gospel finds the community anticipating the end of the world but living out of its experience of the indwelling presence of the Lord who remains with it (Matt 28:16-20; cf. Matt 18:20). Luke's conclusion has the community in Jerusalem (Luke 24:48-49) still awaiting the promise of the Father's power that the author of Luke/Acts takes up in his second volume (Acts 1:1-11).[24] In both Luke and Acts the Lord is absent (Luke 24:50-53; Acts 1:9) but is clearly expected to return (Acts 1:11; cf. Luke 21:25-28). His expected return, however, is not the primary foundation for community life and action; rather, it is the coming of the Holy Spirit whose presence and power grounds and motivates Christian life in Luke/Acts (cf. Luke 1:15, 35, 41, 67, 80; 2:25-27; 4:1, 14; 10:21; 11:13; 12:12; Acts 1:2, 8; 2:4, 33, 38; 4:8, 31; 5:3, 32; 6:3, 5, 10; 7:51, 55; 8:14-24, 29, 39; 9:17, 31; 10:19, 37-38, 44-48; 11:12, 15-16, 24, 28; 13:2, 4, 9, 52; 15:8, 28; 16:6-7; 19:1-7; 20:22-23, 28; 21:4, 11; 28:25).

Another foundation of the community is also found in the past in Tanak. Each Gospel writer draws upon Tanak as constituting the divine oracles of God whose "predictions" are fulfilled in the ministry of Jesus of Nazareth. This reliance on the past for clarifying in concert with the past the community's present self-understanding as Christians can be seen to some extent in Mark (cf. Mark 1:2-3; 7:6-7; 12:10-11; 14:49) and Luke (3:3-6; 4:8, 10-11, 16-21; 7:27; 20:17-18; 21:22; 22:37; 24:44-49). Yet it can best be seen in the formula quotations (e.g., "in order that the scripture may be fulfilled") in Matthew (1:22-23; 2:5-6, 15, 17-18, 23; 4:14-16; 8:17; 12:17-21; 13:14-15, 35; 21:4-5; 27:9-10) and John (10:34-35; 13:18; 15:25; 17:12; 18:9, 32; 19:24, 28, 36-37; 20:9). These authoritative oracles of the past both dictated the inevitable events of the community's foundation and served in the community's present to clarify those events. In either case the community looks to the past for its authority in the present.

Hebrews[25]

The author clearly uses apocalyptic language, although descriptions of the events accompanying the end are made with restraint (1:2; 2:5; 9:9-10, 26-27; 10:25; 13:14). While the author believes that he is living in the "last days," the final events of that end have not yet started. Jesus is not described as one whose "coming" is imminent but he is described as seated at the right hand of God (1:3). Hence the end may be drawing near (10:25), but unlike Paul the author does not describe the end as having begun. Habakkuk 2:3-4 (10:37-38) is quoted as predicting a delay in the timetable of the end and therefore the faithful must continue to endure the present suffering (10:32-34). The heroes of the faith, who died before they received what God had promised, serve as an example to the faithful who also must endure a period of suffering (11:13-16). The numerous quotations from Tanak show that the author looked to the past for the source of religious instruction and authority for life in the present (3:7-11; 1:5-13; 2:5-8, 12-13; 4:3; 5:5-6; 4:11-12; 6:5; 7:17, 21-22; 8:8-13; 10:5-7, 15-17, 37-38; 12:5-6, 26-29; 13:5-6). Thus the writer encourages and admonishes the reader by a steady look to the past (11:1-40; 13:7-9) in particular to the example of Christ (9:14; 10:19-25; 12:1-4). The encouragement of the reader is based not on the soon appearing of the Lord but on the abiding presence of Christ (13:5-6). He speaks of the end and of the Lord's appearing as "our hope," i.e., an as yet unrealized experience. It is in fact an object of the indefinite future (3:6, 14; 6:18; 10:23). The primary future *hope* was the distant eternal city "whose builder and maker is God" (11:10, 16; 13:14), but the source of life in the present was the assured results of the past.

The Johannine Letters (1, 2, 3 John)[26]

The Johannine letters reflect all the characteristics of an emerging orthodoxy, except they do not address the delay of the parousia (1 John 2:28; 3:2-3; 4:17; 5:19). The author believes that the community is living in the last days and apparently that the events of the end have already begun (1 John 2:8, 18; 4:3; 2 John 7). One may suspect, however, that 2:18 suggests a sense of the delayed parousia: If antichrist comes in the last time, why is it that *many* antichrists have come? Nevertheless, the writer does not use this nearness of the end as a sanction for governing life in the present. The authority for community life-style comes from the past in terms of the apostolic tradition (1 John 1:1-5; 2:3-6; 2:22-24, 26-27; 3:16, 22-24; 4:21; 5:2). True faith is expressed in terms of propositional statements that appear to be intellectually perceived and rationally confessed (2:22-25; 4:2-3, 14-15; 5:1-5; 2 John 9-10). These authoritative statements constitute the true authority for the Christian. However, along with the standardization of faith and the propositional confessional statement comes an unusual emphasis on a caring response to a brother's need as an additional concrete standard for judging behavior (1 John 2:7-11; 3:10, 13-18; 4:7-12, 16, 20-21; 2 John 5-6; 3 John 5-7). Indeed, these passages seem extremely radical, since in them love is not the standard; rather, response to human need becomes the standard for judging love (4:20-21; 2 John 5-6).

JAMES[27]

The author expects the parousia and a coming final judgment (5:3, 7-9) but he does not base a proper lifestyle on the immediacy of that event. Instead, it would seem that the end is delayed, because the writer must encourage the readers to faithfulness in their present trials (1:2-4, 12; 5:7-8, 10-11). Indeed, they may probably expect to die before the end (1:10-11; 4; 13-15). The practical basis for behavior associated with the end (probably of the believer's life and not of the end of the world) is the crown of life (1:12). The true authority and guide for life comes out of the past in the form of the apostolic tradition, in particular Paul and Matthew (1:25; 2:8-9, 12; 4:11-12; 5:12). While the author draws upon Torah and Tanak as religious authorities for the Christian community (2:23-26; 3:9; 4:5-6; 5:17-18), Torah is clearly regarded as superseded by the "royal law" and the "law of liberty" (2:8-12). But even this "Christian law" comes to the reader as an assured guide from the past. The general appeal to do what is "right" (4:17) must be understood in the context of Torah, Tanak, and the apostolic tradition (5:19). One also finds an additional standard for Christian behavior that is grounded in one's compassionate response to human need (1:27; 2:1-7, 14-26) rather than in propositional statements (2:18-20), as we found it in the Johannine correspondence.

REVELATION[28]

The author is an apocalyptist who grounds his guidance for living under persecution on the basis of the near future appearing of Jesus the Lord (1:1-3), and he writes using the dramatic cosmic categories of traditional apocalyptic language (1:7; 6:1-17; 8:1-13; 16:1-21; 19:1-20). In the midst of the crisis in which the church finds itself the author calls for patient endurance (1:9; 2:2-3, 9, 19, 25-26; 3:10; 14:12; 20:4; 21:7), an "overcoming life" (2:7, 11, 17, 26; 3:5, 12, 21; 21:7) in the struggle (11:7; 13:7; 17:14), and faithfulness unto death (2:10-13; 3:5, 12, 21; 6:9-11) on the basis of the near return of the Lord (3:3, 11; 22:6-7, 10, 12, 20); but he gives little attention to practical or ethical questions or to how one should comport oneself in the world under normal living conditions. Even the letters to the seven churches deal primarily with endurance and faithfulness (2:2-3:22). Even the victorious vision of God's ultimate victory (21:1-8) is made to serve as an encouragement to the church in its trials and suffering (21:7). The author does draw upon Tanak (10:7; 18:20) and the apostolic tradition (14:12; 18:20) but the real source of authority and foundation for guiding life in the present is the immediate appearing of the Lord and the inevitable victory of God. One may legitimately question whether or not the author would have focused so exclusively on the end as a source of strength and inspiration had the social context in which he wrote been more favorable to the church, such as that which prevailed in the pastoral letters.

LATER PAULINE CHRISTIANITY[29]

Second Thessalonians

The writer is an apocalyptist (note the cosmic metaphors in 1:7-10) who believes in the future appearing of Jesus and the end of the world. That end, however, is neither imminent, as it was in Paul's letters (1:7, 10), nor does it form a practical basis for human behavior. Indeed, the writer clarifies that the end will *not* be *now*, but there will be a delay before the end comes (2:1-12; particularly 2:2, 3, 7, 8). Authority for Christian lifestyle is drawn from the past and not from the future. The real foundation for Christian behavior is found in the "traditions" which the readers "were taught" (2:15; 3:6) and were shown (3:7-9), and the "gospel" of the author drawn from those traditions (2:14-15). The community is simply directed to withdraw fellowship from whomever will not obey (3:14-15), while Paul has to argue that point (1 Cor 5:1-13).

Colossians

The few eschatological features in the text suggest that the author does not view the parousia as the basis for the Christian's lifestyle. Christ's coming is not sensed as "in progress," rather, he is pictured as now seated at the right hand of God (3:1). He will come, but the text does not appear to expect his return to be in the near future (3:4). Faith is not described as a dynamic experience of life but it appears to be the appropriation of a specific body of "truth" from the past (1:23; 2:6-7) that is available to the Christian. Although the Christian still looks forward to the judgment of the world (3:4, 6, 25) and life after death (1:5, 12, 22), redemption is a present reality (1:13-14). Yet the end is without the sense of immediacy that we find in Paul.

The relationship between ethics and eschatology can be seen in 3:1-11. The ground of ethical behavior is the Christian experience. Because you are "raised with Christ" put to death what is "earthly in you." The situation reflected in the letter suggests a church that is accommodating itself to life in the world. In contrast to Paul's charismatic offices (1 Cor 12:4-11, 27-31) this church has officials whose function is described as a "divine office" (1:25; cf. 1:7, 23). They are concerned with the "image" they project to the world outside the church (4:5). Hence one would have to see the *practical* kind of advice given in 3:18-4:1 as motivated, at least to some small extent, by public opinion. For example to consider the service of slaves to their owners as service rendered to God is an incredible statement (3:24) by modern standards and suggests a complete acceptance of Hellenistic morality where slavery was a long-accepted tradition. Although he does not urge the manumission of Onesimus, Paul's own sensitivities seemed at least to acknowledge that slavery was not to be preferred but because of the nearness of the end it could be tolerated (1 Cor 7:17-24).

Ephesians

Whereas the writer uses apocalyptic language (1:21; 4:30; 6:12; cf. also 1:10, 14), he exhibits no real sense of immediacy with respect to the nearness of the age to come. Rather, the writer seems candidly to acknowledge that there may be a lengthy time before the end occurs (2:7; 3:21). Redemption is a present experience of the church and is not associated with the projected end of the world (1:7, 13-14). Faith in Christ is associated with receiving a specific body of truth (4:4-7, 14, 25; 6:10-17) that comes to the church out of the past built upon "the apostles and prophets" with Christ as "the chief cornerstone" of the household of faith (2:19-20). The practical ethics in 4:25-32 and 5:21-6:9 parallel similar statements in Colossians and suggest a church situation that was concerned with not giving offense to the broader Hellenistic world.

EMERGING ORTHODOXY

By "emerging orthodoxy" I am referring to the tendency toward the standardization and institutionalization of religious life and theology in early Christianity. Among the various strands of tradition that can be identified in the literature of first-century Christianity, one eventually succeeds in assuming a dominant role. This tendency can be seen in the Pastoral Epistles (1 and 2 Timothy, and Titus) and the General Epistles (1 and 2 Peter, James and Jude).

There were a number of historical motives that pushed the church in the direction of such standardization. The fact that the parousia and the end of the world did not occur as quickly as the church assumed, forced it to accept itself as a part of history. The loss of a sense of immediacy in the expectation of the occurrence of the end and the realization that the arrival of the end had been delayed, forced the church to accommodate itself to life in the world. At this point the anticipation of an immediate end of the world no longer served the church as a *practical* sanction for an everyday ethical lifestyle, except perhaps in radical branches declared heretical by the now dominant "orthodox" tradition. Some Christian groups under the influence of what may be described as a type of gnostic speculation had given up the faith in the *future* appearing of Jesus altogether and developed a kind of existential/realized eschatology (cf. 2 Tim 2:18 and the *Epistle to Rheginos* in the Nag Hammadi library). This radical stance was also rejected by the church that found itself able to hold onto faith in the parousia of Jesus but with the clear recognition that his coming had been delayed, and "scheduled" for an indefinite future time (2 Pet 3:1-10; cf. 2 Thess 2:1-12). As pointed out above, the awareness that the end was delayed emerges already in Paul. Nevertheless, for Paul the expected end had already begun to dawn (cf. 1 Cor 10:11) and consequently it served as a practical basis for ordering ethical behavior in the church. For the later church the belief in a (delayed) parousia served as a practical basis for preaching and encouragement but not really for dictating lifestyles, since the practical demands made by the belief in an immediate end were simply too radical and rigorous for a church adjusting to life in the world.

The church began to realize that its own emergence was not really part of the end-time drama; rather, it was a historical phenomenon, a fact of history. With time and history on its hands the church began to accommodate itself to the world in terms of praxis, theology, and lifestyle. It inevitably resorts to the contemporary Hellenistic cultural ethic as a primary ethical foundation to help it get along in the world.

The tendency toward institutionalization and the standardization of life, faith, and theology naturally tends to reduce diversity in the churches. The end of this trajectory is reached when an emerging dominant strand of early Christianity begins systematically to weed out other competing strands as being heretical. The limitation of the Gospels to only four is a good example of one effect such standardization had in the practical life of the churches (see above p. 94 and notes 5 and 6).

With the failure of the parousia to occur as quickly as it was initially expected and the realization that the end would not soon materialize, the church began to live out of its past. The authority for the Christian life became the apostolic tradition that belonged to the dominant strand (orthodoxy) of early Christianity. Such a look to the past was natural since the church had looked to the past all along to the Jewish scriptures and the example and teachings of Jesus.

The orthodox strand of Christianity, in contrast to the charismatic Pauline churches (cf. 1 Cor 12), began to develop ecclesiastical offices that had real power. They accommodated themselves to the culture of the world in which they lived to such an extent that ideal Christianity came to be identified with good citizenship. By this time Christianity no longer stood in tension with Hellenistic and Jewish cultures but actually drew on the social concepts of these cultures as a primary foundation for life in the world. Hence, the church advises its members who are slaves to be *good* slaves, admonishes its women members to remember their subordinate place and instructs its leaders to identify themselves so completely with community moral ideals that there can be no possible basis for criticism of the Christian community life.

The roots of this move toward standardization of Christian communities in matters of theology, praxis, and church hierarchial offices can already be detected in the Pauline correspondence, although it must not be considered to be characteristic of Paul. For example, in Rom 13:1-7 Paul argues that the (Roman) government had been instituted by God and therefore deserved Christian support. Indeed, the governing authorities are the servants of God! He argued against the Corinthian Lord's Supper practice (1 Cor 11:17-34) and sought to standardize it. He directed that the church at Thessalonica should "respect those who . . . are over you in the Lord" (1 Thess 5:12-13; cf. Phil 1:1). It should be noted, however, that Paul never possessed "apostolic authority" in the sense that later Christian texts attributed such authority to him and that he was in constant debate with his churches to achieve his goals. For example, compare how conciliatory he is toward Philemon (8-9, 17-20) with regard to Onesimus.?

The Pastoral Epistles[30]

First Timothy. The author clearly anticipates the parousia (6:14) but he does not describe that event with detailed apocalyptic language. He seems to imply that the church is now living in the "latter times" (4:1), but he clearly projects the final appearing of Jesus to a "proper time" in the future (6:14-15). The author is really more concerned with the state of the church in the world and with preparing the church for the long haul of history, than with offering it direction for the immediate end of the world. For example, the text offers guidelines for the appointment of church officers (3:1-12). In contrast to Paul (1 Cor 7:25-40), this author *requires* that one holding the office of bishop (3:2) and deacon (3:12) be married. The text lays down guidelines for church order (5:17-23). Above all there is reflected in the text a concern about the image of the church in the world (3:7; 5:14). It would not be proper for the church to live a lifestyle that runs counter to the culture of the day. They should pray for kings (2:2), keep the women (2:8-14) and slaves (6:1-2) in their proper subordinate position, and provide for those women who are truly widows (5:9-16). Not to have rigorous standards for the enrollment of widows may open the church to community criticism (5:13-15).

The author encourages marriage (5:14) and indeed even links the bearing of children to the salvation of Christian women (2:15). The latter idea appears to stem from a literal application of Gen 3:16 in response to ascetic gnostic groups that rejected sexual activity (4:3).[31] The author's source of authority seems to come from the past as a body of Christian teaching (1:10-11; 2:13; 4:6; 6:3, 20). Other sources of authority are Tanak (2:13-15), public opinion (5:14), and the duly ordained (5:22) leaders of the church (5:17). Above all the text reflects a church that is settling down in the world prepared for the long haul of history.

Second Timothy. The author anticipates the parousia and the end of the world as being an event of the indefinite future (2:17-18), but does not describe that event in detailed traditional apocalyptic language (1:12; 2:11-13; 3:1; 4:1, 18). It appears that the end-time is clearly delayed, since the author expects to die before the end occurs (4:6-8), and anticipates that there will even be a time of "falling away" before the end comes (4:3-4). Indeed, the author expects to receive and use certain study materials sometime in the future (4:13). Authority for ethical lifestyle comes from the past in terms of a body of revealed truth (1:13-14; 2:15) which must be passed on to others (2:2). Tanak is also a source of authority for the believer (3:8, 14-16). The end-time does serve as a point of reference to admonish the church to faithful preaching (4:1-3) but it does not really function as a practical basis for a personal lifestyle.

Titus. The author anticipates the parousia of Jesus in the future (2:13) but it does not appear to be an immediate event (2:12). The text is primarily concerned about the state of the church and its leadership (1:5-9). The church should be so assimilated into the normal ethical lifestyle of the community that it will not give offense to outsiders (2:5-8, 11-12; 3:1-2). The authority for how life ought to be lived in the Christian community comes from the past as a body of truth that is passed from one generation to the next (1:9; 2:1).

The General Epistles

First Peter.   The writer clearly embraces an apocalyptic eschatology, yet without elaborate descriptions of the end and the bizarre imagery that one usually associates with apocalyptic texts (1:5, 20; 2:12; 4:7, 13; 5:1-4). The end it not imminent, however, but it is to be preceded by a period of testing and persecution of the community of faith (1:6; 4:12). Nor is Christ described as "coming" but as being in heaven (3:22). The judgment of the end-time is held up as a sanction for holy living (4:5-11), but it is the judgment of the delayed parousia that is really being held forth, rather than the imminent event that Paul saw himself experiencing. Authority and models for Christian living come out of the past. The author bases his argument for Christian behavior on Tanak (1:10-12, 24-25; 2:6-8; 3:5-6, 10-12, 20; 4:18), on the Christian "gospel," which is the word of God preached to the church (1:23-25, 2:8), and on the example of Christ's sufferings (2:21-24). The writer is concerned with the personal character of church officers (5:1-11), the church's image in the world (2:12), and he equates Christian living with good citizenship (2:11-17). Hence, the text reflects a concern not to disturb the structures of Hellenistic society: slaves be obedient to your masters, even those who are overbearing (2:18-20); wives be submissive to your husbands, even those who do not belong to the community of faith (3:1-6); and husbands honor your wives as the weaker sex (3:7).

Second Peter.[32]   The writer clearly holds to an apocalyptic eschatology (2:9; 3:3-4) with some graphic descriptions of the destruction of the cosmos (3:7-13). But the end is not imminent. There is a clearly recognizable interim period between the writer's present and the events of the end. Indeed, the writer expects to die before the end occurs (1:13-15; cf. 1:11)! It is even recognized that the non-appearance of the parousia has become a problem to the church (3:3-13). Such a circumstance forces the author to justify the Lord's delay. Reasoning that time with the Lord is relative—one day is as a thousand years and a thousand years as one day—the author implies that the Lord may not return for "1,000 years" (3:8). It is also possible that the delay may be due to the Lord's mercy so that more people may turn to faith (3:9). While an appeal is made to the judgment of the end as a sanction for behavior in the present (3:11-14), it is clearly the delayed parousia to which the author appeals. The real authority for behavior is to be found in the past in the apostolic tradition (1:16-19; 2:21; 3:2), Tanak (1:20-21), and the Pauline corpus (3:14-16).

Jude. This short tract is primarily concerned to denounce (in general and imprecise language) certain false teaching that stands in opposition to the apostolic tradition that serves as the primary authority for the author of the text (3-4, 17). A future judgment (6, 18) is anticipated but it lacks the immediacy of Paul's vision. Nor does that judgment really serve as a practical sanction for life in the present. There is no clear allusion to a parousia of Jesus (cf. 14-15), and the future anticipation of judgment in the text may simply be a reference to the death of the individual Christian (21, 24) rather than a reference to the end of the world. While the author read Tanak and the Old Testament Apocrypha (Enoch) and uses them in the debate (5-7, 11, 14-15), the real authoritative basis for the Christian life is found in the apostolic tradition which the writer had received from the past (3).

CONCLUSION

One common uniform basis for determining proper Christian behavior has not emerged in the New Testament literature. Instead one finds a break between an early Christian situational period (Jesus and Paul) and a later traditional i.e., "propositional" period Perhaps one should describe them as "tendencies," the "tendencies" of an earlier period and the "tendencies" of a later period. In their most extreme, the periods can be contrasted as follows:

EARLIER PERIOD	LATER PERIOD
creative ————————————	*adherence to authoritative tradition*
imminent parousia ————————	*delayed parousia*
situational ————————————	*legalistic*
counter culture ———————————	*synonymous with culture*
looks to future ———————————	*looks to past*
advocates ————————————	*defers*
responsible decision ————————	*individual responsibility*

One does find, however, a common element that is shared by both the situational and traditional approaches: that is, the principle of human need as the basis for Christian behavior in any given context. It is reflected in Jesus, Paul, the Johannine letters, and James (cf. Rom 13:8-10; 1 John 3:16-18; James 1:27). Notice that the basis for behavior recommended by this common element that runs through most of the New Testament literature is a love that prompts a compassionate response to human need. It does not prescribe specific predictable responses for specific situations but it leaves the individual to work out the proper response in the context of the given situation. It only requires that love have a character that moves the individual in concrete ways to meet human need. Hence one comports oneself on the basis of the neighbor's needs and not on the basis of individual rights and prescribed specific responses to legalistic requirements.[33]

NOTES

1. For a discussion see W. G. Kümmel, *The New Testament: The History of the Investigation of its Problems* (S. M. Gilmour and H. C. Kee, trans.; Nashville/New York: Abingdon, 1972 [German 1970]), 206-324.

2. See for example the discussions by Walter Bauer, *Orthodoxy and Heresy in Earliest Christianity* (R. A. Kraft and G. Krodel, eds.; Philadelphia: Fortress, 1971 [German 2nd ed. 1964]), and Wilhelm Bousset, *Kyrios Christos: A History of the Belief in Christ from the Beginnings of Christianity to Irenaeus* (J. E. Steely, trans.; Nashville/New York: Abingdon, 1970). See also R. H. Fuller, *The Foundations of New Testament Christology* (New York: Scribners, 1965).

3. See the recent challenge to these dates by J. A. T. Robinson, *Redating the New Testament* (London: SCM Press, 1976).

4. The use of John's Gospel in reconstructing the teachings of the "historical" Jesus has virtually been given up by contemporary scholars; see H. K.

McArthur, ed., *In Search of the Historical Jesus* (New York: Scribners, 1969), 82-108.

5. For an inexpensive collection of t¹ ꝛ earliest non-canonical gospel material see R. Cameron, *The Other Gospels: Non-Canonical Gospel Texts* (Philadelphia: Westminster, 1982).

6. For such new sayings see J. Jeremias, *Unknown Sayings of Jesus* (2nd ed.; London: S.P.C.K., 1964); N. Perrin, *Rediscovering the Teaching of Jesus* (New York/Evanston: Harper & Row, 1967), 126-28 and C. W. Hedrick, "Kingdom Sayings and Parables of Jesus in the *Apocryphon of James*: Tradition and Redaction," *NTS* 29 (1983):1-24.

7. A. Schweitzer, *The Quest of the Historical Jesus* (W. Montgomery, trans.; J. M. Robinson, ed.; New York: Macmillan, 1968 [German 1906]).

8. W. Wrede, *The Messianic Secret* (J. C. G. Greig, trans.; Greenwood, SC: Attic Press, 1971 [German 1901]).

9. For a brief discussion of the current situation see J. Tyson, *The New Testament and Early Christianity* (New York/London: Macmillan, 1984), 147-58.

10. For the most recent discussions of Mark's structure and style see C. W. Hedrick, "What is a Gospel? Geography, Time and Narrative Structure," *Perspectives in Religious Studies* 10 (1983): 255-68; and "The Role of 'Summary Statements' in the Composition of the Gospel of Mark: A Dialog with Karl Schmidt and Norman Perrin," *NovT*, 26(1984): 287-311.

11. See the earliest evaluation (ca. A.D. 130) of the Gospel of Mark by Papias bishop of Hierapolis in Eusebius, *Ecclesiastical History* 3:39.

12. See the discussion of the criteria by Perrin, *Rediscovering the Teaching of Jesus*, 15-53 and N. Perrin, *The New Testament: An Introduction* (2nd ed. rev. by D. Duling; New York/San Diego/Chicago/San Francisco/Toronto: Harcourt Brace Jovanovich, 1982), 405-6. To declare a saying "unoriginal" does not *prove* that it was *not* spoken by Jesus; it only means that the scholar cannot *demonstrate* beyond a reasonable doubt that it *was* spoken by Jesus. Hence the scholar cannot affirm its "probability" as opposed to its "possibility."

13. What I have done is to work from those ethical sayings of Jesus affirmed by those New Testament scholars who apply these criteria most rigorously: R. Bultmann, *Jesus and the World* (L. P. Smith and E. H. Lantero, trans.; New York: Scribners, 1934 [German 1926]); H. Conzelmann, *Jesus* (J. R. Lord, trans.: J. Ruemann, ed.; Philadelphia: Fortress, 1973 [German 1959]).

14. See the essay by E. Käsemann, "Primitive Christian Apocalyptic," pp. 108-37 in *New Testament Questions of Today* (W. J. Montague, trans.; Philadelphia: Fortress, 1969 [German 2nd ed. 1965]). For an excellent discussion of ethics and eschatology in the teaching of Jesus see A. N. Wilder, *Eschatology and Ethics in the Teaching of Jesus* (New York: Harper, 1950 rev.). For brief summaries of the character of apocalyptic see M. Rist "Apocalypticism" in the *Interpreter's Dictionary of the Bible* (4 vols.; New York/Nashville: Abingdon Press, 1962) 1:157-61 and P. Hanson, "Apocalypticism," *IDB Supplement* (1976): 28-34.

15. T(A)N(A)K is an acronymn for the three divisions of the Hebrew scriptures: *T*orah (Law or teaching), *N*eviim (Prophets) and *K*ethuvim (writings).

16. See the discussion by P. Feine, J. Behm and W. G. Kümmel, *Introduction to the New Testament* (14th rev. ed.; A.J. Mattill, Jr., trans.; Nashville/New York: Abingdon, 1966 [German 1965]), 176-282.

17. Note that some suspects that 1 Cor 11:2-16 and 14:33-36 are interpolations into the letter: see H. Conzelmann, *1 Corinthians* (J. W. Leitch, trans.: G. W. MacRae, ed.; Philadelphia: Fortress, 1975 [German 1969]), 182 and 246.

18. See Conzelmann (*1 Corinthians*, 189) for a discussion of this difficult passage.

19. See Cameron (*The Other Gospels*) who dates material from all but one of

his selections from the apocryphal gospels within the 1st century A.D.; see also the review in *Biblical Archaeology Review* 10 (1984): 14-17.

20. See H. Conzelmann, *The Theology of St. Luke* (G. Buswell, trans.; Philadelphia: Fortress, 1982 [German 1953]), 95-136. See also Matthew's allegorizing interpretation of the parables of the tares (Matt 13:37-43) and the dragnet (13:49-50).

21. See. M. C. Tenney, "The Footnotes of John's Gospel," *Bibliotheca Sacra* 117(1960): 350-64 and J. J. O'Rourke, "Asides in the Gospel of John," *NovT* (1979): 210-19.

22. For the susceptibility of this saying to such an understanding see Wilder, *Eschatology and Ethics in the Teaching of Jesus,* 51 note 26.

23. For some of the other digressions in John see 7:39; 11:13, 51-52; 12:33; 15:25; 18:9, 32; 19:24, 28, 36-37.

24. See the brief discussion by Feine, Behm, and Kümmel, *Introduction to the New Testament,* 109-12.

25. Compare the discussion by Jack Sanders, *Ethics in the New Testament: Change and Development* (Philadelphia: Fortress, 1975), 106-10. See also the excellent survey by W. Schrage, "Ethics in the New Testament," in the *IDBSup,* 281-89.

26. Compare Sanders, *Ethics in the New Testament,* 91-100.

27. Ibid., 115-28.

28. Ibid., 112-15.

29. Ibid., 67-90.

30. Ibid.

31. For the asceticism of gnosticism see in particular the following Nag Hammadi texts: *The Book of Thomas the Contender, The Teaching of Sylvanus and The Sentences of Sextus.*

32. Sanders, *Ethics in the New Testament,* 111-12.

33. See the very provocative and challenging essay by Herbert Braun. "The Problem of a New Testament Theology," pp. 169-83 in *The Bultmann School of Biblical Interpretation: New Directions?* (R. W. Funk, ed.; New York: Harper Torchbooks, 1965); and also C. W. Hedrick, "Resurrection: Radical Theology in the Gospel of Matthew," *Lexington Theological Quarterly* 14 (1979): 40-45.

Stanley M. Burgess

Stanley Milton Burgess is a Professor in the Department of Religious Studies, Southwest Missouri State University, Springfield Missouri. Born and raised in India of missionary parents, he earned his B.A. and M.A. from the University of Michigan, and the Ph.D. from the University of Missouri-Columbia. After serving as Professor of History and Head, Department of Social Studies at Evangel College, Springfield, Missouri, from 1959-1976, he joined the faculty of Southwest Missouri State University. In 1977 he was named Director, Office of Grants, and in 1981 he became Head, Department of Religious Studies. He is the author of *Johann Eck and Humanism* (1971), *The Spirit and the Church: Antiquity* (1984)—the first in a projected three-volume series on the history of Christian pneumatology—and several articles on the history of Christian spirituality. He is the co-editor of *A Dictionary of Pentecostal and Charismatic Movements*, in preparation.

In this chapter, Burgess compares the perfectionist impulse of the early Christian aberrant sect, the Montanists, with that of three Christian Fathers of the same period. He questions whether the Montanists were rejected because of the severity of their asceticism, or because of their intolerant exclusiveness and the uniqueness of their hermeneutic.

5

MONTANIST AND PATRISTIC PERFECTIONISM

Stanley M. Burgess

NUMEROUS EARLY Christians explained Jesus' admonition to be perfect as the heavenly Father is perfect (Matt. 5:48), but few agreed either on the degree to which one can reach such a level of character and conduct or how one best attains to such an objective. In this chapter the perfectionism of the Montanists, an early aberrant Christian sect, is examined and compared with the positions taken by three important early Christian Fathers—Clement of Alexandria, Origen, and Gregory of Nyssa. These patristic authors have been selected, not because of their opposition to the Montanists,[1] but because perfection is a central theme in their writings just as it is in the teachings of Montanus and his followers. It is our purpose to investigate the unique qualities of Montanist perfectionism which may have led to its persecution at the hands of a disapproving Catholic Church, as well as those concepts of the perfect life which it shared in common with the three early Christian Fathers.

MONTANISM

Montanism first appeared ca. A.D. 160 in the valleys of Phrygia, a province of Asia Minor.[2] Its founder was Montanus, apparently a former prophesying priest of Cybele,[3] who converted to Christianity and continued to prophesy in his new context. His prophetic utterances gained immediate attention, in part because of his manner of delivery, and in part because of their content. An anonymous opponent reports that Montanus lost control of himself, falling into "a sort of frenzy and ecstasy" in which "he raved and began to babble and utter strange things, prophesying in a manner contrary to the constant custom of the church handed down by tradition from the beginning."[4] The message also was novel: Montanus identified a new holy place—Pepuza—where the parousia was to occur, a New Age of the Spirit, a new authority, a new church polity, and a new and more demanding level of discipline which was practiced with a new extreme of intolerant exclusiveness. Indeed, Montanus proclaimed his words to be a "New Prophecy"—the fulfilling of Jesus' promise of the coming of the Paraclete (John 14:12-18)—which was reserved for the New Prophets whom Jesus anticipated in Matthew 23:24.[5]

Montanus soon was joined by Maximilla and Priscilla (or Prisca), two women who deserted their husbands with Montanus' sanction and claimed to possess a similar prophetic charisma to that of Montanus.[6] All three of these New Prophets believed that their prophecies were to be the final word of God to men. Maximilla is reported to have declared, "After me there will no longer be a prophetess, but the end."[7] A literal reading of their statements suggests that they claimed to be God himself. Epiphanius reports two such statements by Montanus: "I am the Lord God Omnipotent dwelling in man,"[8] and "I am neither an angel nor an envoy, but I the Lord God, the Father, have come,"[9] while Didymus records, "I am the Father and the Son and the Paraclete."[10] In each case, however, it seems more likely that the prophets uttered words which they believed that God had put into their mouths, as he had with prophets in the Old and New Testaments. Biblical prophets frequently used the first person singular. With the Montanists the New Age of the Paraclete had arrived, and they believed that God spoke through them. With that in mind, the fact that the New Prophets spoke in the divine first person is quite understandable.

Maximilla, the last of the original trio, died in A.D. 179-180, and there were no Montanist prophets for several years. Montanist prophecy revived around A.D. 200 after which time the movement spread not only in the province of Asia, but also in Egypt, in Gaul, in North Africa, in Spain, and even to the cities of Constantinople and Rome. Pope Zephyrinus (d. 217) favored the New Prophecy and was preparing letters of peace to the Montanists of Asia and Phrygia when Praxeas, a Modalistic Monarchian, convinced him to reverse himself. This incident is recorded by the famous church father Tertullian in his

Montanist writing against Praxeas, whom he lamented had crucified the Son afresh and put the Paraclete to flight.[11]

Tertullian championed the Montanists late in his illustrious career. The extreme asceticism of the New Prophecy, and its teaching that the Holy Spirit was still operating in the church undoubtedly attracted him. Tertullian apparently did not fully identify ideologically with the Phrygian founders. The two decades that had passed inevitably had changed the Montanists. Indeed, Tertullian may well have changed the movement as much as he was changed by it. While he approved of ecstatic prophetic speech there is no hint that he accepted the excesses which had characterized the utterances of Montanus and his two priestesses. Tertullian describes, for example, a woman who fell into ecstasy during the church service, but assures the reader that she did not communicate her revelation until the congregation had departed.[12] Tertullian held to the fullness of the Spirit in the apostolic period, in direct contrast to the claims of the Phrygian Montanists who had taught that the full gift of the Paraclete was reserved until their time. He does not even mention Pepuza, since he expected that the soon-coming parousia would take place at Jerusalem.[13] Moreover, in sharp contrast to the prominence assumed by the Phrygian prophetesses, and using Paul (1 Cor. 14:34-35) as his authority, he would not allow a woman "to speak in the Church, neither to teach, nor to baptize, nor to offer, nor to claim to herself a lot in any manly function."[14]

Montanist apocalypticism revived first-century Christian anticipation of the imminent return of Christ to earth. The New Prophets taught that their reception of the full measure of the Paraclete prepared the spiritual for the parousia. Since the apostles had received the perfection of the Spirit in limited measure, the final and full gift of the Spirit lay reserved for the prophets of whom Christ spoke, "Wherefore, behold, I send unto you prophets, and wise men, and scribes: and some of them ye shall kill and crucify; and some of them shall ye scourge in your synagogues, and persecute them from city to city."[15] The perfect Spirit was being given for the perfection of the new saints whom Montanus called to experience the consummation of the ages at Pepuza. Tertullian follows this reasoning by directly linking the achievement of human perfection with the Age of the Paraclete: "Hardness of heart reigned till Christ came, weakness of the flesh reigned till the Paraclete came."[16]

Tertullian judged the Old and New Testaments to be primitive writings in comparison to the Montanist prophecies.[17] Like other Montanists he attached final and ultimate authority to a third testament comprising the new prophecies which in Montanist belief were inspired by the Paraclete and served as the final and perfect revelation of God to man. Montanists used these prophecies to legislate the perfect preparation for the establishment of God's Kingdom on earth. This was in effect, if not by intention, an enlargement of the canon.

Although oral Montanist prophecies were collected in numerous books, none of these have survived. There are, however, fragments preserved in the writings of anti-Montanist church fathers, which include several that reflect the Montanists' understanding of their special mission:

> Montanus: "Behold, man is as a lyre, and I hover over him as a pectrum; man sleeps but I watch; behold, the Lord is removing the hearts of men and giving them (new) hearts."[18]

> Maximilla: "The Lord sent me as a partisan of this task, a revealer of this covenant, an interpreter of this promise, forced, whether I will or not, to learn the knowledge of God."[19]

> Prisca: "Appearing as a woman clothed in a shining robe, Christ came to me in sleep; he put wisdom into me and revealed to me that this place is sacred and that here Jerusalem will come down from heaven."[20]

The Montanists' apocalypticism and emphasis on prophecy naturally led them to establish a new hierarchy of authority. Montanist inspiration by the Paraclete ranked higher than the authority of the apostles. The channels of ultimate revelation, the New Prophets, elevated the prophetic office over the authority of the bishops. Montanus, Maximilla and Priscilla claimed to receive their offices in a line of prophetic succession. Their prerogatives were those of the bishops. They had, for example, the power of absolution,[21] and they shared it with the martyrs or confessors.[22] According to the Montanists, the bishops enjoyed no such authority, since they were lowest in ecclesiastical rank.[23]

Montanist leaders included women—at least in the early days of the movement. Maximilla and Priscilla as prophetesses and leaders contributed to Montanist teaching and probably prophesied in the congregation.[24] Female bishops and priests, as well as virgins, continued to officiate in the congregation of

Pepuza after the death of the founders.[26] Tertullian knew that women continued to prophesy, although he does not report that they prophesied in his North African congregation. Bishop Firmilian of Caesarea tells us of a third-century Cappadocian prophetess, probably a Montanist, who baptized converts and celebrated the Eucharist.[26]

Above all else, Montanism stood out for its rigorous asceticism—a perfectionist lifestyle motivated by an apocalyptic awareness of the imminent end of the age and given definition and authority by the new prophetic revelations. Although this disciplined mode of life was at first a means to the end of achieving a restored, pure, and spiritual Church—the perfected bride for the coming Lord—the new discipline with the authority of divine sanction soon became a set of unalterable laws which were as much ends in themselves as means of obtaining perfection.

The new Montanist code included certain laws regarding fasts.[27] Previously, individuals were at liberty to add to the regular fasts according to their devotion. Bishops announced special fasts to meet social needs in their dioceses. The Montanists, however, eliminated the element of individual free will or episcopal flexibility in such matters, requiring all Christians to observe all fasts. The prophetesses ordained that, in addition to the ordinary annual paschal feast of the church, two weeks of what came to be called Xerophagy (from the Greek *xērophagia*, or the eating of dry food) must be observed. During this fast the Montanists abstained not only from fresh food and wine and the use of the bath, but from certain succulent foods such as juicy fruit. On Saturdays and Sundays, however, there was no abstinence.

The Montanists also rejected as fornication second marriages for Christians, a practice which the mainline church had discouraged without questioning its validity and lawfulness. Tertullian, the primary extant source here,[29] takes his reaction against second marriages back to his understanding of the concept of the priesthood of all believers. No believer should perform priestly functions without submitting to priestly regulations. Just as Christ had abrogated the divorce which Moses had permitted for a time, so the Paraclete had withdrawn permission for second marriages, although they had been allowed by Paul (Rom. 8:3, 1 Cor. 8:39) because his followers of Christ were not able to bear all things. Now that the end of the world was approaching, that which was perfect could be revealed and was to be enforced by a law which allowed no exception.

As a Montanist, Tertullian also teaches that idolatry, murder, fornication and adultery are irremible sins for which absolution should never be granted.[30] While the Catholic Church maintained that such offenses could be pardoned on condition of due performance of penance, the Montanists argued that God alone could grant pardon in such cases. In addition, Tertullian insists that a sin into which man runs because of the mere allurement of pleasure was less worthy of indulgence than the sin of apostasy into which he might have been forced by torture.[31]

The adoption of a perfectionist lifestyle led not only to legalism, but also to a spirit of intolerant exclusiveness. Montanism asserted that the gifts of the Spirit were not present in the church because of its moral laxity. Against this Jerome complains:

> Perish Montanus and his mad women! Montanus, who would hurl the fallen into the abyss that they may never rise again. Every day we all sin and make some slip or other. Being then merciful to ourselves, we are not rigorous towards others.[32]

> They close the doors of the Church to almost every faith, whilst we read daily, "I desire the repentance of a sinner rather than his death," and "Shall they fall and not arise, saith the Lord," and once more "Return ye backsliding children and I will heal your backslidings." Their strictness does not prevent them from themselves committing grave sins, far from it; but there is this difference between us and them, that, whereas they in their self-righteousness blush to confess their faults, we do penance for ours, and so more readily gain pardon for them.[33]

Intolerance was met with intolerance. It was impossible, of course, to stamp out Montanism while the church was only one of the many faiths tolerated and at times persecuted in the Empire. But once the Edict of Milan (313) provided freedom of worship to mainline Christians, they in turn sought to stamp out religious dissent, including fringe groups such as the Montanists. Sozomen[34] tells us that an edict of Constantine deprived the Montanists of their places of worship and forbade their religious meetings. Penal laws became increasingly stringent. Montanist buildings were confiscated, their books were destroyed, and they no longer could make wills. Their slaves were given freedom to leave them, and their nearest Catholic relatives given the right to claim their property. Despite these measures, however, the movement did not completely disappear until the sixth century. At that time persecution under Justinian forced the remaining Montanists to gather their wives and children together in their places of worship, to set fire to the buildings, and to perish there.[35]

The church's rejection of Montanism was not the repudiation of a perfectionist world and life view per se. Indeed, numerous church fathers espoused a life of perfection, although none of these writers, aside from Tertullian, defined perfection in terms resembling those of the Phrygian prophets. Three such Fathers—Clement of Alexandria, Origen, and Gregory of Nyssa—share not only a criticism of the Montanist conception of the perfect human state, but also illustrate the evolution of perfectionist views in the patristic period. A study of each follows.

CLEMENT OF ALEXANDRIA

Head of the catechetical school at Alexandria and one of the first important post-apostolic Christian scholars, Clement (ca. 155-ca. 220) used Greek philosophy, for him a gift of God to man, to formulate a Christian theology. In part, this effort grew out of his struggle against heretical gnostics who disparaged the faith of ordinary Christians as an inferior gift since they did not enjoy a "higher level knowledge." Clement's understanding of Christian perfection was a product both of his Neoplatonic training and of his ongoing struggle against heretical gnostics.

Clement's debt to Greek philosophy is evident throughout his writings. For instance, he denies original sin, to the extent that in Socratic fashion he perceives sin as an act of will rather than as a result of evil forces operating in man. "Darkness is ignorance, through which we fall into sins, purblind as to the truth. Knowledge, then, is the illumination we receive, which makes ignorance disappear, and endows us with clear vision."[36] True knowledge issues in proper action.

> True instruction is desire for knowledge; and the practical exercise of instruction produces love of knowledge. And love is the keeping of the commandments which lead to knowledge. And the keeping of them is the establishment of the commandments, from which immortality results. "And immortality brings us near to God."[37]

Clement's definition of true knowledge is the real key to his understanding of Christian perfection. True gnosis is a gift of Christ, the Great Teacher. Because no savior-redeemer is needed to counter the effects of original sin, Christ's passion and death play only a minor role in the drama of redemption. The emphasis falls to Christ the Giver of true knowledge who leads the believer to forgiveness of sin, to perfection, and to immortality. In *The Instructor,* which Clement directs to new Christian converts, he states that those who have been regenerated have "attained the perfection after which we aspired."[38] "Being baptized, we are illuminated; illuminated, we become sons; being made sons, we are made perfect; being made perfect, we are made immortal. . . . Now we call that perfect which wants nothing. For what is yet wanting to him who knows God?"[39] Perfection results from illumination or acquaintance with God. One cannot be imperfect who knows the One who is perfect.[40]

While in *The Instructor* Clement spells out his belief that all Christians are in reality perfected in the sight of God, he writes the *Stromata* or *Miscellanies* to help Christians find the highest stage of character and spiritual perfection. Clement urges such individuals to press on from faith to knowledge, although knowledge is only for those who are fit and selected for it. Clement holds to a progressive view of perfection, which allows for three steps to the ultimate and endless state. "In my view, the first saving change is that from heathenism to faith . . . and the second, that from faith to knowledge. And the latter terminating in love . . . and perchance such as one has already attained the condition of 'being equal to the angels.' "[41]

Although a first reading of the passages in *The Instructor* and the *Stromata* suggests a confusion about when one attains the perfect state, a closer examination reveals that the perfection described in *The Instructor* is imputed to all Christians, while that in the *Stromata* is a higher level reserved for those who truly reach beyond, who strive to attain to the summit of knowledge which Clement calls the highest life of all.[42] Those who have become Christian or true gnostics and have been perfected should ascend to the summit of knowledge and the perfection of love.[43] True knowledge, then, is perfection, and the summit of knowledge is higher level perfection. But even the latter is not equal to the perfection of God, which is an unattainable goal.[44]

All Christian gnosis involves more than mere wisdom, which is the result of human teaching.[45] Christian gnosis perfects faith. It leads man through mystical stages of advancement and is consummated in an acquaintance with divine things. It serves to purify and to return the pure in heart to the crowning place of rest, teaching one to gaze on God face to face with knowledge and comprehension.[46]

In contrast to the teachings of heretical gnostics, true gnosis involves ethical perfection as well as intellectual insight. It is impossible to gain true knowledge by bad conduct. Those who strive after perfection must "give no offense in anything, but in everything approve themselves not to men, but to God . . . purified from all filthiness of the flesh and of the spirit."[47] They never surrender themselves to the babble at the theaters, or allow even in a dream those things which are spoken, done and seen for the sake of fleshly pleasures. They pray for the truly good things which appertain to the soul.[48] Knowledge is the illumination they receive which makes ignorance disappear and endows them with clear vision. The abandonment of what is bad is the adopting of what is better. "For what ignorance has bound ill, is by knowledge loosed well. . . . We are washed from all our sins, and are no longer entangled in evil."[49] The true gnostic does good, not from fear of punishment or hope of reward, but only for the sake of good itself. According to Clement, good works follow knowledge as the shadow follows the body.[50]

Knowledge also generates a disposition of complete disinterestedness to the passions of the soul. The goal is not moderation of passion, but *apatheia* (emotionlessness or impassivity) with complete eradication of desire.[51] In the *Stromata* Clement defines divine perfection as *apatheia*.[52] Human moral perfection, therefore, must be complete disinterestedness in all the distractions of matter. The Christian life should be a continuous passionless state in which one contemplates heaven.[53] This passionlessness which Clement attributes to the true gnostic is the avenue by which the perfection of the believer advances by love, until he "comes to a perfect man, to the measure of full stature," by being assimilated to God.[54] Again, we are alerted to Clement's strong dependence on Greek philosophy. As LaRondelle has suggested,[55] *apatheia* is a virtue which could only have been learned from the Stoa.

Unlike Origen and Gregory of Nyssa, Clement does not advocate extreme asceticism. Withdrawal is from passions alone, not from life itself. Christian gnostics strive to be as perfect as they can while still abiding in the flesh.[56] They allow the body its necessities so that it does not perish;[57] they have strength to serve others, to teach, to attend, and to discipline.[58] In so doing, they represent "the truly kingly man, the sacred high priest of God."[59]

On the question of whether perfection requires sinlessness, Clement is less than certain. In *The Instructor* he writes that the Christian is washed from sin and no longer is entangled in evil. "This is the one grace of illumination, that our characters are not the same as before our washing." He poses the question, however, "Does this . . . take place on the advent of this instruction?" His answer is: "You cannot know the time."[60] Perfection is the renunciation of sin, and regeneration into the faith of the only perfect One, and forgetting our former sins."[61] These are cautious statements. In the *Stromata* he is more direct: "The Gnostics who tread in the footsteps of the apostles ought to be sinless, and, out of love to the Lord, to love also their brother; so that, if occasion call, enduring without stumbling, afflictions for the Church, 'they may drink the cup.' "[62] Clearly, Clement requires a higher level of perfection for those who reach beyond the level of the initiates.

The price for receiving true gnosis—the gift of insight—includes both an intellectual struggle requiring purity and moral discipline and prayer or communion with God as well.[63] One who holds uninterrupted conversation with God by knowledge, life, and thanksgiving, "grows at every step superior to himself in all respects—in conduct, in words, in disposition."[64] The true gnostic is very closely allied with God, especially as love draws the soul into knowledge of divine beauty, and knowledge is perfected.

No one is perfected in all things at once in this life, except for Christ.[65] The prophets were perfect in prophecy, the righteous in righteousness, the martyrs in confession, and others in preaching. Ultimately, the apostles were perfected in all.[66] Each person is proficient in those virtues to which he or she is appointed. In each case, the perfection of the true gnostic exhibits the perfect beneficience of God.[67]

ORIGEN

Origen (ca. 185-ca. 254), a student of Clement in the catechetical school in Alexandria, became one of the most formative of the pre–Nicene fathers in the doctrinal development of the early church. Like Clement, Origen was profoundly influenced by classical Greek thought. His concept of human perfection, however, differs from Clement's in that it begins with his doctrine of rational creatures rather than with an overriding concern to define true gnosis.

Plato's arguments in the *Phaedo* supporting the concept of the immortality of the soul were adopted by Origen. In this view God created first the spiritual world of rational creatures (angels, powers of wickedness, animating spirits of the heavenly bodies, and human souls) and only later the material world. All created spirits were equal and immaterial. They cooled off, however, in different degrees in their relationship to God.[68] Angels ranked as the highest of rational creatures, while the powers of wickedness, including those who had sinned most grievously, were furthest from God. The rational spirits which animate the heavenly bodies were bound to materiality until the consummation of the ages. Human souls had been devils before, and might with the help of Christ raise themselves up to become angels again. They suffer with grossly material bodies as punishment for sin, but also as the means whereby they can be disciplined and trained for their return to God. The Fall did not result in the impairment of an existing material world. It brought the material world into existence. By sin human souls, which were once minds, lost their purely intellectual character as part of their fall from God. They were trapped in a material world, which is God's provision for rational creatures who have failed to abide with Him.

Origen teaches that ultimately God restores all spirits, including devils, to their original perfection. The material world then comes to an end and the human body rises as a pure spirit so that its end will be as its beginning.[69] But this restoration of all things (*apokatastasis*) is only a preliminary to future evolution, for world follows world in an endless succession.

Man can rise in this life to perfect virtue, but only gradually after a long period of ascent, after passing through numerous stations. Those who strive for moral perfection must turn their backs on the material world and human emotions. They must enter the secret chamber with its special gnosis, and not be led astray by the senses. Origen insists on the freedom of human will as part of man's status as a rational being.[70] Man made in the image of God cannot be regarded as essentially corrupt.[71] He is capable of gaining a rational understanding by which he advances "from small things to great, and from things visible to things invisible, attaining to a more perfect knowledge."[72]

The ascent of the human soul to perfect virtue, however, is not perpetual or without interruption. Because of human freedom to choose evil, one cannot guarantee that, even though the soul has been satiated in its contemplation of God, it will not choose to turn away.[73] For Origen all created beings are necessarily unstable, and the journey of the human soul is an ongoing process of rise-statiety-fall-return. This process ends only when God becomes "all in all."[74]

Moses stands as the great example for those who reach beyond, who attempt to ascend above all created things.[75] His law served as a schoolmaster to conduct men to Christ to receive his more perfect principles.[76] Long before Plato, Moses had taught the distinction between the sensible and the ideal world.[77] Christians understand this distinction better than pagans, for followers of Christ can, by closing their eyes in prayer, ascend in soul beyond the visible world to God.[78] Unlike those who sin and still fight against flesh and blood (the body), individuals who strive for perfection and have overcome the flesh wrestle against demonic powers alone.[78]

The children of Israel, whom Moses led out of the land of Egypt into years of wandering, serve as a type of those followers of Christ who strive to reach beyond to perfection. Just as the liberated Hebrews progressed through forty-two stages in their travels to the promised inheritance, so the Christian pursuing perfection passes through forty-two steps of faith and virtue.[80] Beginning from Ramesse the Hebrews traveled from Egypt to the Red Sea. In like fashion, the Christian soul starts out from this world of agitation, embarking on a journey to a life of virtue and knowledge. Virtues are only developed through training, hard work, and many testings. At the Bitter Waters (at the Red Sea) the soul learns to be calm and unalarmed. Testings continue intermittently throughout the entire journey until finally one realizes that no virtue is to be complete without them. Even in a most perfect state, the "beehive of temptation," there is an element of testing which serves to heighten virtue and knowledge of divine plan and provision.

Provision for refreshment follows each testing state. After passing through the Bitter Waters the soul comes to Helim, or the place of Rams, where twelve springs of water and seventy-two palm trees revive the traveler. As rams are the leaders of flocks, the ascending soul serves as a spiritual teacher to those who have not yet begun their journey. Such virtues as self-control, calmness, the ability to discern evil from good spirits, freedom from lusts of the flesh, patience, holy fruitfulness, frugality of the mouth, and a scorn for all earthly things are attained in the climb. As the soul ceases to be driven by things of the flesh, it experiences completed visions and gains perfect understanding as a radiance of true heavenly light. Childlike notions are given up in favor of a more perfect comprehension of the purposes of a man.

For the traveler there are times of conflict as well, for the soul which is armed with many virtues also is fitted for warfare against principalities, powers, and world rulers. Origen refers especially to Mount Shepher, the "sound of trumpets," for the trumpet is a sign of war. The trumpet is sounded by the preacher and the teacher as well, so that the person who hears the sound can prepare himself for battle.

Finally, after the soul has climbed to the height of perfection, it passes from the world, separating from it as Enoch did. As Israel arrived east of Moab by the Jordan, the soul comes at last to the river of God. Here the soul is a neighbor of flowing Wisdom and is watered by the waves of divine knowledge, so that it is made worthy to enter the promised land. The soul has risen to perfect virtue, the highest state that the human rational creature can attain in this life.

While Moses is the archetype for humans who reach beyond, Christ plays the supreme role in the ascent of the aspiring soul to perfection, not so much as a savior to sinners but as a teacher of divine mysteries. He unfolds the divine life of grace to the individual soul. Day after day, in sweet mystical communion with the human soul, He enlightens until man achieves perfection in mystical union with the Word. The Master assists in man's attainment of self-knowledge to help in his struggle against sin. In his *Commentary on the Song of Songs* Origen likens the ascent of the soul toward perfection to the preparation of the bride to enter the bridal chamber. Christ the Groom leads the obedient bride through practices of asceticism to the mystical ascent, and finally to the bridal chamber wherein "are hid the treasures of His wisdom and knowledge," where she is united with the Christ-Logos.[81]

In his writing *Against Celsus* Origen equates perfection in man to the Pauline concept of being crucified with Christ. By continually dying with the Lord, one is converted from sin and placed on the road to ethical perfection. Christ's death, then, is a type for those who struggle against sin even to death.[82] Origen's own life was one of unusual asceticism in obedience to commands in the Gospels. He owned only one cloak, wore no shoes, fasted regularly, and slept on the floor. Eusebius tells us that early in life Origen castrated himself, applying Matthew 19:12 literally.[83] Later he repudiated his youthful folly, arguing that asceticism did not imply hostility to the body. Rather, it is an appropriate means to prepare a fitting vehicle for the soul's ascent to God. Asceticism is an opportunity to imitate the overflowing goodness of God through detachment from worldly concerns and emotions (*apatheia*). By rejecting the false gnostic's dualistic foundation for antagonism to the world, Origen laid a more satisfactory, and, therefore, a more permanent basis for asceticism. He has justifiably been called the precursor of monasticism.[84]

According to Origen, all of the ascetic saint's life is one great unbroken prayer. That such prayer involves much more than the actual act of conversing with God is clear from Origen's recommendation that the Christian pray only three times a day, which is intermittent—a long step from unbroken prayer. But Origen also considers virtuous works as part of prayer, joining prayer to works and good works to his prayer. The soul reaching for perfection will live a life of good works and fulfilling the commandments, as well as of contemplation.

Prayer benefits one in many ways. It recalls the God in whom one believes; it places one before God who is present and anticipates every thought. The frequent practice of prayer helps one to avoid a great number of sins and to perform many good deeds.[85] In fact, Origen is convinced that prayer, which involves forgetting past things and stretching forward to those which are ahead, will lead to additional and more inspired thoughts.[86] It is a vital part of the mystical ascent to divinity for it helps to free the soul from bodily affections.

Origen's treatise *On Prayer* traces the mystical ascent of the soul through several phases of prayer: petition, adoration, supplication, thanksgiving. The highest level of prayer is reached when the soul expresses itself to God without words. This is the vision of the mount of God. A bright cloud of the Father, Son, and Holy Spirit overshadows the genuine disciple of Jesus.[87] Once this level has been achieved, vision overflows into intercession for one's fellows.

From childhood Origen's heart was aflame for martyrdom. The idealization of a heroic Christian death remained strong until his death, which was hastened by the horrible tortures he endured at the hands of the hostile Roman Empire. In this tendency Origen contrasts with his teacher, Clement, who preferred a life of moderate asceticism. Martyrdom was appealing to Origen philosophically as well as pietistically.[88] It provided the swiftest way to follow Christ and to experience unspeakable joy. It also was the real test of the Christian's willingness to prefer spiritual over corporeal realities. This was, after all, an ultimate measure of one's growth in perfection.

GREGORY OF NYSSA

Gregory of Nyssa (330-ca. 395), one of the three Cappadocian fathers, decisively influenced Christian spirituality in the Eastern Church. He based much of his teaching concerning perfection on the writings of the Alexandrian luminaries: Philo, Clement, and Origen. Origen's emphasis on the freedom of human will, on perfection as freedom from bodily affections, and on the vision of God as the ultimate goal of life, remains little changed in Gregory's writings. This is true also of Gregory's understanding of the meaning of Christianity as imitation of the divine nature, which is based upon the Platonic principle that resemblance to God is the end of human activity.[89] Like Origen, Gregory reminds his readers that man is made in the image of God, that this image was tarnished by his fall into sin, and that Christ took human form in order to restore man to his original nature. Humanity has freedom to choose between good and evil. When man chooses good, God's grace cooperates with his moral effort.

Gregory's goal, however, is different than Origen's. While Origen admits to the presence of temptation and the power of sin throughout the journey of the soul, Gregory portrays the ascent to perfection as one of continual progress for the saved or blessed. Evil has no inherent existence.[90] Furthermore, its hold on man is finite and not as strong as the power of good.[91]

So man has the capacity to move towards God. For Gregory, perfection is perpetual progress in virtue, a progress which is without limit.[92]

Everett Ferguson has shown that Gregory's doctrine of perpetual progress is based upon his understanding of God's infinity and man's mutability.[93] God is unlimited and infinite, absolute Good and absolute virtue, lacking nothing that is regarded as good. He is totally self-sufficient and necessary, as well as invisible, incomprehensible, and unknowable. The creation attains excellence by partaking in something better than itself. By participating in God all creatures have their being and virtue.

Creation is defective because of man's fall into sin, and thus to be distinguished from the Creator.[94] Because of the power of the devil, the inventor of evil, the body is bound by mortality and passions and continues its thrust downward.[95] Human feet cannot ascend to where the light of truth may be seen unless the dead and earthly covering of skins first be removed.[96] The soul of man, on the other hand, is incorporeal and, once released from earthly attachments, rises upward to God unless hindered.[97] Man has freedom to choose between right and wrong, and places himself in what sphere he wishes to be.[98] Because God is by nature infinite, He exerts upon creation a ceaseless attraction towards himself which is greater than any power of evil.[99] The Holy Spirit cooperates in any attempt by man to move toward divine virtue, for he now is counted worthy having been freed from earthly desires.[100] The soul of man reaches beyond in an effort to experience the infinity of God and to participate in his perfection.[101]

God's virtue also is infinite. He is unlimited in the good. His eternal substance contains all perfection within itself and cannot be limited.[102] Every perfection that God is conceived to have is present in an infinite and unlimited degree. In turn, the human soul that has divested itself of natural emotions copies the divine life and is thereby conformed to the divine nature.[103] Participation in the enjoyment of God also is infinite, for the more that is grasped, the more will be discovered. Man's reach beyond will never be satiated because God is inexhaustible. The search after God and the growth that accompanies that search is ceaseless. "All that is acquired becomes by participating a beginning of its ascent to something still greater, and it never ceases. . . ."[104] The soul stretches itself forward to things that lie ahead, always passing from the present stage to enter more deeply into the interior of God in the next. As a bride who ever runs toward her spouse, the soul never finds rest in its progress towards perfection. Desire for the Good constantly expands as the soul progresses toward the Good. This craving is never satiated because greater horizons for growth are recognized at each point in the journey.[105] Participation in virtue is never expressed as attainment, only as movement.[106] Gregory's portrayal of Christian progress in perfection is not one of several distinct stages, such as his brother Basil envisions. It is continuous and perpetual. Gregory even suggests that progress in virtue is not limited to the present life. Those who share in divine Goodness will enjoy a greater participation in grace throughout all eternity.[107]

There is a strong note of optimism in Gregory's comments about men who have freely chosen to follow the instincts of the flesh and the cunning leadings of the devil. Progress in evil, unlike progress in good, cannot go on indefinitely. The soul will continue to move, and if that be in evil, once the course of wickedness has been run, it will of necessity turn its motion toward the good. Because Good is infinite and evil is not, Gregory argues for universal salvation.[108]

David Balás has shown the importance of Gregory's theme of participation in divine perfections.[109] God possesses and is every perfection essentially. The creatures possess perfection only by participation. Participation is the presence of the transcendent God in the participant. The fundamental and all-encompassing divine quality is goodness, which includes all other perfections or virtues. This is shared with human participants by God who is both source and exemplar. Such sharing is a mysterious union of divine grace. Man's advancement in virtue increases with his participation in God.[110] Progress must be in all of the actions of life, not just in mind and soul, so that holiness may be complete.[111]

As with Philo and the Christian Alexandrians, Clement and Origen, Gregory chooses the life of Moses to highlight certain qualities of the spiritual life. Moses is both a human exemplar and a precursor and type of Christ. Like Jesus, Moses withdrew to solitude for a season before returning to society to serve. On Sinai, with the people left below, he approached very darkness itself and entered invisible things where he was no longer seen by human eyes.[112] His spiritual life already had passed through two stages in which he had a vision of God in light and later heard the divine voice in a cloud. Now as he rose higher and became more perfect, he saw God in the darkness. This imagery suggests that by natural human power a knowledge of the divine essence is impossible. In the darkness, only the grace of God permits the invisible to become recognizable. But even at this level man becomes aware of the ultimate inaccessibility of the transcendant God. It is in the divine darkness that man sees the invisibility of God. Moses had a new knowledge that God was ultimately unknowable. The finite creature had experienced the true infinity of the Creator. Gregory now has arrived at a negative or apophatic theology in which the darkness is a positive reality that helps us to know God. While mind has encountered the obscurity of darkness, the soul can by faith grasp the transcendent Godhead. One must be satisfied in not pressing beyond these limitations. Additional speculative questions are not to be asked. This is the summit of the spiritual life where the soul has experienced a high degree of union with God by divine love.

Knowledge of God must be coupled with right conduct. After Moses was taught those things he needed to know about God, he was taught the other side of virtue, namely, by what pursuits the truly virtuous life is perfected.[113] Here Gregory places much emphasis on the ethical side of virtue. One's life must be regulated in accordance with the ascetic ideal of austerity. Passions must be controlled. The virtuous life is to be like the pomegranate. This reddish-yellow fruit has a stiff and sour outer cover, but inside is pleasant, both to the eye and to the taste. So the life of virtue should be philosophical and severe. Yet the divine Gardener opens the pomegranate of one's life at the appropriate time and reveals the hidden beauty, the peace and goodness, of the fruit.[114]

In his *De Perfectione* Gregory analyzes the various names applied by the Apostle Paul to Christ. By this he attempts to identify those virtues which should be apparent in Christians who strive for perfection by imitating their Master. They are to be identified with Him in virtues which He demonstrates as the power and the Wisdom of God, Peace, the Splendor of Glory and Figure of His Substance, Spiritual Food and Drink, Rock and Water, the Foundation of Faith, the Image of the invisible

God, the King of Justice, and many others. For example, because Christ as the image and exemplar of the invisible God
became man to restore in us the image of God, we are to become the image of the Image. Because Christ is the True Light,
our life must be illuminated by the rays of the true Father so
that we do all things in the light.[115]

Gregory also wrote an essay[116] attacking a contemporary
Arian, Eunomius, who apparently had maintained that his doctrine alone was sufficient for perfection, and that fleshly in-
dulgences did no harm to the soul. Gregory insists that
Eunomius was lacking both in purity of life and in proper
teaching that such purity of life was necessary. Again we
encounter the notion that true virtue has both an ethical and a
doctrinal part. To be sure, this philosophical union of the intellectual and the moral life was common among the ancient
Greeks, as well as the Alexandrians. Within this framework,
however, Gregory places a special emphasis on the incom-
prehensibility of God and upon the austere life.

Gregory gives to the Christian tradition a new ideal of ascetic
perfection based upon the Greek philosophical ideal of life. His
doctrine of the perpetual progress of perfection is influenced by
Plato's ideal of imitating the divine. Gregory asserts that man is
attracted to God, and, consequently, that he seeks to follow his
Maker. Werner Jaeger argues most convincingly that Gregory's
definition of perfection involves a linkage of his Christian faith
and the hellenic tradition.[117] He points out that in the Scriptures there is no absolute equivalent for the word "perfection"
in the classical Greek sense. Furthermore, the concept of virtue
(*aretē*) is not common in the thought of Jesus and the apostles.
(The term only appears in four passages: Phil. 4:8, 1 Pet. 2:9,
and 2 Pet. 1:3, 5.) Notwithstanding, Gregory chooses to interpret the Christian concepts of sanctification (*hagiasmos*) and
end or goal (*teleios*) in the sense of the term "perfection" as
inherited from Greek philosophers. From this hellenized
perspective Gregory defines perfection as "life in accordance
with virtue," or perfect *aretē* (the sum of good qualities that
make up character).

CONCLUSIONS

The Montanists, including Tertullian, shared with the Eastern
fathers a commitment to asceticism as a necessary step to

achieve perfection. Long before monasticism had elevated asceticism to the rank of the ideal Christian life, the Montanists had gained the attention of a generally disapproving Church. Despite institutional opposition, Montanism was successful in helping to revive Church interest in asceticism—a lifestyle long advocated by Greek and Judaeo-Hellenic philosophers and popular among many first-century Christians. The New Prophets helped to popularize a partial fast during the weeks before Easter, to increase the severity of church discipline, to stimulate the acceptance of voluntary virginity as an ideal, and to prepare Christians to accept martyrdom as the most blessed avenue to paradise.

This ascetic emphasis also emerged strongly in the theology of the school at Alexandria, where the challenge from heretical gnostics was strongest. Like the Stoics and many gnostics, the Alexandrian fathers assumed that ascetic action purified the soul from its passions—a necessary step in attaining to contemplation and in loving God more perfectly. Clement is more moderate than Origen. For example, although he vigorously attacks Christians who used fine clothes and sought to enjoy other worldly pleasures, he also upholds the right of personal property and the sanctity of the marital condition.[118] Again, while he pleads for a Stoic-like *apatheia* in order that the body not be indulged, he recognizes that the flesh must be provided with necessities for health.[119]

Both in lifestyle and in his writings, Clement's student, Origen, went far beyond his teacher, advocating all forms of world-renunciation and such practices as fasting and other forms of abstinence. He advocates not only chastity for the unmarried, but also abstinence from sexual intercourse for the married.[120] For Origen, mortification of the flesh ultimately meant martyrdom, a fate he sought as a young child at the time that his father was led away to his death, and which he encouraged on others in his *Exhortation to Martyrdom*.

By the mid-fourth century, when persecution had passed and the ideal of physical martyrdom had faded, extreme asceticism became the standard for those who reached beyond. Gregory of Nyssa, who closely followed the teachings of the great Alexandrians, actively sought out the ascetic life, disdaining the work of ecclesiastical office. His older brother, Basil, had popularized the principle of monastic perfection. It came to be Gregory's task to mould monastic life by giving it theological

substance through his writings. Above all else, he was concerned with the mystical metamorphosis by which the image of
God is restored in man.[121] This can only be accomplished
through an eternal process which begins by man exercising his
free will in removing all that is mortal and corruptible in him
("garments of skins"). The Holy Spirit then cooperates by adding grace to man's moral efforts. Every perfection in God is
found by imitation in God's image in man. Once the perfections
in man are restored to their original splendor, man can by con-
templating these perfections see and contemplate divine perfection as they are reflected in the mirror of the human soul. One
can contemplate these divine perfections, but not the divine nature in its essence.

While the Montanists and the Eastern Church fathers agreed
in general terms on the necessity for an ascetic life, Tertullian
and other devotees of the New Prophecy were much more vig-
orous than Clement, Origen, or Gregory of Nyssa in condemning what they considered to be an undisciplined or worldly
Church. Tertullian gives vent to the intolerant exclusiveness of
the Montanists by calling his Catholic contemporaries
"psychics" or "animal men," as opposed to his colleagues,
whom he refers to as the "pneumatics" or "Spirit-led."[122] By
contrast, Clement, Origen and Gregory of Nyssa attribute the
lack of discipline in the Church to an absence of divinely-given
knowledge, and they seek to educate simple Christians to a
higher-level understanding and imitation of God. Their intolerance is reserved more for heretics than for imperfect
Catholics.

This contrast in attitude toward the imperfect can best be
understood in the larger context of their respective anthropologies. Tertullian and his fellow Montanists had a profound awareness of man's sinful human nature. Just as children
derive their bodies from their parents, so too is original sin inherited. Sin is a crime against the sovereignty of God which calls
for satisfaction. Christ has offered himself up to God for man's
offences. He is man's satisfaction.[123] His work is one of
atonement and of mediation between a righteous God and fallen
man.[124] Tertullian borrowed the term "satisfaction" from
Roman law to signify the ensemble of painful acts imposed on
man to obtain from God remission of his fault and of the eternal punishment due to his sin. "By confession satisfaction is
settled, of confession repentance is born; by repentance God is

appeased."[125] Christ is able to reconcile God to man and man to God because He has united in His own self flesh and spirit.[126] Without satisfaction, without reconciliation, there is no hope for man. He is eternally lost, despicable in the eyes of a just God and of His true followers.

While Tertullian's emphasis is on Calvary and the forgiveness it brings, Clement and his Eastern fellows find ultimate meaning in the Incarnation. The Word of God, source of all knowledge and of every creature, became incarnate in Jesus Christ.[127] With the Incarnation Christ invaded the dominions of the devil, and thereby began His victorious work. Redemption must consist in lifting up the whole human race from its evil state, in restoring to man the gift of life, and in effecting his ransom. The Logos (the "Word") became flesh so that humans could learn how to become God.[128] Once man's freedom is set free from the tyranny of sin, it is blessed by the example of the Logos-incarnate, which induces all free creatures to return to the good. One is freed from the power of the devil and then is shown the way of salvation. And salvation amounts to man's deification.

Perhaps because of their tendency toward the allegorical method of interpreting Scripture (looking for additional mystical levels of meaning in each verse), because of their Platonic backgrounds which identify two levels of reality, and because of the claims of contemporary heretical gnostics to special knowledge, Clement, Origen, and Gregory of Nyssa also distinguish between two levels of Christians: the simple or primitive and the "true gnostics." The former operate on a level of mere faith, not fully understanding the biblical message and the teachings of the church, but always taking them literally. They never move beyond the first stage of redemption. The latter, who have been given the charisma of gnosis, the grace of knowledge, mount to a new mystical level of understanding through divine assistance. These true gnostics reach beyond both ethically and intellectually to a higher level of perfection, discovering higher intellectual truth and living a life of a higher order. From these more lofty heights they bear a responsibility to teach simple souls the way of perfection.

Both the Montanists and the Eastern patristic writers identify a spiritual elite who have special knowledge. For the Montanists revealed truth comes through the prophecies of the specially gifted. To Clement, Origen, and Gregory of Nyssa knowledge is a sharing of divine character with those who are capable of understanding and willing to walk the rigorous path to perfection. In both cases theology is influenced by environment. Montanism appears to have appealed originally to the persecuted and dispossessed who sought direct communication from God and a place in His coming Kingdom. By Tertullian's time the movement also had reached educated Christians who longed for the ascetic life. In time, the Eastern fathers discovered a way for converted, educated Greeks, who wished to fuse truth from Athens with that from Jerusalem, to become perfect Christians.

The Montanists clearly differed from the Eastern fathers in matters of hermeneutic. The New Prophecy was dominated by a sense of the apocalyptic. Ecstatic utterances, supplementary revelations, and the proclamation of a New Age of the Paraclete with its more rigorous lifestyle were directed towards a single all-encompassing goal—preparation for the end of the world, whether that was to be at Pepuza or Jerusalem. The New Prophets believed that the Holy Spirit was fulfilling the promise of Jesus for a Comforter who would lead believers into all truth. They also taught that "when He which is perfect is come" His followers would be perfected for the end of the world. In declaring the New Prophecy, the Montanists rejected church tradition which taught that the revelation of God to man was complete in Christ, and that the apostles already had received the Spirit in His fulness. Their emphasis was upon newness, for each new revelation was seen as bringing the faithful ever closer to cosmic climax.

Church fathers in both East and West from the time of Hippolytus of Rome onward began to admit that the church was not necessarily living in the last times. In contrast to the Montanists, they defended the process by which the church was accommodating itself to the delay in the Lord's second coming. As the parousia was pushed forward, prophecy was pushed backward. The canon was established and church authorities reasoned that inspired prophecy had ended with St. John. The impulse in Christianity towards perfection in the third and fourth centuries, therefore, was not apocalyptic. Rather it grew out of a rising tendency towards philosophical speculation.

The impact of Hellenism encouraged Christian thinkers to explore the implications of their faith, and with the aid of reason to work for a resolution of the problems it raised. Great respect was paid to the past. In contrast to Tertullian who asked, "What indeed has Athens to do with Jerusalem?"[129] Clement reasoned that philosophy had been given by God to the Greeks, as the law had been given to the Jews, to bring them to Christ. Philosophy combined with established Christian truth would lead man to a higher level of truth. Whether or not the development of Christian theology involved the hellenization of Christianity, as Harnack claims,[130] apologists such as Clement and Origen found a place for Greek philosophy within the Christian system. For Clement, *philosophein* was defined as a striving for the perfect life.[131] A certain knowledge of God, as manifested in his works, is innate in every man. Through abstractions, philosophy purifies the concept of God of its anthropomorphism. What results is negative theology or the quest of the invisible, and ultimately, an awareness that God in His essence is wholly unknowable. He is transcendent and to be found only in the mystery of the dark cloud of unknowing—a decidedly different position than the Montanist vision of an imminent God who reveals His purpose in ongoing revelations through His New Prophets. According to the Fathers, those who would be perfect must seek divinely given gnosis, higher and hidden truth, in their search to know the perfect One, and thereby to participate in divine perfection.

Montanist perfectionistic asceticism as such was not rejected by the mainline church. The efforts of the New Prophets to reach beyond were no more extreme than that of many church fathers. The Montanists, however, rejected much existing Christian tradition, and declared their New Prophecy with intolerant exclusiveness by denouncing all other Christians as immoral and their teachings as false. In turn, those who expected an early parousia were soon disappointed, and Montanist apocalypticism ran its course.

Meanwhile, the Fathers examined their own tradition in light of time-honored hellenic principles as they attempted to develop a new synthesis of Christian doctrine. Their thought survived in part because it adjusted by addressing questions raised by the ongoing life of the Church. Perfection was to be sought after, not to bring the immediate return of Christ to earth, but rather to gain a true knowledge of God as a step in this life toward eventual union of creature with the Creator.

NOTES

1. Clement only briefly mentions the Montanists as "the [heresy] of the Phrygians," in *Stromata* 7.17, ANF 2:555. Origen ignores them in his writings, and Gregory of Nyssa does not include them in his list of heresies in *The Great Catechism* Prologue, NPF 2nd Series 5:473-474.

2. The exact date of the founding of Montanism is uncertain. An anonymous opponent quoted in Eusebius *(Church History* 5.16.7, NPF 2nd Series 1:231) tells us that Montanus began to prophesy when Gratus (probably Quadratus) was proconsul of Asia. A Quadratus was proconsul in Asia Minor in 155 and another in 166. The same anonymous writer states that fourteen years had passed since the death of the Montanist prophetess, Maximilla. (Ibid., 5.7.4, NPF 2nd Series 1:23.) The author must have written ca. 192-193, and therefore, Maximilla must have died in 178 or 179. The best guess as to the origin of Montanism is sometime between 155 and 166.

3. Didymus of Alexandria, *De trinitate* 3.41, PG 39:cols. 989-990.

4. Anonymous author in Eusebius, *Church History* 5.16.7, NPF 2nd Series 1:231.

5. Clement of Alexandria, *Stromata* 4:13, ANF 2:426; Serapion in Eusebius, *Church History* 5.19.1, NPF 2nd Series 1:237.

6. Anonymous in Eusebius, *Church History* 5.14, 5.16.9-22, NPF 2nd Series 1:229, 231-233. Didymus, *De trinitate* 3.41.3, PG 39:col. 381.

7. Epiphanius, *Panarion* 43.2, PG 41:col. 857.

8. Epiphanius, *Haereses* ("Medicine chest") 48.11, PG 41:col. 872.

9. Ibid.

10. Didymus, *De trinitate* 3.41.1, PG 39:col. 983.

11. Tertullian, *Against Praxeas* 1, ANF 3:597.

12. Tertullian, *A Treatise on the Soul* 9, ANF 3:188.

13. Tertullian, *Against Marcion* 3.24, ANF 3:342-343.

14. Tertullian, *On the Veiling of Virgins* 9, ANF 4:33.

15. Matthew 23:34.

16. Tertullian, *On Monogamy* 14, ANF 4:71.

17. Tertullian, *On Monogamy* 4, ANF 4:61; *On the Resurrection of the Flesh* 63, ANF 3:594.

18. Epiphanius, *Haereses* 48.4, PG 41:col. 861.

19. Ibid., 48.13, PG 41:col. 875.

20. Ibid., 49.1, PG 41:col. 879.

21. Tertullian, *On Modesty* 21, ANF 4:99.

22. Eusebius, *Church History* 5.18.7, NPF 2nd Series 1:236.

23. Jerome, *Letter* 41.3, NPF 2nd Series 6:56.

24. Hippolytus, *Philosophumena* 8.19, PG 39:cols. 987-990; Didymus, *De trinitate* 3.41.3, PG 39:cols. 987-990; Eusebius, *Church History* 5.16.9, NPF 2nd Series 1.231.

25. Epiphanius, *Haereses* 49.2, PG 41:cols. 881-882; Didymus, *De trinitate* 3.41.3, PG 39:cols. 987-990.

26. Firmilian, *Letter to Cyprian,* ANF 5:393.

27. Eusebius, *Church History* 5.18.2, NPF 2nd Series 1:235; Hippolytus, *Philosophumena* 10.25, PG 16:col. 3440; Tertullian, *De Jejuniis* 13, PL 2:cols. 971-973.

28. Jerome, *Matthew* 9, PL 26:col. 57; Tertullian, *De Jejuniis* 15, PL 2:cols. 974-5.

29. Tertullian, *On Monogamy* 14, ANF 4:70-72.

30. Tertullian, *On Modesty* 1, 4-5, ANF 4:75, 77-78.

31. Ibid., 22, ANF 4:101.

144   STANLEY M. BURGESS

32. Jerome, *To Pammachus Against John of Jerusalem* 2, NPF 2nd Series 6:425.
33. Jerome, *Letter to Marcella* 41.3, NPF 2nd Series 6:56.
34. Sozómen, *Ecclesiastical History* 2.32, NPF 2nd Series 2:280-281.
35. Procopius, *Secret History* 11, trans. by Richard Atwater (Ann Arbor, MI: The University of Michigan Press, 1961), 59.
36. Clement of Alexandria, *The Instructor* 1.6 ANF 2:216.
37. Clement of Alexandria, *Stromata* 6.15, ANF 2:508. Cf. *Stromata* 6.9, ANF 2:496.
38. *The Instructor* 1.6, ANF 2:214.
39. Ibid.
40. Ibid., 1.6, ANF 2:215.
41. *Stromata* 7.10, ANF 2:539.
42. Ibid., 7.11, ANF 2:540.
43. Ibid., 7.7, ANF 2:536-537.
44. Ibid., 7.14, ANF 2:549.
45. Ibid., 7.10, ANF 2:538.
46. Ibid., ANF 2:539.
47. *Stromata* 4.21, ANF 2:433. Cf. 2 Cor. 6:3-7, 16-18, 7:1.
48. Ibid., 7.7, ANF 2:533.
49. *The Instructor* 1.6, ANF 2:216.
50. *Stromata* 7.13, ANF 2:547.
51. See *Stromata* 6.9, ANF 2:496, in which the Christian gnostic is encouraged to emulate the impassivity of the Great Teacher.
52. Ibid.
53. Ibid., 7.11, 13, ANF 2:541, 547.
54. Ibid., 7:14, ANF 2:547.
55. H. K. LaRondelle, *Perfection and Perfectionism* (Berrien Springs, MI: Andrews University Press, 1971), 297.
56. *Stromata* 4.21, ANF 2:433.
57. Ibid., 6.9, ANF 2:496-497.
58. Ibid., 6.17, ANF 2:518.
59. Ibid., 7.7, ANF 2:533.
60. *The Instructor* 1.6, ANF 2:216-217.
61. Ibid., ANF 2:222.
62. *Stromata* 4.9, ANF 2:422.
63. Ibid., 7.8, ANF 2:537.
64. Ibid., 7.7, ANF 2:533.
65. Ibid., 4.21, ANF 2:433.
66. Ibid., 4.21, ANF 2:434.
67. Ibid., 7.7, ANF 2:534.
68. Origen, *De Principiis* 1.5, 7, 8, ANF 4:256-260, 262-267.
69. *De Principiis* 1.6, ANF 4:260-262.
70. Ibid., 3.1, ANF 4:302ff.
71. Ibid., 4.1.37, ANF 4:381-382.
72. Ibid.
73. Ibid., 2.3.3, ANF 4:272.
74. Ibid., 3.5.6, 3.6.3, ANF 4:343, 345.
75. Origen, *Against Celsus* 1.19, ANF 4:404.
76. *De Principiis* 3.6.8, ANF 4:348.
77. *Against Celsus* 7.31, ANF 4:623.
78. Ibid., 7.45, ANF 4:629.
79. *De Principiis* 3.2.4, ANF 4:332. CF. *Against Celsus* 8.25-27, ANF 4:648-649.
80. Origen, *Homily 27 on Numbers,* in Rowan A. Greer (trans.), *Origen*

(New York: Paulist Press, 1979), 245-269.

81. Origen, *Commentary on the Song of Songs,* Prologue 1.1, 1.5, 4, in R. P. Lawson (trans.), *Origen: The Song of Songs, Commentary and Homilies,* Vol. 26, *Ancient Christian Writers* (New York: Newman Press, ca. 1956), 50, 60, 84-85.

82. *Against Celsus* 2.69, ANF 4:459.

83. Eusebius, *Church History* 6.8, NPF 2nd Series 1:254.

84. R. Newton Flew, *The Idea of Perfection in Christian Theology* (New York: Humanities Press, 1968), 156.

85. Origen, *On Prayer* 8.2, in John J. O'Meara (trans.), *Origen: Prayer, Exhortation to Martyrdom,* Vol. 19, *Ancient Christian Writers* (New York: Newman Press, 1959), 37-38.

86. Ibid., Epilogue, pp. 139-140.

87. Origen, *Commentary on Matthew* 12.42, ANF 10:472-473.

88. In A.D. 235, at the beginning of the persecution under Maximinus the Thracian, Origen wrote *An Exhortation to Martyrdom* to Ambrosius and Protectetus, urging them to stand firm in the face of death. Nowhere is Origen's ability to synthesize Platonism and Christian piety more evident.

89. Gregory of Nyssa, *De professioni christiani,* PG 46:col. 244.

90. Gregory of Nyssa, *The Great Catechism* 5, NPF 2nd Series 5:480.

91. Gregory of Nyssa, *On the Making of a Man* 21.1, NPF 2nd Series 5:410.

92. Gregory of Nyssa, *Life of Moses* 1.10, in Abraham J. Malherbe and Everett Ferguson (trans.), *Gregory of Nyssa: The Life of Moses, The Classics of Western Spirituality* (New York: Paulist Press, 1978), 31 (hereafter CWS). Also see Brooks Otis, "Nicene Orthodoxy and Fourth Century Mysticism," *Actes du XIIe Congres International des Études Byzantines, 1961* (Belgrade, 1964), 2:475-484.

93. Everett Ferguson, "God's Infinity and Man's Mutability: Perpetual Progress According to Gregory of Nyssa," *The Greek Orthodox Theological Review* 18, no. 1/2 (1973):59-78.

94. *Life of Moses* 2.45, CWS 64. Gregory of Nyssa, *Against Eunomius* 8, NPF 2nd Series 5:210-211.

95. *De professione christiana,* PG 46:col. 248.

96. *Life of Moses* 2.22, 224; CWS 59, 113.

97. Gregory of Nyssa, *On the Soul and the Resurrection,* NPF 2nd Series 5:450; *Life of Moses* 2.224-225, CWS 113.

98. Ibid., 2.80, CWS 72.

99. *Against Eunomius* 1.22, NPF 2nd Series 5:62.

100. *Life of Moses* 2.121, CWS 82-83.

101. Gregory of Nyssa, *Commentary on Canticles* in Herbert Musurillo (trans.), *From Glory to Glory: Texts from Gregory of Nyssa's Mystical Writings* (New York: Charles Scribner's Sons, 1961), 190 (hereafter *Glory*).

102. *Glory,* 189.

103. *On the Soul and the Resurrection,* NPF 2nd Series 5:450.

104. *Against Eunomius* 8.5, NPF 2nd Series 5:210.

105. *Commentary on Canticles, Glory* 268; *Life of Moses* 2.238-239, CWS 116.

106. *Life of Moses* 1.6, CWS 30.

107. Gregory of Nyssa, *Sermon* 8, *Glory* 212.

108. Gregory of Nyssa, *On the Making of Man* 21.2, NPF 2nd Series 5:410.

109. David L. Balás, *Man's Participation in God's Perfections According to Saint Gregory of Nyssa* (Rome: Libreria Herder, 1966).

110. *Life of Moses* 1.7, CWS 31.

111. Gregory of Nyssa *On Perfection, Glory* 83.

146   STANLEY M. BURGESS

112. *Life of Moses* 1.46, CWS 43.

113. Ibid., 2.166, CWS 96.

114. Ibid., 2.193, CWS 104.

115. See Sister Mary Emily Keenan, *"De Professione Christiana* and *De Perfectione:* A Study of the Ascetical Doctrine of Saint Gregory of Nyssa," *Dumbarton Oaks Papers* 5 (1950):169-207, for a detailed analysis of Gregory's treatment of the Pauline names of Christ.

116. Werner Jaeger, *Two Rediscovered Works of Ancient Christian Literature: Gregory of Nyssa and Macarius* (Leiden: Brill, 1965), 27-35.

117. Gregory of Nyssa, *Against Eunomius*, NPF 2nd Series 5:33-248.

118. Clement of Alexandria, *The Instructor* 2.11-13; *Stromata* 2.23, ANF 2:263-270, 377-379.

119. *Stromata* 6.9, ANF 2:496-497.

120. Clement of Alexandria, *Homily 23 on Numbers*, PG 12:cols. 745-755.

121. See J. T. Muckle, "The Doctrine of St. Gregory of Nyssa on Man as the Image of God," *Mediaeval Studies* 7 (1945):55-84.

122. Tertullian, *On Fasting* 1, *On Monogamy* 1-2, ANF 4:102, 59-60.

123. Tertullian, *An Answer to the Jews* 13, *Scorpiace* 7, ANF 3:171, 639-640.

124. Tertullian, *On the Resurrection of the Flesh* 63, *On Repentance* 7, ANF 3:593, 662-663.

125. *On Repentance* 9, ANF 3:644.

126. *On the Resurrection of the Flesh* 63, ANF 3:587.

127. Clement of Alexandria, *Exhortation to the Heathen* 11, ANF 2:202-204.

128. Clement of Alexandria, *The Instructor* 1.8, ANF 2:225-228.

129. Tertullian, *On Prescription Against Heretics* 7, ANF 3:246.

130. Adolph von Harnack, *History of Dogma* (New York: Dover, 1961), 2:516.

131. *Stromata* 6.17, ANF 2:516.

This essay is a study of perfectionist varieties in the medieval Eastern and Western Christian churches. Stanley M. Burgess examines the perfectionism of four major figures—two mystics, an apocalyptist, and a rationalist—who shared a common pietistic urge to "reach beyond" their contemporaries. They reached beyond in somewhat different directions, however. Burgess suggests that their contrasting hermeneutics and anthropologies in large measure account for their perfectionist differences.

6

MEDIEVAL MODELS OF
PERFECTIONISM

Stanley M. Burgess

N O PERIOD in the history of Christianity has exhibited greater interest in human perfection or has spawned more varied forms of perfectionism than the Middle Ages. Monasticism was in full bloom throughout the era, encouraging both men and women to strive heroically for salvation, with the underlying assumption that both God's grace and human efforts play an important role in salvation. Rules of several new orders and reformed older orders became increasingly exacting as the religious reached beyond fellow Christians in hope of drawing closer to God. The search for vivid symbols of the working of divine grace helped to shape the cult of the saints, who, through their abundance of good works, were said to have merited grace in excess of what was actually required for their own salvation. During the first centuries of the Christian Era, saints were proclaimed informally by local bishops or by popular acclamation. From the late tenth century onward, however, papal officials studied the lives of deceased holy men and women for evidence of piety and verifiable miracles produced by prayer prayed to them since their death. In turn, these individuals became heroes of the faith, to be emulated by those in succeeding generations who desired to achieve Gospel perfection.

This chapter examines the lives and teachings of four medieval models of perfectionism: the Eastern spiritual, Symeon the New Theologian, and three Western ecclesiastics—the apocalypticist Joachim of Fiore, the rationalist Thomas Aquinas, and the mystic Bonaventure. These luminaries have been selected for inclusion because of the diversity of their perfectionism—especially in hermeneutic and anthropology—as well as because of their individual importance to our theme.

THE EASTERN MYSTIC: SYMEON THE NEW THEOLOGIAN

Symeon the New Theologian (949-1022) was born in Galatia in Asia Minor, the son of Byzantine provincial nobles. He early became the pupil of Symeon the Pious at the famous monastery of Constantinople, the Stoudion. Because his father would not permit him to become a monk until he was twenty-seven years of age, Symeon learned to combine life in the busy world with living the interior life of the monk, which he experienced during his night vigils at the monastery. Within three years of his entrance into full monastic life, Symeon was elected abbot of a nearby monastery at Saint Mamas, which was in a state of physical and spiritual decay. There he labored for more than twenty-five years to upgrade both physical structures and the spiritual life of the monks, until conflict with a dissident party of monks within the community and the opposition of Archbishop Stephen, the chief theologian at the emperor's court, led to his exile in the town of St. Marina.[1] Although the exile later was lifted and he was offered the archbishopric as reparation, Symeon chose to spend his last days at Marina, guiding fellow ascetics and composing spiritual writings of great mystical originality.

As occurs so frequently in the history of Christian spirituality, Symeon's concern with perfection grew out of a profound sense of dissatisfaction with the tradition-minded Byzantine church in which theology was taken over by scholasticism, with mysticism or authentic religious experience largely unappreciated and unpracticed. Byzantine Christianity was developing in the direction of greater liturgical and ceremonial richness and order; yet monasticism had become ossified, in part because of inherent formalism, in part because it had attached itself to the emperor and had, thereby, acquired vast worldly goods and land holdings. Monks and laymen alike had assumed a legalistic view of Christianity, limiting the faith to the performance of obligations, which most insisted were outside the possibility of achieving. The new heresy, declared Symeon, was believing that it was impossible to obey the gospel as did the early Fathers.[2] Quite the contrary, he argued that the Kingdom of God was indeed an attainable reality in this life. What that required was for the Christian to return to a radical living of the gospel, with brokenness of spirit, austere ascetic lifestyle, and perfection of the heart through compunction and tears. Then he would receive grace—the indwelling of the Trinity. Through the Holy Spirit he experiences the resurrection, not just in the life to come, but as a present reality. Perfection is experiencing the Kingdom of God within, transforming not just the spiritual or the intellectual part of man, but the entire existence. Through directly experiencing God, man is deified or metamorphosed into a perfect being, a living book, in the here and now.

Symeon's confidence in the perfectability of man in his present mortal state is consistent with the anthropologies of many of the Eastern fathers. Origen, Athanasius, Gregory of Nazianzen, Gregory of Nyssa, and Maximus struggled with the possibility of integrating a Platonic theory of divine "ideas" about the world into a consistent Christian view of creation. Byzantine theology came to understand man as God's special creature, the only one "created in the image and likeness of God" (Gen. 1:26). As the image of God, the ruler over creation and co-creator with the uncreated Maker, man has the responsibility to reflect God in creation, to transform all that exists into the paradise of God. To bear the image of God is to be like Christ, the uncreated Image of God. It is to become by divine grace all that God himself is by nature. Human nature is created by God to grow and develop through participation in the nature of God for all eternity. Man is made to become ever more godlike forever. That human nature progresses eternally in perfection within the nature of God constitutes the meaning of life for man, and remains forever the source of his joy and gladness.

The Fall meant that mankind failed in its God-given vocation, namely, to live in union with God's divine life, and to rule over all creation. It failed to keep its image pure and to retain the divine likeness. Notwithstanding, humanity still remains the created image of God—this cannot be changed. God's provision of salvation is provided through the death and resurrection of Jesus Christ, whereby Jesus provides the perfect image and example of human life as filled with the grace and power of God, whereby man is reconciled to God, and whereby death itself is made to die. Gregory of Nazianzen declares that man has the potential to become divine for Christ's sake, since for us He became man.[3] Gregory of Nyssa proclaims that man now can progress in perfection "from glory to glory" both in time and eternity. Maximus identifies man's growth in the knowledge of God with "deification." For all of the great Eastern fathers before Symeon, participation in the life of God is restoration of that friendship with God which was man's state before the Fall—the state in which God wanted man to live and which was restored through Jesus Christ.

Symeon refers to this restoration as partaking of Christ's resurrection. By this he does not mean the resurrection of bodies at the end of time, but rather the spiritual regeneration and resurrection of the dead souls that takes place in a spiritual manner every day. In resurrection the recipient is introduced by the Holy Spirit to the Kingdom of God, the indwelling of the Trinity which is to be directly and immediately experienced by all Christians through a continual penitential conversion.

This doctrine of the primacy of personally experiencing God grew out of Symeon's own encounter with the indwelling Trinity. At the age of twenty, while he prayed as a sinner for mercy and shed tears of penitence, Symeon received his first vision of God as light. He lost all awareness of his surroundings, seeing nothing but the light of divine radiance appearing from above and filling the room. He sensed that he also had been turned into light. Filled with tears and inexpressible joy, his mind ascended to heaven where he beheld yet another light.[5] His second vision of God as light occurred while he was a novice at Stoudion. Again, he was moved to tears and was in prayer for the mercy of God when he suddenly was overwhelmed by the divine presence. A great light shone on him and he was aware of being lifted outside of himself, forgetting the place where he lay prostrate. He found himself conversing with the light, unaware who was moving his tongue. Every earthly care disappeared, his limbs and muscles seemed to be stripped of the garment of corruption, and an indescribable spiritual joy, perception and sweetness flooded his soul, as the light had filled the room. Symeon came to recognize that he was experiencing not just present ecstasy, but also the manner of the departure from this present life.[6] After the vision faded Symeon heard a divine voice reminding him to continuously cultivate penitence and purity of heart.[7]

In a manner strikingly similar to modern Pentecostals and Charismatics, Symeon's theology of experience included an emphasis on a stage beyond conversion or baptism of water. This is the Baptism in the Holy Spirit, with the accompanying gift of tears.[8] The Spirit alone unveils the treasury of mysteries reserved by God for His children.[9] He is the divine light,[10] the key of knowledge,[11] the key to unlocking the door which is the Son,[12] by whom man becomes the dwelling-place of God.[13] All those who have been baptized in the Holy Spirit—who have experienced the Spirit as a pool of light descending on them, encompassing them in an unutterable manner—have put on Christ completely.[14]

Symeon the New Theologian received the theology of tears from his teacher, Symeon the Studite. While Symeon the Younger's spirituality allows a large place for ecstatic experience, he places an even greater emphasis on repentance, which is preliminary to all spiritual experiences. Tears are based on true compunction (awareness of one's guilt before God) and *penthos* (an abiding sorrow for sin). Compunction—the chief work of the Holy Spirit—is the divine fire that melts mountains and rocks and levels all things, transforming the soul into a paradise garden with a flowing fountain which cleanses from filth those who participate in it. All of this compunction produces through tears.[15] The gift of tears is necessary and should be sought by all Christians.[16] Once received, this supernatural gift must be exercised throughout one's own lifetime, for spiritual warfare never ceases,[17] and there is no true contrition without it.[18] Unless compunction and tears are present, there is no holiness, no perfection. It is not enough to attend the compulsory offices or to wear the habit.[19] Many monks who are technically in compliance with the rules of their order exhibit careless behavior in the church or live deceitfully by pretending love for their fellows.[20] Spiritual gifts, such as that of tears, are essential for true holiness.

In order to receive the gifts of the Holy Spirit and to enjoy His presence, man must first lay a basis of faith and works.[21] The mind, which is in constant motion and incapable of total inactivity, must necessarily be concerned always in practising the commandments of God.[22] The Spirit of God rewards the faithful believer with the chrism of tears by which he then is more quickly lifted up to perfect purification and holiness. Compunction and tears produce the fruits of the Spirit.[23] Symeon encourages his monks to bear fruit for Christ thirtyfold, sixtyfold, and a hundredfold of the things which the Holy Spirit has cultivated within them—namely, love, joy, peace, kindness, goodness, long-suffering, faith, meekness, self-control[24]—so that they will be fed and grow in virtue until they attain to the perfect man, "to the measure of the stature of the fullness of Christ" (Eph. 4:13).

Symeon's efforts to bring his monks back from their low spiritual state to a life of genuine holiness seemed too radical for many of his contemporaries, and was in part responsible for his acute conflict with a group of his monks. In addition, his mystical approach of experiencing God immanently present, and his desire to call monasticism back to a prophetic, charismatic role within the Church, as exhibited in the lives of the ancient saints, frightened several in his own household, as well as Archbishop Stephen. His opponents viewed his message as a new form of enthusiasm, dangerous because it seemed to denigrate hierarchical authority and foster an independent spirit among mystics who felt that they were directly empowered by God to preach and absolve sins, even without ordination to the priesthood.

It was against such as would argue that mankind cannot partake of the Holy Spirit and that the operations of the Spirit are actually the work of Satan that Symeon writes his thirty-second discourse. Distressed by such "blasphemy against the Spirit," he declares that these reprobates are like the Jews of old who saw the miracles performed by Christ, yet insisted that such things could only be explained by drunkenness and demonic activity. They blaspheme who argue that individuals who fulfill the commandments of God and claim to be personally led by the Spirit are actually being deceived by demons. Indeed, retorts Symeon, it is impossible to be saved unless first man has been baptized by water and then has experienced the second baptism—that of the Spirit,[25] whereby he receives adoption as a son of God and is enabled to become like Him—light from Light, true god from true God.[26]

Symeon stands as an important medieval witness of the inevitable tension in the Christian Church between all forms of institutional "establishment" and the freedom of the Spirit.[27] His teaching that renewal and the attainment of perfection are only possible through a life in the Spirit is characteristic of a long tradition among renovators in orthodox Christianity—extending from Basil of Cappadocia (ca, 329-279) to Symeon

the New Theologian, to Gregory Palamas (ca. 1296-1359), to
Seraphim of Sarov (19th century)—who have reminded Christians that the very essence of life itself is the "acquisition of
the Holy Spirit of God." Above all others, however, Symeon
emphasized that man is made perfect in this life by experiencing the indwelling Trinity from whom mankind can share in the
very resurrection of Christ, not only in the final resurrection of
the body, but also in resurrection to life in the present state.

THE PROPHET: JOACHIM OF FIORE

Perhaps the most important prophetic figure of the Middle
Ages, Joachim of Fiore[28] was born at Celico, near Cosenza, ca.
1130, and was raised in the court of Roger II of Sicily where
his father was a notary. He traveled to the Holy Land as a
young man,[29] nearly dying from hunger and thirst en route.
Several of his companions fell victim to the plague while on the
journey. Joachim fell asleep in the desert and had a vision of a
river of oil, and of one standing by it who told him to drink. In
his dream he drank and discovered, when he awoke, that he
understood the entire significance of Scripture. On Easter Day
he is said to have received a second vision in which the substance of what became his three principal books was revealed.[30]

When he returned to Italy he entered a Cistercian monastery
at Sambucina as a layman. Here he had yet another vision—
this time of an angel who offered him a jar to drink. Joachim
drank and returned the jar. The angel responded, "O Joachim,
if thou hadst but drunk it to the last drop, no knowledge would
have escaped thee!"[31]

Shortly thereafter Joachim entered the Cistercian monastery
at Corazzo, where he soon became abbot. He was particularly
disturbed by monastic discipline and began to seek reform.[32] In
that quest, he proceeded to Rome where he presented certain
of his early writings to the pope. Subsequently, Pope Clement
III asked to see all of his writings. Clement, together with two
other popes, Lucius III and Urban III, encouraged Joachim to
write out the rest of his prophecies.[33] This he did in three
major works: the *Exposition of the Apocalypse,* the *Concordance of the Old and New Testaments,* and the *Psalterium of
Ten Strings.*

Having discovered that monastic life at Sambucina was too
demanding given his other work, Joachim was released from

Cistercian obedience and founded the new Order of Flora, which was approved by the papacy in 1196.[34] His order never became large and disappeared in the sixteenth century. Notwithstanding, the prophet was considered a saint by the Calabrians, and kings, queens, popes and princes sought his counsel. After his death on March 30, 1202, attempts were made to have Joachim canonized. Largely because of his criticism of Peter Lombard's trinitarian views, such efforts came to naught.

Joachim had a reputation as a prophet, although he disclaimed the title, arguing instead that God had given him the spirit of understanding the mysteries of Scripture, and of discovering in its pages the whole history of mankind: past, present and future.[35] In this role he developed a coherent new theory of hermeneutics.

Apocalyptic heremeneutics were not new. The Christian Church from the first century depended upon classical Jewish and Greco-Roman apocalypses, such as the Book of Daniel and the Sibylline Oracles. After the establishment of the New Testament canon, Christian apocalypticism grew, stimulated by the Book of Revelation and the growth of the genre of the commentary. By the eleventh century, however, such commentaries had evolved along moralistic lines, rather than for specific application. Joachim's apocalypticism grew out of the twelfth-century tendency to make use of prophecy for identifiable historical events, some already fulfilled, others still to come. At times he prophesied on contemporary events. Many of his prophecies involved the soon-coming of the antichrist. He looked for the return of Christ to inaugurate His millenial reign upon earth in the year 1260. This date was determined by reckoning forty generations since the beginning of the Age of the Spirit which began with St. Benedict (ca. 480-ca. 527).[36] Events in Joachim's own day, such as the aggression of the Saracens, the Crusades, and the rise of the monastic orders, all became signs of the times fulfilling the predictions of the Book of Revelation.

Joachim's writings are a nightmare of apocalyptic allegory and exegesis, for his philosophy of history rested not only on dispensations and three *status* or states, but also upon the imagery of apocalyptic scriptures, the genealogy of Christ, and the symbolism of numbers and letters. Most twelfth-century exegetes understood that Scripture was to be interpreted in four senses: the literal, the allegorical or doctrinal, the moral or tropological (the compiling of tropes—figurative modes of speech stressing moral meanings), and the anagogical or heavenly. Joachim enlarged this number to include the historical, moral, tropological, contemplative, and anagogic.[37] He attempted to show the historical concordance (*concordia*) between the unfolding of history in the Old and the New Testaments.[38] By this he tried to harmonize texts, but also to understand the future, especially the coming third stage of history, because he believed that the knowledge of things past is the key to things to come.[39] But Joachim also had a basic theological motivation, namely, that of understanding the mysteries of the Trinity.

Joachim's theory of interpretation stems from Neoplatonism and is notoriously complex. He reasoned that through the use of number symbolism one could conceive a finite and orderly universe. Numbers were the means whereby the intellect of God becomes intelligible to human comprehension. While he used a variety of numbers, Joachim emphasized a pattern of twos and a pattern of threes in his effort to structure history. The number three is that of perfection—the essence of all things. There are two Testaments and three periods of time (*tempora*) or states (*status*). The pattern of threes and twos is apparent in the Trinity as well. While the Persons are three in number, the Holy Spirit proceeds from two: the Father and the Son.

Joachim is endlessly ingenious and imaginative in the symbolic designs he discovers. For example, the three chief patriarchs, Abraham, Isaac, and Jacob, are in concord with Zacharias, John the Baptist, and Christ,[40] and, of course, typify the three Persons of the Trinity and, in consequence, the three status of history. Isaac, prefiguring the second status, had two sons, Esau and Jacob. So in the second status arose the *ordo clericorum* and the *ordo monachorum*, first in the Greek Church and then in the Latin. The hairiness of Esau signifies the Greek clergy, the smoothness of Jacob signifies the "smoothness" of the true monk of the West.[41]

The Calabrian prophet was a "picture thinker," with many of his most complex and interesting theories available to us only in his celebrated *Book of Figures*. Of these, perhaps the most important for an understanding of his concept of perfection are the several figurae which picture his three ages, especially the one entitled the "Three Trinitarian Circles."[42] Herein

Joachim relates the course of history to three interlocking rings. The first circle in green belongs to the Father and forms the time of the Old Testament, a time which saw the flourishing of the Jews and a lesser growth for the Gentiles. This is the age of the married (*ordo conjugatorum*), the time of the twelve Patriarchs. The middle blue circle, that of the son, interlocks with both extremities, the median that joins the extremes. Now the Gentiles are more fruitful than the Jews. This is the age of the clerics (*ordo clericorum*), the time of the twelve churches. The final flaming red circle of the Holy Spirit indicates the double procession of the Third Person by its intersection with both the green and blue sections. This is the age of the monks (*ordo monachorum*), the time of the twelve monasteries. The internal rubric of *novum testamentum*, which extends from the Age of the Son through the entire Age of the Spirit, shows that the New Testament is not to be superseded. On the other hand, the noninterlocking area of this last circle suggests a coming special era in history, not unrelated, but still superior to what has gone before. Here will be a more abundant outpouring of the Holy Spirit.

According to Joachim's calculations, the Age of the Father extended from Adam to Christ. The Age of the Son reaches from Elisha (ninth century B.C.) or King Josiah (seventh century B.C.) to A.D. 1260. The Age of the Spirit, in which mankind will be perfected, takes its origin from St. Benedict (ca. 480-ca. 527) and the establishment of monasteries in the West, and will last until the end of the world.[43] The first status was under the law, the second status under grace, the third status will be under a more ample grace. To the first belonged *scientia* (knowledge or expertness), to the second *sapientia* (practical wisdom, knowledge of the world), to the third will be that of *plenitudo intellectus* (full or perfection of understanding). The first is the age of slaves, the second the age of sons, the third will be that of liberty. The first was a time of exasperation, the second a time of action, the third will be a time of contemplation. The first was lived in fear, the second in faith, the third will be in love. The first was under slave bondage, the second in freedom, the third will be in friendship. The first was the age of children, the second that of youth, the third will be that of the aged. The first was in starlight, the second in moonlight, the third will be in full daylight. The first was in winter, the second in spring, the third will be in summer. The first age was one of water, the second wine, the third will be that of oil.[44] The three epochs are respectively those of work, of learning, and of praise.[45] This represents spiritual progress, with mankind ultimately conforming in the third status to the monastic ideal.

In order to lead the Church across the Jordan into the Promised Land, from the second to the third status, Joachim anticipated the coming of two new orders of spiritual men,[46] who were both human and, at the same time, divinely commissioned and inspired. Again, the prophecy is based upon the many concords of "twos" which Joachim finds in the Old and New Testaments—the raven and dove of Noah, Moses and Aaron, Joshua and Caleb, Paul and Barnabas, etc. These orders are not "religious" in the traditional sense of withdrawing from the world. Instead these were to be intermediates between the life of contemplation and the active life of secular clergy and laity. There were to be two degrees of involvement in the world: one order would live the hermit life on the mountain top, interceding for the salvation of the world, but finally descending in fiery denunciation of sin.[47] The other would preach among the people, living an active life.[48] One order is given the teaching gift of counsel by the Holy Spirit, the other is made up of perfect students (*predicatores veritatis*) who translate to the hearts of the laity what they have learned from these teachers.[49] One order is likened to the Son of Man seated upon a white cloud, the other to an angel who descends from the Temple in heaven. One will be the order of perfect men, serving the life of Christ, the other, the order of hermits emulating the life of angels.[50]

The third status will see the evangelization of the world, because the new order would be spiritually equipped to evangelize. All peoples, including the Jews, would be converted. The Greek Church would return to its true obedience.[51] While the third age is the best or most perfect time, Joachim is emphatic that the structure and authority of the Roman Church would remain. The new age would not replace, rather it would serve to strengthen the spiritual life of the Church of Rome. The third status is within history, yet not a third set of institutions. This age is to experience a new and higher quality of living which transforms former institutions. The Church of Peter, the *vita activa*, would not be superseded by the Church of

John, the *vita contemplativa*, in the third status.[52] The Church of Peter would remain unshakable in authority until the end of time. However, the *ecclesia contemplativa* would help to lift the *ecclesia romana* to new levels of spiritual understanding and holy liberty, as well as to ecumenism.

The new age was to experience a renewal of monasticism in which there was to be an eruption of the power of the Holy Spirit. But it also was to be an age of progress. It was not merely a prelude to the Day of Doom, but also a great forward step in man's religious education and awareness of God in the framework of a new status or economy.

For the age of the *ordo monachorum* (or even the *ordo hermitarum*), the age of the twelve monasteries, Joachim is prepared to name five great Cistercian abbeys as representing the early period of the status, but will not name the seven mystical and spiritual houses which will characterize the real age of the Spirit. In the Twelfth Table of his *Book of Figures* Joachim describes these houses of the *novus ordo* as follows:

1. The Oratory of the Holy Mother of God and of Holy Jerusalem. This is the Dove, the Seat of God, the Spirit of Counsel, the Nose, the mother of all other houses, in which the Spiritual Father who is over all will live.

2. The Oratory of St. John the Evangelist and of all the Holy Men and Cloistered Nuns. This is the Eagle (Rev. 4:7), the Spirit of Wisdom, the Eye, with approved and perfect men who are aflame with spiritual desire and wish to lead contemplative lives of prayer and singing the psalms.

3. The Oratory of St. Paul and of All the Holy Doctors. This is the Man (Rev. 4:7), the Spirit of Understanding, the Ear, with learned men who devote themselves to reading and apply themselves to spiritual teaching.

4. The Oratory of St. Stephen and of All the Holy Martyrs. This is the Calf (Rev. 4:7), the Spirit of Knowledge, the Mouth, with brethren who are strong in manual labor, but are not able to advance far in spiritual discipline.

5. The Oratory of St. Peter and of All the Holy Apostles. This is the Lion (Rev. 4:7), the Spirit of Fortitude, the Hand, with old and weak brethren who strive to walk according to the purity of the rule insofar as they can.

Between the fifth monastery and the clerics' place (the sixth house) there will be a distance of about three miles.

6. The Oratory of St. John the Baptist and of All the Holy Prophets. This is the Dog, the Spirit of Piety, the Food (Ps. 67:24), a place where chaste priests and clerics will live in common. These will teach boys and young men Latin and help them memorize the Old and New Testaments. In addition, they will devote themselves to other duties which involve contact with the laity.

Between the sixth and seventh oratories there ought to be a distance of about three *stadia* (each *stadium* was an eighth of a Roman mile).

7. The Oratory of Saint Abraham the Patriarch and of All the Holy Patriarchs. This is the Sheep, the Spirit of Fear, the Body (Ps. 94:7-8), in which the married with their children will live in common. Marriage will be for procreation only, idleness will not be tolerated, and tithes will be given to the clerics to support the poor, strangers, and boys who are studying doctrine.

The new order then is many-divisioned. It is sevenfold according to the seven gifts of the Holy Spirit.[53] All men would be brought into the new religious life in which they are inspired by the love of God to despise this world and worldly things. Even the *ecclesia laicorum* has its place in the divine scheme.[54] Clearly, Joachim is a mystic who sees the supreme life only in the silence of contemplation, but nevertheless is aware of the needs of the people at the mountain-foot. The new order bears responsibility for all—they must meditate, they must intercede for souls, and they must labor as well as rest.

The third status would appear in full bloom (*fructificatio*) with a purified Church under monastic leadership, embracing all men in an atmosphere of peace, freedom and contemplation.[55] The realization of the perfect state was dependent upon the direct intervention of the Holy Spirit, who would complete the teachings of Christ and impart to each man knowledge and grace to achieve perfection and to persevere in it, walking in light and truth up to the end.[56] This was the age of which the apostle spoke, ''Where there is the Spirit of the Lord, there is liberty'' (2 Cor. 3:17).[57] This was to be a time of utopian perfection structured on the principles of monasticism in which the various members of Christ's mystical body would achieve great spirituality and harmony of purpose.[58] The process of individual perfection would be completed. The natural man, whom Paul declared (1 Cor. 2:14) did not receive the teachings of the

Spirit of God, would be brought to spiritual maturity, the end of mankind's perfection which is in the heaven of spiritual intelligence.[59]

The rule of Benedict was spirit and life to the monastic institution. Joachim denied the finality of the New Testament as well as the Old Testament. It was not that either Testament had lost its validity, nor were they completely abrogated. In the new age, however, man was not to be fettered by the letter. This was to be an age of the Eternal Gospel, the gospel of the Holy Spirit.[60] This he based on Rev. 14:6, 7, "And I saw another angel fly in the midst of heaven, having the everlasting gospel to preach unto them that dwell on earth, and to every nation, and kindred, and tongue and people, saying with a loud voice, 'Fear God, and give glory to him; for the hour of his judgment is come.' " The third epoch would not receive a new canon, but rather the Holy Spirit would reveal a special understanding of existing Scripture through the gift of spiritual understanding.[61] Thus a new interpretation of the Old and New Testaments and a new form of contemplative worship would evolve.

The spiritual man of the third age would know the truth without veil and would receive directly from the Holy Spirit all the charismatic gifts necessary for perfection. While the church and all of its institutions were fully valid in the present state, they were not the final form of divine revelation. A new form of religion, which would be altogether free and spiritual, would replace the obsolete ecclesiastical order, which struggles over the letter of the gospel.[62] Just as Christ rose from the dead on the third day, so in this third age of history the church would be raised. What would rise, as from the grave of the old church, was a new spiritual church, into which the true lovers of Christ would pass over just as some Jews who believed in Christ had passed over from the synagogue to the church.[63] With the coming again of the Lord in the Holy Spirit there would be a basic change in attitude, for in the spiritual church men would cease being zealous for those institutions that have been established temporarily. The sacraments would be replaced with more spiritualized means of grace, just as they in their turn had replaced the observances of the Old Testament. After all, if God abrogated his law once, He could do it again.[64]

In the new age of the Spirit a new leader, a universal pontiff of the new Jerusalem, would arise. Therefore, the papacy could not continue in the form it had in the twelfth century.[65] In turn, as the institutional church would be transformed into the spiritual church, so the kingdoms of this world would yield to the Kingdom of God. This globe would then become "spiritualized" and heaven would descend upon earth. Spiritual men would feed joyfully in scriptural pastures, with the illumination of spiritual understanding and jubilation of psalmody emerging from the silence of contemplation.[66]

As with most prophecies, Joachim's description of the new age seems less than clear or complete. Precisely what forms of earthly institutions would emerge in the new order is very much open to question. In the words of Marjorie Reeves, "Joachim did not exactly know what the new order would be—like Moses he viewed the promised land, but could not enter it himself."[67] He is hesitant over, and chary of, details about his third age and its implications. Perhaps this is the very reason why so many and varied orders and groups subsequently could see themselves as Joachim's "spiritual men," the agents designated to lead the world into the new age.[68]

Without question, Joachim opened the door for new revelations, a road which was seized by more than one heretic in the late Middle Ages. Certain of his successors, including the fanatical Gerard of Borgo San Donnino, announced in ca. 1254 that the third status was to be found in a book composed of Joachim's chief writings and one of his own, together forming the Eternal Gospel which superseded the Old and New Testaments. The two Testaments were no longer valid, for the spirit of life had departed from them in ca. 1200.

The doctrine of the Eternal Gospel was condemned and the book ordered burned in 1255, just five years before the prophesied beginning of the new era. But in spite of suppression, Joachim's ideas remained a guiding force. Almost immediately after his death many Cistercians, Franciscans and Dominicans began to foster their hopes for the future upon the new ideas of their orders as they related to Joachite eschatology. Fringe groups, such as the Franciscan Spirituals and the Fraticelli conceived themselves as the *novus ordo*, and understood their mission in light of Joachite ideology, especially his expectation of the *renovatio mundi*.

THE RATIONALIST: THOMAS AQUINAS

The greatest philosopher and theologian of the medieval Western church, Thomas Aquinas (1224-1274) was born near Naples and subsequently enrolled at the new university there. At the age of twenty he entered the Dominican Order and was sent to the University of Paris to study theology. There he fell under the spell of the great Dominican, Albertus Magnus, who was investigating the uses of Aristotle's writings for Christian philosophy. Thomas became convinced, as was his mentor, that Aristotle had come to stay, and that Christianity must make terms with him if the church was not to lose the confidence of intellectuals. During his highly productive career as a teacher and writer, Aquinas developed a vast synthesis of Aristotelian philosophy and Christian thought. Predictably, his concept of perfection began with Aristotle's concept of the unmoved mover, which he then molded to be compatible with the Christian idea of God.

Aristotle argued that, because motion must always continue without interruption, there must necessarily be something eternal that imparts motion, but is itself unmoved.[69] Of all qualities known to man, the most divine is that of thought.[70] The highest level of thinking is thinking on thinking, i.e., the divine thinking is one with the object of this thought. The unmoved mover ceaselessly contemplates himself. He cannot do otherwise. Likewise, man's highest function is thinking, and this act is at its highest when man thinks about things divine. When man is guided by intelligence he is most akin to the gods. This kind of human life is most pleasant and the happiest.[71]

Aquinas rethought Aristotle critically as he built up his own synthesis, adopting what he considered compatible with Christian doctrine. In his *Summa contra Gentiles,* written to win converts to the faith, he remoulds Aristotle's concept of the unmoved source of motion into the Christian idea of God. In large measure, this involves an expanding of divine potential and divine function. For example, Aristotle's god, who thinks only of himself, becomes in Thomas's theology a Being who knows all creatures before they exist, whose knowledge is the cause of all things, whether they be forms or matter. Certainly He knows individuals as well as universals, the finite together with the infinite. His knowledge belongs to His perfection.[72]

God, being perfect, [73] directs all of His creation to its proper end which is good,[74] and the greatest good is God himself.[75] Therefore, all things tend to become like God.[76] Things created by a perfect God obtain perfection from Him. It is part of the fullness of perfection to be able to communicate to another being the perfection one possesses. It is God's function to make all things best.[77]

Man cannot be like his Maker in His essence.[78] God's very Being is goodness. Created beings, however, must be improved in the various ways that they fall short of the ideal in order to attain perfection.[79] Therefore, all beings strive in accordance with their nature to the good, aspiring through the achievement of their perfection to God as the final cause and the first cause by imitating Him inasmuch as is possible. The beginning of this effort for virtue lies in one's natural inclinations.[80] Man's striving, however, must always be directed towards an object whose value and perfection has been grasped by the intellect.[81]

God's essence is His love, [82] and His perfection is evidenced foremostly in His love which binds Him to others for whom He wills good.[83] From this is deduced the ultimate human perfection which is the willing of good to someone else.[84] True perfection, according to Aquinas, must combine knowledge with love—love of God and love of our neighbor.[85] Love unites us with God, who is the last end of the human mind. Indeed, to love things divine is even more excellent than to know them.[86] Characteristically, Aquinas's reasoning on this issue takes him a step beyond Aristotle, for whom a life guided by intelligence is the most perfect.

In the garden Adam knew God with a loftier sort of knowledge (ratio) than after the Fall, although he did not see God in His essence as man will in heaven.[87] Knowing the essence of God would have made sin impossible for Adam.[88] Adam knew everything except God's essence without having learned anything. This natural knowledge was divinely infused.[89] Perfection is the restoring of the original harmony of human faculties and desires as in the garden. But in the world to come, perfection also will involve knowing God in His essence. This will be perfect intellection (intellectus) or a knowledge of the complete range of truth which results from an influx of divine light.[90]

In his discussion of whether prayer is an act of reason, Aquinas further differentiates between ratio and intellectus.[91]

The two are not diverse powers in man, but differ as do the perfect and the imperfect. Intellectual creatures, which understand but do not reason, namely angels, are distinct from rational creatures such as man. Prayer is a function proper to rational creatures who are recipients of grace.[92]

Ultimate perfection as will be experienced in the world to come will include *intellectus* or perfect intellection, like that experienced by the angels. Similarly, while man's fellowship with God—the life of mind and spirit—is imperfect in this life, it will be perfected in his final home, where he will see God face to face.[93]

Aquinas considers the contemplative life, the life of prayer or inward communion with God, as superior to the active Christian life which seeks to extend the Kingdom of God on earth. Both are seen as essential to perfection. By the active life man reaches out to help his neighbor and performs works of justice. The good active life performs acts of moral virtue and is a disposition towards and preparation for the contemplative life.[94] Certain kinds of active work, such as study, preaching and teaching, are to be preferred to almsgiving and hospitality, because they demonstrate both the contemplative and the active lives.[95]

The mind of those in religious communities which minister and teach (including the Dominican Order to which Aquinas belonged) already has ascended to contemplation and then returned to the active life to share the fruit of the knowledge of divine life. The contemplative individual experiences the delight of the knowledge of truth and of having seen God whom he loves. The ultimate perfection of the contemplative life is that the divine truth not only be seen, but also loved.[96] When the contemplative and active lives are so combined, when knowledge is coupled with love, the ideal or perfect life is achieved on earth.

In his *Summa Theologia* Question 184 Aquinas asserts that there are three states or stages of perfection in the spiritual life, culminating in the final ultimate state to which the other states are directed. The first state is contemplative life activated by love, the highest perfection attainable in this life. In this condition everything incompatible with love, including mortal sin, is eliminated, although imperfection, including venial sins, still are present. Man must reject anything that would prevent the soul from being directed totally to God.[97]

The second state of perfection is achieved by individuals in heaven, when love is directed to God in its full capacity. This is the stage spoken of by St. Paul in 1 Cor. 13:10: "When that which is perfect is come, that which is in part shall be done away." Aristotle describes this perfection as one in which nothing is lacking,[98] and Aquinas adopts this concept of completeness or absolute totality as the highest level of perfection the human soul can reach.[99]

The third and ultimate state is absolute perfection which is to be found in God alone. God is loved to the extent that He is lovable. Such a perfection is not possible for any creature, whether on earth or in heaven, but is proper to God alone, whose essence is goodness.[100]

In both the *Summa Theologia* and the *Summa contra Gentiles,* as well as in a short treatise, *The Perfection of the Spiritual Life,* written to encourage men and women in religious orders, Aquinas identifies several "counsels" for perfection—recommendations to practices that help to eliminate obstacles to Christian perfection. These include vows of poverty, chastity, and obedience—the renunciation of earthly possessions and earthly ties and matrimony, and the abnegation of one's own will—by which one's disposition consists in detachment of the mind for God.[101] Monasticism, or following the "counsels" is not perfection, but the means of attaining to perfection.[102] Those who take monastic vows are called "religious" because they offer their bodies, their goods, and their will to God as a special kind of sacrifice.[103] The religious state is the short cut to perfection because man merits much more from God when he acts under vow than not. Anyone who is truly wise will take vows.[104]

Aquinas then considers whether such perfection is more obtainable for those who are in religious orders or hold ecclesiastical office. He argues that bishops belong to the state of perfection because they receive the care of souls and their office gives them authority to confer grace and enlightenment to those in their charge. They are the perfectors while those in religious orders are the perfected. It follows then that bishops are in a higher state of perfection than the religious, who are in turn in a higher state than parish priests and archdeacons.[105]

Aquinas's idea of the unity of truth—that truth, whether derived from reason or revelation, is one and comes from God—led him to believe that reason was a sort of preamble to faith, leading man by its light towards a God who created him to participate in divine life. In man's rise to this perfection he could experience God in three ways: first through the natural light of reason, then by revelation of divine truth which exceeds human intellect, and, finally, by the human mind being elevated in the life to come to gaze perfectly upon things revealed.[106] In each state man's mind is the vehicle used by God to perfect the human state.

This elevation of human intellect as the primary receptive agent in man's quest for perfection broke new ground in the Christian West. To be sure, Aquinas's rationalism was severely attacked in condemnations by the bishop of Paris in 1277, and was almost universally rejected by the foremost Christian philosophers of the late Middle Ages, who were anti-rationalists. In the modern church, however, his influence has been enormous. Following the publication of the encyclical *Aeterni Patris* by Leo XIII in 1879, which praised the work and thought of Aquinas, there has been a revival of Thomism in the Catholic Church. Among the most prominent Neo-Thomist scholars are Gabriel Marcel and Jacques Maritain. Vatican II concurs with Thomas in his teaching that faith and reason are "two orders of knowledge" which remain distinct.[107] Aquinas's influence on modern Protestants also is significant, especially for those who take philosophical theology seriously. Among these are the followers of Immanuel Kant, who argued that man should seek to achieve moral perfection, the very idea of which presented to us though our reason should give us the power to achieve through emulation of the Son of God.[108] Contemporary theological concern with human wholeness also reflects Aquinas's awareness that a rational supreme Being reaches out to His rational creatures, seeking to draw them to ever more perfect emulation of himself through the exercise of divinely given reason.

THE WESTERN MYSTIC: BONAVENTURE

John of Fidanza (1221-1274), better known as Bonaventure—a name taken after his entry into religious life, was the most renowned Western medieval mystic. His mystical tendencies

stemmed in part from a close attachment to St. Francis of Assisi, through whose intercession and merits Bonaventure believed that he was rescued from a dangerous childhood ill-
ness.[109] Because of this devotion to Francis and his acquaintance with the Friars Minor at Paris, he entered the Franciscan
Order in 1238 or 1243. In Paris he lectured on the Scriptures
from 1248-1255, and was awarded the doctorate for his commentary on Peter Lombard's *Sentences* and the treatise *De
Paupertate Christi*. At the age of thirty-six he was elected
minister-general of the Friars Minor, replacing the Joachite
John of Parma who had been asked to resign by Pope Alexander IV. Bonaventure served as a healing agent in the order,
managing to preserve its unity despite growing division between the "Spirituals" and Observants. In 1273 he reluctantly
accepted the see of Albano and a cardinalship. Shortly thereafter, he attended the Council of Lyons (1274) where he worked to
achieve reconciliation with the Greek Church. Unfortunately, this
reunion between East and West proved to be short-lived. He died
unexpectedly at the council on July 15, 1274, and was buried the
same day at the Franciscan church in Lyons.[110] Slightly over two
hundred years later (April 14, 1482), Bonaventure was canonized
by Pope Sixtus IV, and on March 14, 1588, Pius V made him the
sixth Doctor of the Universal Church with the title "Doctor
Seraphicus."

Bonaventure's thought is strongly Neoplatonic, being
structured on the threefold movement of emanation,
exemplarism and return—concepts derived in part from
Dionysius the Pseudo-Areopagite, an author who probably
lived in Syria in the fifth or early sixth century A.D. Bonaventure believed that man alone mirrors God as His image, since
he alone can have God as the object of his memory, intellect,
and will. Christ is the exemplar according to which the world is
created, and the model of all perfection—the pattern for all
graces, virtues, and merits. The perfection of Christ is found in
each man, although none fully reflects His plentitude or imitates Him completely. For the man whose eyes are enlightened
by faith together with reason, the world becomes a path that
leads man to God, while through him all material creation is
brought back to its Creator. For Bonaventure mystical theology
is that which teaches man's return to God, and elucidates the
place of divine grace and human cooperation which leads to

that state of perfection. In several of his writings the Seraphic
Doctor deals with both the divine and human roles which make
possible the journey of man's soul to God. His short treatise on
meditation, *The Triple Way,* in which he formulates the idea of
a "threefold way" to spiritual perfection, is perhaps the most
important for our purposes.[111]

Most of Bonaventure's works are geometrically constructed
on a trinitarian frame. In *The Triple Way* the system is particularly elaborate, since it combines several series of threefold divisions. Christ makes provision through three hierarchic acts:
He purges sins, He enlightens man by His example, and He
perfects those who follow in His footsteps. Grace purifies by
sustaining man in his attempt to reestablish clarity of vision and
in gaining for the spiritual eye the upper hand over all the confused tumult of the passions. Grace enlightens, both by removing the obstacles to divine light[112] and by means of revelation.
Grace perfect by bringing man to conformity with the image of
God to the highest degree possible in a creature. In turn, the
Christian must pursue the "triple way" of purgation,
enlightenment, and perfection by responding with three hierarchic acts or interior exercises. These are the three levels of reflective activity: meditation or reading, prayer, and contemplation. The end of these spiritual exercises is spiritual wisdom,
which includes the repose of peace, the splendor of truth, and
the sweetness of love.[113] These ends, in turn, correspond to the
three superior hierarchies of the heavenly spirits: peace, to the
Thrones; truth, to the Cherubim; and love, to the Seraphim.[114]
There are three levels of consciousness by which one may
judge how far he has proceeded along the path to spiritual perfection: imagination (the use of images to discover vestiges of
God), understanding (self-understanding), and affection (leading
to insight into the nature of God).[115] Finally, there are three
degrees of perfection: when the soul is motivated to virtues
which free the soul from improper attachment to worldly
things; when gifts facilitate freedom from evil, acceptance of
Christ as the model, and practising of the virtues; and when
one reaches the level of beatitude, where the soul recovers the
spiritual senses which give a consciousness of directly experiencing God.[116]

The three main divisions of *The Triple Way* center upon the
three levels of reflective activity—meditation, prayer, and con-

templation. Each of these exercises is discussed in connection with the threefold functioning of the soul in purgative, illuminative, and perfective ways. Thus the tract has nine sections: meditation-purgative, meditation-illuminative, meditation-perfective, prayer-purgative, prayer-illuminative, prayer-perfective, contemplation-purgative, contemplation-illuminative, and contemplation-perfective.

Purgation disciplines the outer man or the "old man" by regulating the life of the senses and passions. Man is led to inner peace by examining his conscience and meditating on his own end and on Christ's passion.[117] Illumination disciplines human reason, it enlightens the soul and teaches how to know Christ and to follow Him. In Christ one comes to know the Father and oneself. Through illumination man becomes the image of God and God the final end of human understanding and will.[118] Perfection or union finally brings man to an experiential knowledge of God, which is at once both wisdom and love.[119] While one might anticipate that Bonaventure would view the "triple way" of purgation, illumination, and perfection as three successive steps toward union with God—i.e. the beginning, middle, and end of contemplative activity—they are in reality treated here as correlative aspects of the same spiritual effort.

In meditation proper—the first mode of reflective activity—the soul concentrates on the more cognitive aspects of divine acts, rather than with full affection for God. Conscience must be stimulated, sharpened, and rectified, until the very heart of the soul has been penetrated.[120] In mental prayer or *oratio* one becomes aware of his miserable state, calls out for compassion, and offers devotion. Here there is a definite union of cognition and affection, whereby one develops love for God.[121] The third and final part of the "triple way" deals with the contemplation which leads to true wisdom. Here one gains a knowledge of God which is more perfect than conceptual knowledge or knowledge by way of inference, which is always indirect. This is a knowledge indescribable for one who has not experienced it. In this state the human mind no longer understands by means of concepts, for this is a penetrating knowledge inflamed with love, wherein the greatest energies of the intellect blend together. But even this level of perfection is not equal to that which God reserves for His children in the hereafter—a state which cannot be realized until one has become incorruptible and is mystically united with Christ.[122]

In his better known *Journey of the Soul to God* Bonaventure also recommends the "triple way" of purgation, illumination and perfection according to the threefold law in Scripture, namely, the law of nature, of Scripture and of grace. More specifically, it is the law of Moses which purifies, prophetic revelation which illumines, and gospel teaching which perfects. Bonaventure also suggests a threefold division according to hermeneutic: the tropological meaning of Scripture purifies one in order to be able to live an upright life, the allegorical meaning illumines one so as to understand clearly, and the anagogical meaning perfects one through spiritual ecstasies and sweet perceptions of wisdom.[123]

In 1260 the Seraphic Doctor was commissioned to write *The Life of St. Francis*. As Ewert Cousins has demonstrated,[124] Bonaventure in this work organizes his material according to themes. The first four and the final three chapters provide chronological details on the saint's life, while the middle nine chapters provide an analysis of his virtues according to the categories of the "triple way." Chapters five through seven deal with purgative virtues, including mortification, obedience and poverty. The following three chapters treat affectionate piety, charity and the desire for martyrdom, Francis's zeal for prayer and the power of his prayer—all virtues growing out of illumination. Finally, in chapters eleven through thirteen the reader is introduced to the saint's virtues of perfection—his understanding of Scripture and his spirit of prophecy, the efficacy of his preaching and his grace of healing, and his sacred stigmata.

In *The Life of St. Francis* the saint's virtues of purgation, illumination and perfection appear to be achieved more sequentially than in *The Triple Way*. There seems to be a direct development from the purgation involved in Francis's conversion through illumination of his virtues to the perfection achieved in his stigmata, his passing, his canonization and the extraordinary miracles that flowed from him after his death. Bonaventure recounts in detail Francis's efforts to achieve perfection and to encourage his followers to the same end. Having resolved to be perfect,[125] he began to ascend in stages to arrive ultimately at Gospel perfection.[126] In his rule, Francis insists that if his followers are to be perfect, they must "go, sell all

. . . and give to the poor" (Matt. 19:21), they must take nothing for their journey" (Luke 9:3), and they must deny themselves, take up their crosses and follow the Master (Matt. 16:24).[127] Inspired by a desire for the perfection of Christ and despising the emptiness of worldly things, at first a few, then many, followed Francis's admonitions and personal example.[128]

According to Bonaventure, Francis early achieved the height of perfection obtainable in this life. As if to find means to maintain himself at these lofty heights, Francis tried new ways of punishing his sensual desires by afflicting his body, as if he were beginning the ascent to perfection again.[129] He called his body Brother Ass, for he felt that it should be subjected to heavy labor, beaten frequently with whips, and fed with the poorest food.[130] In order to do everything faithfully and perfectly, Francis used to direct his efforts chiefly to the exercise of those virtues which by the inspiration of the Holy Spirit he knew especially pleased God.[131] To the end of his life his chief desire was to seek means for more effectively reaching the summit of perfection.[132]

Bonaventure addresses his tract *On the Perfection of Life* to those in religious life who seek to reach beyond their fellows.[133] The religious should start at their own level so as to arrive at true self-knowledge and an understanding of how far they yet have to advance. In so doing, they will realize themselves worthless, and, having gained humility, they will more effectively contemplate God, remember Christ's love, and continue in self-examination. The virtue of poverty is absolutely essential in attaining the perfect life. Equally important is the virtue of silence, for it is most unbecoming for the bride of Christ to desire to converse with anyone other than her Spouse. The soul must be trained in constant prayer and devotional exercises, examining all failings, giving thanks, and being concerned for nothing but what one is praying for. Through such exercises, the soul is lifted in devotion, admiration and exultation, finally reaching states of ecstasy. To keep the flame of ardor alive, however, it is necessary to continually remember the passion of Christ. This stimulates the love which leads men to perfection. Finally, Bonaventure reminds his readers that it is absolutely necessary for those in religious life to follow Francis who persevered unto death in the practice of all of these perfecting virtues.

By combining the Eastern mysticism of the Pseudo-Dionysius

with the emerging devotion of the Franciscan order, St. Bonaventure achieved one of the richest syntheses of Christian spirituality. Convinced by the example of his beloved progenitor Frances that mankind could and should reach beyond to Gospel perfection, Bonaventure presents in his rich corpus a vision of the perfect life and a structure for attaining the Christian ideal which still motivates the pious with its depth, power, and wisdom.

CONCLUSIONS

This portrayal of four medieval models of perfectionism is essentially a study in contrasting hermeneutics and anthropologies. While Symeon, Joachim, Thomas Aquinas, and Bonaventure shared a tendency of the period to esteem most highly those in holy orders and to insist that perfection is more readily achieved by the religious, underlying differences in approach and in their doctrines of man resulted in sharply contrasting visions of the perfect.

To be sure, the Eastern mystic, Symeon the New Theologian, and the Western mystic, Bonaventure, shared many common grounds. The Seraphic Doctor, like his Eastern counterpart, was deeply influenced by Neoplatonic thought. Consequently, both mystics present a negative theology which places God outside mere human reach or understanding. Man of necessity is dependent on a vision of God and the illumination of the uncreated Light, symbolic of divine grace by which man is perfected or restored to the full image of God and united at last with the heavenly Groom. Within their common mystical framework, however, subtle but significant differences surface. Symeon's pathway to perfection is marked by an ongoing practice of compunction and tears and a series of direct experiences with God by which one is deified or metamorphosed into a perfect being in the here and now. In this he is consistent with Eastern Christian anthropology which recognizes that the Kingdom of God is indeed an attainable reality in this life, and that man can be perfected in his present mortal state. While Bonaventure shows strong traces of Eastern Christian influence, he nevertheless follows Western anthropology, allowing for experiential knowledge of God in its fullness only when man is united with his Maker, and as a consequence, attains ultimate perfection. If one wishes to experience God in the present state, he must participate in the sacraments administered by the ecclesiastical hierarchy and descend by grace into his own heart. He then will be transported in ecstasy above the intellect to a beautific vision of God—an experience of the mind that transcends the mind, going beyond intellectual understanding to existential desire.

According to Joachim, those who would be perfect must wait, not on divine light or experience, but rather for a third age vivified by the Holy Spirit during which spiritual men would lead a purified Church in an ideal environment of peace, freedom, and contemplation. This dispensational perfectionism was shared not only by the Joachites, but also by most medieval millenialists who believed in a coming age when the world would be inhabited by a humanity at once perfectly good and perfectly happy.[134]

Unlike the mystics, Thomas Aquinas did not look to a realm of unknowing or to an experience of beautific vision in his quest for perfection. Nor did his world and life view lend itself to dispensational interpretations. He reasoned that the perfect state attainable on earth is the restoration of that harmony of human faculties and desires which man enjoyed in the Garden of Eden. Because of His supreme goodness, God shares with mankind His knowledge and love, both of which belong to His perfection. Man's striving for true perfection must begin with an intellectual understanding of God who is man's pattern, and is completed by combining that knowledge with divinely given love. Again, because of his Western anthropology, Thomas asserts that the perfection attainable in the present life is not equal to that to be experienced by man in paradise. In turn, man cannot ever attain to ultimate perfection—a state which is reserved for God alone.

While each of the four medieval perfectionists described in this chapter were at one time or another considered to be heroes of the faith, three of them also experienced resentment and even rejection. The sole exception was Bonaventure who, because of his active role in reconciling differing factions in the Church, escaped much of the antagonism which befell the others. Symeon's monks and even his archbishop resisted his doctrine of the immediacy of God's presence and power, and his encouragement of those around him to rise to higher levels of perfection through the direct assistance of the gifts of the Holy Spirit. He was removed as abbot at Saint Mamas and exiled. Joachim suffered the antagonism of schoolmen for his critique of Peter Lombard's *Sentences* and because of the extremism of certain followers after his death. These reasons, coupled with the fact that no new age dawned around the year 1260, resulted in his apocalyptic system falling into institutional disrepute and efforts to canonize him being unsuccessful. Thomas Aquinas, unfairly linked with more radical rationalists such as the Averroist Siger of Brabant, was condemned three years after his death by the bishop of Paris in a series of 219 propositions which decried the use of reason in understanding things divine.

This study of selected medieval perfectionist systems has demonstrated that in this period the thirst for perfection was intense, superseding geographic boundaries, as well as hermeneutic and doctrinal differences. It also is clear that those who sought to be perfect were not always heroes to the faithful, but also were subject to misunderstanding and scorn. Perhaps this always was and always will be the fate of those who "reach beyond."

NOTES

1. See Hieromonk Basil Krivocheine, "The Most Enthusiastic Zealot," *Ostkirchliche Studien* 4 (1955): 108-128.

2. Symeon the New Theologian, *Catechetical Discourses* 27 (henceforth Cat.). English translation in C.J. deCatanzaro (trans.), *Symeon the New Theologian: the Discourses* (New York: Paulist Press, 1980).

3. Gregory of Nazianzen, *Oration on Easter* 5; *Nicene and Post-Nicene Fathers* (Grand Rapids, MI: Eerdmans, 1978), 7:203.

4. Gregory of Nyssa, *Commentary on Canticles*, in Herbert Musurillo (trans.), *From Glory to Glory: Texts from Gregory of Nyssa's Mystical Writings* (New York: Charles Scribner's Sons, 1961), 268.

5. Cat. 22.89-105.

6. Cat. 16.79-108.

7. Cat. 16.142-144.

8. Symeon also claimed the gift of tongues, although this was to him insignificant in comparison with the greater gifts. See Patrick Thompson trans.), "A Prayer to God of St. Symeon the New Theologian," *Sobornost* no. 6 n.s. (June, 1936): 20.

9. Cat. 24.101-120.

10. Cat. 33.36, 32.80-82.

11. Cat. 33.80-95.

12. Cat. 33.96-109.

13. Cat. 33.156-175.

14. Cat. 32.80-82; Jean Darrouzes (ed.), *Chapitres Théologiques, Gnostiques et Practiques*, in *Sources Chrétiennes*, 3:43.14-22.

15. Cat. 4.422-452.

16. Cat. 29.209-234.

17. Cat. 4.494-573.

18. Cat. 4.574-623.

19. Cat. 4.155-208, 9.331-333.

20. Cat. 4.209-326.
21. Cat. 10.49.60.
22. Cat. 10.94-98.
23. Cat. 4.360-402.
24. Gal. 5:22-23.
25. Cat. 32.59-730.
26. Cat. 32.105-109, 34.371-373.

27. See especially Stanley M. Burgess, *The Spirit and the Church: Antiquity* (Peabody, MA: Hendrickson Publishers, 1984), 3ff.

28. The sources of Joachim's life, as found in the *Acta Sanctorum* 7 (May), are the biographies by Luke of Cosenza (thirteenth century) and Jacobus Graccus Syllanaus (sixteenth century), and an account of his miracles by James the Greek (early seventeenth century).

29. Joachim of Fiore, *Tractatus super quatuor Evangelia,* edited by Ernesto Buonaiuti (Rome: Tipografia del Senato, 1930), 93 (henceforth TSQE).

30. Joachim of Fiore, *Expositio in Apocalypsim* (Venice, 1527; reprint edition, Frankfurt/M: Minerva, 1964), 39^r (henceforth EA); *Liber Concordia novi ac veteris Testamenti* (Venice, 1519; reprint edition, Frankfurt/M: Minerva, 1964), 1 (henceforth LC).

31. TSQE 97^v

32. In EA 80^r-81^r Joachim complains about those neglecting their monastic rules.

33. LC pref., EA 1^r.

34. Philipp Jaffe ed., *Regesta Pontificum Romanorum,* (Graz: Akademische Druck- u. Verlagsanstalt, 1956), 1:no. 17425.

35. Ralph of Coggeshall, *Chronicon anglicanum . . . ex codicibus manuscriptis editit Josephus Stevenson* (London: Longmans, 1875), 68.

36. LC 134^r, *Psalterium decem chordarum* (Venice, 1527; reprint edition, Frankfurt/M: Minerva, 1965), 272-277 (henceforth PDC).

37. Joachim's understanding of Scripture "according to the Spirit" (*secundum spiritum*) is to be found in LC 60^r-61^v, EA 26^{r-v}, and PDC 264^r-266^r, 271.

38. EA 39^r.

39. EA 3 .

40. LC 8-10^r, 26^v.

41. LC 26^v.

42. *Il libro della figure dell'abate Giochino da Fiore di Leon Tondelli, Marjorie Reeves e Beatrice Hirsch-Reich,* second edition (Torino: Societa editrice internazional, 1953), plate 11b (henceforth LF).

43. EA 5^v, LC 8^r-10^r.

44. LC 112^r.

45. PDC 224^v-247^v.

46. LC 16^v, 19^r, 21^v. 67^r-68^v, 76^r-78^v, 83^v, 85^v, 88^v-90^r, 103^v, 115^v, 133^v; EA 49^r, 64^{r-v}, 75^r, 84^r, 128^r, 137^r, 184-187^r, 196^r, 206^r, 217^v, 222^r. See also a work often attributed to Joachim, *Super Hieremiem,* pref., 31-32.

47. LC 68^r.

48. LC 185^v.

49. LF plate 3.

50. Later Joachim's famous prophecies of two new orders became inextricably associated with the two great mendicant orders. Joachim's conception, however, was of two bodies of men fulfilling quite different functions.

51. EA 5^v, LC 85^v.

52. EA 141^v-143^r.

53. EA 22^r, 48^r.

54. LC 100^r.

55. LF plate 14.

56. LC 111, EA 106.
57. LC 112^v.
58. LC 71^r.
59. LC 6^v.
60. EA 95^v. Joachim never called his writings the Eternal Gospel.
61. LC 9^r, 10^r, 18^r, 103^v; EA 9-10, 86^v, 99^r, 115^r, 128^v.
62. TSQE 1.
63. LC 95^v, TSQE 3.
64. LC 103^r.
65. LC 103^r.
66. LC 133^r, EA 84r-86^v.
67. Marjorie Reeves, *Prophecy in the Later Middle Ages*
Oxford: Clarendon Press, 1969), 146.
68. Perhaps this is the very reason why so many and varied orders and groups subsequently could see themselves as Joachim's "spiritual men," the agents designated to lead the world into the new age.
69. Aristotle, *Physics* 8.10, *Metaphysics* 11.7.
70. Aristotle, *Metaphysics* 12.7.
71. Aristotle, *Nichomachean Ethics* 10.7.30, 10.8.25.
72. Thomas Aquinas, *Summa Contra Gentiles* 1.49-50, 52, 66-67 (henceforth SCG); *Summa Theologia* Ia.14.8-11, Ia.70 (henceforth ST).
73. SCG 1.23.
74. SCG 3.2-3.
75. SCG 3.17-18.
76. SCG 3.19, 115.
77. SCG 3.69.15-16.
78. SCG 3.53.
79. SCG 3.20. Cf. 1.29.
80. ST I.II.9.1.5, 19.3.5.
81. ST I.II.94.2, 27.1.3, 16.3.
82. ST Ia.20.3. Cf. Aquinas, *The Perfection of the Spiritual Life* 3 (henceforth PSL).
83. SCG 3.116.
84. ST Ia.20,1.
85. SCB 3.116-119, PSL 2.
86. ST I.II.66.6.
87. SCG 3.47.
88. ST Ia.94.a.
89. ST Ia.94.d.
90. SCG 3.53.
91. ST II.II.83.10.2.
92. ST II.IIae.83.10.
93. ST II.II.23.1. Cf. SCG 4.1.5, in which Aquinas interjects an intermediate level of knowledge of things divine: that of revelation of divine truth which exceeds human intellect.
94. ST II.II.181.4.
95. ST II.II.1876.6.
96. ST II.II.180.7.
97. ST II.II.184.2.
98. *Physics* III.6.207.8.
99. ST II.II.184.2.
100. Ibid. See also SCG 1.28.
101. ST II.II.184.3, SCG 3.130, PSL 6-14.
102. ST I.II.108.4.
103. SCG 3.130.6.

104. PSL 12.

105. ST II.II.184.7-8.

106. SCB 4.1.5.

107. Walter M. Abbot (ed.), *The Documents of Vatican II* (New York: Guild Press, 1966), 265.

108. Immanuel Kant, *Religion Within the Limits of Reason Alone,* trans. T. H. Greene and H. H. Hunson (La Salle, IL: Open Court Publishing Company, 1960), 3, 79, 110.

109. *Analecta franciscana* 10.558, 678.

110. Ibid., 3.356.

111. Jose de Vinck (trans. and ed.), *The Works of Bonaventure,* I *Mystical Works* (Paterson, NJ: St. Anthony Guild Press, 1960), 59-94. The medieval concept of the triple way of purgation, illumination and perfection as the classical way of formulating the dynamics of spiritual growth was derived from the writings of Pseudo Dionysius (see especially *De Coelesti Hierarchia* 3.2, 7.3, 9.2, 10), although the notion also is present in St. Basil of Cappadocia (*On the Holy Spirit* 9.23, 26.61) and certain of the Alexandrian fathers.

112. Compare Bonaventure's concept of God as inaccessible light (*The Triple Way* 3F in Vinck I) with that of Symeon the New Theologian.

113. *The Triple Way* 2.12.

114. Ibid., 3.1, 3.14.

115. Ibid., 3.6

116. Ibid., 3.14.

117. Ibid., 1.3-9.

118. Ibid., 1.10-14.

119. Ibid., 1.15-18.

120. Ibid., 1.

121. Ibid., 2.

122. Ibid., 3.

123. Bonaventure, *Journey of the Soul to God* 4.6. English translations include Vinck I, and Ewert Cousins (trans.), *Bonaventure* (New York: Paulist Press, 1978). Cf. to the moral, allegorical, and mystical hermeneutics given in *The Triple Way* prologue.

124. Cousins, 42-44.

125. Bonaventure, *The Life of St. Francis* 1.5 in Cousins.

126. Ibid., 1.6.

127. Ibid., 3.3 On poverty also see 7.1, 3.

128. Ibid., 4.7

129. Ibid., 4.7.

130. Ibid., 5.6.

131. Ibid., 12.1.

132. Ibid., 12.2.

133. Bonaventure, *On the Perfection of Life,* in Vinck 1.

134. See especially Norman Cohn, *The Pursuit of the Millennium* (New York: Oxford University Press, 1977), for examples of these medieval millennialists.

Gerrit J. tenZythoff

Gerrit J. tenZythoff was born and educated in The Netherlands, earning the equivalents of both the B.A. and M.Div. degrees at the University of Utrecht. In 1951 he emigrated to Canada where he served as pastor of the Reformed Church in America among Dutch immigrants. He earned the S.T.M. degree at the Union College, University of British Columbia, Vancouver, B.C. He earned both M.A. and Ph.D. degrees from the University of Chicago. He taught at Western Theological Seminary in Holland, Michigan; the Ohio State University; and in 1969 he founded the Department of Religious Studies at Southwest Missouri State University and served as its first head, a position which he held until 1981. Since that time he has continued to serve as Professor of Religious Studies. Among his publications is *The Dutch in America*. His volume on the ecclesiastical background of those Dutch who came to the United States in 1847 is in preparation.

This essay reexamines the question of John Calvin's influence on the history of perfectionism. The author argues convincingly that Calvin opposed the widespread notion that man could and should be made perfect. Instead, the great Reformer believed that, under the tutelage of the Bible, man's condition could be ameliorated. Important clues to his position are to be found in his education and development. "The Non-Perfectionism of John Calvin" focuses on these clues.

7

THE NON-PERFECTIONISM OF JOHN CALVIN

Gerrit J. tenZythoff

JOHN CALVIN was born in the ancient city of Noyon, located in Picardie about seventy miles northeast of Paris. The year was 1509. By this time Noyon had been already a Christian city for over a thousand years. As early as 530 it had been made a bishop seat. Charlemagne was crowned here in 768, as was Hugh (987), the first of the Capetian kings of France. Noyon was never a large town, presently with a population of approximately 12,000; but its institutions were well established by the time John Calvin was born here, the fourth son of Gerard Cauvin.[1]

Father Cauvin had come from a humble family of skippers on the river Oise. He had successfully moved up in Noyon: from fiscal agent of the city to secretary to Bishop Charles de Hangest, and finally becoming the attorney of the cathedral chapter.[2] John's mother was Jeanne Lefranc, the daughter of an innkeeper at Kamerijk who had moved to Noyon. John later recalled how his devout mother would take him as a small boy to the churches in and around Noyon where they would pay homage to the numerous statues of saints and their relics. Mother Jeanne died early. Father Cauvin remarried, but very little is known about his second wife.[3]

John received an excellent education. Not only had father Cauvin enrolled him in the Collège des Capettes, a boys' school at Noyon, but he also managed to have his son John participate in the private home schooling of the children of the prominent Hangest-Montmor and the Hangest-Genlis families.[4] From this kind of exposure John Calvin acquired early an air of aristocracy in thought and behavior that never left him.

Nevertheless, John was an obedient son who faithfully followed the directions of his father who succeeded in having his son, at the age of twelve, receive the income of a chaplain from the cathedral at Noyon. As was the custom of the time, the chaplain's work did not have to be performed by the recipient of the income but could be assumed by a substitute, usually from a lower social class, who in turn would be paid but a small percentage of the official salary.

ON THE WAY TO PRIESTHOOD

In 1523, when his gifted son was fourteen years old, father Cauvin sent him to Paris to complete there his education for the priesthood.[6] John's serious personality had given his father the strong impression that this withdrawn, shy son would indeed be at home in the priesthood. John was not satisfied to know for himself what was right and to act accordingly; he concerned himself with people around him and the way they conducted their lives. His classmates would later remember him as the strict "censor" of their mistakes and improprieties.[7]

John took schooling very seriously. But he also enjoyed the hospitality of his blacksmith uncle Richard as he attended the Collège de la Marche. Although these happy days lasted but a few months, the excellent teaching of his Latin instructor Mathurin Cordier gave John a lifelong superior knowledge of Latin and the classical authors.[8] When Calvin left the Collège de la Marche to join the Collège de Montaigu, he did so at the instruction from Noyon. The chapter authorities there wanted their student, supported by one of their prebends, to be under the more strictly ecclesiastical instruction and supervision of the Collège de Montaigu. Lefranc makes the point that no young student at the University of Paris would voluntarily have chosen Montaigu because it had the reputation of being a dirty place with a poor kitchen. Its instructors made liberal use of the whip to keep the students in line.[9]

Calvin used his time at Montaigu to best advantage, enjoying particularly the Scottish theologian John Mair who made Calvin familiar with medieval philosophy, the church fathers, and especially Aristotle. Calvin learned to debate in the course of his four years at Montaigu; it became almost his second nature. In later years Calvin would denounce the "absurdities, childish arguments, and follies" of Montaigu's methods, but during his time there he gave no evidence that its strict Roman Catholicism had come into question at all.[10]

Several historians later depicted Calvin as withdrawn from the world, somber, with hardly any friends. Typical is Florimond de Raemond who compared Calvin to a bat and other birds of the night which do not appear unless it is getting dark.[11] The truth, however, is that Calvin made many new friends during this time. They introduced him among others to the Swiss born Dr. Guillaume Cop, professor of medicine at the University of Paris and personal physician to Francis I, king of France. Of the four sons of professor Cop[12] whom Calvin befriended, the oldest, Nicolas, was on most intimate terms with Calvin.

REFORM IN FRANCE

In August of 1523, Calvin had entered Paris to study for the priesthood. That very same month Jean Vallière was here burned to death, an Augustinian monk who had joined the heresies of a brother monk in the same order—Martin Luther.[13] There is no evidence that young John Calvin at this time had been won for Luther's views, although the writings of the German reformer were circulating in France as elsewhere.[14] Reformation scholars are agreed, although not to the same degree, that Luther's influence at the time was widespread enough in France that Calvin could readily have joined the movement, or at least more readily sympathized with it, had he wanted to do so.

Nor was France without its native movements toward reformation. Erasmus had strong groups of followers here. Humanists all, they desired to bring about renewal by remaining loyal to the church of old. A typical example was Guillaume Budé, perhaps the strongest influence among them. He had defended Luther as early as 1519, but by 1521 he was no longer willing to support him. The teachings of the Wittenberger monk had begun to cause the kind of social changes that Budé would not support. As Johan Huizinga typified so aptly: "The philologist Budaeus, even more strongly than Erasmus, was of the opinion that faith was a matter of learning."[15] Erasmus and the humanists who followed in his train were first and foremost educators. There was in Erasmus' life no road to

Damascus.[16] He was the man "who was too smart and too modest for heroism."[17] Huizinga characterizes the tragic aspect of Erasmus and the Erasmian humanists as that rather rare group of people

> who are simultaneously complete idealists and in everything moderate. They are unable to tolerate the imperfection of the world, but they don't feel at home with the extremists; they shudder at [the thought of] action, and thus they withdraw, and they continue to call out that everything has to be changed, but when the crisis comes they choose reluctantly the part of tradition and conservatism. Here too is [to be found] a part of the tragic in Erasmus' life: he was the man who saw the new and what was to come more clearly than anyone else, the man who inevitably would get into conflict with the old and yet could not accept the new.[18]

Humanists shared the convictions of Erasmus in their own way, and so did Calvin.[19] Any thought Calvin may have had about perfection at that time would have been in terms of being unable to tolerate the imperfection of the contemporary world. But Calvin had no plan at all to work toward reform outside the church and society of which he was a part.

FUNDAMENTAL CHANGE?

It is true that Calvin discontinued his studies for the priesthood in 1528 after his father instructed him to switch to the study of law. And so, not quite twenty years old, Calvin enrolled first at Orleans[20] to read law with Pierre Taisan de l'Estoile, alias Petrus Stella. A year later Calvin enrolled in Bourges. When l'Estoile was attacked for his views, it was Calvin who joined his friend Nicholas Duchemin to defend their teacher. l'Estoile was certainly no reformer but was instead one of Luther's sharpest critics.[21] Calvin's shift from theology to law had not been inspired by a desire to join Luther's or anybody's more radical reformation.

In the *Preface* to his *Commentary on the Psalms,* written almost thirty years later in 1557, Calvin summarized the motivation for this sudden shift in financial terms: clerics made less money than lawyers.[22] But this is hardly the whole truth. In May of 1531 Calvin had been called home to Noyon. His father was so seriously ill that he died, May 26. The Calvin family found itself in the embarrassing situation that the earthly remains of father Gerard were not to be given an ecclesiastical funeral because the old man had been excommunicated in 1529, apparently as the result of a battle over documents he had been unwilling to handle the way the cathedral chapter of Noyon had wanted. The sons succeeded in having the excommunication nullified when the documents were turned over. Thus the funeral could be completed.[23] Father Calvin's fight at Noyon was probably a factor in the decision to have his son John leave Paris and enroll at Orleans. Whatever sympathies for the budding Reformation the Calvin family may have shared, these feelings were at this time not strong enough to break with the church.[24]

This is not surprising. Although many members of the church were dissatisfied with the church's current condition, few were ready to break away. Thus it was quite normal for John Calvin, after his father's funeral, to return to Bourges, one of the three universities in France at which, according to Theodore Beza, Protestant thought had begun to blossom.[25] At Bourges, Calvin had started to learn Greek under the great German-Swiss scholar Melchior Wolmar. Calvin had liked Wolmar very much, as is clear from his *Commentary on II Corinthians* which he dedicated to Wolmar.[26] Doumergue was to write later that Wolmar and Calvin were reading the New Testament in Greek.[27] Florimond de Raemond wrote in 1605 that Calvin had become known by the nickname "le petit grec," the little Greek, and added that Wolmar had been the "foreigner who had inspired the poison of heresy in the soul of this young man."[28]

Calvin was certainly influenced by Wolmar, but he was not as yet seeking to perfect church and society the way he would later. While at Bourges, Calvin would on occasion preach at Lignières, a village in the county of Berry. There was nothing illegal about this activity. In 1529 Calvin had been awarded the priest's income of the church at Pont l'Évèque on the river Oise. This made him the nominal priest whose pastoral work was performed by a lower paid cleric hired for that specific purpose. Such an arrangement was very common, and because of it Calvin shared with many others the status of *presbyter curatus*, who had the necessary status in the church to preach but who was not permitted to administer the sacraments.[29] As preacher Calvin was popular because of his eloquence. Besides, he knew his Bible well and combined his learning, including the use of Greek, in felicitous ways with his obvious piety.[30] Philbert de Beaujeu, local landlord at the time, observed that Jean Calvin in his sermons would get right into the heart of the matter and was a better preacher than the monks.[31]

NOT YET THE REFORMATION

Following the death of his father, John Calvin was no longer bound by his wishes. Now free to determine his life's direction, Calvin changed indeed, but not yet in the direction which was to establish him as one of the great reformers. The "sudden conversion" of which Calvin speaks in the *Preface* to his *Commentary on the Psalms* was still to take place.[32]

Calvin returned briefly to Bourges where he had earlier earned his licentiate in law. The presence of Wolmar and the opportunity to preach at Lignières, as well as possibly elsewhere in the realm of Queen Margaretha of Navarre, were not strong enough to prevent a second major shift in Calvin's academic training. He returned to Paris.

Calvin was able to pursue further studies because the cathedral chapter at Noyon had decided to let difficulties with the father not influence its support of the son. Thus Calvin continued to draw the income from the prebend at Pont l'Évèque.

Late in June of 1531, a month after his father had died, Calvin wrote to his friend François Daniel at Bourges that he had weathered the summer heat on his arduous but safe journey to Paris.[33] He reported further that he was now trying to find living quarters close enough to the lectures being presented in the new Royal College.

King Francis I had chosen to follow the advice of his confessor, father Etienne Poncher, the bishop of Paris, and other humanists like Budé and Cop, to start a Collegium Trilingue where one could study Greek and Hebrew in addition to Latin. Beza wrote that

> the Sorbonne opposed all of this with such fury that, if one had wanted to believe our instructors, to study Greek and to be even a little involved with Hebrew would be one of greatest heresies in the world.[34]

In March of 1530 the Royal College began its lectures. It was literally unable to open its doors because a permanent building had not yet been constructed. The five professors, known as *regii interpretes* or "royal interpreters," had to lecture without the security of funded chairs. But all courses were open to anyone and free of charge. The Sorbonne tried to scare stu-

dents away by accusing the "royal interpreters" of
Lutheranism. This tactic failed. Abel Lefranc observed in his
history of this remarkable College that "the intellectual eman-
cipation, the most precious of which the modern world can
boast, dates in truth from this movement."[35]

Calvin came to the Royal College in order to study classics,
especially under Pierre Danès who was lecturing on Aristotle's
Ethics. Calvin wrote in retrospect that he had always liked for
himself "the shadow and quietude," for he had wanted to
spend his days "without fame."[36] And, indeed, Calvin worked
hard toward his goal of being just a scholar. It is probable that
Danès's lectures strengthened Calvin's resolve to make his
mark as a humanist by way of a commentary on Seneca's *De
Clementia*. But by choosing this direction for his life Calvin
would find himself at the watershed of Renaissance and
Humanism so clearly delineated by Erasmus in his
Ciceronianus.[38] Many humanists at the time shared Erasmus'
hope for a more perfect civilization on the basis of classical
studies which were to serve the purification of the church. But
some of these humanists would not so use the classics at all.
They preferred the paganism of the classical period to the
Christianity which had conquered that world and some of the
humanists were now even practicing such paganism.[39]

Following the example of Erasmus, John Calvin considered
the classics as a way of life, for there was a church to be
purified. Although a law student, he had used his status of
presbyter curatus to preach the gospel at Lignières. Now that
he actually had become a student of the classics under Danès,[40]
Calvin continued his concern for the church and its purification. This aspect of John Calvin is uniquely revealed in his letter of 27 June 1531 to François Daniel in which he includes a
report of his visit to the monastery for nuns where François'
sister was a novice about to complete her vows.[41]

> Sunday I went to the monastery, accompanied by Cop who had offered to
> come along, in order to determine a day on which your sister might take her
> vows, as you requested me to do. While he negotiated [the date] with the
> Abbess, I tried to examine your sister's inclination. Would she be able to
> accept this yoke in humility? Would she accept it on a patient-or rather a
> broken back? Again and again I encouraged her to speak freely to me about
> everything that was in her heart. Never did I see stronger eagerness and
> preparedness, as if her desire could no longer bear delay. One might say that
> she was playing with dolls every time she heard [me] mention her vows. I
> did not want to change her resolve because I had not gone there for that

purpose; but with a few words I admonished her to rely not too much on her own strength, nor to promise herself blindly to the deity, but to rely completely on the merciful strength of God in whom we are and live.[42]

The church in which Calvin grew up was at this time still *the* church for him. And it is fair to add that Calvin never lost his zeal for this church. On the contrary, as Calvin later denied Cardinal Sadoleto's charge that the reformers were "homines novi," new people, "who had taken the Scriptures in mouth and hands" only to substitute new doctrines for old truth,[43] he insisted "we honor her (the church) as a mother and we wish to remain in her bosom."[44] With great intensity he denied Sadoleto's accusation that the Reformation was "the very own work of Satan and not of God."[45] Calvin did not deny the growing chasm, but he refused to deny that in the church of Rome nothing was to be found of Christ's church, although only certain "sparse and lacerated vestiges" of the true church did remain.[46] Calvin ended his response to Sadoleto with an emotional prayer:

It is to you, O Lord, to declare with whom rests the guilt. Both in words and deeds, I have always demonstrated what love for unity inspired me. For me, however, only that was the true unity of the church which had its beginning and end in you. For as often as you offered us peace and unity, you showed us at the same time that you are the only bond (able) to keep that unity.[47]

This letter also includes the following reminiscence of his earlier years: "As I had been educated since childhood, O Lord, so have I always confessed the Christian faith."[48] This claim is certainly born out by the role Calvin assumed when visiting Daniel's sister on the eve of her profession as bride of Christ. Reformation of the church was needed, but the improvement would have to be made internally. Characteristically, Calvin was very frank about the matter in his response to Sadoleto:

While I observed somehow all of these (matters of faith), and even found some rest in it, I was still far removed from the tranquil certainty of conscience. For as often as I descended into myself, or lifted up my soul to you, extreme fear would come over me of which no sacrifices or penitences could cure me. And the sharper I observed myself, my conscience would prick me with sharper stings, so that no way out remained than to phantasize forgetfulness. Since nothing better offered itself, I continued the road on which I had set out, while in the meanwhile a very different form of doctrine was raised up which was not to turn us away from the Christian confession but was to return (that confession) to its own source and, having cleansed it from its impurities, was to restore it to its own purity. I, however, was offended by its novelty and hardly lent it an ear; from the beginning, I must confess, I resisted it strenuously and proudly. . . . One thing in particular turned my spirit away from these things: my reverence for the Church.[49]

Calvin wrote this reflection in April of 1539 when the memory of Danès and the other royal lecturers was only eight years old. At the time the consequences of one's choices with respect to the church were far reaching. Supporters of Luther and "radical" reformers like De la Forge paid with their life for the choice they made. Even moderates like Le Fèvre d'Étaples were neither secure in their positions nor certain of their lives. King Francis's decision to open the Royal College seemed to offer the most promising way to obtain the much needed reform at last. Calvin was among those who chose the classics as the most likely way in which one could help prevent further disruption and best participate in the restoration and healing of church and society.

Seneca's *De Clementia*

In a fascinating study, A.M. Hugo has given a detailed account of John Calvin as a classicist who set out to establish himself as a scholar-reformer within the church.[50] Hugo points out that the work of Erasmus and other humanists had revived interest especially in Hellenistic antiquity. No serious student at the time could avoid the question of how Christianity related to that classical world.[51] Since Erasmus had provided new editions of Seneca's writings in 1515 and 1529, interest in Seneca had greatly increased. At the same time, Erasmus had discredited the general belief that Seneca, not unlike Nicodemus, had been a Christian.

Hugo came to the conclusion that Calvin chose Seneca's *De Clementia* for several reasons. Seneca was one of Emperor Nero's instructors who urged him to practice clemency. The striking comparisons between, on the one hand, the Seneca who instructed Nero, and, on the other hand, the Apostle Paul who advised Christians at Rome to obey their God-instituted government (Romans 13) do not concern us here except as a reminder that Calvin who had earned his licentiate in law was now turning more to the classics, becoming even more of a humanist in the process. Calvin himself referred in retrospect to this period in his life when he wrote his *Responsio ad Sadoletum* (Response to Cardinal Sadoleto) in 1539.[52]

I do not like to speak about myself. However, since you do not permit me to keep silent, I will say as much as I can say in modesty. If I had wanted to serve my own interest, I would never have left your side.[53] Nor do I wish to boast that I could have attained to all kinds of offices in her, for I did never desire those and I was never able to bring myself to go after them. Nevertheless, I do know no few of my contemporaries who crawled up to some position (in the church) and whom I could have equalled in part or whom I could have surpassed in part. Therefore I will say no more than this: what I then had imagined for myself as highest ideal I could have reached without difficulty, namely to enjoy quiet study of literature coupled with an honorable and well-financed position.

Indeed, as Hugo has argued, the fact that Calvin dedicated his *Seneca* commentary to Claude de Hangest, one of the Hangest-Genlis boys with whom he had been permitted to study and now the abbot of the monastery of St. Eloy at Noyon, was indicative of more than a boyhood friendship and a sense of loyalty.[54] In 1529, Claude de Hangest had proposed John Calvin as the recipient of the Pont l'Évêque parish income.[55] The customs of the time were such that "the highest ideal" mentioned by John Calvin was often realized because friends would do each other a good turn. Accepting the "living" of Pont l'Évêque indicated that Calvin fully intended to stay within the church. He wanted to work for whatever perfection would be possible within the church, not outside of it.[56]

Calvin had his *Commentary* printed at his own expense. Louis Blaauwblom in Paris published the book of just over 160 pages in April of 1532. The costs were higher than Calvin had anticipated and he had to promote its sale by writing to his friends urging them to buy and use the book. But the *Commentary* did not score the success for which Calvin had hoped.[57] It would not be the only setback for the twenty-three-year-old young man. The struggle for the reform of church, state, and society was soon to take a more ominous turn.

JOHN CALVIN: REFUGEE AND EXPATRIATE

Although King Francis I (1515-1547) was popular in France as an energetic ruler and likable personality, he was unable to manipulate the forces for reform in his favor. Domestically, he succeeded in arrogating power unto himself, but his foreign policies and ambitions got him into trouble. By the Concordat of Bologna, 1516, Pope Leo X acknowledged Francis's right to nominate the bishops and abbots in France. But Leo did not want to support Francis's candidacy as the Emperor of the

Holy Roman Empire of the German Nation, preferring instead the young Habsburg monarch Charles V with whom he concluded a secret treaty (1521). Charles seemed to be the early winner, especially as he succeeded in taking Francis prisoner at Pavia (1525); but the French king reneged on the treaty and sought not only the support of the Muslim Turks, but also an alliance with the Lutheran princes of Germany (League of Schmalkalden, 1531). This helps explain why Francis supported the reform movement in France sufficiently to keep the Lutherans in Germany on his side, but not enough to completely alienate the Roman church and its hierarchy. The king's policies seemed self-contradictory. On the one hand, his appointees to the Royal College[58] were expected to teach classical studies, including the biblical languages, but the fiery protests of the University of Paris and the conservative hierarchy against this new learning were ignored. Nor did the king prevent the undermining of Rome's "official" version of the Bible, the Latin Vulgate, as he protected Jacques Lefèvre d'Étaples whom he appointed as instructor at the royal court at Blois, even though the Roman hierarchy had earlier attempted to have him tried as a heretic for his translation of the New Testament in French (1523).[59] On the other hand, it was under King Francis that the Augustinian monk Jean Vallière was burned at the stake, August 1523, because he was suspected of Lutheran sympathies. Still, the same king, ten years later in the season of Lent (1533), had Gerard Roussel preach for his court at the Louvre permitting other citizens to join in so that crowds of over four thousand people would hear reformation sermons. The king even allowed open-air preaching by "prescheurs évangeliques"[60] drawing the attendance of the Royal Lecturers and the vast majority of students.[61]

Whatever motivated Calvin, after his father's death on 26 May 1531, to return to Paris for humanistic studies at the new Royal College, his considerations must have included how he could function best in the France being governed by the policies of King Francis. Living in the house of Étienne de la Forge, Calvin witnessed from closeby what a rich merchant who feared God was willing to risk for the spreading of the Bible in the vernacular, to make Luther's works available, and to host secret meetings at which royal chaplain Gerard Roussel would lead a circle of would be reformers.[62] But Calvin was equally at home with other prominent families in Paris such as

Connan, Cop, and Budé who were equally concerned as Étienne de la Forge, but less "revolutionary."

Circumstances developed that determined some of Calvin's life decisions as much as did his own predelictions. This was especially the case when his close friend Nicholas Cop was chosen to be the rector of the University of Paris for the academic year 1533-34. Nicholas was the son of medical professor Guillaume Cop who served also as personal physician to King Francis. Since 1530, Nicolas had been professor of philosophy at the College of Saint Barbara in the University and now it was his task as rector to address the academic community on the first day of November—All Saints' Day. Everybody was well aware of his preference for the reform movement, if for no other reason than that he had just disciplined some students for their production of a play that ridiculed king Francis's sister Marguerite of Angoulême, Queen of Navarre, an eager protector of the budding Reformation.

Nicolas Cop was a brave person. In his address on All Saints' Day he reflected on the biblical verse: "Blessed are the poor in spirit" (Matthew 5:3). Cop discussed the need to distinguish well between law and gospel. He reproached the "sophists" for stressing minor matters rather than dealing with faith, God's love, and the truly good works. Cop objected to the performance of good works for the purpose of earning eternal life and posed the question "How can a son claim to *earn* the inheritance which his father *gives* him?" Eternal bliss could never be secure if it depended on man's good works. Cop closed his address by sharply criticizing the people responsible for the current persecution of those as heretics who wanted to follow the Word of God. He underlined the point by quoting from the Beatitudes, "Blessed are those who are persecuted because of righteousness," urging his audience to believe the gospel, to serve God, and if necessary to suffer for His name's sake.[63]

Within a few days the Parliament of Paris had to act upon a complaint against Cop for tainting the University of Paris with Lutheran heresies. Summoned by Parliament and already on his way there in full academic regalia, Nicolas received a warning from a friendly member of Parliament that he was about to be condemned. At the very last moment Cop bolted and in the melee that followed made good his escape. King Francis ordered a nationwide alert to arrest Cop and, more ominously, "to exterminate in our kingdom the damned Lutheran sect which appears to be growing." In spite of the price of three hundred livres on his head, Nicolas managed to elude his persecutors and surfaced three months later in Basel, Switzerland.

Calvin had a narrow escape, too, hastily fleeing his apartment at the College Fortet, as the story goes, by tying sheets together and lowering himself from a rear window while the authorities were knocking at the front door. His friendship with the Cop family, and especially with Nicolas, was well known. Many believe that Calvin had been the author of Cop's address. But Dankbaar points out that parts of the speech were taken directly from writings by Erasmus and Luther, not reflective of Calvin's thought at the time. Furthermore, Dankbaar calls attention to the fact that Beza indeed wrote in the first (Latin) edition of his *Vita Calvini* (Life of Calvin) that Calvin had counseled Cop with the respect to this address; but in the French edition (*Vie de Calvin*) of 1564 Beza did not make any mention at all of Calvin's authorship. In this later edition Beza gave the friendship with Nicolas Cop as the only reason for Calvin's flight. Besides, Calvin was only one of some fifty suspects to be apprehended.

It is true that in Geneva a copy of Cop's address has been found, part of which is in Calvin's handwriting. But the copy of the same speech found in Strasbourg is in a different handwriting. Dankbaar believes that Calvin had made a partial copy for himself but that the original was lost.

What Calvin did share with Cop was that both of them now were hunted heretics and had become expatriates and refugees. Even then there was no collusion between the two friends, however. Cop settled in Basel, while Calvin—late in 1533 or early in 1534—joined Louis de Tillet, his friend who was priest at Claix in the province of Saintonge and also canon of the cathedral at Angoulême.[64] Tillet had an impressive library in which Calvin could study uninterruptedly. But the two friends took the precaution that the newly arrived friend was to be known only by the assumed name of Charles d'Esperville. Not unlike Martin Luther, who had lived as Junker Georg at the Wartburg where he worked on his translation of the Bible, so did Charles d'Esperville work on his account of the Christian faith reformed according to the Scriptures, the *Institutes of the Chris-*

tian Religion.[65] A definite change had occurred in Calvin. He had obviously chosen for less compromise and more reformation.

CONVERSION

On the subject of Calvin's conversion many viewpoints have been expressed and the literature is vast. Dankbaar is most helpful by calling attention, on the one hand, to Calvin's reticence, and by pointing out, on the other hand, that two dates provide rather clear clues as to when the conversion occurred.[66] The first of these two dates was 23 August 1533 when Calvin discussed with the cathedral chapter at Noyon how to organize a procession and public prayers in the city as it was stricken by the plague. These conversations took place two months before Nicolas Cop was to deliver his All Saints' address. No convert from Roman Catholicism of Calvin's calibre would have attempted to make such arrangements. Therefore Calvin was still a Roman Catholic at the time.[67]

The second date is May of 1534 when Calvin was back in Noyon. This time he had not come to participate but to separate. No longer did he wish to receive the income from the parish Pont l'Évêque. Only one reason could have brought Calvin to this step. He had given up his ideal of becoming a scholar, doing his work somewhere in quiet.[68] But giving up his status as a *presbyter curatus* in the church and now refusing the income this position had given him did not mean that Calvin was leaving the church. As he was later to write in his "Humble Admonition to Charles V" (1543):

> we did not separate ourselves from the church, nor do we stand outside of her communion. . . . Our struggle against the pope and all of his supporters is nothing other than the present day counterpart of the battle which prophets and apostles did wage against the degenerated church of their day.[69]

The step he took in May of 1534 signaled that Calvin would now firmly and openly belong to the reforming party. But it appears that for Calvin this action was less dramatic than it has been for later generations; that is, while Calvin never found it necessary to elaborate on his conversion, students of his life have chosen to do so ever since.

Compared to what Calvin wrote about himself, Luther's account of his own life is truly an open book, and perhaps it is

Luther's example that some are trying to force upon Calvin. But Calvin's autobiographical statements are slim indeed. In fact, only in two instances did Calvin talk about his conversion. The clearest reference is found in the *Preface* to his *Commentary on the Psalms* in which he wrote:

> At first I was so tenaciously devoted to the superstitions of the papacy that it was not easy to pull myself out of that deep abyss. But by a sudden conversion God subdued into obedience my heart that at my age was too hardened. And when I had thus gained a taste for true piety, such zeal kindled in my heart for making further progress that I, while not pushing my other studies aside, did indeed spend less energy on them. Before a year had passed, all who desired the pure doctrine came to me, the novice and beginner, in order to learn from me.[70]

A second reference may be the following passage in his letter to Cardinal Jacopo Sadoleto, written so that the paragraph would not refer to himself but rather to a supporter of the Reformation who is speaking to God.

> As often as I turned into myself or lifted my heart to Thee, I was seized by a terrible horror that no propitiation or penance could cure. And the closer I looked at myself, the more my conscience was pricked by sharp thorns, so that no other consolation remained than to forget about it and thus deceive myself. Because nothing better presented itself, I continued on the road I had chosen. In the meanwhile, a totally different doctrine had emerged which did not pull us away from the Christian confession but led the confession back to its real source, and, cleansing it from impurity, restored it to its purity. But I took offense at this novelty and listened to it with difficulty. And initially—I admit it—I offered vehement and furious resistance because, due to the steadfastness or obstinacy with which man is born to stay with what he has learned, only reluctantly did I allow myself to get to the point of admitting that I had spent my entire life in error and ignorance. One thing especially held me back: my respect for the church. But once I did open my ears and allowed myself to be instructed, I understood it was needless to fear that the church's majesty would be offended. I was made to see that it makes a big difference whether a person secedes from the church or tries to correct her shortcomings with which she has defiled herself.[71]

If this last statement may be understood as autobiographical, it reveals that Calvin's conversion was preceded by a long, hard struggle of conscience. The course of his studies and his actions as a student speak as eloquently as his words. By his studies Calvin progressed on the way to reforming the church until the definitive decision was made by his heart, his heart of devotion to the church and her Lord. This is perhaps the deepest reason why Calvin never separated mind and heart. For Calvin conversion did not mean that he would belong to a church consisting of "reborn" Christians who by virtue of their conversion had regained paradise. It is important to make this point because in those years such a restoration was beginning to take place at Münster. Since those saints were of the truth, no oath was required of them. Since they had the Spirit, the sword and war became superfluous. Since the "saved" had regained the innocence of paradise, a government was no longer needed. Christ's Church and God's Kingdom were visibly one on the earth.

Such a high view of man's regenerated nature could quickly lead to the disaster that soon took place at Münster. What happened there gave King Francis I an excuse to oppress all reform movements, insisting with the Lutherans in Germany that, like them, he had to guard against such excesses.

When Calvin published his *Institutes of the Christian Religion*, he penned an open letter to King Francis to accompany it. In that letter he objected to the king's distortion of the Reformation.

> You, yourself, O noble king, can be our witness with what kind of false slander this doctrine [i.e. Reformation doctrine] is accused daily in your presence as being solely intent on wresting the scepter from the hands of kings, to overthrow courts and all jurisdiction, to bring down all states and civil governments, to disturb the peace and quiet of the people, to abolish all laws, to disperse all properties and possessions, in short to turn everything upside down. . . . It will be your task, O illustrious king, to turn away neither your ears nor your heart from such rightful protection, the more so because such an important matter is at stake, namely how the honor of God can exist on earth without injury, how the truth of God can keep its dignity, how the dominion of Christ can remain among us without injury. This issue is worthy of your ears, worthy of your examination, worthy of your judgment seat. For it is this consideration that makes a king the true king when he acknowledges that in governing his dominion he is God's servant. And he who does not govern to serve God's honor, holds the reins no longer but commits robbery.[72]

At issue here, again, is the way in which society and man were to be perfect. Calvin expressed very clearly that perfection was out of reach here on earth, but that did not mean one could not live to the glory of God.

NON-PERFECTIONISM

Abraham Hulshof, in his still very readable doctoral dissertation on the history of the Baptists at Strasbourg, included a chapter under the title "Calvin and the (Ana-) Baptists."[73] He raised the specific question why Calvin succeeded so much more than his ministerial colleagues like Martin Bucer, Wolfgang Capito, and Matthias Zell in converting Anabaptists to the Reformed interpretation of the faith. Hulshof mentioned as potential factors Calvin's well-defined convictions, his stricter and deeper exposition of the Scriptures, and his greater eloquence. But Hulshof documented as the single most important cause that the

> Doopsgezinden did find in his [Calvin's] congregation what they found missing in the congregations of the Strasbourg ministers, namely strict ecclesiastical discipline. That those ministers failed to supervise the moral life of the members, did not have the Lord's Supper preceded by a sifting of the worthy and unworthy, and did not even exclude the unrepenting sinner from the communion, was precisely what they threw in their faces again and again.[74]

These contacts with Anabaptists gave Calvin firsthand knowledge of a more radical reformation than practiced by Luther, Zwingli, or himself. Of particular importance may have been Jean Stordeur, from Luik (Liège), who had first come to Geneva and later to Strasbourg (1537) where Calvin was able to bring him and his family into the Reformed Church. After Stordeur's death, Calvin married his widow, Idelette van Buren.[75]

This is not to say, however, that this firsthand information provided Calvin with an exhaustive knowledge of the radical Reformation. Uprisings and wars ravaged Europe at the time, making postal connections difficult. Important letters were usually sent in duplicate, each by different route and courier, but even so not every letter reached its destination. Nor was one able quickly to double-check the written information. Even the eyewitness accounts of refugees who reached the relative safety of Strasbourg and Geneva did not constitute in-depth and balanced accounts of the different movements within what is now called the left-wing or radical Reformation.[76] Even today, four centuries later, scholars have not reached a consensus regarding who should be included in that phase of the Reformation.[77]

While Calvin did not have full and adequate information about the movement, he did not make the "mistake" of a Luther and a Bullinger who considered all Spiritualists, Anabaptists, Fanatacists, and Enthusiasts as one and the same.

Calvin published two works about them. The first appeared at Geneva in 1544 under the title "Brief Instruction to Arm all the Good Believers [or Faithful] against the Errors of the Communal Sect of the Anabaptists."[78] About this sect Calvin was willing to grant: "There are two sects, of which one, however full of many bad and pernicious errors, nevertheless maintains greater simplicity. At least, it accepts Holy Writ as do we."[79]

Calvin followed a year later (1545) with a work entitled "Against the Phantastic and Furious Sect which calls itself Spiritual."[80] Calvin characterized this group as

> a labyrinth of such foolish dreams as there is no other [second] to be found. It is amazing that creatures, who have a human form, can be so deprived of their common sense and reason that they allow themselves to be deceived to the point of falling into more than brutal [affronting] phantasies. This sect calls itself the Libertines. And they claim to be so "spiritual" that they have no more need of the Holy Word of God than they have of fables, except when they arbitrarily choose to do so, at their convenience, when they are able to pervert it [the Word] to serve their diabolical opinions.[81]

In his opposition to these sects Calvin was a true humanist in that he was not willing to revive and renovate the church (and society) by jumping backwards across the centuries to the time in which the church at first emerged. Nor was he willing to abandon the present time as so evil that it was only good enough to serve as the moment for the Lord's return. Calvin had developed a deep appreciation for the classics which he would never abandon. In fact, he stated very clearly that he considered this admittedly extra-biblical learning as gifts from the divine Spirit:

> Can we deny that the truth has shed its light on the ancient lawyers who regulated civil order and discipline with so much justice? Can we say that the philosophers were blinded in their exacting observation of nature and in their artful description thereof? Can we say that those who invented rhetoric and taught us to speak rationally did not have understanding? Can we say that those who practiced healing and benefitted us by their art have been fools? And with respect to mathematics, should we consider that to be the ravings of madmen? On the contrary, we shall read the writings of the ancients pertaining to these matters only with great (enormous) admiration. . . . In the meanwhile, let us not forget that these matters are excellent gifts of the divine Spirit.[82]

Still, Calvin was well aware of the limitations these classics had for the Christian. Unlike some of his humanist-contemporaries, he did not expect that knowledge of the classics alone would result in "the certainty of God's favor toward us." On the contrary, he writes:

> I do not deny that one can read in the philosophers, here and there, insightful and fitting sayings about God, but these sayings witness always to a dizzying imagination. . . . The certainty of God's favor toward us they [the philosophers] have never even smelled. Human reason does not get close to

that truth, does not strive after it, does not understand that it [reason] could fathom who the true God is and what He wishes to be toward us.[83]

Calvin made very clear that he was well agreed with his Anabaptist opponents in the matter of discipline.[84] The disagreement with them occurred over the relation with the church from which reformers took their (different!) distances and with which they might break. Where a church might be impure, but not yet void of biblical truth, Calvin was not willing to separate and secede. He sought the antidote in biblical preaching informed and undergirded by a rigorous education in the very disciplines which he considered "excellent gifts of the divine Spirit."[85]

This meant also that for man on earth, either in or out of the church, no instant perfection was available. Important as his humanism may have been to Calvin, this influence never got the better of his Christianity. Calvin was a *Christian* humanist. When the matter of "being saved" came up, Calvin did not rely on a source other than the Bible. In the *Institutio* he wrote that

> If one seeks salvation, by the very name of Jesus we are taught that salvation is with Him; if one desires whatever other gifts of the Spirit: they will be found in His annointing; if one seeks strength: it exists in His dominion; purity: it reveals itself in His conception; mercy: in His birth by which He became our equal in everything in order that He might learn compassion; if one seeks deliverance: it is to be found in His suffering; acquittal: in His condemnation; forgiveness of the curse: in His cross; satisfaction: in His sacrifice; purification: in His blood; reconciliation: in His descent into hell; mortification of the flesh: in His grave; newness of life: in His resurrection; immortality: likewise, in His resurrection; inheriting the heavenly kingdom: in His ascension into heaven; protection, unconcern, abundance and richness of all goods: in His kingdom; a calm expectation of the judgment: in the power given Him to judge. In short, since in Him are the treasures of all sorts of goods, they will have to be drawn to full satisfaction from Him and not from elsewhere.[86]

It is this Christo-centrism, this refusal to admit other sources as truly revelatory, that marked Calvin's position consistently, and also in the matter of perfection.

To Calvin an important Bible text was Romans 7:26. He acknowledged readily that Paul described how he served the law of God *mente*, in or by spirit. Calvin commented that *mens* is

> that part of the soul that has been enlightened by the Spirit of God so that it [*mens*] feels and wills correctly. For not only is here talk of intelligence, but added thereto is the earnest desire of the heart.

Calvin understood Paul to say that man on earth does not arrive at perfection but that God works an honest desire for it in
our hearts. For

> as long as the faithful dwell in the flesh, they never arrive at the end (goal)
> of righteousness. . . . Paul confesses that he has surrendered to God in such
> a manner that, while living on the earth, he still gets defiled by many im-
> purities. This is a remarkably [good] place (or statement) to expose the per-
> nicious doctrine of the Cathari which at present certain restless spirits are
> trying to revive.[87]

Obviously, Calvin and the radical reformers were not in disagreement with respect to the importance of Jesus Christ. But
they parted ways when they related Christ to the believers. The
perfectionists in the radical wing had total confidence in the
all-overcoming grace of God to make the sinner whole. Calvin
believed no less in the power of God's grace but considered
perfectionism as an overrating of oneself. Nevertheless, perfection was entirely possible for Calvin, provided it was understood as an eschatological gift. But even then this gift was
never to be separated from and always to be connected with
Christ.

Calvin raised the question whether Christ was just a historical figure in a past long gone. If not, in what sense can
Christ be said to be present? And by being present, in what
measure does Christ cause perfection in the believer? Walter
Krusche has observed that for Calvin Christ is indeed one with
the believers but not to the point where there is no distinction
between the two. Christ is at one with the Spirit and he has the
Spirit completely, and wholly, and without measure. To be
anointed with the Spirit means for Christ more than just a quality
of his own (individual) being. While Christ is His own person, He
is not a person in isolation. His baptism took place on His person
but was performed in behalf of the believers, the members of His
body.[88]

In commenting on 1 John 1:7-10, Calvin observed:

> Each member (believer) receives gifts of the Spirit. These gifts are adequate
> to maintain, preserve, the body (of Christ), but are not anywhere near the
> state of perfection. . . .
> As long as we are in the flesh, we must progress constantly (nos in continuo
> profecto esse oportet). What He (God) once began in us, He will continue to
> work in us every day until He does (finally, at last) complete us (absolvat:
> acquits himself of the task). Thus Paul says (Col. 1:22) that we are elect in
> order that we may appear before God without blemish.[89]

It is clear, then, that Calvin did expect believers to make

meaningful progress in the faith. But that progress is never completed on earth. Calvin claimed: "No perfection can be found (on earth) that measures up to God's judgment," commenting on Zephaniah 2:3: "Seek the Lord, all you humble of the land, who do his commands: seek righteousness, seek humility; perhaps you may be hidden on the day of the wrath of the Lord." Calvin understood the "humble of the land" to be the best (optimos). Even for them it is true that God's rod of discipline exhorts them to cultivate piety (colendam pietatem) with more ardor and eagerness than before.[90]

In the *Institutio,* Calvin stated this exegetical comment in more theological language:

> In our time, some of the Anabaptists who do not differ much from the Novatians have fallen into the same foolishness. For they teach that the people of God in baptism are born again (from above) to a pure and chaste life like that of the angels which is not desecrated by the defects of the flesh. But if someone sins after being baptized they leave the person nothing but the unrelenting judgment of God. In short, to a sinner who stumbles after having received grace, they leave no hope for forgiveness at all; for they acknowledge no other forgiveness than the one by which we are born again to begin with.[91]

Calvin wanted no such "foolishness" at all. The *Confession of Faith* that he submitted to the City Council of Geneva stated unequivocally that

> We remain in these mortal bodies, and there remains in us as yet so much imperfection and infirmity that before God we remain always poor and miserable sinners. And however much we have to grow and increase daily in the righteousness of God, there will never be completeness or perfection until Christ will return to restore everything.[92]

By insisting on the imperfection of the believer, however, Calvin did not deny the realities of consolation and progress in the faith. Balke admits that it is not always clear in each instance whether Calvin did battle against the perfectionism of the Anabaptists or the Libertarians. Over against the former he is moved more by pity, because they believed, erroneously in his view, that perfection was a goal that can be reached. But he resisted the Libertarians vehemently because he considered them far more dangerous in their presupposition that perfection is what has made a person into a believer.[93]

Calvin's objection to both of these groups, and others like them, stemmed from his pastoral concern that a person needs to be related to Christ now and always. In his commentary on Jeremiah 29:13, "you will seek me and find me when you seek me with all your heart," Calvin encouraged the faithful to believe that it is not perfection that can be found among people but rather integrity and sincerity.[94]

Calvin's pastoral concern is especially apparent in what he taught and practiced concerning the Lord's Supper.[95] Persons partaking in the Eucharist in a worthy manner signified by that very act not perfection attained, but rather, in the words of M. Eugene Osterhaven, "faith, repentance, and the pursuit of a godly life." For Calvin, faith was always imperfect, although not insufficient,[96] and he relates faith as a necessity to the celebration of the Supper, for "to say that Christ may be received without faith is as inappropriate as to say that a seed may germinate in a fire."[97]

Osterhaven correctly points out that for Calvin repentance issued from faith. Faith did not mark the end of repentance but rather the elevation of it into the very presence of the merciful God. This means that in Calvin's thinking about the Supper "the question of discipline is no less essential than the question of doctrine."[98]

As a consequence, Calvin also was convinced that the Lord's Supper could not be exclusively for the "mature believers, but that it was especially for the weak and imperfect." Osterhaven quotes Calvin's insistence upon our worthiness as "consisting in our faith and love even though these be weak and imperfect." That is why Calvin could advocate celebrating the Supper "very often . . . at least once a week" (IV, 17, 43). He considered the Supper as a "sacred feast . . . medicine for the sick, solace for sinners, alms to the poor." Conversely, Calvin did not see how the Supper could bring "benefit to the healthy, righteous, and rich—if such could be found." In sum, Calvin stated:

> It would be excessive stupidity—not to mention foolishness—to require such perfection in receiving the Sacrament as would make the Sacrament void and superfluous. For it is a sacrament ordained not for the perfect, but for the weak and feeble, to awaken, arouse, stimulate, and exercise the feeling of faith and love, indeed, to correct the defect of both.[99]

This view of the Supper did not lead Calvin to allow the believer an easy conscience on the grounds that perfection was unattainable in any way. Calvin stressed the need for repentance and rectitude alike. That is clear, for instance, in his comment on Genesis 6:9 which describes Noah as "a righteous man, blameless in his generation." Calvin observed:

> Let us realize that not these are being called just and whole (integros) who are perfect in every respect (absoluti omni ex parte) and who lack nothing, but rather those who cultivate rectitude purely and heartily (pure et ex animo). For we know that God does deal with his own according to strictest law (summo iure) not so that he measures their lives according to that norm but in order that in them would not rule hypocrisy but rather that the right eagerness for purity would fill their hearts; it is to that end that He pronounces them righteous because of his grace (indulgence).[100]

On that premise Calvin could tell believers: "It behooves us to pray God that it please Him to draw us unto Himself and to wash and cleanse us."[101] Perfection is thus an eschatological event for man. Precisely the most "perfect" among the believers are conscious of their imperfection. That consciousness draws and brings them to Christ in whom alone perfection is found, but who is gracious, willing, and able to share what is His with all who believe in Him, both in this life and the life to come.

NOTES

1. The name Calvin derives from the latinized name Calvinus adopted by Jean Cauvin for scholarly purposes. The registers of Noyon spell the name always as Cauuin, although it appears elsewhere in many different forms such as Cauvin, Chauve, Chauvin, and Calvus.

2. His biographers contradict each other on the details of John Calvin's youth. See (a) Emile Doumergue: *Jean Calvin: les hommes et les choses de son temps*, (Lausanne: G. Bridel Cie, 1899-1927), 7 vols.; (b) Aimé Louis Herminjard: *Correspondance des Réformateurs dan les pays de langue française récueillie et publiée avec d'autres lettres relatives à la Réforme et des notes historiques et bibliographiques*, (Geneve: H. Georg, 1866-97), tomes I-IX; unfortunately, this work is incomplete, as it contains Calvin's correspondence only till 1544; and (c) Abel Jules Maurice Lefranc: *La Jeunesse de Calvin* (Paris: Librarie Fischbacher, 1888), which is the most reliable work.

3. John Calvin was one of six children. Of the two girls only Marie is known by name. Charles was the oldest of the boys. He became chaplain at Noyon and later priest at Roupy. Accused of heresy, Charles was excommunicated and died in 1537 without the last rites of the church. John was the second son. The youngest of the sons was Francois who died at an early age. Antoine, the third son, like his sister Marie, opted for the Reformation and the two of them came to live in Geneva.

4. See the introduction to John Calvin's *Commentary on Seneca's De Clementia*, Paris, 1532. Although this *Commentary* is the first of Calvin's publications, the earliest "complete" editions of Calvin's works, dated 1552, 1563, and 1566, appeared without it. Beza included the work in his so-called *Editio Latina* of Calvin's works that was published in 1576. In the editions of Calvin's *Opera* of 1597, 1611, and 1667, the *Commentary* was placed as an Appendix to

the *Tractatus Minores*. It took two centuries before the editors Wilhelm Baum, Ed. Cunitz, and Ed. Reuss removed the *Commentary* from its location as an appendix to the very first place of Calvin's works; see volume V of their formidable publication: *Corpus Reformatorum. Ioannis Calvini Opera omnia quae supersunt* (Brunsvigae-Berolini: apud C.A. Schwetschke et filium, 1865-1900), 59 volumes. The Calvin Translation Society published an English translation of this work in 52 volumes at Edinburgh, 1844-59. In their *Prolegomena*, the editors of the *Corpus Reformatorum* (C.R.) expressed admiration for this "first and in this genre unique document" of the barely twenty-three-year-old Calvin. They wrote: "one must begin by reading this *Commentary* if one wants to gain an understanding of that great and never to be sufficiently admired conversion whereby this immortal man transferred from the circle of philologists (among whom he would certainly not have occupied the last place, if one may judge on the basis of such a beginning) to the study of theological authors, and already from the start found a large degree of support for his first effort, and shortly thereafter to carry off the palm branch (of victory) and to leave all others far behind" (see pp. xxxii-xxxiv).

5. Later, in September of 1527, Noyon's cathedral chapter appointed John Calvin as the *presbyter curatus* to St. Martin's church at neighboring Martheville. Again, John received the ecclesiastical income but never fulfilled priestly duties in the parish.

6. This is Calvin's own account in the *Preface* to his *Commentary on the Psalms*, published in 1557, thirty-four years after the fact. It is one of the few places where he talks about himself.

7. See Theodorus Beza, *Vita Calvini*, in *C.R., C.O.*, volume XXI, col. 121. There is even a tradition that Calvin was known by the nickname "accusativus," the accuser. Doumergue strongly protested against this slur: 1:74.

8. Calvin publicly honored Mathurin Cordier in the *Preface* to his *Commentary on I Thessalonians*. In 1562, Calvin brought Cordier to Geneva where he was appointed to the "schola privata," although this position was meant mostly to honor the octogenarian. Cordier was among the first in Europe to practice the new pedagogical concepts of Erasmus.

9. See A. Lefranc, *La Jeunesse de Calvin*, 62-64. See also Doumergue, 1:68ff. The Collège de Montaigue, like the Collège de la Marche, was one of many colleges making up the University of Paris. Montaigue had enjoyed an excellent reputation since Standonc, in 1485, had organized it in the pious spirit of the Brethren of the Common Life. Rector Noel Bédier had transformed it into a staunch bulwark of orthodox scholasticism. Erasmus and Rabelais were among Montaigu's alumni, both of whom later denounced the College with all the powers of their sarcasm. Erasmus went so far as to describe Noel Bèdier as "more a hunk of flesh than a person." The College was popularly called the "collège de pouillerie," the College of bugs.

10. This point is well made by W.F. Dankbaar, *Calvijn: Zijn Weg en Zijn Werk*. (Nijkerk: G.F. Callenbach, 1957), 4-5.

11. A typical example quoted by A.M. Hugo, *Calvijn en Seneca* (for details see note 5;) is Florimond de Raemond: *Histoire de la naissance, progrès et décadence de l'hérésie de ce siècle* whose book was originally published at Paris in 1605.

12. For details see Lefranc: *La Jeunesse de Calvin*.

13. See A. Ganoczy: *Le jeune Calvin, Genèse et évolution de sa vocation reformatrice*, (Wiesbaden: F. Steiner, 1966), 23.

14. J. Cadier: *Luther et les débuts de la Réforme française* (Strasbourg: Positions Lutheriennes, 1958). The Sorbonne condemned Luther's doctrines in 1521.

15. Johan Huizinga, *Erasmus*, in: *Verzamelde Werken*, (Haarlem: H.D. Tjeenk Willink, 1950), 6:128. This text is identical to the third edition published

in 1936. The first edition appeared in 1924. Huizinga gives this characteristic of Erasmus: "He was neither [a] mystic nor [a] realist. Luther was both. For Erasmus the great problem of church and state and society was simple enough. Nothing else was needed than restoration and purification by returning to the original unspoiled foundations of Christendom. A number of accretions to the faith, more ridiculous than abhorrent, had to be removed. Everything had to be reduced to the kernel of the faith, to Christ, and the gospel. Forms, ceremonies, speculations had to yield to the practice of true piety. The gospel was for everyone, easily understandable and accessible for everyone. And the means to all of this was real civilization, *bonae literae*, [arts and letters]." Ibid., 127.

  16. Ibid., 33.
  17. Ibid., 179.
  18. Ibid., 181.
  19. This paper is not the proper place to trace other influences that were working on Calvin at the time. It must here suffice to mention what has been called the "Protestantism of Jacques Lefèvre d'Étaples" or the "circle of Meaux," the city where Guillaume de Briçonnet was bishop. He was also the tutor-friend of Margaretha of Angoulême, sister of King Francis I, later queen of Navarre. When d'Étaples published his French translation of the New Testament in 1523, Bishop Briçonnet helped distribute it among the faithful in his diocese. And yet the bishop removed Guillaume Farel from his "circle" because this student of d'Étaples with his fiery temper had become controversial. d'Étaples himself had discovered the biblical truth of justification by faith long before Luther, and it took the royal protection of King Francis for him to return in safety from Strasbourg where he had fled for shelter when Bishop de Briçonnet proved too weak to safeguard his life. Calvin was well acquainted with this circle as he lived in Paris at the home of the rich textile merchant Étienne de la Forge who financed not only the publication of portions of the New Testament but also French translations of Luther's writings. In his home De la Forge would regularly host secret meetings for proponents of reformation, including some of d'Étaples' students. Gerard Roussel was one of these students, then giving leadership at De la Forge's home. Roussel was the preacher at King Francis's court where his lenten sermons in the spring of 1533 drew record crowds of up to four thousand. Two years later, in the spring of 1535, when King Francis discontinued his liberal policies, Étienne de la Forge became one of the many martyrs for the faith. Gerard Roussel, however, accepted a position as bishop in 1537, bringing a (temporary) halt to his friendship with Calvin. Earlier, in April 1534, Calvin visited his friend Roussel who lived at the time, as did so many of those who saw the need for reform, in Navarre under the protection of Queen Margaret, sister of King Francis I. At the monastery in Clairac Roussel told Calvin "If you want to cleanse the ecclesiastical structure, you can count on my support. But see to it that you do not destroy it, for you and others will then be buried under its rubble" (Dankbaar, *Calvijn*, 28). The first of the following two publications is an excellent guide to Erasmus and the humanist spirit of proponents of reformation in France, while the second work studies in detail the influence of the Modern Devotion on Erasmus as Christian believer:

  a. **Margaret Mann**, *Erasme et les Débuts de la Réforme française (1517-1536);* Bibliothèque litteraire de la Renaissance. (Paris: Champion, 1934).
  b. Otto Schottenloher, *Erasmus im Ringen um die humanistische Bildungsform. Ein Beitrag zum Verständnis seiner geistigen Entwicklung.* Reformations-geschichtliche Studien und Texte, Heft 61. (Münster: Aschendorff, 1933).

  20. The University of Orleans enjoyed an excellent liberal reputation. Not

only Erasmus had taught here, but also Reuchlin, one of the few Hebrew scholars among learned Christians at the time.

21. See for this matter Calvin's letter to his friend François de Connan dated 6 March 1531, in Herminjard, *Correspondance* 2:328. Calvin's introduction to the *Antapologia* by Nicholas Duchemin was Calvin's first publication. Later, King Francis made l'Estoile a member of Parliament. At his death in 1537, l'Estoile was presiding over the "chambre des enquêtes". See G. Beyerhaus, *Studien zur Staatsanschauung Calvins, mit besonderer Berücksichtigung seines Souveranitätsbegriffs.* (Berlin: Neue Studien zur Geschichte der Theologie und der Kirche, 1910), 27ff.

22. See for this *Preface: C.R.*, Vol. 31.

23. Lefranc, *Jeunesse de Calvin.* See especially chapter 2, pp. 15ff., "Opposition de la famille de Calvin contre le clergé."

24. It is not impossible, as Dankbaar suggests, that this episode may later have been a contributing factor in the excommunication of John Calvin's older brother, the priest Charles.

25. *Histoire Ecclesiastique des Églises Reformées au Royaume de France,* par Théodore de Bèze, publiée d'après l'edition de 1580, avec des notes etc., par P. Vesson. (Toulouse: Société des Livres Religieux, 1882), Tome I, p. 6. Forty years earlier this work had been reprinted in three volumes at Lille: Imprimerie de Leleux, 1841-42. A third reprint, in three volumes, was published in Paris: Librairie Fischbacher, 1883-89.

26. Upon completing the *Commentary,* in 1546, Calvin wrote to Wolmar: "For this I owe you much gratitude (non parum debeo) that I was taught the first essentials (rudimentis) which later would be of great aid (majori adiumento) to me. Therefore I am unable to be satisfied in any other way than to establish for posterity a kind of monument to express my gratitude and at the same time to return to you some fruit of your labor." (*C.R.* 12: epist. 814, dated 1 August 1546.) Wolmar had taught Greek at Paris, was there the procurator of the "nation of German students," but had been forced to leave Paris because of his sympathy with Luther. In her capacity as guardian of the University, Queen Margaretha of Navarre brought Wolmar to Bourges.

27. Doumergue, *Jean Calvin,* 1:183.

28. *Histoire de la Naissance,* etc., 883ff. See note 11. Doumergue, *Jean Calvin,* 1:188, points out that subsequent Roman Catholic authors have followed Raemond in interpreting Calvin the reformer as a product of this foreign influence from Germany.

29. Already during Calvin's lifetime it was rumored that he had been ordained to the priesthood. But in a letter of congratulations to Gabriel de Saconay, Calvin wryly observed that this story "certainly honored transsubstantiation quite well, as by pure imagination it made a priest of somebody who had never been anything else than an ordinary lay person, as that is called." *C.R.* 9:443.

30. These facts are well attested by Gilles-le-Duc who later presided over the chapter at Lignières and in 1692 wrote a local history entitled *Memoires inédites pour servir a l'histoire de la ville et des seigneurs de Lignières-en-Berri.* The work was published again in 1890 by L. Jerry.

31. Théodore de Bèze, *Vie de Jean Calvin,* nouvelle édition, publiée et annotée par Alfred Franklin (Paris: J. Cherbuliez, 1849), 16. This work was reprinted in 1869.

32. See for this *subita conversio* the dissertation by F.J.M. Potgieter: *Die Verhouding tussen die Teologie en die Filosofie by Calvyn,* (Amsterdam: Vrije Universiteit, 1939), 16-22. The *Commentary on the Psalms* was published in 1557.

33. The letter is dated 27 June 1531. Calvin was close to François Daniel.

Of the nine known letters which Calvin wrote during the three years between 1530 and 1533. all directed to friends at Bourges, he penned five to Daniel. Some historians believe that Calvin was particularly interested in one of François' sisters named Françoise. At any rate, Calvin ended his letter of 27 June 1531: "Greetings to your mother, your wife, your sister Françoise. Farewell." Herminjard, *Correspondance*, 2:345.

34. *Histoire Ecclésiastique*, 1:2. See for a review of the trilingual colleges Percy S. Allen, *Erasmus: Lectures and Wayfaring Sketches*, (Oxford: Clarendon Press, 1934), in particular the chapter, "The Trilingual Colleges of the Early Sixteenth Century," 138-63.

35. Abel J.M. Lefranc, *Histoire du Collège de France* (Paris: Hachette et Cie., 1893), VII. The Royal College is today known as the Collège de France. Lefranc was later a contributor to and editor of *Le Collège de France* (Paris: Les Presses Universitaires de France, 1932).

36. Calvin wrote this reflection in the *Preface* to his *Commentary on the Psalms* of 1557. Earlier, in 1539, Calvin had written a response to Jacopo Sadoleto, the Cardinal who had been commissioned by the bishops' conference of Lyons to try and win Geneva back for Roman Catholicism. In this response Calvin had also stated how his highest wish had been to find somewhere a quiet position in order to devote himself entirely to literature. *C.O.*, 5: c. 385-416).

37. Herminjard, *Correspondance*, 2:348.

38. Froben in Basel published *Ciceronianus* in 1528. The work was reprinted in Erasmus' *Opera Omnia*, published by Peter van der Aa at Leiden, 1703-1706, Volume 1:972ff.

39. Huizinga observed keenly: "In his battle against humanistic purism, he (Erasmus) is the harbinger of a Christian puritanism." *Erasmus*, 165.

40. Pierre Danès would not qualify as one of the humanists whose paganism had drawn Erasmus' ire. Danès was one of the truly great scholars in France. He remained a loyal son of the church which he later served as bishop of Lavaur. In 1546 the king of France commissioned him as his ambassador to the Council of Trent.

41. For details see note 33.

42. At the time he wrote this letter Calvin was twenty-two years old. A pastoral concern surfaces here that would reveal itself more and more as one of his enduring characteristics.

43. *C.O.*, 5: c. 379-80.

44. Ibid., c. 394.

45. Ibid., c. 382.

46. Ibid., c. 403. The words appear in this context: "We do not deny that the churches under your leadership are churches of Christ. . . . (The church) was almost entirely destroyed. And this would certainly have taken place, if God's special goodness had not prevented it. In all localities occupied by the tyranny of the Roman pope hardly any *sparse and lacerated vestiges* remain visible which [can] make one understand that halfway buried churches are located there" (italics added).

47. *C.O.*, 5: c. 409-10.

48. Ibid.

49. *C.O.*, 5: c. 403.

50. A.M. Hugo, *Calvijn en Seneca: een Inleidende Studie van Calvijns Commentaar op Seneca, De Clementia, Anno 1532.* (Groningen-Djakarta: J.B. Wolters, 1957.)

51. Hugo points out that Calvin was deeply influenced not only by Danès but also by Guillaume Budé, another royal lecturer, who formulated much sharper than Erasmus the difference between classical philosophy and Christian

religion, especially in his book *De Transitu Hellenismi ad Christianismum*, published in 1535. Budé died in 1540, leaving a widow and five children: Mathieu, François, Louis, Jean and Marguerite, all of whom later found shelter in Calvin's Geneva.

52. For details on this letter see note 36.

53. The reference is here to the papal part of the church.

54. Claude de Hangest had become the Abbot of this ancient Benedictine monastery in 1526. The monastery itself originated in 640 and was destroyed by the Protestants in 1591 during the wars of religion.

55. See Hugo, *Calvijn en Seneca*, 171-174.

56. This interpretation contradicts Beza who in his *Vie de Calvin* (1564) tends to make especially the early Calvin more of a reformer than he actually was.

57. Hugo provides excellent details about Calvin and the *Commentary*. He suggests that Calvin was on the one hand ready to speak out because he had earned his licentiate in law while, on the other hand, he had to absorb much new knowledge about the classics. This is not to say that the *Commentary* was not a good study of Seneca's *De Clementia*. The classicist Hugo expresses deep respect and appreciation for Calvin's excellent work.

58. For the Royal College see notes 34 and 35.

59. See note 19 for additional details.

60. The title "prescheurs évangeliques," Reformation preachers or better, perhaps, Bible-preachers, occurs in François Rabelais's *Gargantua* that was published in 1534, reprinted in *Oeuvres de François Rabelais,* in Bibliothèque de Cluny; (Paris; Pierre Grimal, 1939), 34: ch. 24. To translate "evangelical preachers" would be misleading because the word "evangelical" in late twentieth-century America does not mean what "évangelique" meant in sixteenth-century France.

61. A good review of the way sixteenth-century France, in all its different parts, was affected by the revival of classics and religion is given by Pierre Imbart de la Tour in *Les Origines de la Réforme,* (Paris: Hachette et Cie, 1905-1914). A second edition of this work was published by J. de Pins (Melun: Librairie d'Argences, 1948).

62. Étienne de la Forge was one of the many victims who were killed following the so-called *Affaire des Placards*. He was first strangled and then burned at the stake on 16 February 1535. See Doumergue, *Jean Calvin,* 1:338-40.

63. For these and the next paragraphs I am relying on the account of Dankbaar, *Calvijn,* 17ff.

64. Louis du Tillet and John Calvin remained in correspondence long after Calvin was no longer in the Roman Catholic Church which Tillet never left.

65. Thomas Platter at Basel printed the first edition of the *Institutes* in March, 1536. Calvin and Tillet had together arrived at Basel two months earlier. At the time Calvin had protected himself by transposing the letters of his Latinized name Calvinus to Lucianus, adding Martianus as a first name to make the assumed name complete. The book, printed in Latin under the title "Christianae Religionis Institutio," was an instant success. Calvin continued to work on this enormously influential book. Further editions in Latin appeared in 1539, 1543, 1545, 1550, 1553, and 1554. A French translation was published in 1541 in such excellent French that it gained Calvin a place among the classic authors of France. Additional French versions were printed in 1545 and 1551. The famous printer Robert Estienne at Geneva published the "definitive" fourth edition in 1559. In size it had grown five times as large as the first edition. The importance of the *Institutio* was not lost on his opponents who in February of 1544 burnt a copy of the book in front of Notre Dame in Paris.

66. Two of the best studies are

a. Williston Walker, *Jean Calvin: l'homme et l'oeuvre*. Edition française. Traduit avec l'authorisation de l'auteur par E. N. Weiss. (Geneva: A. Jullien, 1909). This translation was produced on the occasion of the four hundredth anniversary of Calvin's birth. Walker had published his book earlier in English under the title *John Calvin: the Organiser of Reformed Protestantism, 1509-1564.* (New York and London: G.P. Putnam's Sons, 1906). A.M. Hugo considers Walker's book the best biography of Calvin.

b. F. Wendel, *Calvin: Sources et Évolution de sa Pensée religieuse.* This work was published as a volume in the Series *Études d'histoire et de philosophie religieuses publiées par la Faculté de Théologie Protestante de l'Université de Strasbourg.* (Paris: Les Presses Universitaires de France, 1950). This work was translated into English by Philip Mairet under the title *Calvin: The Origins and Development of his Religious Thought* (New York: Harper & Row, 1963).

For Dankbaar, *Calvijn*, see 23ff.

67. This point is also made by Wendel, *Sources et Évolution,* 25, who adds that Calvin, in his capacity as a church official, participated in the procession and the prayers.

68. Calvin elaborates on these earlier sentiments in his *Response to Sadoleto* and in the introduction to his *Commentary on the Psalms.*

69. *C.R.,* 6:519. How true Calvin's claim is has been amply demonstrated by Willem Nijenhuis in his doctoral dissertation *Calvinus Oecumenicus: Calvijn en de Eenheid der kerk in het Licht van zijn Briefwisseling* ('s-Gravenhage: Martinus Nijhoff, 1959).

70. *C.R.,* 31:27. The last sentence in this quote may well refer to the fact that Calvin prior to 1533 had not made the Bible and theology the center of his studies. He would remember that well although the *Preface* was written in 1557, almost twenty-five years later.

71. *C.R.,* 5:412.

72. This letter has been reprinted in its entirety by Jacques Pannier, ed. *Épître au roi François Ier.* Préface de la première édition de l'Institution de la Religion Chrétienne, 1541. Texte publié pour la premiére fois, d'aprés l'exemplaire de la Bibliothèque Nationale, avec Introduction et notes. (Paris: Bibliothèque Nationale, 1927).

73. The exact title is Abraham Hulshof, *Geschiedenis van de Doopsgezinden te Straatsburg van 1525 tot 1557,* (Amsterdam: J. Clausen, 1905). Chapter 9, pp. 186-201, is entitled "*Calvijn en de Doopsgezinden.*"

74. Ibid., 199. Within the limits of this essay it is not possible to pursue additional aspects of a similarity between Calvin and representatives of the Radical- or Left Wing Reformation. The relation has been noted by several scholars. A good example is Opeke Noordmans who observed: "I have always been of the opinion . . . that the Reformed person is a twin brother of the Anabaptist (Doopsgezinde). But he (the Reformed) reckoned more with creation-as-opposition and regulated himself accordingly with a certain sobriety. He accepted compromises that Anabaptists refused." *Het Koninkrijk der Hemelen* (Nijkerk: Callenbach, 1949), 58.

75. Idelette died at Geneva, 29 March 1549. For Calvin's intimate thoughts about his happy marriage see the letters he wrote to his friend Farel on 2 and 7 April 1549. In August of 1540 Farel had come from Neuchâtel to Strasbourg to marry Calvin and Idelette. The letters are printed in *C.R.,* 13: epistulae 1171 and 1173. Idelette van Buren came also from Luik (Liège), perhaps the daughter of a Lambert van Buren who in 1533, deprived of all his possessions, had

been banished from Luik for the rest of his life. Hulshof, *Geschiedenis*, 194.

76. A most helpful distinction for the different types of Reformation churches has been made by H. van der Linde in his dissertation *Una Sancta: het oecumenisch vraagstuk en de arbeid van Rome voor de hereniging der kerk* (Nijkerk: Callenbach, 1948). Van der Linde makes a distinction between Protestantism and Reformation. The latter comprises the churches of Luther, Zwingli, and Calvin. Protestantism includes those denominations which, simultaneously with the Reformation, broke with the church of the Middle Ages and later emerged from their midst, but which by their individualism and spiritualism clearly distanced themselves from the Reformation's concepts of faith and church.

77. George H. Williams reviewed the literature in his instructive article: "Studies in Radical Reformation (1517-1618): a Bibliographical Survey of Research since 1939," published in *Church History* (a quarterly published by the American Society of Church History at Wallingforth, PA), 27 (1958): 46-69, 124-160. Williams distinguishes in the movement between Anabaptists, Spiritualists, and Evangelical Rationalists. Kenneth S. Latourette includes in the radical reformers: Anabaptists, Spiritualists, Anti-trinitarians, and Socinians, in his *A History of Christianity* (New York: Harper & Row, 1953), 778-96. Willem Balke in his dissertation provides an even more refined distinction by listing seven groups: Thomas Müntzer and the prophets of Zwickau; Swiss Brethren originating in Zurich including the group of Hubmaier, Denck, and Grebel; the group of Michael Sattler and the Confessio Schlattensis (1527); Melchiorites who followed Melchior Hoffman; the Baptists at Münster; the Mennonites; and the followers of David Joris. See *Calvijn en de Doperse Radikalen* (Amsterdam: Ton Bolland, 1973), 1-3. This book has been most helpful, especially for the later part of this paper.

78. The original title reads, *Brève Instruction pour Armer tous bons Fidèles contre les erreurs de la Secte Commune des Anabaptistes. C.O.*, 7:45-142.

79. *C.O.*, 7:53.

80. The original title reads *Contre la Secte phantastique et furieuse qui se nomme spirituel. C.O.*, 7:145-248.

81. *C.O.*, 7:153.

82. *Institutio*, 2:2, 15-16. A good English translation of the *Institutes*, based on the fourth edition of 1559, has been provided by Ford Lewis Battles in the Library of Christian Classics, edited by John T. McNeill (Philadelphia: Westminster Press, 1960).

83. *Institutio*, 2:2, 18.

84. In his *Brève Instruction* (see above note 78) Calvin stated very explicitly: " . . . nous sommes de bon accord." (. . . we are well agreed). *C.O.* 7:65. Hulshof analyzed this ambivalent relation between Calvin and Baptists very well. See note 73.

85. For the purpose of that kind of education Calvin wrote the *Institutio*. See especially his introduction to the French edition.

86. *Institutio*, 2:16, 19.

87. Commentary on Romans 7:26, in *C.O.*, 49, 136.

88. Werner Krusche, in his *Promotionsschrift* of 1953, published as *Das Wirken des Heiligen Geistes nach Calvin*, (Göttingen: VandenHoeck & Ruprecht, 1959), 136ff and passim.

89. *C.O.*, 55, 304-307.

90. *C.O.*, 44, 34.

91. *Institutio*, 4:1, 23.

92. *C.O.*, 22, 89. This *Confession* was submitted to Geneva's City Council in 1537, a time when public debates with Anabaptists were held. Several

months later, in a public meeting in St. Peter's Church, on Sunday, 29 July 1537, the citizens of Geneva adopted the Confession.

93. Balke, *Radikalen*, 117-122. It should not be forgotten that Libertarians in Geneva, in order to spite Calvin, would support Anabaptists with whom they might not agree theologically.

94. *C.O.*, 38, 59. See for this pastoral concern also Wilhelm Kolfhaus, *Christusgemeinschaft bei Johannes Calvin* (Neukirchen: Buchhandlung des Erziehungsvereins, 1939), 180ff. This work was reprinted in 1949.

95. For this section I gratefully rely on an excellent article by M. Eugene Osterhaven, "Eating and Drinking Christ: the Lord's Supper as an Act of Worship in the Theology and Practice of Calvin," *Reformed Review, A theological Journal of Western Theological Seminary*, 37, no. 2, (Winter 1984): 83-93. See also Osterhaven's observations on perfectionism in his book, *The Spirit of the Reformed Tradition* (Grand Rapids; William B. Eerdmans Publishing Company, 1971) especially the section, "Life in the Holy Spirit," 112-118.

96. *Institutio*, 3:2:4, 18, 20.

97. Ibid., 4:17, 33.

98. This point is well made by Jean-Daniel Benoit, *Calvin: Directeur d'Ames* (Strasbourg: Librarie Oberlin, 1947). This book was available to me in the Dutch translation by A.J.A. Mondt-Lovink, *Calvijn als Zielzorger* (Nijkerk, Callenbach, n.d.).

99. For this and the previous quotes, see *Institutio*, 4:17, 42-43.

100. *C.O.*, 23, 120.

101. This statement is made in his sermon on Daniel 12:8-13. *C.O.*, 49, 165-66.

Richard T. Hughes

Richard T. Hughes is Professor and Chairman of the Department of history, Abilene Christian University. He was educated at Harding College (B.A. 1965), Abilene Christian University (M.A. 1967), and the University of Iowa (Ph.D. 1972). He has taught at Pepperdine University (1971-76), Southwest Missouri State University (1976-83), and Abilene Christian University (1983-present).

For fifteen years, Hughes has studied the role of the restoration ideal in radical Protestantism, and is especially interested in the impact of that theme on American culture, politics, and national self-understanding. He has written several articles exploring these themes and connections. Currently he is writing two volumes, one on politics and primitivism in ante-bellum America, and one on the history of the Churches of Christ for the Greenwood Press "Denominations in America" series. In his essay, "Christian Primitivism as Perfectionism: From Anabaptists to Pentecostals," he identifies Christian primitivism or restorationism as a type of perfectionism, and gives evidence of the variety of primitivist perfectionism which has existed throughout the history of Protestantism.

8

CHRISTIAN PRIMITIVISM AS PERFECTIONISM: FROM ANABAPTISTS TO PENTECOSTALS

Richard T. Hughes

PERFECTIONISM in Christian history has worn many faces. Usually the term signifies emphasis on the sanctification or perfection of the individual believer. But another form of perfectionism has been equally persistent: The concern to perfect the *church* by rejecting Christian history with its imperfections and ambiguities and by restoring instead the primitive church of the apostolic age.

This type of perfectionism—which we may call Christian primitivism or restorationism—has abounded within Protestantism. This paper will review the most prominent of the primitivist efforts within the Protestant spectrum, ranging from Anabaptists and Puritans to Mormons and Pentecostals. Further, it will seek to determine how the primitivist motif has intertwined itself with other theological themes and how it has related itself to cultural and social concerns. In addition, it will seek to impose some semblance of order on the multi-nuanced primitivist world view by distinguishing between *ecclesiastical primitivism,* wherein the forms and structures of the apostolic church are of paramount concern; *ethical primitivism,* wherein the lifestyle of the ancient Christians is the chief concern; and *experiential primitivism,* wherein the apostolic gifts of the Spirit are of ultimate concern.[1] Typologies are always approximations at best, and there are certainly ways in which these categories overlap one another in various combinations. Further, Christian primitivism was sometimes intimately related to the more traditional form of perfectionism which focused on individual sanctification. But the common thread that bound all primitivists together was a mutual striving to live and move in a perfect church, patterned after an apostolic model.

It should be said from the outset that this concern has not been true of all Christians nor even of all Protestants.[2] Luther, for example, is a classic exception. Luther did not pursue the fundamental question of all Christian primitivists, namely, "What was the ancient tradition?" Rather, he raised what to him was the most fundamental question of all, "How can I find a merciful God?" Put another way, the primitivists were concerned with *chronological reform,* that is, returning to the time of beginnings. Luther, on the other hand, was concerned with *ontological reform,* that is, receiving the gift of *ontos* (being) from the God who is Being-itself.[3]

There is a sense, to be sure, in which Luther was a primitivist for as he himself put it, "the crawling maggots of man-made laws and regulations" had "eaten into the entire world" and had "swallowed up . . . all Holy Scripture."[4] Thus, Luther sought to go behind the "man-made laws and regulations" of history and to preach once again the primitive gospel of grace and faith. From this perspective, Luther perhaps could be called a "gospel primitivist." But the essence of that gospel, in Luther's view, was God's activity, not man's, and this was the difference that made all the difference. Thus, once the gospel had been proclaimed, Luther sought not so much to recover apostolic forms or traditions as simply to receive by faith the grace whereby God enabled him to stand.

In point of fact, Luther viewed efforts to recover the traditions and experiences of primitive Christianity as fundamentally at odds with the gospel. Thus, he severely chastised Andreas Karlstadt who had sought to abolish from the Wittenberg church practices he viewed as non-apostolic. "Listen, murderer of souls and sinful spirit!" Luther thundered, "Are you not indeed a murderer of souls who sets himself above us in God's place and takes away our Christian liberty and subordinates consciences to himself?" From Luther's perspective, the contention that the rites and practices of the primitive church were normative in and of themselves was an argument that "destroys faith, profanes the blood of Christ, blasphemes the gospel, and sets all that Christ has won for us at nought."[5] For Luther, primitivism placed man's efforts above God's grace and was therefore the worst sort of idolatry.

ETHICAL PRIMITIVISM

But if Luther rejected all forms of Christian primitivism other than "gospel primitivism," there were others in the Reformation period who disagreed. Perhaps most notable in this regard were the *ethical primitivists* of the Reformation period, the evangelical Anabaptists,[6] who sought to recover the ethical and moral purity—the disciplined lifestyle—of the apostolic communities. According to these Anabaptists, the union of church and state that had dominated Europe since Constantine completely precluded the possibility of an ethically pure church, for within the state-church arrangement, church membership was not by choice but by birth. Obviously, hundreds and thousands of church members would inevitably be unconcerned and uncommitted. Further, the state-church arrangement provided no possibility for church discipline by which ethical purity within the church could be enforced. Therefore, these Anabaptists felt they had no choice but to separate from the established order and to gather congregations of committed believers whose conscious, adult commitment to righteousness and purity would be symbolized by adult baptism. Thus it was that on January 21, 1525, in Zurich, Conrad Grebel baptized George Blaurock upon Blaurock's confession of faith—the first adult baptism in the Reformation era.

The primitivist motif punctuates the early history of these Anabaptists. To them, it was apparent that Christian churches prior to Constantine were communities of committed believers, fully willing to suffer persecution and even death for their commitment to the lifestyle of Christ. But since that time, the world had so thoroughly seduced the church by the allure of power and privilege that, from the Anabaptists' perspective, there was now no substantial difference between the church and the world. This left the Anabaptists no choice but to restore the ethically pure and committed church that they felt existed prior to the Constantinian church-state union. No one made this point more clearly than did Menno Simons. The established church, he wrote, was a "worldly church" and "has left her lawful husband, Christ, and follows after strange lovers." He sought, therefore, "to reclaim this adulterous bride . . . and return her to her first husband.''[7] In a particularly illuminating statement, Menno wrote that

> since it is as clear as the noonday sun that for many centuries no difference has been visible between the church and the world, . . . we are constrained . . . to gather together . . . a pious and penitent congregation or church out of all impure and deceiving sects of the world. . . .[8]

Like Luther, Menno and his colleagues did not emphasize the forms, structures, and rites of the apostolic church. Nor was their principal concern with the theology of faith and grace that meant so much to Luther. Rather, theirs was an ethical, behavioral restoration. While insisting, for example, on adult baptism, the Anabaptists rigorously insisted that outward baptism does not make a Christian. Thus, Menno denied that ''we are one church with the Münsterites, because they and we were baptized with the same baptism externally.''[9] Rather, he wrote that all who were ''quarrelsome, tumultuous, slanderous, defaming, bitter, wrathful, and cruel of heart'' were not ''in His kingdom, even though they do carry the external appearance of being Christians, and are greeted as brethren.''[10] What made one a Christian was a changed life. In 1539 Menno declared that

> no one can be a profitable member in this . . . pure body of Christ who is not believing, regenerate, converted, changed, and renewed; who is not kind, generous, merciful, pitying, chaste, sober, humble, patient, long-suffering, just, constant, heavenly and spiritually minded with Christ.[11]

Balthasar Hubmaier agreed. For him, baptism was a pledge to a new life of righteousness and purity. ''He [the baptismal candidate] has purposed and pledged himself in heart henceforth to lead another and a better life,'' Hubmaier wrote. ''He shall testify this publicly when he receives the water of baptism.''[12]

Their preoccupation with a pure church also explains the Anabaptists' concern for the rigorous exercise of church discipline. Indeed, a candidate for baptism had to promise to submit to exclusion, or the ban, should he or she become entangled once again with the world. While one purpose of the ban was to reclaim the errant believer, it also was intended to preserve the purity of the church. As Menno wrote, sinful members should be excluded ''lest the others be corrupted and the ugly scurvy be transmitted to other sheep.''[13] And Dietrich Philips asserted that ''if open sinners, transgressors, and the disorderly are not excluded, the whole congregation must be defiled (1

Cor. 5:13; 1 Thess. 5:14), and if false brethren are retained, we become partakers of their sins."[14] In such a case, the separatist congregations of the Anabaptists would become no better than the inclusive church of the larger society. Thus, the ban was fundamental to restoring the purity of pre-Constantinian Christianity. Indeed, Menno himself placed the ban squarely in the context of Christian primitivism: "The [ban] was so diligently practiced, first by Christ Jesus and his apostles, and afterward by us, who are intent upon recovering again Christian doctrine and practice. . . ."[15] Clearly, the distinguishing mark of evangelical Anabaptism was its concern for ethical perfectionism in the context of Christian primitivism.[16]

ECCLESIASTICAL PRIMITIVISM

If ethical primitivism focused on an ethically pure church, unspotted by the world, ecclesiastical primitivism focused from its beginning on the forms and structures of the primitive church, especially liturgy, rituals, and church organization. Interestingly, ethical primitivism in the sixteenth century lay for a while in the same cradle with ecclesiastical primitivism and, to some degree, was born of the same womb. But as the children grew, they became increasingly antagonistic toward one another.

The womb of ecclesiastical primitivism was the fascination with Christian antiquity that characterized the Christian Humanists of the sixteenth century.[17] Renaissance Humanism, the mother of Christian Humanism, had sought to recover, translate, and edit the texts of pagan antiquity, and had advocated behavior in keeping with the ethical norms of these ancient pagan thinkers. But when Renaissance Humanism crossed the Alps, it took on a decidedly Christian cast. The concern now was to recover the texts of *Christian* antiquity that had been obscured during the Middle Ages, and to live lives in harmony with the ethical teachings of the ancient Christian thinkers. Through its presence in numerous European universities, Christian Humanism exerted a profound influence on the Reformed wing of Protestant Christianity. Indeed, most of the early Reformed theologians had been schooled in the presuppositions and methods of Christian Humanism and therefore had a profound reverence for Christian antiquity.

If Christian Humanism was the womb of ecclesiastical

primitivism, Zurich was its cradle. Indeed, Huldreich Zwingli, "people's priest" of the Great Minster there from 1519-1531, had been steeped in humanistic learning, studying under Heinrich Woelfli (Lupulus) at Bern, Conrad Celtis at Vienna, and Thomas Wyttenbach at Basel. It is no wonder, then, that Zwingli exhibited a typically humanistic fascination with antiquity which found expression in a thoroughgoing primitivist theology. But Zwingli's primitivism fastened especially on the legal dimensions of the primitive church. Thus, in his *Commentary on True and False Religion,* Zwingli conceived of God as a lawgiver who "rises . . . in the night . . . to arrange and prescribe everything early, that we may not begin to labor before the allotted task has been assigned."[18] Within this legal context, Zwingli condemned both singing and organs in the church since they were not commanded in the apostolic churches and because they pointed away from the true, invisible worship of the heart.[19] Indeed, in Zwingli's Zurich, the mass was reduced to a simple memorial supper; images and organs were destroyed, relics and vestments were abolished, pilgrimages were eliminated, and a plethora of medieval laws and prohibitions were lifted, including prohibitions concerning clerical celibacy.[20] The reason for these changes was simply because such practices failed to conform to the clear word of God and had no precedent in the apostolic tradition.

It is significant that Zwingli's ecclesiastical primitivism and the Anabaptists' ethical primitivism grew from a common humanist womb and lay in the same Swiss cradle. Indeed, Conrad Grebel, acknowledged leader of Swiss Anabaptism, was a resident of Zurich and had learned from Zwingli's own preaching the normative importance of apostolic Christianity.[21] But Zwingli was not prepared to take seriously the ethical implications that those early Anabaptists perceived in the model of apostolic Christianity. To do so would have meant a break with the Zurich Council and a rejection of his position as a minister of the established order. Thus, Grebel himself rebuked Zwingli and the Council for failing to carry out what Grebel perceived as the lifestyle and ordinances of the primitive church. Grebel was particularly concerned with believers' baptism, for it was the one ordinance that would most effectively distinguish the regenerate community of believers from the old, corrupt state church. "Your shepherds have often asserted," proclaimed Grebel, "that the Scriptures must be allowed to speak for themselves to which we may not add nor subtract anything. Although this was the intention it was never carried out. . . . [I] am sure that . . . [Zwingli] has exactly this same understanding of baptism. . . . [I] do not know . . . for what reason he does not declare himself."[22]

In an effort to have his cake and eat it, too, Zwingli had settled for second best. He could maintain allegiance to the primitive church and at one and the same time maintain power and position in the established order by recovering the rites, forms, and structures of primitive Christianity, while essentially ignoring the ethical dimensions of the apostolic communities.

But if Zwingli simultaneously held to ecclesiastical primitivism and the established order, it was left to England to fuse the two. Indeed, nowhere did ecclesiastical primitivism flower more fully than in England, where recovery of the primitive church became a means of enhancing the civic order. The soil for this development was prepared by William Tyndale whose prefaces and prologues to his popular 1534 New Testament emphasized the covenant between God and His people as the central theme of Scripture, and whose prologue to Jonah portrayed England as standing in a covenant relation with God. By 1547, when Edward VI ascended the English throne, the notion of England as a new Israel was becoming increasingly commonplace, and even Archbishop Cranmer, at the young king's coronation, designated Edward as a young Josiah who would "suppress idolatry, remove images, and discharge the tyranny of the bishop of Rome."[23]

Given the extensive influence of Christian Humanism in sixteenth-century England, it perhaps was inevitable that Christian primitivism eventually would be yoked to Tyndale's covenant theology. This did not happen under Henry VIII since most early Christian Humanists in England stopped well short of pressing for recovery of the primitive church.[24] But during the reign of Edward VI, several Reformed theologians from the Continent planted the seeds of ecclesiastical primitivism squarely in England's covenantal garden.[25] This was especially true of Martin Bucer whose *De Regno Christi* of 1550 argued that through proper attention to the ancient church, England could become the kingdom of Christ; of Peter Martyr Vermigli, who for six years as Regius Professor of Divinity at Oxford stressed primitive Christ-

ianity in the context of the national covenant; and of Huldreich
Bullinger, Zwingli's successor in Zurich, whose primitivist influence was felt in England principally through his *Decades of Sermons*. By the time of Edward's death in 1553, many English people
were convinced that the nation would flourish and prosper to the
extent that the Church of England corresponded to the apostolic
Christian communities.

No wonder, then, that when Mary Tudor acceded to the
throne in 1553 and launched her campaign to crush Protestantism
through persecution, many Protestants viewed her reign as God's
curse upon England for their failure to recover primitive Christianity during the rule of Edward. This was particularly true of many
who fled to the Continent to escape possible death at Mary's
hands. Though not all the Marian Exiles were covenantal
primitivists, many were, and these many became in exile England's earliest Puritans. While these Puritans had first learned
covenant theology from William Tyndale, their fellow exile John
Foxe dramatically strengthened this perspective through his *Actes
and Monuments* which portrayed England as an "elect nation."[26]
Armed with this outlook, the Puritans viewed their task as simple
and clear. They had failed to recover primitive Christianity under
Edward, and for this failure God had afflicted them with His
wrath.[27] But when Mary died, they would return to England and
thoroughly transform the established church into apostolic communities. They would spare no means and leave no stone un-
turned. They were determined that never again would England
suffer the warth of God for her failure to embrace the apostolic
Christian faith.

Thus it was that when Mary died and Elizabeth ascended the
English throne in 1558, these early Puritans returned home to
launch their propaganda campaign designed to transform
England into "the kingdom of Christ," to borrow Bucer's
phrase, and thereby to bring God's favor and blessing upon the
nation. To gain these ends, they preached in the pulpits, lectured in the university lecture halls, particularly at Cambridge,
and published pamphlets, broadsides, and books with a fervor
characteristic of desperate men. To be sure, desperation was never
far away, for the stakes amounted to nothing more or less than
salvation of the nation itself.

These earliest Puritans were Presbyterians who, having witnessed Presbyterian polity in Geneva, became convinced not
only of its value for eroding the power of the archbishop and

enhancing the power of the people, but also of its apostolic origins. This was true even for those early Puritans who had not shared in the exile experience. Thus, for example, Thomas Cartwright contended that Presbyterianism "is no innovation but a renovation and the doctrine not newe but renued no straunger but borne in Sion whereunto it . . . ought now of right to be restored."[28] Quite naturally, Anglicans defended themselves with similar appeals to primitive Christianity, and Anglicans and Puritans alike employed the primitivist rhetoric against the traditions of Rome. Thus, Leonard Trinterud has contended that "nothing in early Elizabethan religion was quite so sacred as the primitive church. Upon it hung the entire case of English religion against Rome, whether that case was argued by the Queen, by Bishop Jewel, by John Foxe, or by any other spokesman."[29]

In spite of the rhetoric during her reign, however, Elizabeth herself consistently frustrated the Puritans' attempts to remake the Church of England after a primitive, Presbyterian model. So thorough were the frustrations that by the 1580s, at least some Puritan primitivists were opting for separatism— "reformation without tarrying for anie" as Robert Browne put it in 1582. For these Separatists, the model of primitive Christianity was no longer presbyterian but rather congregational. One thing, however, had not changed, and that was the zeal with which these separating congregationalists defended their churches as fundamentally apostolic. Thus, Henry Barrow rejected the presbyterianism of the earliest Puritans and exalted the primitive church instead as the true model for the church in his day. Just because the fathers erred, Barrow asked, "should we therefore justify or persist in their errors? Especially should we reject the true pattern of Christ's Testament which reproveth our works, and showeth us a better course?"[30]

Similarly, those who became Non-separating Congregationalists shortly after 1600 defended their polity with an equal zeal for primitive Christianity. Thus, Henry Jacob, the father of Congregational Puritanism, advocated "a true Visible or Ministeriall Church of Christ" wherein members observed "all religious & vertuous duties as Christ & the Apostles did institute & practice in the Gospel."[31] And the Separatist turned Congregationalist John Robinson argued that the Congregational way was "cast in the apostolical and primitive mould, and not one day nor hour younger, in the nature and form of it, than the first church of the New Testament."[32]

It is hardly surprising, then, that the various sectarian spinoffs from English Puritanism typically defended themselves by appealing to primitive Christianity. Thus, Baptists found in believers' baptism not only the most logical symbol for congregational separatism but also a rite clearly practiced in the apostolic communities. And the Quakers, originating in 1652, sought to return to an interior spirituality which, it seemed to them, characterized the earliest Christian communities and was prior, both in time and importance, to outward books and ceremonies. It was their cultivation of "that of God within" which William Penn clearly labeled "primitive Christianity revived."[33]

Ecclesiastical primitivism, however, was destined to blossom into full flower not in England but in America. This was due in large measure to the fact that the New England Puritans, who stamped the self-consciousness of all Americans as did no other immigrant group, exerted their bias toward primitive Christianity in powerful ways. Indeed, Professor Dwight Bozeman has argued that New England Puritans were first and foremost biblical primitivists who fled England not to erect a "city on a hill," and certainly not to launch a millennial age for the world, but rather to return, in awesome awareness of their covenant with God, to the ancient order depicted in holy writ.[34] Further, New England Puritans were quite certain of their success in restoring the primitive church. Thus, Edward Winslow could argue in 1646 concerning both Plymouth and Massachusetts Bay that "the Primitive Churches were and are their and our mutuall patterns and examples." And John Cotton was certain that the New England way was as close as could be to what "the Lord Jesus [would erect] were he here himselfe in person."[35]

There were others, however, who disputed these smug assertions and organized their dissent upon the very restorationist premises that sustained the established New England order. Roger Williams was a case in point. Taking his stand on apostolic ground, Williams charged that the Church of England was, in fact, no church at all, and that though the New England churches had made progress toward primitive Christianity, "yet you never came out of the Wilderness to this Day." His advice, therefore, to the New England established order was to "abstract your selfe with a holy violence from the Dung heape of this Earth" and to submit to that "second kind of regeneration" which demanded allegiance even to a New Testament pattern of worship.

Following banishment from Massachusetts, Williams' primitivism moved him to participate in 1639 in the formation of a Baptist church in Providence, Rhode Island. His participation in the Baptist faith, however, was to be short-lived, for he soon concluded that the apostasy from the primitive order had been so complete that no person or persons on earth could possibly hope to recover the purity of ancient Christianity. Attempts to do so would only produce "great mistakes and wanderings from the first Patterns and Institutions of Christ Jesus." Only God could now restore the primitive church in the fulness of its purity, and He would do so through new apostles who would proclaim the ancient gospel and gather apostolic congregations in the impending millennium. Thus, Williams finally emerged as a Seeker, waiting for the millennial restoration.[36]

Williams' millennium never came, and the millennial restorationists of the mid-seventeenth century disappeared. Significantly, however, ecclesiastical primitivism was kept alive in New England principally by Separate Baptists who, after the Great Awakening, were increasingly convinced that the New England Puritans had compromised with modernity, particularly in their Half-Way Covenant of 1662. While Separate Baptists in New England argued for adult immersion as the apostolic mode and rejected creeds in favor of the Bible alone, Separate Baptists in the South after 1755 carried restorationism even further in an attempt to recover numerous practices of the early church (see below, p. 232).

If anyone thought, however, that ecclesiastical primitivism would be confined in America to a radical band of Separate Baptists, they were wrong. For shortly after the birth of the Republic, ecclesiastical primitivism burst upon the scene as the passionate concern of hundreds and thousands of Americans, many of whom eventually found their way into three American restoration movements: the "Christians," the Baptists, and the Mormons.

ECCLESIASTICAL PRIMITIVISM: THREE AMERICAN MOVEMENTS

The American Background

There were solid reasons for the phenomenal growth of these

two movements and for the renewal of the restoration sentiment in American culture at that particular time. First, due to
the pervasive influence of Puritan thought, the restoration sentiment had become the mainspring of much of the Anglo-
American religious experience, regardless of whether that experience was incarnate in Baptist, Methodist, Quaker, or even
Deist forms. The propriety of measuring contemporary religious
life by primordial norms had become an accepted way of doing
theology in America, whether those norms were the norms of
nature in the case of the Deists, or the norms of the primitive
church in the case of more orthodox Christians.[37]

But what factors in American life had focused and
radicalized this sentiment so as to produce such strongly dis-
senting and enormously popular traditions as the Mormons and
the Christians? There were at least five factors that came together during the years of the early Republic to buttress the
traditional primitivist ideology and to make restorationism a
popular expression of the Christian faith.

First, the American democratic experiment appeared to many
Americans to be both radically new and fundamentally primordial at one and the same time, and thereby to transcend both
history and tradition altogether. As the Great Seal of the
United States clearly suggested, America was a "new order of
the ages" emerging from the desolate wilderness of history and
tradition. Now cut loose from the aristocratic and totalitarian
traditions of the Old World, America presented herself, as Tom
Paine suggested, "as in the beginning of a world. . . . We are
brought at once to the point of seeing government begin, as if
we had lived in the beginning of time . . . , unmutilated by contri-
vance, or the errors of tradition."[38]

A second reason for the renewal of primitivism in this period
is closely related to the first, namely, the antiquity and
primeval quality of the American land itself. As John Locke
observed in his *Second Treatise on Government,* "In the beginning, all the world was America." To those pioneers who
settled the frontier in the early nineteenth century, the American wilderness seemed like Eden rediscovered. Significantly,
substantial restorationist ferment emerged in those wilderness
regions.[39]

Third, ecclesiastical primitivism was a powerful way of translating the freedom that already had been won in the civic arena

into the realm of the churches. While Americans were no longer vulnerable to the political tyrannies of princes and kings, many American Christians still felt vulnerable to the tyrannies of clerics, traditions, and creeds. A most effective antidote to these tyrannies was to renounce the jurisdiction of Christian history altogether and to take refuge instead in primitive Christianity. This strategy was characteristic, for example, of the broadly based anti-mission movement which, between 1800 and 1840, sought to reject the power of the traditionally established churches simply by rejecting their traditions and creeds as post-apostolic and therefore illegitimate.

Fourth, ecclesiastical primitivism was an effective rejoinder to religious pluralism in the new nation. Long accustomed to one church for one nation, transplanted Europeans were bewildered by the vast array of churches in America, all competing as equals in the vast free market of souls. Many, therefore, were moved to raise that peculiarly American question: "Which of all the churches is the true church?" And they typically assumed that the true church could be known and the false churches exposed by comparing them all to the standard of primitive Christianity revealed in Holy Writ.

Fifth and finally, ecclesiastical primitivism was a natural corollary to the optimistic post-millennialism that gripped the thinking of so many Americans in the early national period. The successful revolution and the emergence of a free and democratic nation convinced many Americans that the long-anticipated millennium was at last about to dawn. But would it dawn—could it dawn—while American churches were still bound to the bankrupt traditions of history and still badly divided from one another by the persistence of those very traditions? It therefore was clear to Americans like Alexander Campbell that American Christians must unite themselves upon the primitive and apostolic foundations in order to actualize the millennial age.

Ecclesiastical Primitivism: The Christians

All these factors combined to produce an intellectual and cultural climate highly conducive to the rise of various restorationist movements. Indeed, the most striking aspect of the "Christian" movement was its simultaneous emergence in four widely separate locales under four influential leaders, each initially oblivious to the existence of the other three.[40] The first of the four movements was led by James O'Kelly in Virginia and North Carolina and was passionately dedicated to religious freedom. Rejecting the clerical authority of Bishop Asbury and the Methodist Episcopal Church, O'Kelly and several other ministers withdrew in 1792 and took refuge in the primitive church. In 1794 Rice Haggard convinced these "New Lights" that they should reject all names born of history and tradition and be known simply as Christians.[41]

A similar movement was emerging during the same period in New England under the leadership of Abner Jones and, even more importantly, Elias Smith. A radical Jeffersonian, Smith resisted every encroachment on his liberty, perceived or real, that emanated from the established churches, and dedicated himself to shearing those churches of their power. Not surprisingly, he resisted expansion of those churches under whatever guise and therefore became a major figure in the campaign against ecclesiastical missionary societies in the early nineteenth century. Coming from a Separate Baptist background and therefore well-acquainted with the rhetoric of restorationism, Smith called for the recovery of a primitive church in which members would be simply Christians and over which the traditions of men would hold no sway.[42]

Far more important from the standpoint of later institutional developments than either the Smith or O'Kelly movements was another "Christian" movement that originated in Kentucky under the leadership of Barton W. Stone. Once again, power and freedom were central issues. Stone and four other Presbyterian ministers had participated in the highly ecumenical Cane Ridge Revival of 1801, had involved themselves in the revival's charismatic exercises,[43] and had set themselves against the Calvinistic notion of rigid predestination. When one of their number was censured by the Synod of Kentucky for doctrinal deviance, Stone and his colleagues withdrew from the Synod in 1803 and formed the Springfield Presbytery, only to dissolve that body in the spring of 1804 in order to become "Christians only." The Stone movement took root and flourished especially in Kentucky, Tennessee, northern Alabama, and southern Ohio, and it made converts especially among Separate Baptists who already shared a primitivist orientation. By 1811, according to one contemporary source, the Stone movement boasted some 13,000 adherents.[44]

There is a profound sense in which the Stone movement was dedicated to ethical primitivism fully as much as to ecclesiastical primitivism. In the very first issue of Stone's *Christian Messenger* (November 25, 1826) Stone called for "the restoration and glory of the ancient religion of Christ." He defined this concept as walking in the spirit instead of the flesh, as being dead to sin and alive to God, and as being willing to give up wealth, pride, and valued relationships for the sake of truth.[45] Out of this context, Stone and his colleagues rejected slavery, urged compassion for the poor and the downtrodden, and called for separation from the "God-robbing practices" of this world.

At the same time, however, the Stone movement also pursued ecclesiastical primitivism, but their pursuit of this theme amounted far more to a rejection of historic traditions than to a positive reconstruction of primitive Christian practices. The reason for this negative emphasis was their profound commitment to religious freedom in the aftermath of the American Revolution. The fact is that Baptists, Methodists, and Presbyterians in Virginia and Kentucky had been exceedingly zealous for civic liberty during the revolutionary period. As Daniel Trabue, a Separate Baptist of those regions during the Revolution, later recalled:

> Their was meetings Called to consult about the war. Their was Fast Days appointed. The baptist and Prespeteruns was ancious for the war. Then it was that most of the men had hunting shirts and had "Lirbety" marked on their hunting shirts and bucks' tails in their hats. And the Mejority of the people said, "We will fight for out lirbety."[46]

But when the War was over, the clergy's tyranny still persisted, a tyranny that Stone and his colleagues thought was particularly apparent in the treatment they received from the Synod of Kentucky. Thus, Richard M'Nemar wrote of the Stone movement in its earliest years that "it is difficult to paint the zeal for liberty, and just indignation against the old aristocratic spirit, which glowed through every member of this new confederacy."[47]

Indeed, one could argue that if any one theme was more central to the Stone movement than any other, it was this ideal of freedom. From that perspective, these radicals rejected all the encumbrances of history embodied in creeds, clerics, and tradition, and even jettisoned theology itself. As one of Stone's colleagues observed, ''We are not personally acquainted with the writings of John Calvan [sic], nor are we certain how nearly we agree with his views of divine truth; neither do we care.''[48] Their gaze was fixed, instead, squarely on primitive Christianity revealed in Holy Writ.

Their commitment to freedom was so strong that they avoided developing ecclesiastical traditions of any kind, even traditions predicated on primitive Christianity. Thus, for example, even believers' baptism, acknowledged by practically all Stoneites as apostolic, was simply left to the discretion of the individual.[49] Consequently, the Stone movement was, from the outset, both vacuous and amorphous, largely without dogma, form, or structure. The common thread that held the movement together was a commitment to primitive Christianity whose chief role was to legitimize both Christian character and Christian freedom.

But Stoneite primitivism performed another role as well, namely, the hastening of the millennial kingdom of God. Like many other Americans of their time, the Stoneites were convinced that the millennium was imminent. But while most Americans hinged their millennial hopes on the new Republic, the Stoneites argued that no mere nation could hasten the kingdom of God. Nor could the churches of tradition and history perform that task. Only the primitive church which stood prior to history could finally hasten the consummation of history in the glorious millennial age.[50]

The possibility of an imminent millennium led to another central theme in the Stoneite agenda, namely, a demand for Christian unity predicated upon apostolic Christianity. Clearly, a Christendom divided by the traditions of history could never inaugurate the perfections of the millennial dawn. Thus, Stone and his colleagues advocated a restoration of primitive Christianity as a means to Christian unity which in turn would hasten the millennial age.

Further, it was precisely at this point that the Stoneites dealt with the pesky problem of religious pluralism. While admitting that there were Christians in all Protestant denominations, the followers of Stone argued that the denominational structures themselves constituted a Babylonian wilderness of babel and confusion. Therefore, they called upon "Christians in the sects" to "come out of Babylon" and to unite upon the one apostolic foundation. When this task was accomplished, the denominational structures of history would fall, the primitive church would embrace all Christians worldwide, and the millennium would have begun.[51]

It must constantly be borne in mind, however, that Stone and his colleagues defined the primitive church more in terms of negation of tradition than of the creation of new traditions, even primitive traditions. Consequently, the unity for which Stone pled was a unity in freedom rather than a unity in conformity. Freedom, when all was said and done, was the cornerstone of the Stone movement.

The fourth "Christian" movement was that of Thomas and Alexander Campbell. Belonging to the Old Light, Anti-Burgher, Seceder Presbyterian Church in his homeland of Ireland, Father Thomas arrived in America in 1807, settled in southwest (Washington County) Pennsylvania, and began preaching under the direction of his church. For sharing communion with Presbyterians of other stripes, however, he was disbarred from his ministry and subsequently withdrew from the Seceder fellowship. He and several kindred spirits then formed a study group, the Christian Association of Washington, which produced the charter of the Campbell movement, *The Declaration and Address*. This document articulated the chief preoccupation of the Campbell tradition: Christian unity. But how could unity be achieved? Drawing on the Puritan tradition to which he was heir, Thomas proposed what to him was the obvious solution: Recover the common denominator of all Christians, namely, primitive Christianity as reflected in Scripture, and forsake the particularized creeds and traditions of Christian history which had been responsible for maintaining division. The Campbell agenda, therefore, was clear: The restoration of primitive Christianity would be the means of achieving Christian unity.[52]

Thomas's son, Alexander, arrived in America with the remainder of the family in 1809 and very quickly assumed leadership of the Campbell movement. A student of both John Locke and Common Sense philosophy at Glasgow, Alexander began publishing in 1823 his first periodical, *The Christian Baptist*, and began addressing what to him was the heart of the matter, namely, the rational and systematic reconstruction of the apostolic communities entailing a clear distinction between the essentials and the non-essentials of primitive Christianity. Thus, Campbell rejected the holy kiss, deaconesses, communal living, footwashing, and charismatic exercises as non-essential, and argued for congregational autonomy, a plurality of elders in each congregation, and weekly communion as characteristic of the primitive communities, and for immersion for the remission of sins as essential to being a Christian. In this systematic and rational reconstruction, Campbell stood in contrast to Barton W. Stone.

While Campbell's movement spread throughout the western reserve, it was singularly successful in Kentucky, Tennessee, and southern Ohio where hearts had been prepared for many years by the work of Barton Stone. In 1823, Campbell made his first trip into the Stone-dominated region of Kentucky in order to debate the Presbyterian W. L. McCalla on the subject of baptism. As a result of that debate and through the circulation of *The Christian Baptist* in Kentucky, Campbell quickly captured the attention of the thousands of Stone-Christians who, according to contemporary reports, were increasingly unsettled by the radical freedom and the lack of dogma of the Stone movement. For a people already committed to primitive Christianity in principle, Campbell provided form, structure, and a clear and rational definition of primitive Christianity in practice.

Further, the cornerstone of Campbell's rational and systematic portrait of primitive Christianity was his baptismal theology which insisted that baptism was immersion and immersion was *for the forgiveness of sins.* To Kentucky Calvinists uncertain of their election, as was true of many in the Stone movement, this notion offered compelling assurance and certainty. Thus, when the Stoneite preacher B. F. Hall learned this doctrine from a printed copy of the Campbell-McCalla debate in 1826, he was ecstatic. He proclaimed that he had found "the long lost link in the chain of gospel obedience. . . . I now saw the evidence of remission, which I had never seen before."[53] And John Rogers, another Kentucky Stoneite turned Campbellite, hailed certainty of salvation as itself a mark of the primitive faith. The early Christians, he said, were immersed and were therefore "pardoned, & knew it, & rejoiced in it . . . & never spoke in the language of doubt or fear upon the subject."[54] Thus, by providing structure, order, and certainty, Campbell quickly overshadowed Stone and became the undisputed leader of the "restoration movement" even in the upper South.

In responding to the culture around them, the Campbell and Stone movements agreed at many critical points. Campbell was fully as convinced as was Stone that through recovery of primitive Christianity, the millennium would dawn.[55] Moreover, primitivism, for Campbell as for Stone, was a means of winning Christian freedom and shearing the clergy of their power. In addition, the Campbell movement like Stone's was a response to religious pluralism, calling for the unity of believers based on an apostolic model.

But it was around the issue of pluralism that the Campbell movement finally faltered and even divided. Indeed, if Campbell's solution to pluralism had been unity through restoration, by the 1840s that platform already was breaking apart. As if to signal that development, Campbell himself discontinued his *Christian Baptist* and launched a more conciliatory journal, *The Millennial Harbinger,* in 1830. As the years went by, Campbell and his followers in the upper Midwest increasingly accepted unity in pluralistic diversity and subtly downplayed the strict restoration ideal. Further south, however, the Christians clung to the restoration ideal of Campbell in his *Christian Baptist* days and continued to resist the fact of religious pluralism. While this theological rupture was rooted in the ambiguities of Campbell's own theology, a variety of social factors including the Civil War exacerbated the rupture which finally became open division by the end of the century.[56] In 1906, the United States Religious Census showed two churches rather than one: the Disciples of Christ, highly ecumenical and centralized in the Midwest, and the Churches of Christ, fundamentally restorationist and centralized in the upper South.

The fact that Churches of Christ emerged with extraordinary strength in the region once dominated by the freedom movement of Barton W. Stone is highly instructive. To be sure, Churches of Christ ultimately must trace their success in this area to the great numerical strength of the Stone movement long before anyone in that area had even heard of Alexander Campbell. But when the amorphous and structureless Stone tradition finally began absorbing the more regimented theology of Campbell after 1823, a subtle transition occurred: The reality of freedom evolved into a mythology of freedom that performed an important double function. On the one hand, the myth of freedom obscured from the eyes of these Christians the very real dogmas, forms, and structures that were developing in their midst. To be sure, their own Common Sense perspectives enhanced the invisibility of their traditions and made them appear to their proclaimers as essentially natural rather than in any sense historical and developmental. But on the other hand, their myth of freedom also became a dogma in its own right. In this way, their presumed lack of tradition became itself a tradition, their rejection of theology became a fundamental theological maxim, and their commitment to transcend history became the substance of the particular history of this particular people.

Ecclesiastical Primitivism: Baptists

Since Churches of Christ in the mid-nineteenth century had their greatest strength in middle Tennessee, it is striking that a similar movement emerged in the same time frame and in the same region with great success: the Landmark Baptists spawned in middle Tennessee in 1851. The Landmark movement ultimately drew its strength from the same primitivist strand of the Baptist heritage that had nourished the Stone movement in the early nineteenth century: the Separate Baptists. During and following the Great Awakening, "New Light" dissenters in Connecticut and Massachusetts moved to organize Separatist congregations determined to recover the purity of early New England Puritanism.[57] From the ranks of these Separatists came the Separate Baptists who, led chiefly by Isaac Backus, rejected infant baptism as no baptism at all and sought to take the Bible alone as their only standard for faith and practice.[58] In 1755, Shubal Stearns led a band of Separate Baptists to Sandy Creek, North Carolina, which became the center of the movement throughout the South for the rest of the century. Concerned to emulate apostolic Christianity, these Baptists not only practiced immersion of adults, but also footwashing, the holy kiss, the anointing of the sick, love-feasts, laying on of hands, and weekly communion.[59] During the latter half of the eighteenth century, many Separate Baptists pushed farther west to settle in Kentucky and Tennessee.

After the American Revolution, Baptist primitivism, especially in the western regions, was infused with the same cultural concerns that motivated Stone, O'Kelly, Campbell, and Smith: liberty, millennial expectations, and puzzlement over religious pluralism. The dominant note among these Baptists, however, was that of freedom. Their chief concern focused on the once-powerful, eastern religious establishments and their missionary societies which, many feared, were designed to control the nation in the wake of legal disestablishment. Thousands of Baptists, therefore, joined in a nationwide anti-missionary society crusade which typically contrasted the organizational simplicity and freedom of the primitive church with the cumbersome interdenominational societies of the eastern churches. A wide variety of unlikely allies participated in this primitivist, anti-Society crusade, including Deists like Elihu Palmer, Christians like Elias Smith and Alexander Campbell, Baptists like John Leland, John Taylor, and Daniel Parker, Methodists like Peter Cartwright and Lorenzo Dow, and interdenominational propagandists like Theophilus Ransom Gates, whose *Reformer* (1820-1835) spearheaded this movement. But the Baptists, especially in the West, reaped the bulk of the harvest of the anti-society crusade. By 1820, many Baptist churches in Tennessee and northern Alabama had embraced the primitivist, anti-society posture, and between 1836 and 1838, these churches withdrew from churches favorable to mission societies to form the Anti-Mission or Primitive Baptist Church.[60]

The persistence of primitivism in Tennessee, Kentucky, and northern Alabama first among the Separate Baptists and then among the Primitive Baptists, coupled with the strength of the primitivist Churches of Christ in the same region and the same period, provided a favorable milieu for the rise of the Landmark Baptists in middle Tennessee in 1851. But the Landmarkers dramatically transformed the primitivism of earlier Baptists. Rather than emphasizing freedom from tradition and control, the Landmarkers sought to construct a precise model or blueprint of the primitive church which, in their view, defined authentic Christianity. Further, they contended that the true church had preserved itself without interruption from the days of the apostles to the mid-nineteenth century, and could be identified by the "trail of blood" which had marked the martyrs of the true church in every age.[61]

The early leader of the Landmark tradition was James Robinson Graves, assistant editor of *The Baptist* (later *The Tennessee Baptist*) in Nashville, Tennessee, who in 1848 attacked "alien immersions" and refused recognition of pedobaptist organizations as churches in any sense at all. Furthermore, Graves contended, any religious body organized since Pentecost can make no claim to being a church, and Landmarkers therefore contrasted the dates of origin of the various denominations with their own presumed origin at Pentecost. Another Landmark leader, Amos Cooper Dayton, published in 1857 a novel, *Theodosia Ernest: Ten Days' Travel in Search of the Church,* which graphically illustrated the argument from primitive origins. Further, Graves and other Landmarkers taught that any deviation from the New Testament pattern of organization, worship, belief, and practice automatically disqualified a religious body from any legitimate claim to being a church.[62] In this way, Landmarkers clearly identified the true church amidst the claims and counter-claims of the competing denominations.

If freedom was the motivation of the earlier Separate Baptists, concern to locate the one, true church in the midst of religious pluralism had become by mid-century the driving force of the Landmark movement.[63] This shift is significant, for precisely the same sort of shift occurred among the Christians in the South whose earliest concerns were for freedom but whose interests within the Churches of Christ increasingly focused on finding and defending the one true church of the Bible. It is also worth underscoring the Landmarkism and Churches of Christ flourished in precisely the same geographical arena, a fact which warrants research into the possible relations between these two groups. Though Landmarkism gained significant strength in Tennessee and parts of the Southwest by 1880, it was not until 1905 that it was organized into a formal denomination—the General Association of Landmark Baptists—in Texarkana, Arkansas, renamed in 1924 the American Baptist Association.

Ecclesiastical Primitivism: Mormons

Anxiety over religious pluralism also undergirded the rise and growth of yet another restoration movement of the early nineteenth century: the Church of Jesus Christ of Latter-day

Saints.[64] Indeed, the wide assortment of religious denominations competing in the free market of souls in upstate New
York had caused a young lad named Joseph Smith no small
amount of consternation. Bewildered and confused, Smith took
to the woods "on the morning of a beautiful clear day, early in
the spring" of 1820, to put a simple question to the Lord:
which of all the churches is the true church? Significantly, the
Lord responded with a clear rejection of Christian history when
he told Joseph that he "must join none of them, for they were
all wrong," and that "all their creeds were an abomination in
His sight."[65] For the next several years, Joseph, like Roger
Williams two hundred years before, became a seeker, waiting
for the restoration of true Christianity.

But while Williams died a seeker, waiting for the prophet
who would restore the ancient faith, Smith became the very
prophet through whom restoration would occur. The restoration began in 1827 when Smith allegedly unearthed the golden
plates, the basis for the Book of Mormon, from the hill called
Cumorah near his home. That event set in motion a complex
and far-reaching transcendence of history which would make
Mormons a primordial people "engaged in the very same order
of things as observed by the holy Apostles of old," as Smith
put it.[66] Indeed, Jan Shipps has pointed out that the Book of
Mormon, itself, "effected a break in the very fabric of history"
by both prophesying that a book would come forth and then
fulfilling its own prophecy.[67]

But Mormon transcendence of history was not primitivism
alone, looking from the present to primordial beginnings, but it
also involved expectation of an imminent future millennium.
Thus, as Robert Flanders notes, Joseph Smith viewed himself
as "a transitional figure, a hinge between the old profane history and a new sanctified one . . . , called to found the premillennial kingdom of God on earth."[68] No wonder, then, that
early Mormons imagined themselves a sacred people, sojourn-
ing through profane time, but ultimately rooted both in the
primordium and in the millennium, those monuments of perfection bracketing each end of the fallen human experience.

Mormon preoccupation with perfect beginnings and a perfect
end can best be seen in two phenomena: the church's name
and the significance of Jackson County, Missouri. The name of
the church is itself instructive: the Church of Jesus Christ of

Latter-day Saints. The first phrase, "Church of Jesus Christ," implicitly reflects the primitivist impulse, the yearning to recover the true church in its primitive beginnings. The second phrase, "of Latter-day Saints," makes it clear that Mormons had a sense of standing in the last days, on the threshold of the millennial dawn. Further, the fact that restoration of the church had not occurred in some middle point of history but rather in the last days suggests that for Mormons the perfect beginning and the perfect end were fundamentally congruent. One almost suspects that Mormons viewed history not so much as a straight line but as a curved line whose end points finally met and interlocked. Early Mormons thereby blended primordial and millennial perfections into one grand concert whose rapturous chords obscured the hymns of history, long sung out of key.

This suspicion is heightened when one considers the significance of Jackson County, Missouri in Mormon thought. It is well known that Joseph Smith, by revelation, designated Jackson County as Zion, the site from which Christ would finally rule His kingdom in the millennial age. Less well known is a discovery Joseph Smith made of a pile of stones in a barren field north of Jackson County in 1838. Upon consulting the Lord concerning the stones' significance, he learned that they were ruins of an ancient altar constructed by Adam, the father of humankind, and that Jackson County was the site of the Garden of Eden.[69] Once again millennium and primordium had converged, though in this instance the convergence occurred not only in time but also in space. Clearly, Jackson County, Missouri was an *axis mundi*, the center of a fallen world but a center from which the world could once again be restored to the perfections of the first age.

In thus linking primordium and millennium, Mormons shared with numerous Americans of their age for whom history had largely been erased. After all, the American experiment seemed both a replication of the ancient, natural order of things, and at the same time, the harbinger of a millennial dawn. Further, the basically history-transcending structure of the Mormon world view was not at all unlike that of an Alexander Campbell or a Barton W. Stone. But viewing the Mormon standpoint against the backdrop of the Christian movement also illumines some fundamental differences between the two groups.

One such difference lay in the fact that for Christians restoration remained an expectation, while for Mormons it was an accomplished fact. After all, in the case of Mormons, restoration had been inaugurated not by some man or group of men but by God himself. The divine direction of Mormon restorationism, embodied especially in the actual, concrete recovery of the Book of Mormon, lent Mormon claims a finality and authenticity missing from Christian efforts. To be sure, Mormons contended that the gospel was fully restored in the Book of Mormon, and so soon as a church was organized upon its principles, restoration of the church was an accomplished fact as well. Christians, on the other hand, proceeding in a more post-millennial mode without such divine directives, never doubted that through their efforts the church had been partially restored and eventually would be fully restored. Until then, however, their attitude was one of confident expectation while Mormons, on the other hand, were conscious of living in primal structures in the here and now.

This difference leads directly to another, one suggested by Jan Shipps who distinguishes between restoration as "recapitulation" and restoration as mere "ritual recreation."[70] By recapitulation, Shipps means the experiential re-enactment or the "living through" of primal events by which the believer is mythically united with the primal age. Here, present time and primal time become practically indistinguishable. By ritual recreation, Shipps means the self-conscious effort to duplicate through ritualized acts certain primal events, all the while aware of the vast difference that separates one's own time from the time of primordial beginnings. For Shipps, early Mormonism was clearly recapitulation. But in the light of her constructs, it should be added that the early Christian movement, particularly under the influence of Alexander Campbell, was merely ritual recreation. Perhaps this was inevitable, given the coldly logical, Common Sense approach Campbell took to primitive Christianity. At any rate, there is a vast difference, for example, between celebrating the Lord's Supper each first day of the week in imitation of the primitive church and, on the other hand, building a millennial Zion on the site of the Garden of Eden.

A third difference between Mormon and Christian restorationism lay in the sheer scope of their efforts. For Christians, restoration encompassed only the primitive church as described in the New Testament. The history to be transcended, therefore, was only eighteen hundred years of distinctly Christian history. Mormons, on the other hand, attempted a cosmic restoration, simultaneously blending Adam's Eden, the world of the Patriarchs, ancient Israel, and primitive Christianity. All were sacred epochs and were therefore mythically, at least, equally primordial. Thus, Mormons lived for a while in the ancient Garden of Eden and even established a settlement where Adam had once called together his posterity: Adam-ondi-Ahman. They established a Church of Jesus Christ which, under an Aaronic priesthood, would practice in a restored "Jewish" temple the ancient Christian rite of baptism for the remission of sins, and even introduced the ancient patriarchal practice of polygamy.[71] In this way Mormons collapsed the various sacred times of Judaism and Christianity into a single primordium.

But beyond this, Mormons even collapsed space into a single sacred domain. Thus, the chosen people had dwelt not only in Palestine but also in the Americas, and Jesus had appeared on both continents as well. But now in the nineteenth century. Mormons determined to collapse space even further through the repeated reproduction of the city of Zion in adjacent plats until the whole earth would be filled.[72] In this way, Mormons sought to erect a cosmic stage upon which they themselves could continually re-enact the primordial story through the remainder of finite time. Mormons thereby resolved the nineteenth-century debate over whether America should perfect herself in time or extend her perfections through space. As Flanders aptly notes, Mormons would do both.[73]

It was precisely out of this context that Mormons addressed the problem of religious pluralism of which Joseph Smith already had been warned by the Lord in 1820. Because "all their creeds were an abomination in His sight," Mormons embarked upon an effort to collapse pluralism, along with time and space, into one communion of saints that would extend from Adam to Christ's second coming and from Jackson County, Missouri to the remotest reaches of the earth. It is in this context that the Mormon practice of baptism for the dead must be understood. It was not enough to triumph over pluralism in their own time in their own place in America. Even the dead from ages past throughout the earth were to be snatched from the jaws of alien religions and engrafted by baptism into the one, universal church. Indeed, their preoccupation with an overarching unity that would build on primordial models, hasten the millennial kingdom, and embrace all peoples in all time and space was the genius of the Mormons' faith.

ETHICAL PRIMITIVISM: THE HOLINESS REVIVAL

If the restoration theme among Baptists, Mormons, and Christians in the early nineteenth century had focused on the forms and structures of *ecclesiastical primitivism,* the last third of the century witnessed a surge of *ethical primitivism* understood as vivification by the Holy Spirit. This development had significant precedents earlier in the century. Indeed, Professor Grant Wacker has argued that "the whole nineteenth century evangelical movement—Wesleyan as well as Reformed—might well be defined as historic Protestant orthodoxy spiced with a tingling awareness that the theology and power of the Spirit, lost since the days of the apostles, was about to be restored to the life of the church."[74] Especially important in this regard was the emphasis placed on entire sanctification by Charles Finney and Asa Mahan at Oberlin. And in the Methodist fold, Phoebe Palmer sought to revitalize in the 1830s the Wesleyan notion of entire sanctification. She reconstructed Wesley's view of sanctification, however, in a way that became normative for virtually all holiness advocates later in the century. If for Wesley sanctification was a gradual process, Mrs. Palmer viewed sanctification as a second crisis event following conversion in which the Holy Spirit purges the believer of the will to sin, and therefore she viewed her own holiness meetings as "strikingly imitative of the pentecostal."[75]

In the years following the Civil War, ethical primitivism became a powerful force. Significantly, if the earlier ecclesiastical primitivism had been a response to the failures of the historic churches set in stark relief by the optimism of the new Republic, this new variety of primitivism reflected similar themes. On the one hand, as Professor Wacker notes, the astonishing possibilities of the gilded age focused the attention of a variety of Christians, both liberal and evangelical, on the power of God's Spirit to actualize His kingdom in the here and now.[76] But on the other hand, the historic churches seemed to many to be more impotent than ever. The very possibilities of the gilded age had seduced many Protestant denominations into social and economic acculturation, robbing them of authenticity and power. The spirit of the age thereby transformed many Christians into children of modernity, inhabiting fashionable temples which celebrated success, prosperity, and the entrepreneurial spirit. The earmarks of this transition were unmistakable: the construction of ornate and costly sanctuaries where choirs and organs replaced simple congregational singing and where dramatic presentations and church festivals competed with secular organizations for the time and money of the cultured middle class. Thus, the noted evangelical A. J. Gordon noted the "new organs and frescoings and furnishings and . . . strawberry festivals" of the Protestant churches and drew a striking contrast between primitive and modern Christianity.

> Is not this an infinite descent from the primitive records of power and success—the Lord "confirming the word with signs following," and . . . "in demonstration of the Spirit and of power?"[77]

This spiritual decline was particularly apparent within Methodism, which in earlier generations had been unequivocally committed to the cultivation of pious and holy living. As early as the 1830s, one bishop noted that the theme of holiness within Methodism was receiving "less and less attention . . . [and was in] danger of being regarded as a novelty."[78] By 1866, primitive holiness stood increasingly at variance with an acculturated mainstream Methodism wherein some rejoiced that "our church members have as a body risen in the social scale, and thus become socially removed from the great body out of which most of them were originally gathered."[79] But others like John P. Brooks, architect of the "come-outer" theory which legitimated separation from the traditional churches,[80] felt betrayed and roundly condemned the "easy, indulgent, accomodating, mammonized" kind of Methodism that erects "gorgeous and costly temples to gratify its pride."[81] Even the founding of the National Camp Meeting Association for the Promotion of Holiness in 1867 failed to pacify many Methodists for whom the gap between the modern churches and primitive Christianity was rapidly becoming a chasm.

These Methodists, therefore, increasingly rejected mere reformation and insisted instead on a restoration of primitive Christianity centered on entire sanctification as a dramatic and sudden work of grace. Methodist leaders increasingly viewed this posture as disruptive, and their discipline of holiness dissenters fostered rebellion which finally grew into full-blown secession. Many, therefore, finally rejected Methodism altogether to organize holiness churches grounded in the sanctified lifestyle of primitive Christianity.

Somewhat typical of many holiness communities was a relatively obscure denomination which later flowed into a major holiness body, the Church of the Nazarene. This primitivist holiness body was the New Testament Church of Christ, organized in 1894 in Milan, Tennessee. When the West Tennessee Conference of the Methodist Episcopal Church, South, attacked "unauthorized, self-styled evangelists," Robert Lee Harris, a transplanted west Texan, in turn attacked Methodism as "fashionable and worldly" and set about establishing what he called a true "New Testament" church. On July 9, 1894, he and fourteen others gave birth to the New Testament Church of Christ. With the Bible as its only creed, elders governing, deacons serving tables, and both men and women preaching the word, Harris's church also instituted pouring for baptism and sanctification as a second work of grace and rejected all flirtations with the world including jewelry, tobacco, secret societies, and idle amusements. A particularly striking aspect of the New Testament Church of Christ was its geographical continuity both with the Church of Christ of Stone-Campbell lineage and with the Landmark Baptist movement. By 1901, Harris's group had spread through west Tennessee, northern Alabama, Arkansas, and into Texas, centering its activity in Milan, Tennessee in the East and Buffalo Gap, Texas (near Abilene) in the West.[82]

The striking feature of many holiness groups was the way they combined their primitivism with the same themes that intertwined with the primitivism of the Christians and the Mormons a half-century before. Thus, many holiness advocates were deeply troubled by religious pluralism in America and viewed their movement as the key to Christian unity which in turn would usher in the millennial age.

Daniel S. Warner and his Church of God (Anderson, Indiana, 1880) is a notable case in point. Having lost his preaching license for advocating holiness doctrines in the Church of God (Winebrennerian) in 1878, Warner finally concluded that "holiness could never prosper upon sectarian soil, encumbered by human creeds, and party names," and claimed that God had called him to "build up the apostolical [sic] church of the living God."[83] This one true church, he said, had been all but lost during the "Great Apostasy" (sic) of the Constantinian era which gave birth to Roman Catholicism. The Protestant movement had merely perpetuated the abominations of Catholicism and, further, had transformed the church of God into a "Babylon of confusion" through its proliferation of sects. But Warner rejected the denominational premise out of hand and summoned the true sheep of God out of their denominational structures and into "the only holy church of the Bible."[84]

To this point, Warner sounded remarkably like Alexander Campbell or even Joseph Smith. But there was one fundamental difference. If Campbell and Smith had sought to eradicate pluralism and unite God's people by recovering the doctrines and practices of the primitive church, the holiness advocates would achieve these goals by restoring the sanctified lifestyle of the primitive Christians, inaugurated by the baptism of the Holy Spirit. In fact, holiness advocates typically rejected restoration efforts like those of Campbell as incapable of generating authentic Christian unity. Edgar M. Levy was a case in point. "At last," he proclaimed,

> we have discovered the basis for Christian unity. The sanctification of the believers of every name, create unity in the great Christian brotherhood, such as no creed has ever been able to accomplish. [Here is] a unity not in ordinances; a unity not in church government; a unity not in forms of worship; a unity not in mere letter or creed—but in . . . the baptism of the holy Spirit.[85]

For Levy, the arena for restoration would not be cognitive, but ethical and even experiential. Indeed, holiness advocates typically downplayed doctrine in the face of the sanctified Christian life. Hannah Whitall Smith, author of the devotional classic, *The Christian's Secret of a Happy Life* (1870), argued that "the trouble with most of the religion of the day is its extreme complexity," adding that true religion avoids "theological difficulties [and] doctrinal dilemmas. . . . No theological training *nor any especial theological views* are needed."[86]

Daniel Warner agreed. He longed for the unity of all Christians, "not bound together by rigid articles of faith, but perfectly united in love, under the primitive glory of the Sanctifier.

. . ."[87] Indeed, the clear link between sanctification and Christian unity was the love which would eradicate from the heart the selfish interests which built and sustained the denominational creeds and parties. Thus, through the power of the Spirit, the millennial age of unity, peace, and harmony would be realized at last. But, as Melvin Dieter notes, "the dominant theme . . . [in this scheme] was the strong primitivism which was present in all holiness concepts of the church."[88]

EXPERIENTIAL PRIMITIVISM: PENTECOSTALS

Primitivism was equally prominent in the Pentecostal movement which, near the turn of the twentieth century, grew directly out of Holiness longings for recovery of the apostolic church. But if the Holiness tradition emphasized an *ethical primitivism,* concerned with a sanctified way of life, Pentecostalism sought an *experiential primitivism* directed toward recovery of the apostolic gifts of the Spirit, especially glossolalia and healing. Indeed, Pentecostals sought nothing less than a restoration of the Jerusalem Pentecost which began the Christian story.[89] For those who embraced this posture, experiential primitivism was valuable not only in its own right but also because it authenticated to the believer that his or her ethical primitivism was indeed the work of the Spirit and not one's own accomplishment.

To be sure, preoccupation with primitive, experiential Christianity abounds in the records of early Pentecostalism. Thus, the very beginnings of the movement at Charles Parham's Bethel College in Topeka, Kansas were replete with primitivist symbols. After Agnes Ozman received the gift of tongues on New Year's Eve, 1900, the remainder of the Bethel group met in an "upper room," waiting for a similar manifestation. Finally, on the evening of January 3, 1901, members of the group witnessed "clovend tonges as of fire" [*sic*] coming "down into the room." Parham himself reported seeing twelve ministers with raised up hands bathed in a "sheen of white light above the brightness of many lamps," and most in the group proceeded to speak in languages not their own.[90] As Robert Ampes Anderson observes, this scenario was "almost exactly as Pentecost is described in the second chapter of Acts."[91]

That the Pentecostals' fascination with apostolic origins was fully self-conscious and intentional is illustrated by the titles of some of their periodicals: *The New Acts, Apostolic Messenger, Apostolic Evangel, The Pentecostal Record*, and *Pentecostal Wonders*, among others. Indeed, B. F. Lawrence, an elder in the Assemblies of God, contrasted the "historylessness" of Pentecostalism with the "older denominations" which "can trace the beginnings of their church and the course of its history subsequent to its foundation. The time between the beginning and the present has been sufficient to establish precedent, create habit, formulate custom." But, Lawrence declared:

> The Pentecostal Movement has no such history; it leaps the intervening years crying, *"Back to Pentecost."* In the minds of these honest-hearted, thinking men and women, this work of God is immediately connected with the work of God in New Testament days. Built by the same hand, upon the same foundation of apostles and prophets, after the same pattern, according to the same covenant, they too are a habitation of God through the Spirit. They do not recognize a doctrine or custom as authoritative unless it can be traced to that primal source of church instruction, the Lord and his apostles.[92]

Perhaps in none of the various Pentecostal sects was the primitivist impulse more pronounced or the familiar intersection of primitivism, millennialism, and anti-pluralism more evident than in A. J. Tomlinson's Church of God based in Cleveland, Tennessee. Beginning as a Holiness community in a remote mountain region near the juncture of Tennessee, Georgia, and North Carolina, the Church of God embraced the doctrine of tongues in 1908. By 1910, Tomlinson was articulating the standard Pentecostal view of church history, namely, that the primitive church remained true to its original faith for a number of years but then "departed from the faith" and "was lost to view." Now in these latter days, however, the true church of God had been restored in the mountains of North Carolina and Tennessee. Further, Christ soon would erect his millennial kingdom both at Burger Mountain (North Carolina) and at Jerusalem after the true Christians from all denominations had flowed into the one, true apostolic church.[93] Thus Tomlinson's Church of God, like the Mormons years before, acknowledged an *axis mundi* around which primordium and millennium converged. And in that convergence history was eclipsed, the churches of history rejected, and religious pluralism collapsed into a sacred unity once known at Pentecost and soon to be revealed again in the final age.

In forging the familiar triad of primitivism, millennialism, and ecumenism, Tomlinson's Church of God was not only reminiscent of Mormons, Christians, and Holiness advocates, but also more or less typified Pentecostalism at large. The fact is that virtually all Pentecostals articulated their primitivism from squarely within a millennial context. Indeed, recovery of beginnings was simply inseparable from their awareness of living in the shadow of the end, an awareness that lent urgency and meaning to all their efforts to recover apostolic Christianity.[94] The introduction to B. F. Lawrence's *The Apostolic Faith Restored* unflinchingly declared, for example, that "the last times are ushered in. The last days have come, in very truth. The harvest is at hand; nothing can stay the onward march of God and His glorious kingdom."[95] This is the explanation for the Pentecostals' familiar "former rain"/"latter rain" terminology. If the first Pentecost in Jerusalem was the "former rain" which launched the Christian age, these people sought a second Pentecost—a "latter rain" which, through the power of the Spirit, would conclude the Christian age just prior to the millennial dawn. As the *Latter Rain Evangel* put it in 1909, "the first Pentecost *started* the church, . . . the second Pentecost, *unites* and *perfects* the church unto the coming of the Lord."[96] Sometimes the terminology was "morning light"/"evening light." Thus, A. J. Tomlinson compared "the full blaze of light [which] beamed forth from the Pentecostal chamber" in the primitive church with his own age when "the evening light, the true light is now shining."[97] But whatever the metaphor, the conviction remained constant that the sacred history of the primitive church was now being replicated in these latter days in anticipation of a glorious millennial dawn.

Further, like Mormons, Christians, and Holiness advocates, Pentecostals also generally envisioned their movement as the instrument God was using to unify the Christian world before the end of time. Thus through the miracle of tongues, Pentecostals would preach the gospel to the ends of the earth to people of all nationalities in their own language, thus insuring a global unity of all believers and hastening the day of the Lord.[98] In this way, the restoration of glossolalia bore a distinctly functional relation to the millennial dawn. Once again, as so often in the past, primitivism and millennialism had forged an alliance which would slay the demons of history with the double-edged sword of sacred time.

CONCLUSION

The extent to which American restorationist movements almost universally grappled with the problem of religious pluralism lends credence to Sidney Mead's definition of primitivist dissent as "the ploy of throwing part of 'the Book' at the theological and ecclesiastical establishments in which the dissenters have been nurtured."[99] In a nation holding in its bosom scores of Christian denominations, differing among themselves on a variety of theological and ecclesial concerns, the surest path to certainty was a rejection of those churches and a clear appeal to the New Testament and the model of the primitive church. In America, this was at least part of the social meaning of "the search for the ancient order."

Mead's use of the phrase, "part of 'the Book,' " is also instructive. Thus, primitivist movements emphasized ethical, ecclesiastical, or experiential concerns, or some combination thereof, as the burden of their restoration focus. Mead's statement concerning Alexander Campbell is therefore applicable to practically all restoration movements, namely, that they seem to "have been limited to restoring and/or rearranging some of the furniture in one apartment of the sprawling Christian condominium."[100] Mead might well have added that the choice of which furniture to rearrange often was dependent on the objectives the restoration motif would serve. Indeed, seldom did the restoration theme function as a virtue in its own right, but variously served instead to secure religious liberty, to bring Christian unity, to hasten the millennial dawn, or simply to distinguish the true church from false churches in a world of religious pluralism.

Mead's insights clearly are indisputable. At the same time, however, they say nothing about the genius of the restoration ideal which, I would argue, was most clearly embodied in the ethical primitivism of the evangelical Anabaptists. After all, the contest in their case was not between their church and other churches as though religious pluralism were at issue. The contest for them was instead between the values of the church and the values of the world—two opposing perspectives the Anabaptists judged irreconcilable. Their task, as they saw it, was to form separate Christian conventicles outside the prevailing religious/political establishment where a disciplined and perfected lifestyle could be rigorously pursued. To their minds, the significance of the outward ordinances of primitive Christianity, especially baptism and the ban, was the deeper meaning of disciplined Christian perfection which these ordinances symbolized. And they stridently opposed the established church precisely because the church was established, that is, yoked in an unholy alliance with the power of the state and thereby with the values of the world.

The American situation, however, tended to trivialize the restoration ideal and to undercut its deeper meaning. Since no denomination in the new nation was established and all denominations were therefore free of official church-state entanglement, Christians tended to assume that they had won their battle with the world and to ignore their more subtle entanglement with the values of their culture. In this new context of disestablishment and religious pluralism, the restoration ideal often therefore failed to discriminate between the church and the world. Instead, it frequently became a tool of denominational one-upmanship which obscured the real issue of the meaning of sanctification. Thus, American Christians engaged in endless debates over sacramental forms, ecclesiastical structures, and methods of worship and often paid little regard to the deeper meaning which those forms and structures had symbolized for those evangelical restorationists of the sixteenth century. This clearly is the point of John Yoder's comment that the "narrowing of the restitution focus to formal polity issues [especially among American Churches of Christ] . . . may have contributed to discrediting the idea of restitution."[101]

There were exceptions to this pattern, of course, most notably the Stone movement in its earliest years, the Holiness revival, and the early phases of the Pentecostal movement. But typically the dynamic concern for holy living gave way in time to more formal doctrinal and ecclesiastical concerns. This recurring spiritual metamorphosis was contingent in part upon the competition engendered by religious pluralism. But it also was contingent on the periodic collapse of the primitivist view of history. Nor were these two issues unrelated.

The fact is that so long as primitivist Christians could imagine themselves standing with one foot in primordial beginnings and the other in the millennial dawn, straddling history like water under a cosmic bridge, it was relatively easy to stand apart from the values of the world whose end was imminent in any event. But when the millennium failed to materialize, the active presence of the primordium disappeared as well, and primitivists found themselves thrust once again in to the midst of an historic, imperfect, and finite world. It was precisely at that point that American primitivists typically transformed their dynamic conceptions of ethical primitivism into more formal conceptions of ecclesiastical primitivism and their struggles with the values of the world into struggles with competing sects. Thus it was, for example, that the Stone movement, concerned for ethical primitivism in its earliest years when millennial expectations were strong, shifted its focus by the 1840s to questions regarding the "true church" in the context of ecclesiastical primitivism. And when the immediacy of the millennium disappeared from the world of the early Pentecostals, as Robert M. Anderson observes, tongue speaking also lost its function of separating the faithful for the Second Coming and became instead "a largely formal doctrine . . . and the central teaching of the Pentecostal movement,"[102] making Pentecostal groups distinct from other denominations. It is true that in the case of some primitivists, the more formal concerns of ecclesiastical primitivism sometimes symbolized the earlier ethical and moral aspirations. But when the two themes divorced entirely, as often was the case, primitivists were free to hold simultaneously and paradoxically to the values of the world and to the structures of the primitive church.

What all this says is that American primitivism consistently rode the crest of the "sense of historylessness" which was so central to the American experience itself. If America was a *novus ordo seclorum,* cut off from the historical past and tied only to Eden at one end of time and the millennium at the other, American primitivists imagined that the church could not be far behind. Thus, primitivist perfectionism in America took on a decidedly trans-historical cast: To be holy and perfect was to escape the bounds of finitude. And when the bounds of finitude refused to be broken, ethical primitivism gave way to more churchly and, paradoxically, more worldly concerns. The sixteenth-century Anabaptists, on the other hand, entertained no such trans-historical illusions. Primitivism for them meant the recovery of an apostolic lifestyle within the very fabric of history and the contemporary world. They therefore took history seriously in a manner hardly characteristic of most primitivist groups in America.[103]

Finally, it should be noted that the struggle which religious pluralism in America encouraged between competing denominations was at least partly responsible for the great irony of American primitivism. After all, the point at which primitivists finally made friends with the world had little to do with liquor, tobacco, dancing, or similar transgressions—practices roundly condemned by virtually all primitivist sects. Rather, in their zeal to promote their "true church" perspectives in a religiously pluralistic milieu, primitivists ironically embraced the cardinal and bedrock assumptions of the very world they opposed, namely, the use of power, dominion, and even coercion to achieve their ends. Indeed, most primitivists fully expected their moral and ecclesiastical perspectives to triumph not only over their denominational foes, but even over the larger culture itself. This is the inescapable meaning of the recurrent primitivist motif of a final millennial unity predicated upon a particular moral, ecclesiastical, or experiential vision of apostolic Christianity. In the absence of a state church which traditionally had secured both unity and uniformity, this vision of the "true church" became, at least in the minds of many American primitivists, the functional and eschatological equivalent of the older "state church" ideal. This aspect of American primitivism was particularly apparent in the aspirations of Mormonism to dominate both time and space with their Zion restored.

To one accustomed to the primitivist model of sixteenth-century Anabaptism, this American vision is ironic and paradoxical, to say the least. After all, most American primitivists simply turned on its head the Anabaptist understanding of restoration—an understanding which inevitably entailed separation from the world's values of power and dominion—and proceeded on premises more congenial to an establishment of religion. But then the earliest model for American primitivism was not the ethical perspective of Anabaptism at all, but rather the ecclesiastical and legal emphasis of the Zwinglian reform wherein primitivism was a complement rather than a challenge to the established order. Even closer home was the Puritan restorationist agenda which directly linked the welfare of the civic order to recovery of the primitive church.

Coupling this backdrop with the vacuum of religious power mandated by disestablishment, it perhaps was inevitable that so many American primitivists would find the European establishment model so attractive, in spite of the fact that it was alien both to the genius of the American nation and to the genius of the restoration ideal.

NOTES

1. For another typology of restorationist movements, focusing strictly on America, cf. Samuel S. Hill, Jr., "A Typology of American Restitutionism: From Frontier Revivalism and Mormonism to the Jesus Movement," *Journal of the American Academy of Religion* 44 (March 1976): 65-76. In fact, the majority of the articles in this issue of *JAAR* deal with various aspects of the restoration ideal in Christian history. Cf. also Donald F. Durnbaugh, *The Believers' Church: The History and Character of Radical Protestantism* (New York: Macmillan, 1968), esp. 37-204.

2. Hill, for example, notes that for many Christian groups, their sense of catholicity excludes interest in primitivism. For some of these groups (e.g., Roman Catholics, Anglicans, and Orthodox), catholicity is integral; for others (e.g., Lutherans, Presbyterians, Methodists, and Congregationalists) catholicity serves as guideline or inspiration; and for still others (e.g., many Baptists and Quakers) catholicity is subordinated to personal piety. But in each of these instances, catholicity, not primitivism, is fundamental. Ibid., 74-75.

In addition, John Howard Yoder has argued that primitivism characterized the sixteenth-century Anabaptists but not most other Protestants in the Reformation period precisely because the latter refused to challenge the fusion of the church and the world in the *corpus christianum*. "Anabaptism and History" in Hans-Jürgen Goertz, ed., *Umstrittenes Täufertum, 1525-1975: Neue Forschungen* (Göttingen: Vandenhoeck & Ruprecht, 1975), 248-249.

3. For a discussion of *chronological* vis-à-vis *ontological* reform in the sixteenth century, see Richard T. Hughes, "From Civil Dissent to Civil Religion and Beyond," *Religion in Life* 49 (Autumn 1980): 268-269. See this same article (270-272) for an analysis of restorationism in the light of the constructs of Mircea Eliade.

4. Martin Luther, "Preface to the Epistle of St. Paul to the Romans," in John Dillenberger, ed., *Martin Luther: Selections From His Writings* (Garden City: Doubleday, 1961), 34.

5. Luther, "Against the Heavenly Prophets," December, 1524 and January, 1525, in Conrad Bergendoff, ed., *Church and Ministry: 2* (vol. 40 of *Luther's Works: American Edition* [Philadelphia: Fortress Press, 1958]), 90-91 and 150.

6. George Huntston Williams has defined the "evangelical Anabaptists" as those for whom "the New Testament was normative for doctrine, ethics, and polity" and who should clearly be distinguished from both "revolutionary Anabaptists" and "contemplative Anabaptists." *Spiritual and Anabaptist Writers*, vol. 25 of The Library of Christian Classics (London: SCM Press LTD, 1957), 28-31. Franklin H. Littell, however, has observed that the theme of *restitutio* was the common element that bound together all Anabaptists of whatever stripe. *The Origins of Sectarian Protestantism* (New York: Macmillan, 1964), 47-48.

7. Menno Simons, "Why I do not Cease Teaching and Writing," in

Leonard Verduin, tr., and John Christian Wenger, ed., *The Complete Writings of Menno Simons*, hereafter *CW* (Scottdale, PA: Herald Press, 1956), 300. Cf. similar statements from Menno in ibid., 303; "Meditation on the Twenty-fifth Psalm," *CW*, 81 and 85; and "Admonition to the Amsterdam Melchiorites," *CW*, 1026.

8. Menno, "Reply to Gellius Faber," *CW*, 679.

9. Menno, "Reply to False Accusations," *CW*, 548.

10. Menno, Exhortation to a Church in Prussia," *CW*, 1031-1032.

11. Menno, "Christian Baptism," *CW*, 273-274.

12. Balthasar Hubmaier, "A Summary of the Entire Christian Life," in G. D. Davidson, tr., *The Writings of Balthasar Hubmaier*, typescript in William Jewell College Library, Liberty, Missouri, 61-62.

13. Menno, "A Kind Admonition on Church Discipline," *CW*, 415.

14. Dietrich Philips, "The Church of God," in Williams, *Spiritual and Anabaptist Writers*, 246.

15. Menno, "A Kind Admonition on Church Discipline," *CW*, 415.

16. For a discussion of the theme of ethical perfectionism in Anabaptism, cf. Kenneth R. Davis, *Anabaptism and Asceticism: A Study in Intellectual Origins* (Scottdale, PA: Herald Press, 1974), 135-145 ff.

17. Cf. Abraham Friesen, "The Impulse Toward Restitutionist Thought in Christian Humanism," *Journal of the American Academy of Religion* 44 (March 1976): 29-45.

18. Huldreich Zwingli, *Commentary on True and False Religion* ed. by Samuel Macauley Jackson and Clarence Nevin Heller (Durham, NC: The Labyrinth Press), 339.

19. The classic statement of Zwingli's rejection of music in Christian worship is Charles Garside, Jr., *Zwingli and the Arts* (New Haven: Yale University Press, 1966), especially pp. 43-47. Garside also discusses at length Zwingli's rejection of images and other art forms within the church.

It should be mentioned that some Anabaptists also objected to singing in the church for precisely the same reasons raised by Zwingli. Thus, for example, when the evangelical Anabaptist Conrad Grebel learned that Thomas Müntzer had translated the mass into German and had introduced new German hymns, he wrote to Müntzer arguing that "Paul very clearly forbids singing in Eph. 5:19 and Col. 3:16 since he says and teaches that they are to speak to one another with psalms and spiritual songs. . . ." Grebel even argued against singing from the silence of Scripture: "whatever we are not taught by clear passages or examples must be regarded as forbidden, just as if it were written: 'This do not; sing not.' " "Letter to Thomas Müntzer," in Williams, *Spiritual and Anabaptist Writers*, 75.

20. Cf. Bernard J. Verkamp, "The Zwinglians and Adiaphorism," *Church History* 42 (December 1973): 486-504. Verkamp fully admits that Zwingli and his circle "preferred a church that would feature the sort of simplicity and interiority it had enjoyed in apostolic times." But Verkamp also takes issue with John T. McNeill's assessment that for Zwingli, "what is not authorized in Scripture [is to be] rejected." (McNeill, *The History and Character of Calvinism* [New York: Oxford University Press, 1954], 32, 39, et al). Verkamp finally concludes that Zwingli, like most other magisterial reformers, was an adiaphorist who did not hold to the negative Scripture principle of, for example, many of the Anabaptists.

21. Cf. Emil Egli, *Aktensammlung* No. 797, p. 378, as cited in Harold Bender, *Conrad Grebel, c. 1498-1526, The Founder of the Swiss Brethren Sometimes Called Anabaptists* (Goshen, IN: The Mennonite Historical Society, 1950) 261, n. 107.

22. "Conrad Grebel's Petition of Protest and Defense to the Zurich Council in 1523," ed. by E. Correll and Harold S. Bender, *Goshen College Record Review Supplement* 27 (January 1926): 23.

23. Cf. James C. Spalding, "Restitution as a Normative Factor for Puritan Dissent," *Journal of the American Academy of Religion* 44 (March 1976): 49-52.

24. Ibid., 49; and Friesen, "The Impulse Toward Restitutionist Thought in Christian Humanism," 40-45.

25. Spalding, *Restitution,* 52-59 and Hughes, "From Civil Dissent," 274-275.

26. Cf. William Haller, *The Elect Nation: The Meaning and Relevance of Foxe's Book of Martyrs* (New York: Harper & Row, 1963).

27. Cf. Ronald J. Vander Molen, "Anglican Against Puritan: Ideological Origins During the Marian Exile," *Church History* 42 (March 1973): 49-56, where the author explores the struggle between John Knox and Richard Cox over this very issue. Vander Molen does argue, however, that Puritan restorationism was not initially a means to achieve a pure church. Rather, early Puritans adopted restorationist rhetoric in order to justify their claims that their practices, admittedly modelled after Reformed churches in the Netherlands, France, Italy, Spain, and Scotland, were nevertheless pure. Pp. 50-51. Cf. also Dan G. Danner, "The Theology of the Geneva Bible of 1560: A Study in English Protestantism" (Ph.D. dissertation, Univ. of Iowa, 1969), 67-68.

28. Thomas Cartwright, preface, *A Replye to An answere made of M. Doctor Whitgifte* (1574). On Cartwright as primitivist, cf. John K. Luoma, "The Primitive Church as a Normative Principle in the Theology of the Sixteenth Century: The Anglican-Puritan Debate over Church Polity as Represented by Richard Hooker and Thomas Cartwright" (Ph.D. dissertation, Hartford Seminary Foundation, 1974).

29. Leonard J. Trinterud, ed., *Elizabethan Puritanism: A Library of Protestant Thought* (New York: Oxford University Press, 1971), 235.

30. Leland H. Carlson, ed., *The Writings of Henry Barrow, 1587-1590* (London: Allen and Unwin, 1962), 126.

30. Champlin Burrage, *The Early English Dissenters in the Light of Recent Research, 1550-1641* (Cambridge: The University Press, 1912), 2:157.

32. Robert Ashton, ed., *The Works of John Robinson* (Boston, 1851), 2:43.

33. Cf. William Penn, "Primitive Christianity Revived, in the Faith and Practice of the People Called Quakers" (1696), in *A Collection of the Works of William Penn,* II (London, 1726), 855-875, an excerpt of which appears in Smith, Handy, and Loetscher, *American Christianity,* 1:239-247.

34. Edward Winslow, *Hypocrisie Unmasked,* cited in Perry Miller, *Orthodoxy in Massachusetts* (New York: Harper & Row, 1970), 136.

35. John Cotton, "A Replie to Mr. Williams," cited in Miller, *Orthodoxy,* 160.

36. This section on Williams, including quotations from Williams, is dependent upon the superb analysis by Leonard C. Allen, " 'The Restauration of Zion': Roger Williams and the Quest for the Primitive Church" (Ph.D. dissertation, University of Iowa, 1984), 143 ff.

37. Cf. Hughes, "From Civil Dissent," 268 ff.

38. Moncure Daniel Conway, ed., *The Writings of Thomas Paine,* 2 (New York: G. P. Putnam's Sons, 1894), 428-429.

39. Cf. Byron Cecil Lambert, *The Rise of the Anti-Mission Baptists: Sources and Leaders, 1800-1840* (New York: Arno Press, 1980), 2-45, 110-111, et. al.

40. The standard history of the early years of all four movements is

William E. Tucker and Lester G. McAllister, *Journey in Faith: A History of the Christian Church (Disciples of Christ)* (St. Louis: The Bethany Press, 1975). See also Earl I. West, *The Search for the Ancient Order,* 3 vols. (Indianapolis: Religious Book Service, 1949, 1950, 1979). An excellent analysis of the cultural backgrounds to the four wings of the "Christian" movement is Nathan O. Hatch, "The Christian Movement and the Demand for a Theology of the People," *The Journal of American History* 67 (December 1980): 545-567.

41. For O'Kelly, see W. B. MacClenny, *The Life of Rev. James O'Kelly* (Indianapolis: Religious Book Service, 1950). See also Rice Haggard, *An Address to the Different Religious Societies, on the Sacred Import of the Christian Name* (Lexington: 1804; reprinted in Nashville: Disciples of Christ Historical Society, 1954).

42. Cf. Lambert, *The Rise of the Anti-Mission Baptists,* pp. 63-116; Nathan O. Hatch, "Elias Smith and the Rise of Religious Journalism in the Early Republic," in William L. Joyce, et al., eds., *Printing and Society in Early America* (Worcester: American Antiquarian Society, 1983), 250-257; and Thomas H. Olbricht, "Christian Connexion and Unitarian Relations: 1800-1844,"

43. John Dunlavy, *The Manifesto, or A Declaration of the Doctrine and Practice of the Church of Christ* (New York: Edward O. Jenkins, 1847), 463; and Richard M'Nemar, *The Kentucky Revival* (New York: Edward O. Jenkins, 1846 [orig. printed 1807]), 63. For Stone, cf. William Garrett West, *Barton Warren Stone: Early American Advocate of Christian Unity* (Nashville: The Disciples of Christ Historical Society, 1954).

44. Joseph Thomas, *The Travels and Gospel Labors of Joseph Thomas . . . Through Various Parts of the Western Country* (Winchester, VA: J. Foster, 1812), 90.

45. Barton Stone, n.t., *Christian Messenger* 1 (November 26, 1826): 1-4.

46. Chester R. Young, ed., *Westward into Kentucky: The Narrative of Daniel Trabue* (Lexington: University Press of Kentucky, 1981), 42.

47. Richard M'Nemar, *The Kentucky Revival* (New York: Edward O. Jenkins, 1846), 59. This document was printed originally in 1807.

48. Robert Marshall and John Thompson, *A Brief Historical Account of Sundry Things in the Doctrines and State of the Christian, or as it is Commonly Called, The Newlight Church* (Cincinnati: J. Carpenter & Co., 1811), 17.

49. Thomas, *Travels and Gospel Labors,* 88; and Barton Stone, "History of the Christian Church in the West—No. VIII.," *Christian Messenger* 1 (October 25, 1827): 267.

50. Cf. Richard T. Hughes, "Primitivism and Culture: New Light Christians in the Upper South," unpublished paper presented at American Historical Association, December, 1983, 12-17.

51. Ibid., 17-20.

52. Thomas Campbell, "Declaration and Address" in Charles A. Young, *Historical Documents Advocating Christian Union* (Chicago: The Christian Century Company, 1904; repr. Rosemead, CA: The Old Paths Book Club, 1955), 71-209. For a comparison of the Campbells and Anabaptist primitivism, cf. Richard T. Hughes, "A Comparison of the Restoration Motifs of the Campbells (1809-1830) and the Anabaptists (1524-1560)," *Mennonite Quarterly Review* 45 (October 1971): 312-30.

53. Benjamin F. Hall, "Autobiography," typescript in University of Texas Libraries, 57-58.

54. "Life and Times of John Rogers, of Carlisle, Kentucky, By Himself," *John Rogers Books* #2659 in Southern Historical Collection, University of North Carolina, I, 8. An abridged edition of this material is in "The Life and

Times of John Rogers, 1800-1867, of Carlisle, Kentucky," *Lexington Theological Quarterly* 19 (January-April 1984): 6-89.

55. Cf. Richard T. Hughes, "From Primitive Church to Civil Religion: the Millennial Odyssey of Alexander Campbell," *Journal of the American Academy of Religion* 44 (March 1976): 87-103.

56. Cf. David Edwin Harrell, "The Sectional Origins of the Churches of Christ," *Journal of Southern History* 30 (August 1964): 261-277. Cf. also Harrell, *The Social Sources of Division in the Disciples of Christ, 1865-1900* (Atlanta: Publishing Systems, Inc., 1973), esp. 1-158.

57. C. C. Goen, *Revivalism and Separatism in New England* (New Haven: Yale University Press, 1962), 159.

58. Ibid., 208-211. Cf. William G. McLoughlin, *New England Dissent, 1630-1833* (Cambridge: Harvard University Press, 1971), 1:428. There were limits to early Separate Baptist primitivism, however. Cf. Edwin S. Gaustad, "The Backus-Leland Tradition" in Winthrop Hudson, ed., *Baptist Concepts of the Church* (Philadelphia: Judson Press, 1959), 113-114.

59. John Henderson Spencer, *A History of Kentucky Baptists* (Cincinnati: J. R. Baumes, 1885), 1:583, cited in James E. Tull, *A History of Southern Baptist Landmarkism in the Light of Historical Baptist Ecclesiology* (New York: Arno Press, 1980), 96; and Robert B. Semple, *A History of the Rise and Progress of the Baptists in Virginia* (Richmond: John O'Lynch, Printer, 1810), 81-83, cited in Errett Gates, *The Early Relation and Separation of Baptists and Disciples* (Chicago: The Christian Century Company, 1904), 76-77.

60. Lambert, *The Rise of the Anti-Mission Baptists,* 2-400. The antimission posture of the Primitive Baptist Church was also a function of the church's extreme Calvinism: if it is a foregone conclusion who is saved and who is damned, then why send missionaries at all?

61. Tull, *A History of Southern Baptist Landmarkism,* 170 ff.

62. Ibid., 172.

63. Ibid., 188.

64. The standard history of Mormonism is Leonard Arrington and Davis Bitton, *The Mormon Experience: A History of the Latter-day Saints* (New York: Alfred A. Knpof, 1979).

65. The text of Smith's first vision is reprinted in Edwin S. Gaustad, ed., *A Documentary History of Religion in America: To the Civil War* (Grand Rapids: Eerdmans, 1982), 350-352.

66. Joseph Smith, Jr., *History of the Church of Jesus Christ of Latter-day Saints,* ed. B. H. Roberts, 1 (Salt Lake City: Deseret Book Co., 1964), 85.

67. Jan Shipps, typescript of *Mormonism: The Story of a New Religious Tradition,* chapter 3, forthcoming from University of Illinois Press.

68. Robert Flanders, "To Transform History: Early Mormon Culture and the Concept of Time and Space," *Church History* 40 (March 1971): 110.

69. Ivan J. Barrett, *Joseph Smith and the Restoration* (Provo: Brigham Young University Press, 1973), 372-373.

70. Shipps, op. cit.

71. Ibid.

72. Flanders, "To Transform History," 113-114.

73. Ibid., 108-111.

74. Grant Wacker, "The Holy Spirit and the Spirit of the Age in American Protestantism, 1880-1910," unpublished paper, 1983, 15.

75. Cited in Melvin E. Dieter, *The Holiness Revival of the Nineteenth Century* (Metuchen, NJ: Scarecrow Press, 1980), 39.

76. Wacker, "The Holy Spirit," 23-26.

77. Cited in Wacker, 31.

78. Cited in Dieter, *The Holiness Revival,* 25.

79. Cited in Winthrop Hudson, *Religion in America,* 3rd ed. (New York: Charles Scribner's Sons, 1981), 345.

80. Timothy L. Smith, *Called Unto Holiness: The Story of the Nazarenes: The Formative Years* (Kansas City: Nazarene Publishing House, 1962), 28.

81. Cited in ibid., 29.

82. Ibid., 153-159.

83. Cited in Dieter, *The Holiness Revival,* 247-248.

84. Ibid., 250-252.

85. Cited in ibid., 241.

86. Cited in Wacker, "The Holy Spirit," 20-21.

87. Cited in Dieter, *The Holiness Revival,* 250.

88. Ibid., 251.

89. Several scholars have pointed to the centrality of primitivism in the Pentecostal world view. Cf. Robert Mapes Anderson, *Vision of the Disinherited: The Making of American Pentecostalism* (New York: Oxford University Press, 1979), 80-81 ff.;   Donald Dayton, "Theological Roots of Pentecostalism," unpublished paper presented at American Academy of Religion, October, 1974, 2-3; and   Grant Wacker, "Primitive Pentecostalism in the Southern Highlands," unpublished paper presented at American Historical Association, December, 1983, 8-10, and "The Functions of Faith in Primitive Pentecostalism," *Harvard Theological Review* 77 (3-4, 1984): 353-375.

Wacker notes (p. 10) that "as the years passed this restorationist impulse gradually faded, but in the beginning it illumined the pentecostal horizon, leading the first generation into a complex 'Latter Rain' or 'Evening Light' theory to account for their place in God's 'Plan for the Ages.' "

90. This account is taken from the description given in Anderson, *Vision of the Disinherited,* 53-54.

91. Ibid., 57.

92. B. F. Lawrence, *The Apostolic Faith Restored* (St. Louis: The Gospel Publishing House, 1916), 11-12.

93. Vinson Synan, *The Holiness-Pentecostal Movement* (Grand Rapids: Eerdmans Publishing Co., 1971), 84-87.

94. For the backdrop of this awareness, see Timothy P. Weber, *Living in the Shadow of the Second Coming: American Premillennialism, 1875-1925* (New York: Oxford University Press, 1979).

95. Lawrence, *The Apostolic Faith Restored,* 7.

96. Cited in Anderson, *Vision of the Disinherited,* 89.

97. Cited in Synan, *The Holiness-Pentecostal Movement,* 85.

98. Anderson, *Vision of the Disinherited,* 84 and 90.

99. Sidney E. Mead, "The Theology of the Republic and the Orthodox Mind," *Journal of the American Academy of Religion* 44 (March 1976): 106.

100. Ibid.

101. Yoder, "Anabaptism and History," 255.

102. Anderson, *Vision of the Disinherited,* 96.

103. Yoder, "Anabaptism and History," 249-253.

Edith L. Blumhofer

Edith L. Blumhofer is an Associate Professor of history, Evangel College, Springfield, Missouri. She earned A.B. and A.M. degrees from Hunter College, and the Ph.D. from Harvard University. She has served on the faculty of Hunter College and Southwest Missouri State University. Her publications include "A History of Speaking in Tongues and Related Gifts" (with George Williams), "The Christian Catholic Church and the Apostolic Faith," and several articles in *The Encyclopedia of Southern Religion,* edited by Samuel Hill. At present she is completing a history of the Assemblies of God.

Blumhofer presents both Wesleyan and non-Wesleyan backgrounds of Pentecostal perfectionism. She identifies dual motivations for Pentecostals who have attempted to reach beyond to perfection—a desire for spiritual purity and a preparation for the parousia. Of particular value is the author's explanation of the tendency among Pentecostals to correlate a "life in the Spirit" with the perfectionist lifestyle.

9

PURITY AND PREPARATION: A STUDY IN THE PENTECOSTAL PERFECTIONIST HERITAGE

Edith L. Blumhofer

AMERICAN PENTECOSTALISM, with its strong stress on the Holy Spirit, emerged as a discrete religious phenomenon in 1901. Initially a small, struggling, and internally divided movement, it has become a dynamic and influential force on the religious scene. Its doctrine challenges adherents to continuing experience in the Spirit in which glossolalia plays a prominent role as the initial evidence of the crisis reception of the baptism with the Holy Spirit. This view of glossolalia with the concomitant distinction between the functions of tongues as initial evidence and tongues as spiritual gift has traditionally separated Pentecostals from other Christians who share their nineteenth-century evangelical heritage. Pentecostalism emerged in the broad mainstream of American evangelicalism among those who, at the end of the nineteenth century, for a variety of reasons were pursuing experience in the Spirit. A significant number of these were part of a contemporary quest for perfection.

Perfection, the elusive goal of Christians over centuries, had both negative and positive connotations in nineteenth-century America. Before the Civil War, the perfection of society had been a general Christian concern. The postmillennialist framework of much contemporary Christian thought supported the efforts to "usher in God's kingdom" that combined with the Wesleyan-perfectionist perspective in evangelicalism to shape the varied social reform and missions enterprises of the day.[1]

The perfection of individuals proved a less popular cause than the perfection of society, and with apparent justification. Critics of the notion of individual perfectibility pointed to extremes associated with the effort. For example, the Shakers, followers of Mother Ann Lee who had been influenced by radical Quaker teaching, believed perfection attainable by the elimination of greed, pride, and sex. After their arrival from England in upstate New York in 1774, they worked out complex forms in which these evils could be addressed and overcome. They lived in communities where the sexes were separated and where life was carefully regulated by hundreds of "orders" designed both to shield residents from "the world" and to protect them from pride and greed. In the early nineteenth century, the Shakers followed in the wake of revivals, challenging new converts to obey the essential command they believed most Christians ignored: "Go on unto perfection." [2]

Tourists admired the order and industry in Shaker communities but found the theology less attractive. Ritual dancing, shaking, and speaking in tongues were only the most obvious divergences from the norms in worship. Communal living, celibacy, the insistence that Ann Lee was the female expression of Christ, and the spiritualism that became part of the ritual in some Shaker families further separated Shakers from the denominations. Believers remained convinced "that Mother Ann was really anointed of God to usher in the latter day of glory, and bring in the Kingdom of righteousness and peace, and make an end of sin," but membership declined sharply after mid-century. [3]

Another contemporary expression of the radical tendencies of a stress on perfection was the Oneida community in upstate New York. If Ann Lee could be scorned as a virtually illiterate, impressionable woman, whose earliest religious impressions derived from a setting influenced by the French Camisards, John Humphrey Noyes—Oneida's leader—could not be so easily dismissed. Noyes received the B.A. degree from Dartmouth in 1830, attended Andover Seminary, 1831-32, and studied theology at Yale, 1832-34. As a Yale student, he was attracted by the doctrine of perfectionism which he understood as a call to sinless union with Christ. Noyes concluded that the challenge to perfection was the essence of Christianity and that perfection could best be attained in a community where discipline could enforce the forsaking of "special loves."

Like Ann Lee, Noyes maintained that the second advent had

already occurred. He dated the event in A.D. 70 when, he claimed, Christ's spiritual return had abolished the "law of sin" and had made perfection available to all who accepted the inner presence and reign of Christ. For Noyes, the quest for full understanding of perfection led to the establishment of communities in which experiments in the practical aspects of the doctrine could instruct believers outside in the full implications of commitment to Christianity. Noyes came to the conclusion that the marriage relationship, stressing as it did "special love," was a hindrance to perfection. His community in Oneida, New York from 1848 until it disbanded in 1880 endorsed for true believers complex marriage and selective breeding.[4]

The pursuit of individual perfection, then, was fraught with danger, having the potential to promote disregard for the moral law. There was, however, another side to the story in nineteenth-century America—a quest for personal perfection directed by men and women aware of the potential pitfalls yet convinced that the call to perfection was at the heart of the Christian message. Those individuals drew inspiration from the teaching of John Wesley.

THE WESLEYAN HERITAGE

Wesley dated his interest in perfection to 1725 when, at the age of twenty-three, he had read Bishop Jeremy Taylor's *Rule and Exercise of Holy Living and Dying* and had been challenged to "dedicate all [his] life to God, all [his] thoughts, and words, and actions." The next year, the writings of Thomas à Kempis challenged him to "inward religion," to the "giving of all his heart" to God. A third formative influence on Wesley's understanding of perfection came through the writings of William Law. Law, a graduate and Fellow of Emmanuel College, Cambridge, lost his academic and clerical privileges in the Anglican Church when he refused to take the oath of allegiance to the House of Hanover. He had devoted his life to teaching, humanitarian efforts, and writing. Two of his books, *Treatise on Christian Perfection* and *A Serious Call to a Devout and Holy Life*, directly influenced Wesley's developing views.

The *Serious Call*, directed against the strong Arianizing tendencies in contemporary Anglicanism, challenged Wesley just after his election as a Fellow of Lincoln College, Oxford (March 1726), and as he was preparing for his ordination as an

Anglican Deacon that September. In *Christian Perfection*, Law
developed the argument that perfection was "the highest
standard for the Christian to emulate" and "the lowest degree
of holiness which the gospel allows."[5] Law's importance to the
molding of Wesley's early spirituality must be acknowledged.
The call to perfection and to mystical union with Christ continued to motivate Wesley throughout his life. His views would
develop over several decades until he had distilled, on the basis
of observation, experience, and theology, the content and
method of Christian perfection into a doctrine that would become an integral part of the Methodist heritage. His developing
thought would be influenced by the Catholic mystical tradition
in church history in which he focused on the practical aspects
of union with Christ.

Within Anglicanism, Wesley drew on a rich Catholic heritage
of involvement in the quest for perfection and combined that
"ethic of holiness" with the Protestant "ethic of grace" to
formulate in synthesis his own doctrine.[6] The currents on
which Wesley drew led him to the mystics of earlier generations. The Anglicanism of his own day referred often to the
subject of perfection but identified it with good works. The influential Churchman of the preceding century, John Tillotson,
archbishop of Canterbury, was a model orator for eighteenth-
century Anglican clergy. With regard to holiness he had declared: "Let us then do all the good that we possibly can . . .;
let us serve God industriously . . . knowing that no good action
. . . shall lose [its] reward."[7]

Wesley objected strenuously to this popular view because it
ignored the essential challenge to inward perfection and
equated holiness with works. In 1739 he and his brother,
Charles, published a volume of *Hymns and Sacred Poems* in
which they incorporated their doctrine of inward holiness:

> Heavenly Adam, life divine,
> Change my nature into Thine;
> Move and spread throughout my soul,
> Actuate and fill the whole.[8]

The experience Wesley envisioned connoted "no more and
no less than giving God all our Heart; loving him with our
Heart, and our Neighbour as ourselves."[9] The Christian life, he
maintained, should be characterized by "absolute unreserved
dependence upon Christ, as the fountain of every good and perfect gift, of all holiness and happiness."[10] Such perfection

neither implied "dispensation from attending all the ordinances of God" nor "doing good unto all men" nor "entire deliverance, either from ignorance or mistake" from sin or temptation.[11] Wesley was less concerned with the timing of the experience than with its occurrence:

> Concerning the circumstances we need not dispute, whether it be wrought gradually or instantaneously. Only let the change be wrought. Only let our souls be renewed in the whole Image of God. Only let that mind be in us, which was also in Christ Jesus: Let him reign in our hearts without a rival; at all times and in all places. Let us be all devoted to him in soul and body: And let all our thoughts, and words, and actions, be continually offered up to God, as holy sacrifices acceptable to God, through Christ.[12]

In Wesley's perception of Methodism the notion of perfection was central: it was "the reason God hath raised up the people called Methodists," the "grand depositum" of Methodism. Although his consideration of the subject began some thirteen years before the Aldersgate experience when his heart was "strangely warmed," it was only after that moment that his evangelistic activity began to assume the dimensions that would bring him notice. Wesley attributed his success to his proclamation of Christian perfection.[13]

For him, perfection involved inward identification with the death and resurrection of Christ and the full apprehension of Christ's atoning work. It was Christ revealed within, a gracious gift rather than an earned reward or a human achievement:

> Jesus, to Thee we look,
> Till saved from sin's remains,
> Reject the inbred tyrant's yoke,
> And cast away his chains.
>
> Our nature shall no more
> O'er us dominion have;
> By faith we apprehend the power
> Which shall for ever save.
>
> Jesus, our life, in us appear,
> Who daily die Thy death:
> Reveal Thyself the finisher;
> Thy quick'ning Spirit breathe!
>
> Unfold the hidden mystery,
> The second gift impart;
> Reveal Thy glorious self in me,
> In every waiting heart.[14]

Wesley was deeply influenced by the contemporary German mystic Gerhard Tersteegen (1697-1769), some of whose poetry he translated into English. Tersteegen, a pietist and mystic, led a religious community and popularized in German the writings of French Quietists and Christian mystics.[15]

For Wesley, Christian perfection connoted dependence on Christ—a close relationship with an indwelling Lord. Just as one could "fall" from saving grace, so could one forfeit Christian perfection. Only persistent humble dependence assured continued holiness.

THE AMERICAN ADAPTATION

In American Methodism, particular interest in Christian perfection became apparent in the 1820s and became a significant force in the 1830s. One who influenced its course was Timothy Merritt, author of *The Christian's Manual, A Treatise on Christian Perfection* (1825). Merritt distinguished clearly between justification and sanctification, noting the need for an experience of entire sanctification to complete the sanctifying process begun at justification.[16] Methodist Adam Clarke, in his well-known *Commentary* published in 1826, endorsed the doctrine of perfection (entire sanctification) as an instantaneous experience, attainable in this life, and centering in the experience of purity.[17]

Popular interest in the doctrine was greatly stimulated by the activities of Phoebe Worrall Palmer, who after 1835 with her sister Sarah Lankford, directed the Tuesday Meetings for the Promotion of Holiness—interdenominational prayer gatherings conducted in homes—in which entire sanctification (or Christian perfection) was pursued. Palmer also wrote extensively on the subject, developing the theme that holiness was instantaneously available through faith in Christ. It was also essential: God claimed "by virtue of the great price paid for the redemption of body, soul, and spirit, the *present and entire service* of all these redeemed powers."[18] Her daughter, Phoebe Palmer Knapp (wife of an insurance executive) pictured the experience as a "plunge" into a cleansing stream. In the words of the popular holiness gospel song she authored (which would later be a Pentecostal favorite), one emerged from this experience transformed:

> I rise to walk in heaven's own light
> Above the world of sin
> With heart made pure and garments white,
> And Christ enthroned within.[19]

Phoebe Palmer used an "altar terminology" to convey her teaching: by "laying all upon this altar" [Christ] one "laid [himself] under the most sacred obligation to *believe* that the sacrifice became 'holy and acceptable' . . . even by virtue of the sanctity of the *altar* upon which it was laid." Thus the "altar" sanctified the "gift" as long as the "gift" remained on it: Removal of the "gift" from the "hallowing altar" would negate its sanctification.[20]

American Methodists used various terms to characterize the discrete experience they stressed: Christian perfection, entire sanctification, entire consecration, second blessing, second definite work of grace, holiness. They inspired the Holiness movements which emphasized the present availability of the experience, insisting that, once believers had met divine conditions, they had the right to "claim the blessing." Testifying to its reception was believed important to establishing it in one's experience. Although holiness advocates stressed the continuity of their teaching with Wesley's, their shift in emphasis and terminology ultimately produced significantly different results: "Wesley's followers developed a discipline for seeking perfect love; Mrs. Palmer's, a discipline for the sanctified life." Whereas Wesley's goal had been "pure, godly intention," Phoebe Palmer's was, in effect, a "sudden crisis accompanied by emotional exuberance."[21]

In pre–Civil War America, interest in the Wesleyan doctrine was interdenominational, and a focus on perfectionism characterized many groups and causes in the culture. Teaching on perfection developed in other evangelical settings, most notably at Oberlin College under the influence of Asa Mahan and Charles Finney. Asa Mahan experienced "perfect sanctification" before Finney, but Finney, because of his wide reputation, became especially important to the promulgation of the doctrine. During the 1830s, Finney became concerned over his failure to instruct his converts in holiness and concluded that he needed to know Christ in a more intimate way. As a result of this conviction he became convinced that an experience of the Spirit's fulness should be normative for Christians. He and Mahan were influential in popularizing the terms "baptism" and "filling" with the Holy Spirit as designations for the second crisis experience they espoused.[22]

THE HIGHER LIFE

Another perspective on holiness was developed by William Edwin Boardman, who called his emphasis the "higher Christian life." In an effort to spread the doctrine of "full salvation" among those whose roots were in non-Wesleyan traditions, Boardman, influenced by Finney and Mahan (and familiar with the work Charles Cullis of Boston), taught that it was "God's work to cleanse and keep . . . from sin. . . . There's nothing to get hold of, it is letting go all hold of everything but Jesus."[23] He instructed believers to "claim by faith the presence and reign of Christ within the soul" to enter a fuller Christian experience. Boardman's book, *The Higher Christian Life*, popularized his message. In association with Robert Pearsall Smith (a Pennsylvania Quaker by birth, although for much of his life a Presbyterian), Boardman brought the teaching to London in 1871 where its promulgation resulted in the creation of the Keswick movement in 1875.[24] Smith had been stimulated by Methodist teaching to pursue perfection and had, at about the same time, been influenced by the Plymouth Brethren to intensive Bible study. His wife, Hannah Whitall Smith, would, at his urging, write the book that became the classic statement of the practical implications of "higher life" teaching, *The Christian's Secret of a Happy Life*.

Boardman and Smith maintained that the majority of contemporary Christians never experienced salvation as it had been intended because they expected, after justification, to continue to sin. God had provided for "victory" over sin in each individual experience; it could be achieved by allowing Christ to reign in the heart "moment-by-moment." Smith stressed the necessity of "death to self" in an experience of "present" salvation. "The cross isn't a reprieve to the flesh to do as we please," he cautioned, "but a sentence to death. . . . If we come to a full death of the old Adam, there will be a full resurrection of the new."[25] Smith claimed to understand this in his own life:

I find my peace to flow as a river, with rare cross currents, or return tides. As from day to day I feel this increasing power of God to raise me above the snares and sorrows of life, the Christ formed within and giving dominion over the world, the heavenly and continuous joy that fills my soul, the presence of Jesus to my consciousness in all my life, I find myself involuntarily exclaiming again and again, "THIS IS SALVATION—a salvation worthy of its Author!"[26]

In spite of the fact that Smith seemed clearly to assert that the ideal Christian life should be one of constant death to sinful self and of apprehension of the perfect reign of Christ in the soul, he warned his followers against perfectionism. "It must not be forgotten," he counseled, "that Perfectionism is a real danger." He cautioned against self-confidence or emphasis on a spiritual "attainment," claiming that such a presumption would provoke a "fearful fall."[27] On the other hand, he challenged believers not to oppose authentic spiritual experience in their zeal to protect themselves from the fanatical. This teaching was similar to Boardman's focus on the constant, conscious, subduing reign of Christ within the believer, and it met with considerable favor in some British evangelical circles of the period. After extended ministry in England, Smith toured parts of continental Europe where his ministry was widely acclaimed. He returned to England, claiming "all Europe is at my feet," only to fall victim to some of the inherent tendencies in his own teaching and to be forced to retire from his ministry. Accused of fanatical teaching (he was reported to have privately inculcated what were vaguely termed "dangerous doctrines" regarding the relationship of believers to the moral law) and immoral behavior, Smith suffered a nervous breakdown, returned to the United States, and lost his faith.[28]

Smith's difficulties had serious implications for the future of the movement with which he was so closely identified. It became necessary for those organizing what would become the Keswick movement to disassociate themselves explicitly from sinless perfection and to affirm their commitment to the moral law. The charges of critics seemed justified in the disrepute of a key leader. In general, Christian critics of "higher life" teaching claimed that it tended to "lightness and flippancy," minimizing injunctions to "watch, pray, struggle, fast, work." It also seemed to deemphasize steady growth in faith and to substitute crisis experiences for steady development.[29] Princeton's prolific Benjamin Warfield agreed with Boardman and Smith that salvation in Christ was complete, but he objected to the claim that believers received this "complete" salvation in two distinct acts of faith. The separation of the higher life from justification and conversion was, in Warfield's opinion, essentially the Wesleyan error expressed in different terms.[30]

Another accusation raised against higher life advocates pertained to their supposed desire for personal ease and comfort: "Men grow weary of serving the Lord; they do not wish to fight to win the prize; they prefer to be carried to the skies on flowerly beds of ease."[31] The teaching tended toward "comfortableness" rather than toward Christian warfare. Higher life spokesmen substituted the idea of "freedom from all known sin" for the more typically perfectionist claim of eradication of the sinful nature. This stress was sometimes presented in terms of "entire consecration." Its central thrust was the insistence that all responsibility for keeping the soul from sin be transferred to Christ and that the believer "rest" in this assurance. The object of the experience was the individual's advantage: faith for "deliverance, peace, and power" was qualitatively different, critics maintained, from faith "because God deserves it."[32] Efforts to persuade the critics that higher life teaching was not in fact perfectionist (in the sense of advocating sinlessness) were never really successful, and the charges persisted:

> When Satan wants to give the doctrine of sinless perfection currency among mankind, he does not always entrust it to some rotten hypocrite or crackbrained enthusiast. He manages to secure John Wesley . . . C. G. Finney . . . an eminent devotional writer like [the popular South African Keswick author and spokesman] Andrew Murray.[33]

American Wesleyan-holiness advocates stressed purity; "higher life" teachers emphasized "overcoming." Both pursued freedom from sin—perfection of heart and life in the present age — through a discrete religious experience, apprehended and maintained by faith. They regarded this experience as both biblical and essential and therefore sought to make it normative. For those involved, it was neither primarily Wesleyan nor Reformed, but essentially *Christian*. Like the revivalistic challenge to salvation, its appeal was universal, and its challenge clear.

THE LATE NINETEENTH CENTURY HOLINESS MOVEMENT

After the Civil War, groups within both units of a divided Methodist Episcopal Church placed renewed emphasis on holiness. In an age that seemed to many increasingly secular and alarmingly skeptical, some found certainty in a reaffirmation of the pietistic core of Methodism, including its stress on perfection. In 1867, the organization of the National Camp Meeting

Association for the Promotion of Holiness attracted the support of some of Methodism's leading figures. An extradenominational association, this fellowship specifically committed itself to the promulgation of the "second blessing" in a camp meeting setting. Interdenominational from its inception, the association operated outside Methodist jurisdiction and, as local associations proliferated, teaching developed under its general auspices which official Methodist leadership could not endorse.[34]

The tension that surfaced in Methodism toward the end of the nineteenth century was due in part to the failure of some holiness advocates to incorporate their message into a broader theology. Critics perceived a tendency in the holiness ranks to place inordinate stress on the "second blessing" and to claim a monopoly on the true Wesleyan message. Holiness advocates, on the other hand, believed the denomination, both North and South, neglected Wesley's doctrine of perfection. The quarrel was, of course, part of the broader tension in the religious culture related to the growing acceptance of liberal theology; it was also influenced by the independence of the holiness associations from formal control by the denomination.

The stress on religious experience and Christian perfection fostered by the holiness associations of the late-nineteenth century included a stronger emphasis on outward evidences of inward grace than had been generally apparent before the Civil War. Sanctification connoted "separation" from "the world," and came to include abstinence from such products as coffee and pork as well as from alcohol and tobacco; the prohibition of theater attendance and dancing; and the proscription of mixed bathing (i.e. swimming), stylish clothing, the cutting of women's hair, the wearing of neckties, involvement in spectator sports and a long list of other such activities. The accepted external evidences of holiness differed to some extent from region to region and even from local group to local group, but in the absence of a widely held consensus on concrete biblical evidence of the "second blessing," an emphasis on particular behavioral norms became typical, especially in the more radical holiness groups.[35]

The Premillennialist Incentive

The holiness movements of this period derived much of their momentum from their Wesleyan base, but they always served a constituency considerably larger than that represented by Methodism (which was, by this time, the largest single Protestant denomination in America). A sizable group of evangelicals disagreed with the central holiness interpretation of sanctification. These individuals denied that instantaneous sanctification was possible, stressing rather a progressive sanctification to be completed only in eternity. Toward the end of the nineteenth century, however, an emphasis emerged among these non-Wesleyan evangelicals that resulted in their stressing, from a different perspective, but with some similar results, the concept of inward purity.

After the Civil War, the premillennial understanding of Christ's second advent had become increasingly important in American religion. The view of the "any moment" and "always imminent" return of Christ articulated by those called "Plymouth Brethren" gradually stimulated other evangelicals to affirm their conviction of the rapidly approaching "end of all things."[36] Those who accepted the emphasis regarded their apprehension of the imminence of Christ's return as a second conversion experience which profoundly altered their lives and ministries. Reflecting on his acceptance of the doctrine, Reuben Archer Torrey claimed, for example, that it had marked an epoch in his spiritual life. The "blessed hope," he asserted, "transformed my whole idea of life; it broke the power of the world and its ambition over me."[37] Such an attitude was typical of those among Torrey's contemporaries who were similarly convinced, many of whom were in non-Wesleyan denominations. One of the few Methodists among early premillennialist leaders, W. E. Blackstone, wrote a standard book on the Second Coming in which he listed forty practical implications of the doctrine. Among these he included the "blessed hope" as incentive to purity, to abiding in Christ, and to separation.[38] Among those who accepted premillennialist teaching were several who would develop these aspects of the doctrine and thus be stimulated to reconsider their understanding of the Holy Spirit.

Probably the most prominent contemporary advocate of a "walk in the Spirit" and an experience of "enduement with power for service" was Dwight L. Moody. R. A. Torrey, A. J. Gordon, and A. T. Pierson clearly shared these concerns and developed them in ministries associated with Moody. Albert B.

Simpson, their contemporary, shared their vision and created independent ministries through which to articulate his convictions.

Their premillennialist persuasion prompted these men to consider the role of the Holy Spirit both in purifying the believer in preparation for the advent and in empowering believers to evangelize the world. Concern for personal purity and preparedness led them to reflect on an "overcoming" life in which "daily, hourly, constant victory over the flesh and over sin" was possible. Torrey expressed it as follows:

> The Spirit's power may be in such fulness, that one is not conscious even of the presence of the flesh—it seems dead and gone—but it is only kept in the place of death by the Holy Spirit's power. If we try to take one step in our own strength we fail. We must live in the Spirit and walk in the Spirit if we would have victory.[39]

Such relationship with Christ through the Spirit brought personal purity, but not full inward perfection. There was always more to be "overcome" and subdued. The experience was progressive in nature, "not the extinction of evil" but "the putting off, the laying aside of evil."[40] The sanctified life was highly disciplined "growing in grace," a gradual transformation into the image of Christ which would only be perfected in eternity.

In order to evangelize the world rapidly and effectively, these premillennialists concluded that they needed a specific "enduement with power for service" that they believed was the baptism with the Holy Spirit. This experience, they maintained, was not a work of grace and it did not sanctify, but it was specifically an empowering for evangelism which was a requisite to any effective outreach.[41] They recognized, however, that this enduement also contributed to the "overcoming" life. Moody called Spirit baptism the "short cut to holiness," claiming that the Spirit revealed Christ, and the "quickest way of getting the world out" was "to get Christ in."[42]

The attitude of these biblical literalists toward Spirit baptism was straightforward: "If I *may* be baptized with the Holy Spirit, I *must* be."[43] Furthermore, anyone in any form of Christian work who had not received Spirit baptism "ought to stop his work right where he is," claimed Torrey, "and not go on with it until he has been clothed with power from on high."[44] He took the challenge of Spirit baptism seriously: "If I am not willing to pay the price of this Baptism, and therefore am not so baptised, I am responsible before God for all the souls that might have been saved but were not saved through me because I was not baptised with the Holy Spirit."[45]

This emphasis on a crisis experience of Spirit baptism evoked a largely negative response in the denominations represented by these men. Most Reformed thinking supported the claim that the Acts 2 account of Spirit baptism described a "peculiar" and "unique" event which should not be expected to recur.[46]

These non-Wesleyan premillennialists rejected instantaneous sanctification, substituted a "walk in the Spirit" or "overcoming" life, and promoted teaching on a crisis experience of baptism with the Holy Spirit as enduement with power for service. In asserting their view of the close personal relationship between the Holy Spirit and the believer, they in effect affirmed attitudes similar to those of contemporary holiness advocates toward such amusements as card playing, dancing, and theater attendance. Torrey maintained, for example, that true communion with the Holy Spirit destroyed interest in "worldly" amusements.[47] Fellowship with the Spirit was to be cherished and cultivated: its "cost" was absolute obedience. "How carefully we ought to walk in all things," Torrey wrote, "so as not to grieve Him who dwells within us."[48]

THE PENTECOSTAL CONCEPT

By the end of the nineteenth century, then, a small but important segment of American evangelicalism was committed to a specific dimension of inward purity and experience in the Spirit which they regarded as essential for believers in fulfilling their Christian mission. In contexts influenced by the Wesleyan tradition, Christian perfection was the challenge and dynamic; in other settings where non-Wesleyan thinking predominated, premillennialism beckoned the devout to inward purity as well as to evangelistic service. The two basic perspectives had, in practice, much in common, but they remained apart on the critical issues of definition of sanctification and Spirit baptism.

American Pentecostalism emerged in a context influenced by such thinking. Its distinctive claim that speaking in tongues was the uniform initial evidence of an enduement called the baptism with the Holy Spirit was articulated by Charles Fox Parham, an itinerant Kansas-based holiness preacher, in 1901. This baptism Parham understood as subsequent to the Wesleyan second blessing; it was an enduement for the one already living the "clean, sanctified life."[49] Thus perfection was perceived as requisite to power, and this became a focal doctrine of early Pentecostalism.

Parham's conclusion relative to uniform initial evidence was the result of his effort to ascertain the biblical sign of Spirit baptism. By 1900 there had been, in some holiness groups, teaching on spiritual crisis experiences subsequent to the "second blessing."[50] The use of the term "baptism with the Holy Spirit" to describe the holiness experience had also been customary for some time. Parham, an independent young preacher who had attended a Methodist college and obtained Methodist licensing, described himself as a holiness advocate but admits to no specific influence on his thinking but the Bible. Although it is difficult to ascertain which phases of the broad holiness revival directly inspired his ministry, it seems apparent that much of his religious understanding derived from two sources: the contemporary holiness movements and the influence of his wife's Quaker relatives.[51]

In his work on perfectionism, R. Newton Flew maintains that "Quakerism is one of the most significant facts in the history of the Church."[52] Certainly in the quest for perfection, George Fox and his followers, drawing as they did on the mystical tradition of the church as well as on Reformation teaching, suggested important innovative concepts. "There is within every man," Quaker William Penn wrote, "a divine principle, informing him of his duty and enabling him to do it."[53] Submission to this Principle would lead to perfection. At the heart of Fox's idea of perfection was the crucified Christ:

> Now that ye know the power of God and are come to it . . . which is the Cross of Christ, that crucifies you to the state that Adam and Eve were in, in the Fall, and so to the world, by this power of God ye come to see the state they were in before they fell, which power of God is the Cross, in which stands the everlasting glory; which brings up into the righteousness, holiness, and image of God, and crucifies to the unrighteousness, unholiness, and image of Satan.[54]

For Fox, the significance of the Cross was its internalization in the experience of every believer—death to self that resulted in perfect love. Perfectionism, then, had been an integral part of Quaker thinking throughout that movement's history with varying implications for local meetings in terms of a lifestyle expressing the ethic of love. For Parham, who depended heavily on his own interpretation of biblical passages, the hours of conversation with Quaker relatives had profound significance in the molding of doctrine, although the Quaker perception of the obligations of perfection in the social life of man, at least as expressed in commitment to reform, had virtually no place in his thinking.

Convinced by his personal Bible study (as well, perhaps, as by some of the holiness teaching around him) that there were two essential crises subsequent to conversion in the biblical pattern for believers, Parham concluded that the baptism with the Holy Spirit was not sanctification, but rather it followed sanctification and it was an enduement with power for service. Asa Mahan, who had been influential in the popularization of the term "baptism with the Holy Spirit" as synonymous with the "second blessing," had stressed the enduement aspect of Christian perfection.[55] Parham now clearly separated the two experiences, made cleansing the requisite for power, and began to consider the question of evidence of Spirit baptism. In his separation of sanctification and enduement, Parham moved closer to the non-Wesleyan understanding of Spirit baptism. He refused, however, to accommodate his doctrine of inward perfection, choosing to make the reception of perfecting grace central to his theology of enduement.

Among the currents that converged and branched in unpredictable ways in the fluid religious culture of late-nineteenth-century conservative evangelicalism were at least three with vital significance for twentieth-century Pentecostalism: perfectionism, premillennialism and restorationism. Each influenced the other, and all were essential to the shaping of the milieu in which Pentecostalism could develop. At the heart of early Pentecostal teaching was the conviction that Pentecostalism was, in its essence, the *restoration* of the Apostolic Faith, and this became Parham's designation for the movement. The hope of Christ's *premillennial* advent aroused desire for Spirit baptism; the pursuit of *perfection,* thus, was central for at least two reasons: The individual needed inward purity both for preparedness for the imminent advent and for the special "enduement with power for service," which alone would enable him to fulfil the Great Commission. Such perfection was a work of grace,

Parham believed, accomplished by God in the individual soul in response to faith. In his ministry, Parham most frequently designated Christian perfection as "entire consecration."[56]

In his use of the term "consecration," Parham was probably influenced by John Alexander Dowie, one of the restorationist teachers of his day who enjoyed a prominent ministry of divine healing in Chicago during the 1890s.[57] As part of his personal spiritual quest, Parham had visited several centers in which the work of the Holy Spirit was stressed, among them Dowie's Chicago-based Zion ministries, A. B. Simpson's Christian and Missionary Alliance headquarters in New York City and Frank Sandford's Shiloh work in Maine. Sandford, a former Free Will Baptist who had launched an independent ministry, had been influenced by Simpson and Moody, but by the 1890s had become increasingly radical in both his claims about himself and his vision for ministry.[58] When he determined to open a "faith" Bible school in Topeka in 1900, Parham modeled the school on Shiloh. Like Sandford, he operated without tuition charges, with one Teacher, the Holy Spirit (illuminating Parham), and one textbook, the Bible. Although he adopted Sandford's model for his ministry and was influenced by Dowie, Simpson, and other in his views on perfection and consecration, Parham remained dissatisfied with the lack of consensus on the evidence of Spirit baptism until the conclusion that glossolalia was the biblical initial evidence was reached in his school in December 1900. This insistence became an integral part of his message and ultimately became the criterion for the emergence of a distinctive Pentecostal movement from among those who had been stimulated to pursue perfection and enduement in both Wesleyan and non-Wesleyan contexts in the preceding decades.

Parham preached his holiness-Pentecostal message for five years before it received acclaim outside the Midwest. In April 1906 William J. Seymour, a black holiness Baptist preacher, brought Parham's doctrine to Los Angeles, where revival meetings in an abandoned warehouse on Azusa Street became the catalyst for the emergence of an international religious movement.[59]

Opposition immediately emerged. From the holiness perspective, the Pentecostal message was "third blessing" heresy, and charges of fanaticism abounded. Some declared that the reputed tongues evidenced demon possession. Newspapers characterized the meetings as gatherings of uneducated and emotionally unstable worshippers. The group accepted controversy as an indication of divine approval: "Apostolic power will mean apostolic persecution. Hell with all its powers will be turned loose."[60]

Non-Wesleyan evangelicals who accepted the validity of Spirit baptism for their day objected to the notion of a uniform initial evidence, claiming that the Pentecostal case for glossolalia was weak and that other spiritual gifts as well as simple practical effectiveness could also be evidence of the experience. Others among the premillennialists, particularly those leaning toward dispensationalism, rejected the notion that the "upper room" event of Acts 2 could recur. Among those whose teaching had helped shape a context favorable to the emergence of Pentecostalism, an apparent tendency among Pentecostals to overemphasize glossolalia gave rise to concern.[61]

Pentecostal teaching spread from Azusa Street across the country. Among the many who traveled to Los Angeles to examine the revival firsthand were several individuals whose ministries would play a key role in the diffusion of the message: G. B. Cashwell, through whose ministry the Pentecostal Holiness Church would be created and the restorationist ministry of A. J. Tomlinson in the Church of God would become Pentecostal; C. H. Mason, whose acceptance of the Pentecostal message would result in the division of the Church of God in Christ into a Pentecostal group of that name and a holiness body, the Church of Christ (Holiness) U.S.A., led by C. P. Jones; and Florence Crawford, who for a time assisted at Azusa Street and then launched an independent Apostolic Faith ministry in Portland, Oregon. Peripherally, A. B. Simpson's Christian and Missionary Alliance was another group permeated by Pentecostal teaching, and whole congregations identified with the new Pentecostal movement.

Some six months after the Azusa Street revival had begun, Charles Parham accepted an invitation to bring the Pentecostal message to Zion City, Illinois where John Alexander Dowie had formed a Christian community. Parham's successful establishing of a Pentecostal center in Zion City proved significant for the course of American Pentecostal history, for out of Zion

City came a disproportionate number of Pentecostal leaders who would be extremely influential through their association in the Assemblies of God.

Until 1910, most Pentecostals accepted without question the insistence that an experience of Christian perfection preceded Spirit baptism. Leaders reportedly taught in some places that, unless one had received the "second blessing," enough sin remained in him to damn him. In most areas, the nineteenth-century Wesleyan holiness notion of the necessity of two works of grace in salvation was propounded: justification which procured pardon and sanctification which "rooted out" the Adamic nature.

As the decade progressed, however, increasing numbers of Pentecostals representing a non-Wesleyan heritage organized Pentecostal ministries. Some of these never fully accepted the second work of grace teaching (or gave it only qualified allegiance, perhaps stressing consecration rather than perfection); others did not question it particularly but were not strongly committed to it. One center where non-Wesleyan Pentecostalism would become increasingly important was Chicago where in 1910 William Durham, a local pastor, provoked the first serious division in American Pentecostalism.

Durham, a native of Kentucky and a Baptist in background, pastored a holiness mission in Chicago until his curiosity led him to Azusa Street where he received Spirit baptism March 2, 1907. After that experience, he returned to Chicago where he attracted capacity audiences in his small North Avenue Mission and became noted as an able Pentecostal leader. In 1907 he began to question the teaching on sanctification as a second definite work of grace which he had promulgated since 1901. Like his non-Pentecostal contemporaries in the Keswick and "higher life" movements of the day, he focused rather on Christ's atoning work. By 1910 he articulated the "finished work" teaching that rejected the perfectionism that many regarded as a cardinal Pentecostal truth and that would permanently divide the nascent Pentecostal movement, eventually aligning more than half of its adherents with a non-Wesleyan American evangelical heritage.

In his rejection of perfectionist teaching, Durham maintained that "the living faith that justifies a man, brings him into Christ, the Sanctifier, in Whom he is complete, not with regard to sanctification only, but everything else that pertains to his salvation."[62] No subsequent work of grace was needed: in the conversion experience, Christ cleansed the soul, forming a "new creature." The believer [was] "saved from sin, death and hell, [was] a real child of God, possess[ed] eternal life, [did] not need another work of grace, but need[ed] to abide in Christ, receive and walk in the Spirit . . . grow in grace and in the knowledge of God and of Christ."[63] This teaching, Durham asserted, exalted Christ's atoning work as holiness doctrine could not do. Holiness teachers, Durham added, were deluded by Satan, and preached a doctrine "so deadly that all men ought to avoid it, as they would the most deadly poison."[64]

Claiming that "the Finished Work is by far the most important teaching in the Bible," Durham determined to proclaim it in the Pentecostal center, Los Angeles, where meetings continued at Azusa Street and numerous other Pentecostal groups worshiped. Accordingly in February 1911, Durham left his Chicago base to begin his West Coast ministry. When Los Angeles's largest Pentecostal church, the Upper Room Mission, rejected his message, Durham conducted services at Azusa Street until its leader, William Seymour, returned from an evangelistic mission and locked him out. Eventually Durham and some six hundred followers established another assembly which promulgated his "one work" Pentecostalism and which became the headquarters for his ministry.[65]

From that time, controversy raged around Durham. Holiness Pentecostal leaders (some of whom reportedly taught openly that "when God pardoned sinners He left them full of sin and corruption, and that it required a second work of grace to save them from hell") labeled Durham's teaching a "devilish theory from the pit of hell."[66] In January 1912, Charles Parham publicly accused Durham of "counting the blood of the covenant an unholy thing," charged him with having "committed the sin unto death" and "prophesied his destruction within six months." Under what he claimed was "the constraint of the Spirit" Parham prayed, "If this man's doctrine is true, let my life go out to prove it, but if our teaching on a definite grace of sanctification is true, let his life pay the forfeit."[67]

In a similar vein, Durham maintained that the obvious success of his ministry validated his teaching. In this instance, however, immediate events seemed to vindicate Parham. On July

7, 1912, after a "general breakdown" during a convention in Chicago the preceding week, Durham died in Los Angeles. Parham noted, "How signally God has answered."[68]

Durham's untimely death hardly interrupted the controversy surrounding his message. His paper, the *Pentecostal Testimony*, begun in 1908, had circulated it more widely than his own personal ministry and had convinced many, particularly those whose spiritual heritage was in a non-Wesleyan tradition, of its validity. These often gathered in hundreds of independent urban Pentecostal missions across the nation, some of which associated in 1914 in the Assemblies of God. Durham's message had virtually no effect on the Pentecostal groups that had organized earlier. These retained their perfectionist stance. For the next generation, their influence would be predominantly local and largely southern.

As his teaching became more pervasive in the unorganized areas of the general movement, Durham's supporters found it necessary to reaffirm often their belief in sanctification and their exaltation of the blood of Christ against the persistent claims of holiness Pentecostals that, in effect, their doctrine neglected the subject of holiness.[69]

From its inception, the Pentecostal movement incorporated a strong perfectionist impulse. The experience of perfection was presented as an essential step in the *ordo salutis*. From this perspective, one could not be truly Pentecostal with a "second blessing," because an authentic Spirit baptism could only be received by one who had been instantaneously sanctified. The "discipline for the sanctified life" that Phoebe Palmer had promoted in her adaptation of Wesley was also apparent in much of early Pentecostalism. Parham's encouragement of his followers in the wearing of stylish clothing and jewelry was the exception rather than the rule.[70] The Pentecostal groups that have continued to stress the necessity of a distinct perfectionist experience have tended to be more radical in their legalism than those which have followed Durham and endorsed the "finished work" view of sanctification.[71]

The quarrel over perfectionism which was the first issue to divide Pentecostals internally has never been resolved, but time has lessened its intensity. The larger groups on both sides have established warm fraternal relations, although the smaller and more radical perfectionist Pentecostal bodies continue to con-

tend for their distinctives and to uphold strict codes of behavior. The largest non-holiness Pentecostal organization, the
Assemblies of God, although not officially endorsing perfectionism, has always included in its ranks some who do. Even in
Pentecostal groups where the Wesleyan-perfectionist heritage
to which some Pentecostals subscribe is not professed, the pursuit of the qualified perfection idealized by nineteenth-century
"higher life" teachers continues. One's perfection may be valid
only on a "moment-by-moment" exchange basis, but in that
moment, as sin is "overcome," the believer approximates perfection as completely as possible in this life.

Pentecostals identify readily with the Christian perfectionist
tradition, quoting widely from Catholic saints and Protestants
whose theology they may not understand but with whose mystical inclinations they can empathize. The *Journal* of George
Fox, the writings of John Wesley, Thomas à Kempis's *Imitation of Christ*, Madame Guyon's *A Short and Easy Method of
Prayer*, or Brother Lawrence's *The Practice of the Presence of
God* all have a significant Pentecostal readership. Pentecostalism has also made a contribution to that perfectionist stream.
Its emphasis on the Holy Spirit has encouraged individuals to
an avid pursuit of a perfection which adherents agree comes
from God to the individual. Desire to cultivate relationship with
the Spirit early contributed to an emphasis on separation from
the world that has typically had specific implications for lifestyle and that has raised the issue of the relationship between
perfection and "works."

The perfection Pentecostals pursue defies full definition and
is undoubtedly as varied in texture as the multifarious individuals who comprise the movement. At its best, it challenges
them, as it has Christians throughout history, to a fuller comprehension of the potential of humanity in relationship with
God. The function of the teaching has changed. Only the smaller, more radical groups still insist that a valid baptism of the
Spirit must always be preceded by a discrete sanctification experience, but a consensus remains that perfection, whether attainable in this life or not, is at the heart of Christianity as an
essential challenge in man's pursuit of fellowship with God. In
the heritage of perfectionist teaching which Pentecostalism
appropriates, a dual emphasis on Christ and on the Holy Spirit
is apparent. Part of the Spirit's role is the inward revelation of

Christ: perfection is, in one sense, the full reign of Christ in the soul. Pentecostals may disagree over when and how this reign is realized, but they perceive in their strong emphasis on the dynamic relationship between the Holy Spirit and the believer a particular advantage in the quest for perfection. William Law contended that perfection through the indwelling Spirit was the purpose of salvation:

> All that Christ was, did, suffered, dying in the flesh, and ascending into heaven, was for the sole end, to purchase for all His followers a new birth, new life, and new light, in and by the Spirit of God restored to them, and living in them, as their support, Comforter, and Guide into all truth.[72]

Pentecostals echo these sentiments with the supreme confidence that they, in fact, have come to know the Comforter within in a crisis experience of Spirit baptism evidenced by speaking in tongues.

NOTES

1. See Timothy L. Smith, *Revivalism and Social Reform* (New York: Harper & Row, 1965).

2. For the story of the Shakers, see Edward D. Andrews, *The People Called Shakers* (New York: Dover Publications, 1953).

3. See the testimony of Richard Treat in *Testimonies Concerning the Character and Ministry of Mother Ann Lee, First Witnesses of the Gospel of Christ's Second Appearing,* (Albany, NY: n.p., 1827), 38-46.

4. A study of the Oneida concept of perfection is Richard DeMaria, *Communal Love at Oneida* (New York: E. Mellen, 1978).

5. William Law, *Christian Perfection,* ed. Erwin Rudolph (Carol Stream, IL: Creation House, 1975), 19.

6. See, for example, George C. Cell, *The Rediscovery of John Wesley* (New York: Henry Holt & Co., 1935).

7. Quoted in John Leland Peters, *Christian Perfection and American Methodism* (New York: Abingdon Press, 1956), 19.

8. John Wesley, *Christian Perfection,* ed. Thomas S. Kepler (Cleveland: World Publishing Co., 1954), 11.

9. John Wesley, *An Extract from the Journal of Mrs. Elizabeth Harper* (London: n.p., 1796), 3-4; idem, *A Plain Account of Christian Perfection* (London: J. Paramore, 1785).

10. Ibid.

11. Wesley, *Perfection,* 34.

12. Wesley, *Extract,* 4.

13. R. Newton Flew, *The Idea of Perfection in Christian Theology* (London: Oxford University Press, 1934), 313.

14. Wesley, *Perfection,* 51-52.

15. See, for example, Gerhard Tersteegen, *Geistliches Blumengaertlein inniger Seelen* (Germantown, PA: Christoph Saur, 1773). See also the Th.D. Thesis (University of Utrecht) published by Cornelis Pieter van Andel, *Gerhard Tersteegen* (Wageningen: Zeeman & Sonen, 1961).

16. Peters, *Perfection,* 101-102.

17. Ibid., 102-106.

18. Phoebe Palmer, *The Way of Holiness* (New York: Joseph Longsking 1852), is a concise statement of Palmer's views.

19. This song is included in many collections of gospel songs, Pentecostal, holiness, and "other." One such is the hymnal of the Christian and Missionary Alliance, *Hymns of the Christian Life* (Harrisburg, PA: Christian Publications, 1962), 459.

20. For the altar theology, see Palmer, *Way of Holiness* and other writings.

21. Charles E. Jones, *Perfectionist Persuasion* (Metuchen, NJ: Scarecrow Press, 1974), 4; Palmer, *Way of Holiness*.

22. See Asa Mahan, *Christian Perfection* (Salem, OH: Schmul Publications, 1975); Charles Grandison Finney, *The Promise of the Spirit*, comp. and ed. Timothy L. Smith (Minneapolis: Bethany Fellowship, 1980), especially the introduction and 50ff.

23. Quoted in W. E. Boardman, *Work for Jesus* (Boston: Willard Tract Repository, 1875), 34.

24. See Mary Boardman, *The Life and Labours of the Rev. W. E. Boardman* (New York: D. Appleton & Co., 1887); Hannah Whitall Smith, *The Unselfishness of God and How I discovered It: A Spiritual Autobiography* (New York: Fleming H. Revell, 1903); Robert A. Parker, *A Family of Friends: The Story of the Transatlantic Smiths* (London: Museum Press 1960). A representative collection of Keswick sermons has been compiled in Herbert F. Stevenson, ed., *Keswick's Authentic Voice* (London: Marshall, Morgan & Scott, 1959).

25. R. Pearsall Smith, *Through Death to Life* (London: Morgan & Chase, n.d.), 33.

26. Ibid.

27. Ibid., 34.

28. *The Christian's Pathway of Power, 2* (June, 1875): (July, 1875): 17. Smith recovered, and in the 1880s, the family returned to England. The three children became involved in various reform movements. One became Bertrand Russell's first wife, and all renounced the faith their parents had proclaimed.

29. "A Danger of the Higher Life," *The Presbyterian, 46* (22 January 1876): 8; John Todd, Review of W. E. Boardman, *The Higher Christian Life, the Biblical Repertory and Princeton Review, 32* (October, 1860): 632; H. A. B., *The "Higher Life" Doctrine of Sanctification, Tried by the Word of God* (Philadelphia: n.p., 1877).

30. Benjamin Warfield, *Perfectionism* (Grand Rapids: Baker Book House, 1958), 228ff.

31. Ibid.

32. E. H. Johnson, *The Highest Life* (New York: A. C. Armstrong & Son, 1901), 133-139.

33. R. A. Lapsley, "The Doctrinal Issues Presented by the Case of Dr. M. H. Houston," *The Presbyterian Quarterly, 13* (April, 1899): 261.

34. See Jones, *Perfectionist Persuasion*, 54-61.

35. See, for example, Vinson Synan, *The Holiness-Pentecostal Movement* (Grand Rapids: William B. Eerdmans, 1971), 58, 66-67.

36. For the story of the Brethren, see F. Roy Coad, *A History of the Brethren Movement* (Grand Rapids: William B. Eerdmans, 1968).

37. R. A. Torrey, *The Return of the Lord Jesus* (Los Angeles: Grant's Publishing House, 1913), 21.

38. W. E. Blackstone, *Jesus Is Coming* (Chicago: Fleming H. Revell, 1908).

39. R. A. Torrey, *What the Bible Teaches* (Chicago: Fleming H. Revell, 1898), 251.

40. A. B. Simpson, *Wholly Sanctified* (Harrisburg: Christian Publications, 1925), 14.

41. R. A. Torrey, *The Baptism with the Holy Spirit* (Chicago: Bible Institute Colportage Association, 1895).

42. D. L. Moody, "Christ and the Holy Spirit," in *College Students at Northfield,* ed. T. J. Shanks (New York: Fleming H. Revell, 1888), 170f; D. L. Moody in E. M. Fitt's Scrapbook, Moodyana Collection, Moody Bible Institute, Chicago.

43. Torrey, *Baptism,* 28.

44. Torrey, *Baptism,* 24-25. Simpson agreed: "We are not fit to represent God in the world or to do any spiritual work for Him until we receive the Holy Ghost." A. B. Simpson, *The Holy Spirit, or Power From on High* (New York: Christian Publications, 1895), 1:82.

45. Torrey, *Baptism,* 28.

46. See, for example, Review of R. A. Torrey, *How to Obtain Fulness of Power, The Presbyterian Quarterly, 12* (January, 1898): 125; Review of A. J. Gordon, *The Ministry of the Spirit, The Presbyterian Quarterly, 9* (April, 1895): 346; Benjamin Warfield, *Counterfeit Miracles* (New York: Charles Scribner's Sons, 1918), 23ff; C. I. Scofield, *Plain Papers on the Doctrine of the Holy Spirit* (New York: Fleming H. Revell, 1899), 42-43.

47. R. A. Torrey, *The Person and Work of the Holy Spirit* (New York: Fleming H. Revell, 1910), 97.

48. Ibid., 94.

49. See, for example, Charles Parham, "Address," *Apostolic Faith, 3* (November, 1913): 6-7.

50. Jones, *Perfectionist Persuasion,* 67; Synan, *Holiness-Pentecostal Movement,* 61ff.

51. See Sarah Parham, *The Life of Charles F. Parham,* (Joplin, MO: Hunter Printing Co., 1930), passim; interview with Pauline Parham, Assemblies of God Graduate School, Springfield, MO, 30 November 1983.

52. Flew, *Perfection,* 281.

53. William Penn, *Primitive Christianity Revived,* quoted in Giles Gunn, ed., *New World Metaphysics: Readings on the Religious Meaning of the American Experience* (New York: Oxford University Press, 1981), 80.

54. George Fox, *Journal,* quoted in Flew, *Perfection,* 291.

55. See Mahan's two important books, *Christian Perfection* and *The Baptism of the Holy Ghost* (New York: W. C. Palmer, 1870).

56. Interview with Pauline Parham, Assemblies of God Graduate School, Springfield, MO, 30 November 1983.

57. See Edith L. Blumhofer, "The Christian Catholic Church and the Apostolic Faith: A Study in the 1906 Pentecostal Revival" in the forthcoming Cecil M. Robeck, ed. *Charismatic Experiences in History* (Peabody, MA: Hendrickson Publishers, Inc., 1986).

58. See William C. Hiss, "Shiloh: Frank W. Sandford and the Kingdom, 1893-1948" (Ph.D. diss., Tufts University, 1978). A recent publication by a follower of Sandford gives a lengthy biased account. See Frank S. Murray, *The Sublimity of Faith* (Amherst, NH: Kingdom Press, 1981).

59. Frank Bartleman's book, *How Pentecost Came to Los Angeles* (Los Angeles: Privately printed, 1925) has become the classic account. Edited by Vinson Synan, it was republished by Logos Publishing Co. as *Azusa Street* in 1980.

60. *Apostolic Faith,* 1 (October, 1906): 1.

61. See, for example, R. A. Torrey's pamphlet, "Is the Present Tongues Movement of God?" (Los Angeles: Biola Book Room, 1913); A. T. Pierson,

"Speaking with Tongues," *Missionary Review of the World, 20* (1907): 487-492, 682-684.

62. William Durham, "The Great Battle of 1911," *Pentecostal Testimony, 2,* no. 1, 6.

63. William Durham, "The Finished Work of Calvary—It Makes Plain the Great Work of Redemption," *Pentecostal Testimony, 2,* no. *3, 6.*

64. Ibid., 5-6; William Durham, "Some Other Phases of Sanctification," *Pentecostal Testimony, 2,* no. 3, 9-11.

65. Bartleman, *Azusa Street,* 150-157.

66. Florence Crawford, in the *Apostolic Faith,* quoted in E. N. Bell, "Believers in Sanctification," *Christian Evangel,* 19 September 1914, 3.

67. Charles Parham, "Editorial," *Apostolic Faith, 2* (February, 1913), 9; supplement to the *Apostolic Faith,* July 1912.

68. Supplement to the *Apostolic Faith,* July 1912.

69. See, for example, Bell, "Believers in Sanctification," an article typical of those that appeared in non-holiness Pentecostal publications.

70. For an indication of Parham's standards in this regard, see both Parham, *Parham* and Ethel Goss, *The Winds of God* (New York: Comet Press, 1958).

71. Law, *Perfection,* 140.